James Morton was for twenty-five years a solicitor primarily involved in defence work. He now edits the *New Law Journal* and *The Criminal Lawyer*, and is one of the UK's leading crime experts. He is the author of *Gangland, Gangland Volume 2, Gangland International, Bent Coppers, Supergrasses and Informers* and *A Calendar of Killing*. James Morton has also co-written *Mad Frank* and its sequel, the memoirs of the celebrated villain Frankie Fraser.

SEX, CRIMES AND MISDEMEANOURS

James Morton

WARNER BOOKS

A *Warner* Book

First published in Great Britain by Little, Brown and Company
in 1999
This edition published by Warner Books in 2000

A CIP catalogue record for this book
is available from the British Library.

ISBN 0 7515 2526 X

Typeset by Palimpsest Book Production Limited,
Polmont, Stirlingshire
Printed and bound in Great Britain by
Clays Ltd, St Ives plc

Warner Books
A Division of
Little, Brown and Company (UK)
Brettenham House
Lancaster Place
London WC2E 7EN

Contents

Introduction

On 15 September 1977 Scotland Yard issued a statement saying that its officers were investigating the disappearance of a young Mormon missionary, Kirk Anderson. 'We cannot rule out the possibility that he has been abducted,' said a spokesman. In fact the 21-year-old reappeared within a matter of days and, to the delight of the press, announced that he had indeed been kidnapped. Better than that he said, he had been held captive by a wealthy lovesick woman who had him manacled in a remote cottage for three days. There was still more to come. The alleged kidnapper was the former beauty contestant Joy McKinney, another Mormon. It was alleged that, back in America, she had pursued him and that he had scorned her love before fleeing to Britain.

On 22 September Ms McKinney – a former American beauty queen now at the ripe age of 27 – and Keith May, three years her junior, a trainee architect, were charged with forcibly abducting and unlawfully imprisoning Anderson at a cottage near Okehampton. They were also charged with possessing an imitation firearm. What the allegation amounted to was that Ms McKinney had, if that were physically and legally possible (which the latter certainly wasn't) raped the missionary. Over the next few weeks the pair were repeatedly remanded in custody by Epsom magistrates as their solicitors applied for bail with no success whatsoever. What was good from the public's point of view, however, was that reporting restrictions had been lifted at Ms McKinney's request so there could be glimpses behind the curtain of the peep-show. All was not, she claimed, as it seemed.

For a start, the missionary Kirk Anderson was a fighting-fit 18-stoner. Secondly, Ms McKinney was indeed a good-looking blonde who tore pages from the Bible to hold messages she had written for the press as she arrived at court in the prison van. One claimed: 'He had sex with me for four days.' Another appealed for Christians to pray for her and a third said that Kirk had been a willing partner. The solicitors, Anthony Edwards and Stuart Elgrod, who appeared for Ms McKinney, appealed for witnesses who might have seen Anderson in the Haymarket – scene in the past century of almost unbridled licentiousness – now housing, amongst a number of other offices, that of American Express which the Mormons were said to have visited. Anyone who had seen him in the Hard Rock Café in Piccadilly was also invited to make contact.

The committal proceedings at Epsom Magistrates' Court were high-profile with Neil Dennison QC appearing for the Director of Public Prosecutions, asking the magistrates to commit McKinney and May to the Central Criminal Court. The whole story, rather like a Ross MacDonald mystery, had begun in America some years earlier, although since Kirk was only 21 it could not have been that much earlier. According to the prosecution Joy McKinney – who was also known under the names of Beth Palmquist, Heidi Krazler, Kathy Vaughn Bare and Cathy Van Deusen – claimed she had been impregnated by the missionary who had then deserted her. One of the reasons she had been remanded in custody was the proliferation of identities, but her solicitors explained that this was to fool the Mormon Church rather than to deceive the British authorities.

In fact, in a letter under one of her aliases Ms McKinney explained the reasoning behind her mission.

> Although Kirk took my virtue, got me with child, and did me wrong, I still love him and want to marry him.
>
> There's nothing in the world I would not do to make that man happy.
>
> In order to do this I must find him first.
>
> Beth Palmquist.
>
> Now – go get 'em.

According to the prosecution, Anderson had been kidnapped at gun-point by Keith May – who, in another attempt to deceive the Mormons, was now going under the name of Bob Bosler – outside their church in East Ewell. He was put on the floor and driven for five hours, the roads not being as good as at present, to Devon.

Kirk Anderson accepted that they had dated a couple of times, whatever that may mean in American socio-sexual terms. Presumably in this version it meant they had intercourse, because he felt some guilt about behaving in this way before going off to become a missionary.

According to the defence, once in the cottage, Joy had cooked him a meal and although they spent the night in bed together nothing of a sexual nature took place. The next day was more of the same. He had decided to co-operate in the hope that he would soon be freed and so played along. The next night, however, things went from bad to worse and Keith May and Joy McKinney chained him to the bed and tore off his pyjamas as well as an undergarment which was embroidered with religious insignia designed to remind the wearer of the duty of chastity. McKinney, he said, then stimulated him orally and once he was aroused had sexual intercourse with him. During the night, for fear that he would be chained again, he had sexual intercourse with her on three occasions.

The next day the three returned to London and did, indeed, go to the Hard Rock Café. Arrests took place and, after being remanded in custody for three months, McKinney was given bail. For some time she was the darling of the media, being photographed as she made her way around the London night-spots but on the night before her trial she and May skipped their bail, going first to Shannon and then home to America. Sadly, we shall never know what an English jury would have made of the tale.

But had Ms McKinney been convicted on the charge of indecent assault she would have been liable to a term of ten years' imprisonment. Had her supposed lover Mr Anderson been charged with an indecent assault on her, however, the maximum sentence he would have faced would have been two years.

Over the years there have been many such anomalies in the English criminal law so far as sex crimes are concerned. Until this decade rape could only take place *per vaginam* and not *per anum*, which was buggery, so a male-to-female transsexual who had not undergone reconstructive surgery could not be raped. If a man over 21 had intercourse with a male friend also over 21 in private, no offence was committed. If a man over 21 and his female partner of the same age, in private, had intercourse *per anum* then both could, in theory, be sent to prison for life. Certainly it was the practice of the courts to send the man to prison. A husband could go to prison for consensual anal intercourse; he could not even be charged with raping his wife from whom he might have been separated for 20 years. There again, he could be charged with assisting another to rape her.

There was also an irrebuttable presumption that, despite all physical evidence to the contrary, a boy under 14 could not be guilty of rape.

If two consenting 17-year-olds are found in bed together, then no offence is committed if they are female or one is male and the other female. If they are both male then, depending upon what exactly has happened, in theory they can be sentenced to life imprisonment. If two or more heterosexual or female people take part in consenting sex in private, then no offence is committed. If more than two men do so then, if this includes anal intercourse, they could be sent to prison for life. If a man indecently assaults a woman, the maximum sentence is one or two years. It is no offence for a woman to have sex with a man by fraud or by drugging him.

If two men and a woman have intercourse together, it may be a crime. If one man and two women do so, it is not. There have been similar discrepancies in sentencing. If a man has intercourse with a 13–15-year-old consenting girl, who is no relation, then the maximum sentence is two years' imprisonment. If he has intercourse with an animal of whatever age, the maximum is one of life.

This book then is about the often patently absurd and frequently hurtful laws about sex in and out of marriage, illegal sex and homosexual sex (which for a long time was the same thing) over approximately the past 170 years. It is a story of good intentions gone bad and some bad intentions which have remained bad. It covers a period when Britain changed from a largely agricultural society in which, with few exceptions, women had at best a subservient role and certainly none in law-making, to the present day when, it may be argued, their position in both respects is better but by no means all it should be. At the time of the accession of Queen Victoria there were no women lawyers, certainly no women judges. Women did not have the vote. They certainly did not have seats in Parliament. When divorce became available there was one rule for men and a much harsher one for women. Into the twentieth century they were largely regarded as chattels. Laws relating to sex were man-made. Since there were no women police officers until the beginning of the First World War and no women judges until after the Second World War, they were also male-enforced.

I had intended to take as a starting point the accession of Queen Victoria for no better or worse reason than that her reign saw either a very real or at least a purported – depending on one's perspective – change in attitudes to sexual behaviour. After all her immediate predecessor, her uncle William, had wept bitterly on being told of his own accession in 1830. He was not mourning the death of his relative, he was mourning the loss of his long-time companion the actress Dora Jordan, by whom he had ten children over a 20-year period, and whom royal society had forced him to abandon.

Victoria's accession also followed hard on the heels of the Marriage Act of 1835, and this seemed as neat a place to begin as any. Fortunately or unfortunately I quickly realised my mistake. It was absolutely necessary to look at what had gone before if I, or anyone else, were to understand what has taken place since. After all, syphilis did not drop like a stone on London in 1837. Prostitutes did not suddenly come from out of nowhere and park themselves in Regent Street that year. There had been prosecutions of what were seen as undesirable books and sexual behaviour a hundred years earlier. Nevertheless, I have tried to keep the 1830s as the major starting point.

Although I have not intended to write a history of feminism and the growth of the gay movement, much of the law relating to sex formulated over the period has paralleled their development. I hope that those who see lacunae in that part of the account will accept that I have intended to write a general legal and social rather than a specific history. In the chapter on divorce I have avoided the tedious – other than to the parties – details of financial awards on the breakdown of the marriage. I should, however, mention the first case of the engagingly named 'palimony' which dates back to 1970 in which Michella Triola, the one-time live-in girl-friend of the actor Lee Marvin, unsuccessfully claimed half his property. She may have failed, but just over 20 years later there was the first successful 'galimony' suit when Judy Nelson sued Martina Navratilova, the tennis player, claiming half her fortune. In support of this she provided a videotape which showed a ceremony solemnising their relationship. She obtained a house in Aspen, Colorado and $1 million.

I have also tried to avoid over-complicating things by the use of statistics. One reason is that statistics can be made to do almost anything, even stand on their heads, at the behest of the person who introduces them. An example of this is the controversy in the *Criminal Law Review* after the Abortion Act. Madeleine Simms wrote an article which showed quite correctly a dramatic drop in the number of cases of illegal abortion in Nottingham pre and post the Abortion Act: the number of reported cases had fallen from 94 in 1967 to 3 in 1969. However, what she did not point out was that 1967 must have been a freak year, because apart from that year the figures from 1963 to 1968 had run at between one and five annually. Secondly, perhaps of all offences, sexual ones are the most subject to under-reporting and therefore the true figures bear little resemblance to the official ones.

Another example of the need to regard statistics with caution is the apparent drop in prostitution in London in 1923, when there were 595 convictions, from 2,251 during the previous year. The explanation is that the police had more or less staged a go-slow. Upset by a decision at the London Quarter Sessions that there was insufficient evidence to show that the person said to have been accosted had been annoyed, they had, in a phrase, downed tools.

The various heads of divisions were then circulated asking what magistrates in their area required as evidence before they would convict, and it became apparent (as the women probably knew without this detailed research) that conviction would depend not only on which area you were arrested in but in front of which magistrate or court you appeared. Richmond wanted proof of annoyance such as actions or words spoken. Kingston wanted corroboration of police evidence, preferably by the person annoyed. South Western Magistrates would not convict on the evidence of police officers that a person was annoyed. At both Tower Bridge and Lambeth, one stipendiary but not the other would convict on police evidence only. Highgate was not in a position to comment; there had been only one case in recent times.

This is an account of a trial following an arrest in Streatham:

P.C. Caswill gave evidence on 5 May 1924 that Nellie Stetfall aged 37 was arrested for insulting words and behaviour on Streatham Common. The words spoken were, 'Hello dear, would you like to take me for a walk?'

Mr Forbes Lancaster (Magistrate): Perfect nonsense, she has not insulted anybody. Be more careful in future in arresting women.

Lancaster was a sympathetic man. Earlier that year he had said, 'I have a friendly regard for these kind of women and I shall deal with her under the byelaw. These women are to be pitied. 10/- or seven days.'[1]

---

[1] 1PRO/MEPO/2/7012

There is no thought that, unlike a number of stipendiary magistrates, Lancaster was personally susceptible to their charms. One such, who sat after the Second World War at Marlborough Street in London, was able to convince his wife that the reason he stayed in a seedy hotel on Shaftesbury Avenue was that the terms of his office provided that whilst on duty he remain within the jurisdiction of the court.

Another of the problems I have faced has been that of the young advocate who was told by the judge that he must marshal his facts into some sort of order – historical, geographical even alphabetical. For a time I toyed with the historical and then alphabetical – A is for Abortion and so forth. Finally I have settled on the paradigm of life. I may not, as in the old joke, have encompassed all aspects of sexual behaviour in and outside the law from the erection to the resurrection, but I hope I have dealt with the problems in most cases from the womb to the tomb, more or less in that order.

Some topics will inevitably overlap. It is, for example, almost impossible to separate the attitudes of society towards contraception from the perceived triple vices of prostitution, venereal disease and birth control. It must be remembered that many campaigns have a different aim from their immediate and apparent target. The Incest Act 1908 was not wholly aimed at protecting daughters under the age of consent but rather at improving the morality of the working classes. Over the years, there have been a curious number of cases of women who have contracted multiple marriages to other women. Should these feature under transvestism, lesbianism, bigamy or possibly simply fraud?

Readers may say that I should have imposed more of my own opinions in the text. I disagree. In what I hope would now be called early middle age, I took a degree at the University of Hull where one of the principal lecturers observed a doctrine of students' choice. I do not intend to parody him unkindly when I say some of his talks went along the lines of, 'You may find Robert Merton's theories of anomie helpful, but there again you may not.' He was right. He was not imposing his will on his students, something which would have been easy enough for him to do. Instead we had to decide for ourselves whether we supported or opposed a particular theory. He merely provided the framework on which we had to base our arguments. I hope that, overall, I have provided a similarly unbiased approach.

If I have not, the failings are mine alone. I would like, however, to thank the following who have tried to make sure I have set out the facts and the law correctly; those who have supported the endeavour in one way or another; and those who have allowed me to quote from or paraphrase their own work. In alphabetical order they include Jeremy Beadle, J.P. Bean, Barbara Boote, Keith Bottomley, Martin Bowley, Fenton Bresler, Clive Coleman, Michael Cudlipp, Clifford and Marie Elmer, Wilf Gregg, Martin Harris, Dominique Harvie, Frances Hegarty, Andrew Hyslop, Jonathan Goodman, Ted Goodwyn, Linda Jourgensen, Loretta Lay, Jean Maund, Silvia Perrini-Rice, William Pizzi, Joshua Rozenberg, Louisa Thomas, Jane Thompson, Terrence Walton, Richard Whittington-Egan, Alice Wood, Camille Woolf.

Once again, this is a project I could not have even begun without the unfailing help and support of Dock Bateson.

PART ONE

The Holy Estate

1

Breach of Promise of Marriage and Enticement

> 'What are you doing?' asked the father.
> 'Writing a letter to my girlfriend.'
> 'Just think how it will look in court.'

And many a young man discovered, to his cost, that his words of love were recycled to his disadvantage when, after he had broken off his engagement, he found himself sued for breach of promise of marriage.

Lord Revelstoke was one of the more fortunate ones, although his excruciating letters must no doubt have caused him a great deal of embarrassment. In the 1930s, using the Wooster idiom he wrote to the beauty queen Angela Joyce, calling her Teedles and himself Boodles:

> You are a 100 per cent dreamland girl . . . You are just something that is divine, utterly divine, and supremely heavenly . . . You are the last one left in your race, Angela and you are saving that race from being utterly extinct.

She sued him, claiming $500,000, but after three days the
jury found against her. The trial judge had commented:

> A man doesn't promise to marry merely by saying 'You
> are the sweetest girl I ever met.' A woman doesn't
> promise to marry by saying, 'You are the most adorable,
> desirable, most lovable man I ever met.'

Contracts of marriage did not have to be in writing, nor
even in express words, which accounts for the judge's
comments. An exchange of rings could be clear evidence,
as could fixing a date for marriage or even their behaviour
towards one another. Those under 21 could sue for breach
of promise but not be sued for it.

If the man discovered the woman had been unchaste
before the engagement and he did not know of it until
too late, then he was entitled to break off the engagement.
Even subsequent irreproachable conduct after a little lapse
was not sufficient. A Miss Bench had an illegitimate child
some ten years before she met her fiancé. After someone
kindly told him and he broke off the engagement, the court
held that he was entitled to do so. Gossip was evidence. If
the defence of unchastity was set up, then evidence of her
reputation in her neighbourhood could be given. It was not
quite all one-way traffic, however. The woman could break
off an engagement if, on enquiry, her fiancé turned out to
be of bad character. Proof of bad behaviour provided her
with a defence. If the charges could not be proved and there
was mere suspicion, damages could be reduced.[1]

If it was discovered that the plaintiff was seriously
ill, this might be sufficient to let the defendant back
away – as was the case when, after the engagement, Mr
Atchinson was found to have an abscess in his breast. No

[1] *Bench v Merrick* (1844) 1 Car & Kir 463; *Foulkes v Selway* (1800) 3 Esp. 236.
Baddeley v Mortlock (1816) Holt N.P. 151.

disease or infirmity, however, was sufficient to let the defendant off, even if performance of conjugal duties was life-threatening, though it might persuade the defendant that it was worth paying money not to have to live with this unpleasant person.

Shortly before the First World War, Caroline Gamble became engaged to William Sales. During the War he was badly injured in France and spent years in hospitals, suffering physically and mentally. In 1919 he told her he could not marry her. He was then receiving a compassionate allowance of £40 per annum doing light work in an establishment for wounded soldiers. She sued for breach of promise.

Lord Darling was the judge and he had nothing but praise for Sales in his attitude, saying, 'A great many people now regarded marriage as a mere trifle and bigamy as only a little more serious.' He had little sympathy for Miss Gamble:

> The plaintiff's feelings might have suffered, but if she was a reasonable woman she would say that she had escaped great danger of a miserable life . . . In the circumstances the plaintiff has lost nothing of value.

Bound by the law to find in her favour, he awarded her a farthing damages. When he was asked to award her costs he refused, saying:

> It is not really to the woman's advantage that this action should have been brought. It is for the public interest that such actions should be discouraged.

After the case the defendant fell in a fit and had to be carried to the corridor and attended to by his friends.[2]

---

[2] *Atchinson v Baker* (1796) Peake, Add. Cas. 103; *Hall v Wright* (1859), E.B. & E. 765; *Gamble v Sales* (1920) 36 T.L.R. 427.

From the twelfth century jilted fiancé(e)s had some sort of remedy, at first with the Church-enforced breach of promise cases in that century imposing the threat of excommunication and penances but not damages.

The first recorded dispute was in 1576 over a gold bracelet given by a wealthy Londoner 'as a token at such time as he was a suitor for marriage with her'. She married someone else and he sued and obtained its return. In 1676 Chief Justice North made the same decision in a case

> where a person of quality, intending a marriage with a lady, presented her with a jewel. The marriage not taking effect he brought an action against her. She, taking it to be a gift, claimed to retain it. But the court would not admit her to do it.

In 1730 an elderly Mr Tolson gave several valuable pieces to his younger fiancée, but in the excitement of it all on the morning of the wedding he collapsed and died. His family claimed the jewels, but in the exceptional circumstances she was entitled to keep them.

And 12 years later in 1742 Lord Hardwicke laid down the law:

> If a person has made his addresses to a lady for some time upon a view of marriage and upon reasonable expectation of success makes presents to a considerable value, and she thinks proper to deceive him afterwards, it is very right that the presents themselves should be returned or the value of them allowed to him.

In 1753 the Breach of Promise of Marriage Act, providing what was widely regarded as another in the list of Blackmailer's Charters, became law.

Over the years, breach of promise of marriage actions fell

from whatever status they once had to simply providing the
wronged fiancée with her day in public to vent spite on her
former loved one – and a day of jocularity for the judge
and the Bar. Of course, the press and the public enjoyed
them enormously. So did judges and the Bar, and a breach
of promise action was the opportunity for a good deal of
sycophantic laughter at His Lordship's wit.

When in 1913 the Marquis of Northampton was sued,
traffic was halted in the Strand to allow the throng to make
their way to the court. The evidence rewarded them greatly
for their troubles in getting to court on this occasion. The
plaintiff was the already divorced idol of the West End
stage, the actress Daisy Markham, star of such farces
as the appropriately named *The Glad Eye*. In 1912 she
became engaged to Lord Compton, the 27-year-old son
of the Marquis. He tired, his father died, he jilted. But
when the case began on 2 July 1913 there was very little
scandal to hear. One letter did for the Marquis.

On his death-bed his father had been told of the engagement and had forbidden the union. Now the 'broken hearted
Bim', as the new Marquis signed himself, wrote that whilst
she was his 'ideal of perfect womanhood' and begged her
forgiveness, she could not know 'how these so-called ladies
would treat you' and that he 'could not bear to see you
suffering so'. £50,000, please.[3]

The young gentry very often did get hold of actresses,
or the other way around, to their or their families' regret.
Sometimes the actress was just on the snatch, but some –
even carnival performers – behaved extremely well. One of
those was Emily Finney, the daughter of an impoverished
City businessman, who was a star of the D'Oyle Carte

---

[3] World-wide the highest figure awarded seems to have been against John H.
Castle when in 1929 a Detroit jury awarded his ex-landlady $450,000. It was
later reduced by a judge to $150,000. *Star* (Toronto) *Weekly Magazine*, 18
February 1961.

Opera Company, where she fell under the adoring gaze of Viscount Garmoyle, son of a former Lord Chancellor. They met in 1882 and some months later Garmoyle proposed. Miss Finney, now acting under the name Fortescue, seems to have behaved admirably; she insisted he secure his parents' consent. His mother approved whole-heartedly of the marriage. His father, a missionary churchman, was not so happy but seems to have offered no substantial opposition. The price, however, was that she should give up the stage and this she did. Then it was decided that Garmoyle should join the Army as a career, and again his fiancée acceded. The blow came when after taking lodgings to be with her in Brighton he wrote breaking off the engagement. She wrote back asking the reason, and when he did not reply she departed for a tour abroad and left her solicitors instructions to sue. She also returned to the stage. He went abroad as well.

The breach of promise was admitted, but the stumbling block was the amount of damages. She wanted £30,000. Lord Cairns on behalf of his son offered £2,000 and then doubled it. Miss Fortescue then announced that she would leave things to the jury. The hearing took place on 21 November 1884 and closely resembled a successful first night. A consent judgement of £10,000 was entered for Miss Fortescue, along with a statement in open court that the breakdown of the engagement had in no way been her fault: 'there was nothing in her conduct in any way unbecoming a high-minded English gentlewoman.'

Who could ask more praise than that?

The spectators were enchanted. This was by far the highest award of damages so far. The previous record had stood for nearly 50 years after a solicitor jilted another solicitor's daughter and paid £3,500 for the privilege. Some years later a jury had awarded a milliner's daughter £2,500, but now this was real money. And on the whole the press was with Miss Fortescue. Lord Garmoyle did not fare so well:

> He is clearly a simpleton and a very weak-minded young gentleman, not withstanding that he will become one of our hereditary legislators.
>
> The moral of this case is simple and salutary. The exemplary damages which, by mutual consent, were awarded to the plaintiff will operate as a peremptory admonition to brainless boobies of position not to philander after their inferiors and especially after actresses.

It was generally thought that his parents had not encouraged the rift, but that Lord Garmoyle had another lady in mind when he broke off the engagement. He certainly married one after he returned to England.[4]

When Helen Dunhill was awarded £20,000 in 1951 in her suit against the 70-year-old Samuel Wallrock, the Court of Appeal reduced the award to £11,000. She had been affianced for some six years and the damages may well have been aggravated by the allegation by Wallrock's counsel that she had been paid £25 every time they had sex, something she firmly denied.

At the other end of the entertainment scale came William Bensfield (42) who in 1959 was sued by widow Elizabeth Bowak (38). He gave her various presents, including an Indian mynah bird and a foul-mouthed Indian parrot named Tommy. Six weeks after they met and three days before the wedding, Bensfield broke off the marriage with a note delivered by his mistress of 12 years. He then compounded his bad behaviour by suing for the return of the birds and other presents. Mrs Bowak counter-claimed, alleging

---

[4] For an account of the case, which quotes numerous comments by newspapers, see Horace Wyndham, 'The Case of Viscount Garmoyle' in *Blotted 'Scutcheons*, pp. 129–48.

breach of promise. To general laughter, Tommy was not allowed in court because of his foul language. 'Your honour might hold me in contempt,' wagged counsel. The judge awarded her £300, but said Bensfield could have the birds back. She left the court in tears, saying she would have preferred to keep the birds: 'They call me "Mom".'

Over the years came efforts to do away with the action. In 1879 Lord Herschell, then a Member of Parliament, obtained the assent of the House to a resolution proposing that the action should be abolished except in cases where there had been actual pecuniary loss. It was suggested that the only losers would be 'eloquent junior counsel, needy and speculative attorneys and the proprietors of newspapers'. This was passed but never became law.

Another effort was made in the early summer of 1883 when W.S. Caine gave notice of intention to introduce a Bill. At the time an Irish MP was having well-publicised troubles and it was jocularly known as the Biggar Relief Bill. Joseph Biggar – a great ladies' man – had shortly before been sued by a barmaid who had caught his fancy. Miss Fanny Hyland had gone with him to Paris (where he had proposed) and been given, at her choice, a pendant rather than a ring. Later Biggar had spoken of impediments to the marriage. What, he was asked in court, were these 'impediments'? 'Two illegitimate children,' was the reply. 'Is the mother still alive?' 'Both are.' £400 to Miss Hyland.

Throughout the twentieth century there was a string of articles attacking the Act. No longer was a woman 'ruined' by a broken engagement. Barristers and judges came out against the action. The great advocate Sir Patrick Hastings wrote: 'I suppose that circumstances may exist in which an action for breach of promise is justifiable, although, personally, I have never met them.' And a little later Hilbery J. – to whom the saying, 'You can't patch a broken heart with pound notes' is attributed – commented:

Sometimes if a woman has given herself to a man without talk of marriage it is tempting as a saveface if she can persuade herself that he has asked her to marry him.

If you think that the man has shown himself to be a cad, that in one sense cancels out some of the other considerations in the way of damages. The greater the cad, the greater the escape from marriage to him. One cannot get damages increased both ways.[5]

Unsurprisingly, Mr Justice McCardie was in on the act in the 1930s:

If a man finds that his engagement is a mistake, what is he to do? I have long thought that the contract to marry is not like the commercial contract made in a counting house.

And he dismissed the case.[6]

The plaintiff does not seem to have appealed, but in 1937 the House of Lords took a different view: that a married man's word is binding if he promises to marry as soon as his pending divorce becomes absolute. Anthony St John Mildmay had to pay up £2,000 damages.

In the 1960s a 30-year-old woman from York won £45.8s damages to cover the cost of her trousseau, even though she had married another man by the time the case came to court. Judge D.O. McKee commented, 'This is a unique

[5] Tom Peters, 'What is the price of a BROKEN HEART?' in *Illustrated*, 1 October 1955.
[6] McCardie was himself something of an oddity; a great gambler and seemingly the possessor of a Jewish mistress whom he allowed to visit him only by the backstairs of his flat in St James's. He committed suicide following overwhelming gambling losses on the Stock Market. In his later years at the Bar he became, by accident or design, increasingly involved in cases with a sexual connotation. For a possibly partly fictionalised account of his affair and death, see Sybill Bedford, *Jigsaw*. For an account of his predilection for introducing sex into a case, see Serjeant Sullivan, The Last Serjeant, pp. 311–14.

piece of litigation, a married woman suing for breach of promise.'

There had even been that impossibility, an absolutely unique case, when in the 1920s a middle-aged woman sued the same man twice for breach of promise and was successful on both occasions, the 43-year-old Annie Brain collecting damages from Jesse Dixon, a customs officer ten years older than herself. In 1954 there was the case of the Midlands woman who sued a 74-year-old haulage contractor and this time was awarded a farthing. Earlier she had won £1,000 in an out-of-court settlement against a doctor.

By the 1960s criticisms of the action were coming thick and fast. One lawyer suggested that the root of the trouble lay in the making of the promise and a cooling-off period should exist:

> . . . a new Act of Parliament should make a Contract to marry an essential document prior to a marriage, and should provide that it should be completed and signed by each of the engaged parties, not sooner than, say, 14 days from the time of the engagement – so as to give the couple time to sleep on it.
>
> It is incredible that in this enlightened age the law of this country should be so archaic as to treat a few mere spoken words on such an important subject as binding.
>
> After all, a housewife has four days to think over whether to go ahead with a hire purchase agreement signed on her doorstep.[7]

Actions could be brought by men, but rarely were. When in July 1962 the 60-year-old Albert Edward Brown brought a suit against 41-year-old Dorothy Macgregor, formerly an acrobatic dancer, he cannot have hoped that she would

[7] A Barrister writing in *Weekend*, 11–17 December 1968.

be able to pay substantial damages because she was then working as a chambermaid. His was only the third suit brought by a man in 20 years. Michael Hanzewniak must have read about Mr Brown, because he tried his luck three years later and lost.

Of 500 trials in the Queen's Bench Division in May 1967, only two were for breach of promise and one of these was a retrial. There was no legal aid and defendants usually offered something out of court. These had become blackmailing actions pure and simple. Very often the case was a game of poker between the parties, as in the action of an Australian divorcée who sued for breach of promise when she discovered that her businessman fiancé who had telephoned her from the Law Courts to say his decree *nisi* had been granted had not in fact yet lodged the petition. In turn, during the proceedings he found that he was not the only recipient of her affections and that while he had been working in unhealthy places in preparation for their union, she had been keeping company with an Italian gentleman of indeterminate means. An early settlement was achieved.

The Law Commission thought about it in 1967. Times had changed; no longer did a broken romance kill a woman's chances in the marriage market. The Attorney-General Reginald Manningham-Buller said, 'I recognise the force of the argument, but there does not seem to be sufficient evidence of a general demand for a change.'

There was no need to act immediately on a breach of promise action. Revenge was a dish best eaten cold, and often when the man had married another woman. In 1952 at the Birmingham Assizes the plaintiff was a woman of 57 who was said to have been bedridden with paralysis since 1936 and blind for the past three years. The defendant had been engaged from 1927 to 1947 and during that time had shown her continuous and devoted attention, although he could not afford to marry her and incur the responsibility of a woman requiring constant medical care. Finally despairing of the relationship, he married someone else. His former fiancée then brought the action.

The judge commented that there was a great deal of credit in what the defendant had done, but the jury awarded £200. Since the defendant was now a married man earning only £5.6s a week, it was quite out of proportion to any blame attached to him.[8]

Properly handled, an engagement could last almost a lifetime. In one of the most celebrated and entertaining Canadian cases, *Mott v Trott*, Ethel Trott agreed in 1908 to marry Elmer Mott 'when he had something to marry on'. He was then a Bible class teacher and a school superintendent and she a church organist. In 1919 Elmer Trott's finances had improved and he suggested half-heartedly that they live at the home he had shared with his recently deceased mother. He didn't think she would like that, however, and she agreed.

By 1941 she was convinced that she had been jilted and sued for breach of promise, claiming $15,000. The trial judge ruled that if the engagement still existed in 1919 then there was a breach, but Ethel had waited too long and he dismissed the action. She appealed and the Ontario Court of Appeal ruled there should be a retrial. Elmer appealed that decision and the Supreme Court upheld it. Ethel won at the retrial and was awarded $7,000. Elmer appealed and lost again. Defeated, he proposed.

There was a more modest English example when Ann Rosemary Bennell claimed that after an 18-year engagement she had been jilted by Denis Sherwood. The case was settled for £200 in May 1965.

The action was laid to rest in 1972, along with enticement actions which were also abolished. The earliest case,

[8] A Barrister, 'Should "Breach of promise" Go?' in *Everybody's*, 9 July 1952.

Winsome v Greenbank, dating from 1745, allowed a man or woman to sue another for the enticement of their spouse from their affections. It was not necessary to prove adultery, merely that the will of the husband or wife was overruled by the stronger will of the enticer. Again these cases provided great fun for lawyers and spectators alike. Over the years there were a number of actions brought by men, but it seems that the first suit brought by a woman was in 1948 when Gladys Baker of Maidstone obtained £400 from Miss Margaret Houbigant, a Maidstone beauty specialist.

One of the more curious of the actions was that brought by Elizabeth Welton against May Broadhead over Mrs Welton's husband, Alan. Elizabeth Welton had lost an arm in a train accident in Ostend before her marriage, and May Broadhead had lost both legs in another train accident in 1945. In June 1958 she obtained £1,500 damages from her rival. When Welton's wife taxed him on his liaison, he replied, 'It's the old trouble.' She had known for years that he had a powerful fascination for crippled women – a weakness he tried to overcome. This had started when he was five and had seen a one-legged woman, and he had told his wife that he wished she had a leg off.

Mr Justice Donovan, enigmatically telling them that he was not alluding to anyone in the case, set out this simple analogy for the jury:

> If we leave honey on the table on a Summer day flies will soon be there – but we do not speak of the honey enticing the fly. By comparison a spider weaves his web and represents how nice it would be if the fly comes into his parlour. The spider is enticing the fly.

Afterwards Alan Welton told reporters that if his wife's attitude had been kinder and more sympathetic he might never have left her.

Enticement actions continued intermittently over the next 20 years, with damages for the loss of a husband or wife varying between £400 and £2,500. At the lower end of the scale, in 1952 'The man who came to dinner' and stole 'an admirable wife and a superb cook', John William Harris, now an out-of-work grocer, was ordered to pay £500.

Mrs Parker had worked in the same Co-op branch as Mr Harris, but Mr Justice Cassels – obviously enjoying himself and treating the working-classes as only judges could – said that there was no suggestion that customers were kept waiting whilst Mr Harris and Mrs Parker made love under the counter:

> She admits she had a few extras but most husbands would be delighted if their wives brought home a few extra rations of bacon.
> What more could Mr Parker want? He had a good wife. He knew he was coming home to an excellently cooked meal. His wife won prizes for her cooking. He won prizes for his allotment vegetables. Now she cooks for another man. The break-up of this marriage is a tragedy.

After the hearing, Mr Parker said that he was still registered at the same branch of the Co-op, where there was now a new manager.

One of the later and most entertaining cases was that brought by the Marchioness of Winchester against Eve Fleming, mother of the author Ian. It concerned Monty, the elderly 16th Marquess of Winchester, then aged 90, who in 1953 went to live in a cottage owned by Evelyn Fleming. In October 1951 he had become engaged to Evelyn, then a widow, but the engagement was broken off because it was feared that she would lose her widow's stipend. The Marquess had an impecunious streak and had himself been declared bankrupt as long ago as 1930. The totally eccentric Marchioness (born Bapsybanoo Pavry) had become the third wife of the Marquess on 2 July 1952, but the wedding night was spent in separate hotels. In January 1953, amidst rumours of an action for non-consummation, he left for a winter in Nassau.

The trouble started when he was unable to return to take his seat at the Coronation and the Marchioness was refused entry to the Abbey on the grounds that wives had to be accompanied. Throughout her life she was a great collector of ceremonial occasions and her exclusion rankled, particularly since the Marquess was staying at Mrs Fleming's home on Cable Bay, where she had built him a swimming pool. For the next six years the women exchanged litigation as well as insults. Some of the more entertaining were hurled by the Marchioness who, showing the worth of her education at Columbia University, New York, included the offering, 'May a viper's fangs be forever around your throat and may you sizzle in the pit of your own juice.' She sued Mrs Fleming for enticement in the Bahamas, which ended in a settlement under which they agreed not to interfere with each other's lives – a clause which perhaps could have been better defined. The Marquess then brought an unsuccessful nullity action in the Bahamas. It was thrown out on the grounds that he did not live there.

The Marchioness thought this breached the agreement and she sued in the English courts, claiming that Evelyn Fleming had financed the nullity suit and also that she was harbouring the Marquess. The suit had everything the press and reading public could hope for, including the threat by Mr Justice Devlin that if the Marchioness's behaviour did not improve he would imprison her for contempt. Devlin ruled that if harbouring was actionable at all, then it was because it interfered with the economic process by which a wife, refused food and shelter elsewhere but in the matrimonial home, would be forced to return to it:

> In a society in which everyone is in the last resort to be housed and fed by the state, the bottom has dropped out of the action for harbouring.

He ruled that such an action could not be brought by a wife, but on the enticement found in the Marchioness's favour. Much to her wrath, his decision was overturned in the Court of Appeal on the grounds that on the evidence it could not be held that Evelyn Fleming had financed the nullity petition. The happy couple retired to the Hotel Metropole in Monte Carlo until he died in 1962.[9]

The last action – brought in November 1971 – was almost certainly that of Leonard Charles Lacey, who claimed that barrister Jeffrey Prowse Smith had used his wealth to entice Lacey's wife, Helen. No case to answer, said Mr Justice Browne, adding that the action was a mixture of the desire for revenge and a wish to get some money. And what were all the other actions about then?

Was it really the last action? 'If so, I am not sorry,' said his Lordship.

Enticement actions were not always over matrimonial affairs. There could be actions for the enticing of servants and in November 1921 the boxer Gunner Moir brought an action for enticement after a James Nelson had sued for defamation. Moir had accused him of having an unnatural

---

[9] [1957] 3 All ER 711; the marriage to the Marquess took place when he was 89 and she was 51. He had been born when his father was 60, so she had a father-in-law born in 1801 even before the Treaty of Amiens. The Dowager Marchioness of Winchester spent much of the remaining days of her life attempting, mostly unsuccessfully, to infiltrate high society. She would appear at Ascot with her brother, ignoring the racing and gazing at the Royal box. There was also much lobbying to be done to obtain tickets for events such as the Silver Jubilee Gala at Covent Garden. After the death of her brother in 1985 she returned to India, where she died on 6 September 1995.

relationship with his son and having enticed him away from home. The trial was a bitter affair with the son, who dressed identically to Nelson and shared a bed with him, denying any impropriety, saying he had left his father because of the former boxer's violence to him and his mother. In the witness-box Moir made impassioned appeals to his son to return. The jury was not impressed and awarded Nelson £400. McCardie was more impressed. When asked to impose an injunction against Moir repeating the slander he commented, 'I say nothing whether I agree with the jury or not but I decline to grant an injunction.'

It was one of the earliest actions heard by women jurors, who were repeatedly invited to leave the court rather than to hear the unpleasant evidence thought, by counsel, not to be fit for the ears of men let alone women. The jurors stuck to their guns, saying they had been selected and would do their duty.[10]

[10] *The Times*, 21 November 1921.

2

Crim Con

When, probably in the 1840s, an itinerant beggar appeared before him for sentence after pleading guilty to bigamy, Lord Maule kindly took the trouble to explain the law to him.

> I will tell you what you ought to have done under the circumstances, and if you say you did not know, I must tell you that the law conclusively presumes that you did. You should have instructed your attorney to bring an action against the seducer of your wife for damages; that would have cost you about £100. Having proceeded thus far, you should have employed a proctor and instituted a suit in the Ecclesiastical Courts for a divorce *a mensa et thoro*: that would have cost you £200 or £300 more. When you had obtained a divorce *a mensa et thoro* you had only to obtain a private Act for divorce *a vinculo matrimonii*. The Bill might possibly have been opposed in all its stages in both Houses of Parliament and altogether these proceedings would cost you £1,000. You will probably tell me that you never had a tenth of that sum, but that makes no difference. Sitting here as

an English judge it is my duty to tell you that this is not
a country where there is one law for the rich and another
for the poor. You will be imprisoned for one day.[1]

Which meant his immediate release.

Lord Maule's explanation to the beggar came towards the
end of the struggle for divorce in the courts in England and
Wales. It was also, if not quite the end of a power struggle
between Church and State, certainly a point at which the
State could be seen to have the upper hand.

The beginning of the end of the power of the Ecclesiastical Courts in England came with Henry VIII's break
with Rome over the Church's refusal to allow him to marry
Anne Boleyn. On the advice of Thomas Cromwell in
1533, Parliament made sodomy and bestiality triable in
the criminal courts and punishable by death. Prior to that
the Ecclesiastical Courts had heard, in private, cases (in
alphabetical order) of adultery, bigamy, impotence, incest,
rape and sexual perversion.

James I continued the rot so far as those courts were
concerned. It was in his reign that bigamy became a felony,
and so a capital offence. Being a felony, it carried the added
attraction from the State's viewpoint that the convicted
person's goods became forfeit to it. By the time of Charles
II the rot had become a rout. The criminal powers of the
Ecclesiastical Courts were abolished, along with most of its
civil jurisdiction. Now the cases which had previously been
heard in camera entered the public domain at Westminster
Hall, the Old Bailey and in the Assize towns around the
country. The peerage retained its right to trial by fellow
peers well into the twentieth century.

What the Ecclesiastical Courts did retain was jurisdiction
over matrimonial relations, presided over initially by the

---

[1] There are various versions of the homily. This one is quoted in T.A. Nash,
The Life of Richard, Lord Westbury (1888).

prelates but later by ecclesiastical lawyers. There was an annulment of marriage on very similar grounds to today, such as consanguinity within the prohibited degrees of relationship, for example father–daughter; wilful non-consummation; physical incapacity; lack of genuine consent. These marriages could be ruled null and void. It was also possible to obtain what was called a divorce *a mensa et thoro* (from bed and board) on the grounds of adultery on the part of the wife and adultery and cruelty by the husband. This did not, however, mean that either party was free to remarry during the lifetime of the other, but was in effect a judicial separation. *Pace* Lord Maule, a defended case could take up to three years and cost several thousands of pounds, but uncontested proceedings ran from £300 to £500.

This was not the law in Scotland, where the power to grant an absolute divorce was assumed by the courts in 1560 and enacted in 1573. It should be remembered that the Act of Union between England and Scotland would not take place for another 30 years. Divorce was not allowed in Ireland until the 1970s. Actions there for criminal conversation, or crim con as it was known, were permitted, however.

Just what was this crim con? Neither criminal nor a conversation, it was the forerunner of the divorce petition and an essential part of matrimonial law, although it masqueraded in the King's/Queen's Bench Division as a civil action by which the aggrieved husband could make a claim for damages for the loss of his wife's virtue. There jurors were a 'special jury of gentlemen of fortune', 24 selected from freeholders of substance, knights and urban gentry. They served in a number of trials and were thought to be more inclined to value the honour of gentlemen than the usual run-of-the-mill juror.

Once damages were awarded, and they could be as high

as £15,000, often awarded in a matter of minutes,[2] the defendant either paid up and came to a composition with the husband or he was arrested, his goods seized and he was put in prison. An 1836 Act allowed the defendant to apply for his release after 12 months. Before that the period was ten years.[3] An escape route was to France, to live in Calais or Boulogne.

From 1798 a Private Bill for dissolution of marriage had to be brought in the House of Lords and supported either by a divorce *a mensa et thoro* or by a crim con verdict in favour of a male petitioner. The petitioner had to appear before the Bar of the House of Lords and submit himself – or more rarely herself, since only four women successfully availed themselves of the opportunity. Before 1714 there was a total of ten parliamentary divorces, and only 307 from then until 1856.[4]

Crim con was, however, a course of action brought only by the gentry, and over the years some of the best families in the land either prosecuted or defended such actions.[5] To the delight of the pamphleteers and newspapers, these proceedings were heard in public.

---

[2] Lawrence Stone quotes an 1802 example of £5,000 awarded without the jury leaving the box, and another when in 1815 the jurors halve a £30,000 claim in an hour. In later years they appear to have taken longer in their deliberations, which Stone suggests meant they were taking their responsibilities more seriously (*Road to Divorce*, p. 234). It should, however, be remembered that in 1911 the jury in the capital murder trial of Steinie Morrison, in a case in which the judge was urging an acquittal, took only half an hour to convict him.
[3] 48 G. 3c 123; *Goodfellow v Robings* (1836) 3 Bingham N.C.
[4] *Report of the Committee on One Parent Families*, 1974, Cmnd 5629, vol 2, p. 92.
[5] Damages could be quite low as well. In 1782 Sir Richard Worsley, Governor of the Isle of Wight, claimed £20,000 damages for crim con against his former friend George Bissett. He had succeeded, but received only 1 shilling damages because the jury accepted evidence that Worsley had made a back for his friend to stand and peep through a window in a public bath-house the better to see Lady Worsley naked. Apparently the trio had left the bath-house together, all in high good humour. A month after Worsley's death in 1795, she married a Frenchman, Louis Cochet, with whom she had been living following her separation.

One of the earliest actions which led to an absolute
divorce was that of Henry Howard, 7th Duke of Norfolk,
who had failed to obtain a divorce *a mensa et thoro* in the
Ecclesiastical Courts. In 1700 his marriage was declared
void after he had obtained damages from the soldier of
fortune Sir John Germain. His Lordship had obtained the
evidence in a somewhat fortunate way. The Duchess, Lady
Mary Mordaunt, daughter of the 2nd Earl of Peterborough,
was having her portrait – to make a pair with that of the
Duke – painted by the artist Simon Verelst in an apartment
in Windsor Castle. At the end of one sitting, Verelst put
away his paint and canvas in a cupboard where Germain
had left some of his clothing. Germain then offered Verelst
money to say the clothing was his. The offer was overheard
by the long-eared and -tongued Mrs Verelst and in turn the
Duke learned of his cuckoldry. He sued Germain, claiming
£10,000, and was awarded about £66. The reason the
jury took against the Duke was his undoubted ability as
a swordsman himself and because he had introduced his
wife to the bad company she later maintained. The story
has a happy ending at least for Germain's lawyers. In 1701
– curiously the year when Norfolk died – she married
Germain and in turn died four years later, leaving him a
large estate and £70,000 along with a bitter litigious struggle
with her family.[6]

For centuries damages awarded by the jury, however
unreasonable either way, were not subject to appeal and in
1758 Lord Mansfield refused a retrial in a case where £500
damages were awarded against a clerk earning £50 a year.

> . . . the jury are the proper judge of damages in an
> action founded upon tort and only they can judge the
> particular circumstances of the case.[7]

[6] J.M. Robinson, *The Dukes of Norfolk*, pp. 145–6 (1982).
[7] *Wilford v Berkley* (1758), Eng Rep. 97: 472.

It was not until Lord Ellenborough allowed the possibility of an appeal in 1805 in a case of excessive damages that you could appeal. By now there was a growing concern about what were seen as arbitrary and irresponsible decisions[8].

As Santayana points out, it is curious that we never seem to learn from history. It was not until the late 1990s that steps were taken to curtail what were seen as irresponsibly large awards made by juries in libel cases.

To the delight of the pamphleteers and newspaper proprietors the cases were heard in public and, with the exception of the trial of Queen Caroline before the House of Lords, the one which most entertained the country in the first half of the nineteenth century was that of *Norton v Melbourne*. The Hon. George Chapple Norton was a Metropolitan magistrate sitting at Whitechapel Police Court. Viscount Melbourne was the Prime Minister. The object of both their affections was Norton's wife Caroline, described as beautiful and fascinating and to whom politicians were clearly drawn – Disraeli was another of her admirers. To keep the family finances afloat she wrote some 30 novels and other books as well as turning her hand to a little poetry, the only surviving piece of which is her 'Arab's Farewell to his Horse', which was enormously popular at the time. Norton, eight years older than herself, was by all accounts a mean-spirited and idle man who was fortunate to obtain a paid appointment.

Melbourne had already survived a previous brush with the courts in a similar case brought against him by the elderly and ill-tempered (as a result of his gout) divine, Lord Brandon, who thought that his wife, young and attractive Lady Brandon, had become too close to Melbourne and had finally left him to live in London under an assumed name. The action heard in November 1820 got nowhere.

[8] *Chambers v Caulfield* (1805) Eng Rep. 102: 1285.

The best evidence which could be dragged from a mixture of cab-drivers, gentlemen's gentlemen and a maid of all work was that someone with a name like Lord Merrybone had occasionally visited her ladyship in Lisson Grove – then deemed to be part of St John's Wood rather than being off the Marylebone Road, and a suburb-from-suburb for ladies who preferred not to have husbands, their own or those of others, about the place the whole time. Lord Tenterden, sitting in the Court of King's Bench, threw the case out in double-quick time, non-suiting Brandon, who fared no better at all when he later tried to petition for divorce.

Still, it was a case of lightning striking twice. Melbourne undoubtedly knew Caroline Norton, who had written to him seeking her husband's appointment. He called on her regularly, sometimes leaving brief notes which were held against the Premier: 'I will call about half-past four or five – Yours Melbourne.'

Apparently, according to the social etiquette of the time such notes should have begun 'My dear Mrs Norton'. The fact that they did not do so meant adulterous thoughts if not action. 'They seem to import much more than the mere words convey,' said Sir William Follett for George Norton. Many of Melbourne's other notes seem to be urging Caroline to stay with her husband for the sake of the children, and he firmly believed that the suit was a money-grabbing action.

> You ought to know better than I do and must do so. But you seem to me to be hardly aware what a GNOME he is. In my opinion he has somehow or other made this whole matter subservient to his pecuniary interest.

The case was heard by Lord Chief Justice Tindal in the Court of Common Pleas at Westminster, with Melbourne represented by the Attorney-General, Sir John Campbell.

Again the evidence was a mish-mash of discharged footmen,
pregnant maids and drunken coachmen. One when pressed
agreed that he had been discharged for 'having a drop too
much'. Pressed further, he agreed that when driving his
master and mistress to a ball he had been so drunk that
he was arrested and kept in custody overnight. In an early
example of buying a witness, he also agreed that he had
been given £10 and lodged pending the case at the country
house of Norton's brother.

The Attorney-General could not call Melbourne, for he
was the defendant, and he could not call Caroline Norton
as she was the wife of the plaintiff. He therefore called no
evidence and relied, correctly, on his closing speech. The
jury did not leave the box. *The Times* was not pleased:

> Lord Melbourne has been acquitted by the verdict of a
> jury against the laws of God and man.

In the end it did him no harm, but Mrs Norton fared
badly:

> A cabal of intrigue and innuendo was levelled at her,
> and studied and systematic misrepresentation were her
> lot. Woman-baiting and mud-flinging, it seemed, were
> popular pastimes among a section of the gutter journal-
> ists from whom the general public formed their opinions.
> Some of the mud stuck.[9]

She separated from her husband – with the breakdown
of the action against Melbourne, there was no question
that Norton could petition for divorce. What she did not
realise, however, was that by agreeing to a separation she
had forfeited her rights in the children. Norton now had

---

[9] Horace Wyndham, 'The Case of the Hon Mrs Norton' in *Blotted 'Scutcheons*, p. 234.

sole custody and he denied her access except in degrading conditions. All her appeals were rejected with insults.

She was, however, a woman of indomitable resources and next published a pamphlet, *A Plain Letter to the Lord Chancellor on the Infant Custody Bill*, in which she pointed out the hardships imposed on a woman solely because of her separation from her husband. For the purposes writing in the third person, she adopted the name of Pearce Stevenson and used it to reply to her critics. In 1848 she was also wrongly denounced for wheedling a State secret from Sidney Herbert and selling it to *The Times*. Norton died in 1875 and two years later, in March, she married Sir William Stirling-Maxwell, a long-time friend. She died three months after the marriage.[10]

What promised to be another of the more spectacular actions was that brought in 1843 by Lord William Paget, second son of the Marquis of Anglesey, against Lord Cardigan, yet to lead the ill-fated Charge of the Light Brigade. It arose from Cardigan's affair with Lady Frances, Paget's wife.

Paget was reputed to neglect his wife, and to be unfaithful as well as brutal. Not only that, but he had Lady Frances watched. One day she left her country home, called Cardigan to her house off Berkeley Square and took him into her drawing room. Winter, a known blackmailer employed by Lord William, had concealed himself under the drawing-room sofa and remained there for some two hours. Fortunately for her, she took Cardigan into the back drawing room and so the hidden Winter could not say exactly what did or did not happen. Certainly, after Cardigan drove away there was a bitter quarrel between Paget and his wife, who was later seen to have a black eye.

[10] *Norton v Melbourne* is satirised by Dickens as *Bardwell v Pickwick*. The Herbert incident is fictionalised by George Meredith in *Diana of the Crossways*.

The matter was high drama in the press and followed by the middle and upper classes – few of the lower could read – with great interest. Paget challenged Cardigan to a duel, only to be told that, 'Lord Cardigan could never again fight a duel in England.'

The reason for this was that Cardigan had already fought a duel at 5 p.m. on 12 September 1840 at the Windmill, Wimbledon Common, in which his opponent, Captain Harvey Tuckett, had been seriously wounded. On 20 October a Grand Jury at the Old Bailey had found a true bill of intent to murder, maim, and cause grievous bodily harm to Tuckett. The maximum penalty in the event of a guilty verdict was transportation for life. As a felon, his goods and land would be forfeit to the Crown. Cardigan, sensibly, executed a deed of gift in favour of Viscount Curzon, the son of his favourite sister. As was his right, Cardigan had elected to be tried by his peers.

In fact he was many times fortunate. First, the indictment omitted the wounding, which took away the risk of transportation. Second, it was announced that the recovered Tuckett would not appear to give evidence. Then on 16 February 1841, the day of the trial, both the Lord Chancellor and the Solicitor-General were taken ill simultaneously and the Lord Chief Justice, Lord Denman, took the proceedings[11]. The evidence was clear, but there was a legal loop-hole. Sir William Follett, appearing for Cardigan, told their Lordships: 'The prosecutor is bound to prove the Christian and surnames of the person against whom the offence is alleged; if he fails in either, he fails in the proof.'

---

[11] Denman was later described by Henry Greville as 'an honourable gentleman but no lawyer and one of the feeblest Chief Justices who ever presided over the court of Queen's Bench'. See Lytton Strachey and Roger Fulford (eds.), *The Greville Memoirs 1814–1860*. He is best remembered for his contribution to the Evidence Act 1843, known in legal circles as Lord Denman's Act, which allowed witnesses convicted of crime or with an interest in the case to give evidence.

In fact, because Tuckett was absent from the trial there was no legal proof that Cardigan had shot at him at the Windmill. Not Guilty. It is easy, however, to understand Cardigan's reluctance to fight another duel on English soil after that little escape.

Finally, to the intense delight of the public, an action for crim con was brought and appeared in the Guildhall list for 22 December 1843. As often happens, however, it was a damp squib. Winter failed to appear and the action failed with him. Paget withdrew to conduct a second action in the correspondence columns of *The Times*, claiming that Cardigan was guilty 'of the wicked and infamous crime of having bought and sent out of the way the principal witness against him'. Cardigan was equally abrasive in his denials.

Shortly before the action for criminal conversation was abolished by the Matrimonial Causes Act 1857 came one of the more entertaining of crim con cases. In August 1857 Mr Lyle, an upholsterer, brought an action against his business partner, a Mr Herbert. Fearing that his wife's affections had been mislaid, Mr Lyle had employed a cabinet maker, William Taylor, to construct what the judge called a crimconometer which would show how many people were in the matrimonial bed at any one time. He then rented a room in the next house, bored a hole through the wall and set up the device, which seems to have been in the form of a lever which fell to a level when one person got into bed and dropped further when a second, third and fourth joined.

Once the lever had fallen to the second level, Lyle and Taylor went to the matrimonial home and shone a torch on the offending couple. Mr Herbert was described as 'making the best of his way to the place'. Taylor then stole a bottle of gin from Mr Herbert, taking the view that it was really Mr Lyle's and he should have a bonus. The pair then tipped round to the pub, where they seem to have drunk themselves insensible. Mr Herbert was allowed to remain in the house for the rest of the day and, indeed, to ensure that he did so they confiscated his boots. A farthing damages.[12]

With the abolition of the action, damages in divorce cases could be obtained from the seducer of the errant wife. *Plus ça change.* The action remained a tort in America until 1935, and in Ireland until the 1970s, when in June 1972 a German commercial agent, Werner Braun, brought an action claiming damages from a Mr Roche, who admitted that Braun's wife Heide had gone to live with him but denied that he had caused Braun any suffering. The marriage seems to have been an entertaining one certainly as far as the press was concerned, and one Dutch witness gave evidence of a three-in-a-bed evening. Heide claimed Braun had had affairs with five women, and her counsel argued that as she too had committed adultery she was fairly valueless anyway. Mr Justice Butler, telling an all-male Dublin jury that their task was not to punish the defendant but to put a price the wife, added 'In this country a wife is regarded as a chattel, just as a thoroughbred mare or cow.' Adultery or not, the jury valued Mrs Braun highly, putting a price tag of £12,000 on her.

---

[12] 'A Merry Tale from Croydon', cited by Thomas Boyle in *Black Swine in the Sewers of Hampstead*, pp. 16–17.

3

Wife-Selling

Crim con for the upper and middle classes; wife-selling for the peasantry. In a country in which wife-selling had been a relatively popular pastime for centuries, the sale by Hardy's eponymous Mayor of Casterbridge of his long-suffering wife was greeted by the reading public with some disbelief. It was, they said, as did the critics, just stretching the imagination too far to believe that such things still went on. A relatively modern-day equivalent would, perhaps, be jurors in the sex cases of the 1950s who either did not understand what was alleged to have happened, or who did it themselves. But, in the 1880s, those who did it themselves in all probability could not read the sentiments expressed by Michael Henchard:

> I don't see why men who have got wives and don't want 'em shouldn't get rid of 'em as the gipsy fellows do their old horses ... Why shouldn't they put 'em up for auction to men who are in need of such articles?

If Hardy was correct, the wives themselves were not, on occasion, wholly averse to the practice.

'Will anybody buy her?' said the man.

'I wish somebody would,' said she firmly. 'Her present owner is not at all to her liking.'

To begin to understand the (almost wholly economic) reasons behind the practice, it must be remembered that a marriage could not be easily dissolved before 1853. Until then divorce was by Act of Parliament and extremely expensive. It was thus out of the reach of the large majority of the population. Bigamy was therefore the order of the day and, in case there were any misunderstandings which might linger in the breasts of potential bigamists, the kindly judge Lord Maule had patiently explained the divorce law to the itinerant and bigamous beggar who appeared before him for sentence.

One of the reasons for wife-selling amongst the not-so-rich was the fear that a separation by mutual consent could still lead to later financial complications. A husband was liable for the debts of his wife. When he died, she might make a claim of up to a third of the estate. As for the wife, there was the possibility that the separated husband could take her newly acquired goods. After all, in law they were his. There was always the possibility for an action of criminal conversation. The answer to the problems was a separation agreement. The sale of a wife was often to a lover, and was more of a symbolic act than an outright sale. Moreover, a properly drawn wife-sale contract could be an indemnification against an action for criminal conversation.

What the husband often believed was that by selling his wife he was now absolved from supporting her. Certainly it was usually a belief in the community – and that was what counted – that he was now free from her debts. In the few cases where maintenance was sought the former husband was, however, swiftly disabused of his false belief.

These were not really considerations for the extreme poor, however. They had not the money for a lawyer and they could not read or write anyway. It was a question of the economics of survival. The answer for them was also the wife-sale.

The practice went back to the late sixteenth century, when it was common to exchange money for rights over persons.[1] It was the practice of the church courts to punish such behaviour, but convictions were rare and the punishment was usually only a form of public penance. A period of time stood in a nightshirt and holding a candle in the market place seems to have been the order of the evening. The Marriage Act 1753 appears to have standardised the procedure throughout, at least, southern England and the Midlands, where at its height in the 1830s there were over 50 recorded cases in the decade.[2]

Wives were usually brought to be sold on market day at the Cross, often in a halter and, not infrequently, in a shift so that potential purchasers could see the full extent of the merchandise for which they were bidding. The price realised could range from a few pints of beer to several guineas and would, of course, depend upon the quality and age of the stock. Other factors included both the weather and the time of year. A popular time of sale was after a

---

[1] In Scotland and Northern Ireland in the twentieth century servants could be bought and sold, and if a man wished to obtain work as a farm hand he would often have to bring with him a girl, not necessarily his wife or mistress, who would do the hard domestic labour.

[2] This figure is, of course, hopelessly inaccurate. Lawrence Stone, who believes that there were fewer than 300 cases of wife-sale between 1780 and 1850, considers the figures to have been exaggerated by newspapers who invented accounts for the titillation of their readers. 'Wife-sale was therefore no more than a very rare occurrence, which for about half a century attracted attention far beyond its true significance.' *The Road to Divorce*, p. 146.

 Perhaps the existence was more than Mr Stone would admit. For example, in 1835 two accounts were recorded in one paper alone in a three-month period. This would account for about two-fifths of the annual total. It is perhaps another reason why one should not rely heavily on statistics.

poor harvest, when money had to be raised to keep the livestock through the winter. Something had to go, and that something was all too often the wife. Giving a quasi-legality to the transaction was the fact that a commission was paid to the owner of the market.

> A farmer of the parish of Stowupland sold his wife to a neighbour for five guineas and, being happy to think he had made a good bargain, presented her with a guinea to buy a new gown. He then went to Stowmarket and gave orders for the bells to be rung on the occasion.[3]

Set against this successful transaction is the record of a case where a man called Lees in Sheffield sold his wife for sixpence to a man named Hall. She was delivered to her purchaser with a halter around her neck. The sale cannot have been for money, because Lees paid a guinea to have the unfortunate woman delivered by coach to Manchester the next day.[4]

The following year there is a report of a butcher's wife being sold at Smithfield Market in a double halter. The price was three guineas and a crown and the purchaser was a hog-driver. 'Pity it is there is no stop put to such depraved conduct in the lower order of people,' thundered the writer, only to change his tune the next day in saying, possibly with his tongue in his cheek:

> By some mistake in our report of the Smithfield Market, we had not learned the average price of wives for the last week. The increasing value of the fair sex is esteemed by several eminent writers as a certain criterion of increasing civilization. Smithfield has, on this ground, strong pretensions to refined improvement, as the price

[3] *Ipswich Journal*, 28 January 1787.
[4] *The Times*, 30 March 1796.

of wives has risen in that market from half a guinea to
three guineas and a half.[5]

It was not a steady market. In March 1803 a woman was sold
by a butcher for a guinea in Sheffield Market, but three years
later a John Gosthorpe received 20 guineas for his wife. It is
possible to read between the lines, for the purchaser was a
man named Houseman who had lodged with the pair for a
number of years. Reports of sales were not exactly thick and
fast but not uncommon. A wife went for sixpence and a quid
of tobacco at the Market Cross, Knaresbrough, Yorkshire
in 1807; and in 1820 a man named Brouchet hired a pen in
the cattle market in Canterbury and sold his wife for five
shillings. The rent of the pen was sixpence.

Twelve years later, on 7 April 1832, Joseph Thomson sold
his wife, Mary Anne, in a halter in Carlisle. He delivered a
little diatribe which one might have thought would put off
would-be purchasers:

> She has been to me only a born serpent. I took her for
> my comfort and the good of my home; but she became
> my tormentor, a domestic curse, a night invasion, and
> a daily plague.
>
>   Gentlemen, I speak truth from my heart when I beg we
> may be delivered from troublesome wives and frolicsome
> women! Avoid them as you would a mad dog, a roaring
> lion, a loaded pistol, cholera morbus, Mount Etna or any
> other pestilential thing in nature.

Thomson cannot have been that poorly off because when he
went on to expound on such good qualities as he saw in Mrs
Thomson he said she could 'scold the maid'. He offered her
for 50 shillings and, after an hour, Henry Mears bought her
for 20 shillings and a Newfoundland dog. According to the

[5] *The Times*, 18, 19 July 1797.

report, each pair went their separate ways in 'perfect good temper'.[6]

In 1832, an early version of 'Disgusted, Tunbridge Wells' wrote to *The Times* complaining about an account of a sale of Mrs Thomson of Carlisle. 'Has the magistrate no power to prevent such disgraceful exhibitions?'

The editor was in no doubt of his answer: 'There is no question but that the offence is punishable at common law.'

But it was one of those offences of which no one took that much notice. One of the problems in enforcing the law was that it was suspected that magistrates sometimes did it themselves. Sir Geoffrey Kneller, who sat as a Justice of the Peace for Middlesex, was reputed to have purchased a Quaker's wife. Even higher up the social scale, the Duke of Chandos is said to have bought a chambermaid from her husband and subsequently married her on Christmas Day. When the wife of Sir John de Camoys eloped with Sir William Paynel, in an example of locking the stable door, the cuckolded husband made a gift of her to the seducer. *Spontanea voluntae mea.* After Sir John's death she claimed dower, but judgement was given against her and Sir William on the grounds of her adultery.[7]

Whether it was because of this or mere lack of interest, as a general rule magistrates did not wish to know. The *Laws Respecting Women* and *The Cabinet Lawyer*, both summarising *Delaville*, were clear on the subject.

> There is no doubt that the vulgar and brutal exhibition too often tolerated, of a man selling his wife and delivering her in a halter, is a misdemeanour, both in the buyer and seller, punishable with a fine and imprisonment.

[6] These examples come from William Andrews, *Bygone England*, pp. 202–6.
[7] Baronage 1, 767.

However, Exeter magistrates were amongst those who did not wish to know: '. . . a most disgraceful case and she did not deserve any protection'. It was a view shared by Clerkenwell magistrates, who dismissed a prosecution for assault in a wife-selling case.

Nevertheless voices were raised against the practice. In the 1836 edition the editor of *Blackstone* fulminated:

> It is extraordinary that prosecutions are not instituted against those who publicly sell their wives, and against those who buy them. Such practice is shameful and scandalous in itself, and encourages other acts of criminality and wickedness. It now prevails to a degree, that the punishment of some, convicted of this offence, by exposure in the pillory would be a salutary example. All such acts of indecency and immorality are public misdemeanours, and the offenders may be punished either by an information granted by a Court of King's Bench or an indictment preferred before a Grand Jury at the Assizes or Quarter Sessions.

And what was the attitude of lawyers as opposed to the law? That their opposition to the practice was unequivocal is undeniable. It may, however, have been an early form of trade unionism which produced the announcement that:

> Lawyers intend to petition against the sale of wives in Smithfield; as the practice is a contempt of the Courts in Westminster Hall. The sales there carried on are illegal because they are not sanctioned by the decision of a jury and the contracts must be void because they are concluded without the assistance of an Attorney.

Two years previously, a rather romantic sale had taken place at Clare in Suffolk:

Strange to say, the plan was adopted to transfer the lady
from her first husband to her first love, who had left her
to enlist as a soldier nineteen years ago, but rekindled
old recollections by his recent return. The lady being
brought to the *halter*, the son of Mars offered a *crown*,
which the husband pocketed and walked quietly home
to Stanstead.[8]

There is, however, no record to show that juries were any
more interested than the magistrates, nor for that matter
that judges were appalled. Imprisonment and the treadmill
were sentencing options which seem to have been invoked
only rarely, although in 1837 a man received two months'
hard labour at West Riding Quarter Sessions for trying to
sell his wife.

Juries could usually be persuaded that the vendors and
purchasers did not understand the law or were of honest
intent. When they came, the prosecutions were often for
bigamy and occasionally the errant purchaser was carted
off to the pillory. That in itself was not too bad because
the culprit could expect his friends and, if he had enough
money, his servants and bullies to protect him. So, with
fortune, apart from a little cramp and discomfort for a few
hours coupled with some humiliation, he did not usually
suffer much actual physical harm.

There are a few reports of sentencing at Quarter Sessions.
At Rutland in 1820 the purchaser was fined one shilling and
expenses. More serious punishment was meted out in 1833
when a husband at Marlborough Quarter Sessions was fined
£1 and sentenced to three months in prison.

Many of the records in the latter half of the nineteenth
century relate not to trials for the offence itself, but to
kindred matters such as child care and support. In 1872

[8] *Bury Post*, 25 February 1835.

a purchaser was fined 50 shillings for assault after a brawl
with the husband; he was also ordered to pay the costs of
the case. Nothing was said about the wife-sale itself.

By the end of the nineteenth century the practice was
confined almost exclusively to the industrial north, with
Sheffield said to be a particular stronghold. One of the last
recorded cases appears to have been in Sheffield Market,
which came to light on 13 July 1887 at the County Court.
An agreement was drawn up at the time:

> At the Royal Oak, Sheffield, I, Abraham Boothroyd,
> agree to sell my wife Clara to William Hall, both of
> Sheffield for the sum of 5s.[9]

One of the reasons for the decline of the practice and
the consequent disbelief of the public in Hardy's novel
had been the Matrimonial Causes Act 1857; this enacted
the recommendations of the Royal Commission which had
reported three years earlier. Now a secular Divorce Court
was established which took over the functions previously
exercised by Parliament and the Church.

Even so, divorce was no easy matter. The average cost was
£30, but there was some help for the indigent. Proceedings
could be taken out in Somerset House *in forma pauperis*.
There is little evidence, however, that this was of much
assistance to Somerset farm labourers.

But cases did continue to crop up. As late as 1920
there was a case before the Southend Justices where a
husband had persuaded a man to sign a document taking
over his wife. A year earlier, a woman told Tottenham
Magistrates that she had been given away to another man
by her husband.

A case tried in the 1920s by Mr Justice McCardie was

---

[9] Sheffield County Court, 13 July 1887. Andrews *ibid*, p. 207.

a variation on the theme. An allegation was made that during the War a husband had sold his wife to her lover on condition that he would be kept out of the trenches. Eventually he decided the case – which was over the price of a dress – without making any finding on the allegation.

In 1920 it was alleged, and denied, that Ethel Roberts had been sold as part of the fixtures and fittings of the matrimonial home in Stockton Lane, South Shields, by her husband to a man named Eliott by whom she later had a child.[10]

Certainly in 1929 a miner in the Languedoc, France, sold his wife for a bottle of rum. In August of that year he applied to the police for an official declaration that the sale was invalid.[11]

Perhaps, however, even at the end of the twentieth century wife-selling is not wholly dead in the Western world. In 1988 a Denver man offered his wife in exchange for tickets for the match when the local team, the Broncos, appeared in Superbowl XXII. He was reported as having said, when confronted by his irate wife on television, 'Have I done something wrong, honey?' For the record, Denver lost.

At least a Mexican, burdened by Christmas debts in 1995, only pawned his wife. She had to work for three days in an Acapulco pawnshop before he redeemed her for the $40 he had borrowed against her.

[10] *Empire News*, 3 October 1920.
[11] C. Kenny, *Wife Selling in England*.

4

Divorce

Throughout the 1850s there had been efforts to put a Divorce Bill on the file. The Royal Commission had recommended one in 1853, pointing out that the likely cost of a divorce *a vinculo matrimonii* was some £700 to £800, whereas in Scotland – where these things were differently and better ordered – the cost was £30 for a contested case and £10 less if the petition was unopposed.

Apart from anything else there were considerable difficulties in drafting such a Bill, the principal reason being that the law of marriage itself was in a mess. Over the years the Church had experienced great difficulty in actually defining just what marriage was. There was no doubt that a valid marriage was, at the time, effectively dissoluble. But just what *was* a valid marriage?

Until the middle of the eighteenth century marriage in England was possible at any hour of the day or night in any building. No marriage banns were necessary and there was no need for a clergyman to officiate. Not surprisingly, this led to the stuff from which novels and plays were written. Bigamous and fictitious marriages were contracted to secure the fortunes and seduction of ill-advised and unwitting heiresses. However, it was not until the celebration of clandestine marriages by the clergy at and around the Fleet prison in the 1740s became such a scandal that Lord Hardwicke, then the Lord Chancellor, steered the Marriage Act 1753, commonly called after him, through Parliament to put a stop to these riotous goings-on.[1]

By virtue of Lord Hardwicke's Act, a legal marriage could only be conducted by a parson of the Church of England. Until 1836 Roman Catholic and nonconformist ceremonies were not legally binding. In that year the Marriage Act established Registrars of Births, Deaths and Marriages who could conduct civil ceremonies.

Then, even given that a valid marriage could be successfully defined, what were to be the grounds for divorce? One of the stumbling-blocks was the question of evidence. Adultery could be proved evidentially, as could desertion. But what about the very subjective matter of cruelty?

In 1857 the Palmerston Government mobilised itself and pushed through the Bill. The Bill was supported by the Archbishop of Canterbury but amongst their opponents was the future Prime Minister William Ewart Gladstone, aided and abetted by 'Soapy Sam' Wilberforce, later Bishop of Winchester. For a start, Gladstone did not believe that the general public would avail themselves of this marriage breaker and he spoke virulently against the Bill, regarding it 'a major depredation of the authority of the Church'.[2]

---

[1] In Scotland an oral declaration in front of witnesses before the blacksmith's forge at Gretna Green just over the border from England sufficed.
[2] Roy Jenkins, *Gladstone*, p. 184. As Jenkins points out, Gladstone was on rather shaky moral ground. He had already been instrumental in the Lincoln divorce which had been carried out by Act of Parliament. In July 1849 Gladstone had travelled to Italy to try to persuade the Countess of Lincoln, who had run off with Lord Walpole, to return to the bosoms of her husband and five children. He failed, and second-best gave evidence before the House of Lords of her adultery. Ibid., pp. 93–5.

Here in the Act was an early example of men making laws for men. Adultery by a woman was a ground for divorce, but adultery by the husband had to be coupled with some other form of bad behaviour to enable her to seek a decree.

S.27 provided:

> It shall be lawful for any husband to present a petition to the said court, praying that his marriage may be dissolved, on the ground that his wife has, since the celebration thereof, been guilty of adultery; and it shall be lawful for any wife to present a petition to the said court, praying that her marriage may be dissolved, on the ground that since the celebration thereof, her husband has been guilty of incestuous adultery or of bigamy with adultery, or of rape, or of sodomy or bestiality, or of adultery coupled with such cruelty as without adultery would have entitled her to a divorce *a mensa et thoro*, or of adultery coupled with desertion, without reasonable cause, for two years and upwards . . .

It was an early example of legal double standards and one which was not corrected for many years.

Connivance, condonation and collusion were bars to petitions, while the petitioner's own adultery, delay, cruelty, desertion or conduct conducing adultery were discretionary bars. Out went the old civil action of crim con and in came the opportunity for a petitioner to claim damages from a co-respondent.

The Matrimonial Causes Act came into effect on 1 January 1858 and immediately Gladstone – and other politicians for that matter – was proved wrong. It had been thought that petitions would run in the twenties and thirties annually. In fact, that year there were 326 divorces granted. There was then a fall from 1859 with a low of 236 in 1861, and then an almost unchecked rise until 1901, when the total reached 848. In fairness, there was really no great rush either. In 1868 in America, which then had a population roughly double that of England and Wales, there were some 25,000 divorces.

A year later came the Matrimonial Causes Act 1860, which established the office of Queen's Proctor. Now a divorce could not be made absolute until after the expiration of three months, and the Queen's Proctor could show cause – connivance or condonation were two grounds – why the decree should not be made absolute at all.[3]

One of the earliest of litigants to fall foul of the Queen's Proctor was the Cabinet Minister in Gladstone's Government, Sir Charles Dilke, MP for Chelsea, thought by many to be a strong candidate for Prime Minister. It is ironic that his political and social downfall came because he looked to the Proctor for help in the divorce action in which he was cited as co-respondent. There is little doubt that Dilke was what a century earlier would have been called a rake.

On 18 July 1885 he heard from Mrs Christina Rogerson that she had grave information to pass to him. The grave information was just that: he was to be cited in a divorce action brought by a Donald Crawford, alleging a confession of adultery with Dilke by his wife Virginia. Even a hundred years later it is difficult to unravel the plot of who did what to whom and why, but there is little doubt that the unmarried Dilke had *affaires* with a number of women including Christina Rogerson and also Virginia's friend Mrs Eustace Smith. Virginia Crawford's confession also alleged there had been three-in-a-bed romps with her, Dilke and, worst of all, Fanny Stock or Grey, Dilke's maid.

In fact, Virginia Crawford, along with her sister Harriet,

---

[3] The period was extended to six months by the Matrimonial Causes Act 1866.

led an interesting sexual life. Crawford, a Tyneside ship-owner, was twice her age and the sisters had disported themselves with medical students as well as in a Knightsbridge brothel where they had met a Captain Henry Forster. It is possible that Dilke never slept with Virginia Crawford and his naming in her confession was a smoke-screen to protect the gallant Captain. It is also suggested that Mrs Rogerson may have played a hand. She was none too pleased that Dilke was now engaged to the wholly respectable widow, Emilia Pattison, whom he married on 3 October.

In law there was no evidence against Dilke. The only evidence in the suit was Virginia Crawford's confession, which was evidence against her but not against Dilke. Sir Charles Russell was instructed for Dilke and declined to put his client in the witness-box. He had no need to do so. Then, as is often the case with advocates, he opened his mouth once too often, saying, 'In the life of any man there may be found to have been possible indiscretions.' Mr Justice Butt dismissed Dilke from the suit and granted Crawford his divorce. And down swooped the press, led by W.T. Stead in the *Pall Mall Gazette*, like vultures on a dead donkey.

Stead demanded that Dilke should clear his name and, as many another was to do and find to his cost, Dilke went to law. He applied for the Queen's Proctor to annul Crawford's decree *nisi* before it was made absolute. A second hearing was ordered for the July. Fanny Stock was found and she was happy to deny the threesome story. So far so good, but there was a serious problem. Dilke was now not a defendant but a witness. His lawyers had no right to cross-examine Mrs Crawford. Now she amended her evidence. Yes, she had slept with the gallant Captain, but nothing would shift her from her story that she had committed adultery with Dilke. The jury took a quarter of an hour to find that the decree *nisi* had not been improperly obtained.

Efforts over the years to clear Dilke's name failed. By the time of the re-hearing he had been defeated in his Chelsea constituency and, although he was re-elected to the Forest of Dean seat which he retained until his death in 1911, he never again held public office. Nowadays the consensus of opinion amongst parliamentary historians is that he did not commit adultery with Mrs Crawford.[4]

The story of the Irish leader Charles Stewart Parnell, which ran a little after that of Dilke, was infinitely more sad. His was not a spot of adultery to pass away some boring hours. He fell deeply in love with with Katherine Page O'Shea, known as Kitty, who was sadly, at the time, married to a British Army captain William – described as 'a vain man, with little income from his estate, he soon squandered the money his solicitor father left him'.[5] He lived abroad for much of the marriage, at one time managing a sulphur mine in Spain. In 1880, 13 years after her marriage, she met the dashing Charles Stewart Parnell when O'Shea – then MP for County Clare – sent her to invite Parnell, leader of the Irish Home Rule party, to a dinner. They were both 34. The following year he moved into Wonersh Lodge, bought for her in O'Shea's absence by an aunt. The next year O'Shea challenged Parnell to a duel after he had found his portmanteau in the hallway. Parnell accepted but O'Shea backed down. Parnell moved in and he and Kitty had two daughters; but he still kept a wary eye out for O'Shea, on one occasion climbing down a fire escape at a rented flat in Brighton to avoid a confrontation.

It was W.T. Stead's *Pall Mall Gazette* which upset the matrimonial apple-cart with a little notice to the effect

---

[4] That lady went from strength to strength. Converted to Catholicism, she became a public figure in her own right, a Labour councillor and a major campaigner against Mussolini. She died in 1948. For a detailed analysis of the affair, see Roy Jenkins, *Victorian Scandal*.
[5] Matthew Parris, *Great Parliamentary Scandals*, p. 51.

that Parnell had been involved in a slight accident on
his way home to Eltham. It was surely designed not to
report the accident but to cause mischief, and it succeeded. O'Shea, who must have known perfectly well
what the situation was, now demanded an explanation.
His wife replied that it was an invention of Parnell's
enemies.

In 1889 O'Shea filed a petition for divorce. He had known
perfectly well of the situation from 1886 at the very latest –
it was then that the *Sussex Daily News* reported that Parnell
had been staying with Mrs O'Shea in Eastbourne – and must
have been blind had he not realised what was happening
some years earlier. Everybody else on all sides of the House
of Commons did.

On 24 December 1889 O'Shea sued for divorce, naming
Parnell. His motives are still obscure. In the early 1880s he
had negotiated the Kilmainham Treaty which had obtained
the release of Parnell from prison, where he had been
sent at the times of trouble which preceded the Land
Act. Parnell had never appeared sufficiently grateful for
this. It is possible that money was the real reason. The
wealthy aunt who had bought Wonersh Lodge had now
died, leaving Kitty her fortune. O'Shea saw a share for
himself. His motive may also have been political – he was
not opposing Home Rule.

Neither Kitty O'Shea nor Parnell, by then a sick man,
appeared in court. Kitty's only defence was O'Shea's own
infidelities, some 17 in number. The public and the press
behind him, O'Shea emerged the wronged man and won
custody of all the children. Parnell lost the leadership of
the Irish parliamentary party.

He married Kitty O'Shea in the summer of 1891 and
almost immediately fought a by-election. Bare-headed in
the rain on the hustings, he caught cold. Unable to change
because he had lost his suitcase, he sat up all night in

his wet clothes. He contracted rheumatic fever and died a week later.[6]

It is curious how the Queen's Proctor turned a blind eye to what was surely both connivance and condonation.

What was certainly the best of fun about the whole thing of divorce – for the public if not the parties – was the continual detailed reporting of these divorces in the press, something to which the Queen took exception:

> The Queen wishes to ask the Lord Chancellor whether no steps can be taken to prevent the present publicity of the proceedings before the new Divorce Court. These cases, which must necessarily increase when the new law becomes more and more known, fill now almost daily a large portion of the newspapers, and are of so scandalous a character that it makes it almost impossible for a paper to be trusted in the hands of a young lady or boy. None of the worst French novels from which careful parents would try to protect their children can be as bad as what is daily brought and laid upon the breakfast table of every educated family in England, and its effect must be most pernicious to the public morals of the country.[7]

In fact the Lord Chancellor had tried to do something. He had brought an unsuccessful Bill to try to stop such reporting, but he had failed to get it through Parliament.

As is regularly the case with well-intentioned but ill-thought-through Acts of Parliament, the 1858 statute was muddled and not well drawn. From the start judges were

---

[6] Kitty Parnell fared much worse than Mrs Crawford. Ruined financially by the divorce, from then on she was continually on the move. She never remarried, and died at the age of 76 in 1921. Her daughter Norah wrote, 'She has the happy delusion that Parnell comes back to her at night, when things are worse, and draws her out of the black waves as she lays dying.' For an account of her life, see Joyce Marlow, *The Uncrowned Queen of Ireland: The Life of Kitty O'Shea*.

[7] *Letters of Queen Victoria 1837–1861*, 3 vols.

taxed with a definition of cruelty. There had been little legal
definition in the divorces of the rich prior to the 1857 Act
and really their behaviour had no social relevance to the
middle classes who were now benefiting. In *Barlee* in 1822,
Sir John Nicholl had ruled that 'to amount to cruelty there
must be personal violence, or manifest danger of it'. Later
in *Bray*, where Mr B suggested that his wife had committed
incestuous adultery: 'It is not, I think, possible to conceive
cruelty of a more grievous character'; whilst Dr Lushington
ruled in 1847 that 'Threats of personal ill-usage have been
deemed sufficient to justify a separation.'

In 1850 Lord Brougham had somewhat abdicated his
judicial responsibilities by calling on a Dr Harding to define
cruelty. The good doctor had equivocated: 'There is no
code, or canon, or statute regulating the law of separation
by reason of cruelty. That law is only to be collected from
the decisions.'

Defining cruelty post 1857 was particularly difficult,
since a husband had the right to chastise his errant wife.
In the case of *Smallwood* in 1861, taking Mrs S. by the
throat and throwing her to the floor was not sufficient. In
1862, however, Waddell, who, apart from drinking heavily,
spat at Mrs W., threw cold water over her and indulged in
what was described as minor violence, was deemed to be
cruel. Mrs Scott was also found guilty of cruelty. She had a
tendency to hit her husband with a poker and on the occasion
when he protested she threatened him with a knife.

There was, however, the problem of sodomy. Then as
now, anal intercourse was used as a form of contraception.
S.27 of the Matrimonial Causes Act 1857 had provided that
sodomy was a ground for divorce, but it was not explicit
on whether this was sodomy with a third party or sodomy
with the wife to which, possibly through ignorance, she had
consented.

In 1861 the first judge of the Divorce Court, the elegantly

named Sir Cresswell Cresswell, gave a wife a divorce because her husband had treated her in such a way that passers-by could have thought she was a prostitute. Cresswell died in a carriage accident shortly afterwards and Lord Penzance took over the divorce reins. He seems to have been much more human and less ironic than his predecessor. In 1865 in *Brown*, he was faced with the problem of a husband who had wilfully communicated venereal disease to his wife; he was also habitually drunk. Penzance accepted the evidence but ruled that he was bound by precedent and declined to grant a divorce. However, there were signs that times were changing. In *Knight* he accepted that non-violent conduct could be cruel, and in *Swatman* he ruled that the presence of a mistress in the matrimonial home was of such conduct 'that she [the wife] could not be expected to discharge the duties of married life'. In 1870 he would reaffirm that decision in *Kelly*.

It was not too long before there were signs that perjured evidence was creeping into the petitioners' suits. One of the first of the cases was in the 1860s, *Alexander v Alexander and Amos*. Mr Alexander, who had some property, had, as they say, married beneath him. Mrs A. had to go, and so the servant Amos was cited. The evidence was that a farm labourer Patrick Sullivan had on countless occasions seen them 'go into another room'. He had busied himself and climbing on to a stable had spied through the bedroom window. On another occasion he had caught the pair almost *in flagrante* in an outhouse. When he reported this to his employer, Mr Alexander had at first been dismissive; but when he confronted Amos he had been kicked and abused for his pains. Sullivan added a further titbit in that most of the time Amos and Mrs A. had been three parts drunk.

Of course at this distance in time it is impossible to say whether it was a put-up job; but the Sullivans of this world were then, even more than now, regarded as unsuitable witnesses. The judge, taking the pre-electricity view that intercourse does not take place with the lights on, commented about the improbability of curtains not being drawn and doors being left open. It also may be that whilst masters might topple the maids, in those pre-Chatterley days the courts were not keen to accept that the mistresses granted the servants favours. It is not recorded whether Sullivan went unrewarded for his unsuccessful efforts on behalf of his master.

Servants were not always regarded as unreliable witnesses, however. In an earlier suit, Lady Anne Foley paid the penalty for believing that her coachman was blind, deaf or at the very least mute. He gave evidence that he had peeped through the blinds which covered the coach windows and had plainly seen Lady Anne

> . . . lying upon the back seat of the said coach, with her naked thighs exposed, and the said Lord Peterborough lying upon her and between her naked thighs, and they were in the very act of carnal copulation and the said coach was then in motion occasioned thereby, notwithstanding the horses were standing still.

All very grand language for the coachman, but at least the horses had not been frightened. Lady Anne's husband, Edward Foley, was awarded £2,000 damages.[8]

Penzance took things a step further with his Matrimonial Causes Act 1878, which gave magistrates the power to make a separation order coupled with maintenance in favour of a wife in a case of aggravated assault. This now took 'divorce' law into the realms of the poor. It was followed

[8] *The Life and Amours of Lady Anne F-l-y* (1782) quoted in H. Montgomery Hyde, *A Tangled Web*, p. 22. He goes on to record that Lord Peterborough did not do the gentlemanly thing and marry Lady Anne, who in turn married a Captain Samuel Wright.

by the Maintenance of Wives (Desertion) Act 1866, which gave the magistrates power to award a deserted wife up to £2 a week. But even as late as 1909 the County Courts Committee maintained that 'The Divorce Court in London [was] outside the reach of the poor.'

If divorce spelled ruin to a parliamentarian, it did not do so to a wronged divine. During the 1890s even the clergy were using the divorce courts, and one of the more popular of cases was that of the much-admired Methodist preacher Newman Hall, who preached in the Surrey Chapel. He had been married for some 20 years to the rather younger and certainly sporty Charlotte Graham. She smoked, rode, and after 25 years refused him his conjugal rights. She also took up with Frank Richardson, a riding-master and a rather younger man, indeed what would now be called a toy-boy. It was not a story out of which any of the players comes with that much credit. The subsequent contested divorce suit was meat and drink for press and public alike and provides a few shafts of light on the attitudes of the time. As the years of the marriage progressed Mrs Newman became more and more flighty, sitting at all hours with Richardson (now a guest in the house), smoking in a locked kitchen, visiting Brighton with him and going off with the local hunt whilst her husband in vain besought her to visit the Holy Land with him. Instead he travelled with a Harriet Knipe whom he met there. In 1873 he presented a petition alleging adultery and naming Richardson, and almost at once withdrew it. Six years later he presented a second petition also naming Richardson. Mrs Newman cross-petitioned, claiming that he had misconducted himself with Mary Wyatt at Llandudno. After all, what else was there to do on a wet Sunday afternoon in that town?

The petition was heard by the President of the Divorce Division, Sir James Hannen, a jury and a huge public gallery which, much to the distaste of Hall's counsel Sir Henry

James, enjoyed itself immensely: '. . . instead of reading the evidence in their own homes where their blushes of shame could not be seen, the public galleries have been thronged with women.'

As for the jury at least one member was shocked when, opening the petitioner's case, Sir Henry said, 'She even refused her husband conjugal intercourse.'

'Surely not,' protested a juryman.

Sir Henry was clear that since Mrs Hall had refused her husband his lawful privileges for 16 years, 'the petitioner was fully justified in now looking elsewhere for feminine companionship and consolation'. To many people the withdrawal of the first petition had the smell of condonation about it and Hall was pressed on the subject. His answer was frank if not wholly engaging:

—I was building a church at the time. This was costing £60,000 and I thought it unwise to expose my domestic affairs to the world.

What about remarriage?

—Have you anyone in mind to marry if you could and have you told her so?

Condoner he might have been, but on this point Hall was not a liar.

—Yes. I have.

Although evasive, perhaps.

—Did you deliberately take a Captain Cotton into your wife's bedroom and leave him there?
—I can't remember.

A housemaid then was called to say she had seen Mrs Hall leaving Richardson's bedroom wearing only a petticoat and bodice.

In her turn Mrs Hall proved quite sparky. Why had she refused to cohabit with the good clergyman?

—My reason was my utter dislike to it.

She admitted kissing Richardson, and he her, but both denied adultery. Miss Wyatt was dropped from the suit without a stain on her character, whilst the President laid into Mrs Hall and Richardson. The learned Sir James had a fixed impression that indulgence in tobacco by a woman was, when combined with conjugal obduracy, clear proof of infidelity.[9]

Hall was granted a divorce but he did not escape unscathed. *The Standard* commented:

A middle-aged man with a young wife who allows her to sit up at night and smoke with her riding master, may fairly be said not only to deserve but to have brought about, his own disgrace and dishonour.

There were thoughts that Hall would drop from the pulpit, but after a month's recuperation from his ordeal he was back:

If at any time during my long pastorate, any husband, parent or brother has had occasion to complain that I have ever overstepped the limits of gentlemanly deference or Christian purity . . .

and so on and so forth. His congregation certainly believed

[9] Horace Wyndham, *Victorian Parade*, p. 208.

in him. He was presented with a set of psalms and a bust modelled by Onslow Ford. Then came the announcement of his marriage – not as it turned out to the long-suffering and slandered Miss Wyatt, who it was now claimed had something of a religious mania, but to the travelling Holy Land companion Harriet Knipe. The wedding took place on 17 February 1880, when the bridegroom declared somewhat infelicitously, 'A new stop – *Vox Angelica* – has this day been heard on the organ.'

Mrs Hall was not at all pleased when she heard of the granting of the decree absolute and endeavoured unsuccessfully to have it overturned. The best she could do was to write to *The Times*, which had been sympathetic towards her the previous summer: 'I will ever protest against the injustice of the verdict recorded against me.'

She pointed out that the 1869 petition had been abandoned and dismissed with costs. There were two acts – Salisbury Street in April 1870 and Elstree in 1878 – alleged against her in the new petition, and the jury had not indicated which of the two they had found proved. So far as the Salisbury Street charge was concerned, she maintained that an alibi had been proved by the production of the diary of the deceased friend of her husband's but that for legal reasons it had been withheld from the jury. As to the Elstree affair, a perfect stranger had come forward at the time of the trial to disprove the charge.

> To the mind of a woman smarting under a sense of cruel wrong, these things are unintelligible. Other women, perhaps more helpless even than I, have suffered and found no remedy, unless it is to be found in the emphatic protest which I trust your columns will allow me to make.[10]

[10] *The Times*, 18 February 1888.

As for the middle classes, even towards the end of the century generally they saw adultery as little better than prostitution:

> In fact, she was, if anything, rather worse, for she had not only sinned against a divine commandment but violated the earth-made contract (total fidelity in return for maintenance) upon which the institution of marriage was based. Accordingly, there was nothing unusually narrow-minded or maniacally puritan in believing that a woman who committed adultery put herself beyond the social pale. On the contrary, this was the view expected and, indeed, demanded of 'men of the world' and 'men of honour'.[11]

What had happened was that Dr Playfair had discovered his sister-in-law to have miscarried in circumstances in which it seemed clear that she could not have had intercourse with her husband at the time of the conception. He was proposing the woman should leave London, and was on the point of telling his wife so that she would not visit her. In fact his rectitudinous attitude cost the good doctor dearly. Mrs Kitson sued because the slander for the ears of his wife was passed on to Sir James Kitson, a relative of the unfortunate woman. Playfair had the choice of pleading either privilege – that is, that his remarks were made in circumstances of legal or medical confidentiality – or justification – that Mrs Kitson was indeed pregnant. Wrongly he chose privilege and she received £12,000 reduced on appeal to £9,200.

---

[11] Giles Playfair in *Six Studies in Hypocrisy*, p. 140.

5

Dum Casta

One of the more unpleasant provisions in a Victorian separation agreement was the so-called *dum casta* clause – the wife would be paid maintenance or an allowance provided she led a sole and chaste life; *dum casta et sola vixit*. Or put more simply, provided she didn't have sex. After all, the husband was paying out of his hard-earned money to keep her. All too often the clause caused great hardship, sometimes to both the wife and husband alike, not least in the case of the great advocate of the English Bar, Edward Marshall Hall, and his estranged wife.

Hall had known Ethel Moon, the youngest of six daughters of his father's colleague and neighbour in Brighton, from childhood. By the time he went to Cambridge, where he was reading law but determined on a life in the Church, he was in love with her. At the age of 17, to his utter astonishment, she refused to marry him.

He met her again at a dance in the spring of 1880, after his return from a trip to Australia. One version of events is that the same evening he proposed once again and she accepted him. In all events they were married in June

1882, he being then 23. Ethel was not accepted by the Hall family, particularly Ada Labouchere, Marshall's snobbish sister, who was now a leading light in county society. The reason was plain; Miss Moon had a relative in trade.

Hall's marriage was a disaster from the start. He recorded in his diary kept on his honeymoon: 'Ethel told me she would be just as happy without me as with me, which is not exactly a cheering prospect.' The marriage limped on until early 1886, when she asked Hall for a divorce, which he refused. She then went on a trip to Australia, financed by selling some of her jewellery.

When she returned in 1889 Hall hoped they would be reconciled, but this was far from his wife's mind. Instead a separation agreement was drawn up including as Clause 4 the infamous *dum casta* provisions. It was to prove disastrous. Within months she had met and fallen in love with an Indian Army officer of French extraction, Lieutenant Raoul de Ponthieu of the Bombay Staff Corps. By April 1890 they were living together in Berners Street (off Oxford Street) in the house belonging to a Mrs Grandt who described herself as a music teacher and, whilst she did just that, was rather more at home in the Alhambra Music Hall and certainly knew a number of louche people.

On 5 May, de Ponthieu took Ethel to see a Dr Vintras in Hanover Square. She believed she was pregnant, but Vintras said it was too early to make a firm diagnosis. Mrs Grandt introduced them to a Belgian known as Dr Laermann – who also called himself the Viscount de Lerma – who ran the White Lion dispensary in the Pimlico Road and who was probably a drug-trafficker as well.

On 15 May de Ponthieu sent a telegram in the name of Mrs Grandt and, driving with Ethel in a separate carriage from Mrs Grandt, they all arrived for a consultation with the doctor. It was perhaps unfortunate that at the time his rooms were under observation by the police, who suspected him of forging cheques to pay his rent. Mrs Grandt and Ethel Hall went into his rooms, where Laermann performed a minor surgical operation described in his notebook as the removal of a polypus. He was paid £15 in cash. The next day Ethel Hall moved from Berners Street to Duke Street in Mayfair. Once de Ponthieu had called on her, they again sent for the compliant Mrs Grandt and a second operation was performed by Laermann. This was no more successful than the first. The third operation, on 24 May, followed a bottle of champagne shared by the doctor and the ladies. He injected a corrosive substance; she shrieked and bit his hand; the music teacher, anticipating George Joseph Smith, whom Marshall Hall would later defend, played the piano to drown her cries.[1]

Back in Duke Street, Ethel collapsed in agony and de Ponthieu went for Dr Vintras, who, suspecting an abortion, refused to help. Laermann was summoned, diagnosed dysentery and provided a prescription. Later Dr Phillips, Ethel Hall's own doctor, was called but by this time she was showing signs of mercurial poisoning. In her delirium she repeatedly called for Marshall Hall, who was on holiday in Paris. He was sent for but, by the time he arrived, she had died.

Laermann was arrested on the forgery charge and his notebooks were found to record a series of 'operations'.

---

[1] George Joseph Smith was the celebrated 'Brides in the Bath' murderer. Hall defended him under the Poor Prisoner's Defence Act for £3 5s. 6d. At the time, and indeed for many years afterwards, it was accepted that the way a man charged with murder could pay for his defence was to sell his story to a Sunday newspaper. The arrangement was that on a conviction the man would provide a death-cell confession for printing on the Sunday after he had been hanged. Smith, confined in Brixton prison, was willing to do this but the Home Secretary refused to allow him to sign the necessary contract on the grounds that it was contrary to public policy. Had he been on bail there would have been no problem. Smith drowned a number of women whom he had married. With them in the bath, he played hymns on the harmonium. He was executed after the jury had retired only 22 minutes before bringing in a guilty verdict.

He was charged with using an instrument and feloniously administering a noxious drug to Grace Ethel Hall, thereby causing her death. De Ponthieu was arrested in Hastings where, he said, he was under immediate orders and on his way to rejoin his regiment in Russia; he had reached Berlin and then returned to answer the accusation. Now he was charged with being an accessory before the fact and so liable to the same penalty as Laermann.

The committal proceedings were held at Bow Street Magistrates' Court before Mr D'Eyncourt. Charles Matthews appeared for the Crown and the celebrated London solicitor, George Lewis, for de Ponthieu.[2] Bernard Abrahams appeared for Laermann. In a statement to the police, de Ponthieu had said he did not know Ethel Hall was seeking an abortion. Had he done so he would have advised her against it and told her to 'go through with it' – that is the pregnancy. Mrs Grandt was called as a witness and said she did not know that Laermann was a doctor. She denied ever having been told that Ethel was pregnant, or that she had gone to the surgery with her. She had, however, received a commission of £2 for her introduction.

De Ponthieu was undoubtedly fortunate in having George Lewis as his solicitor. Not only did he obtain bail for him but this classy advocate, the equal of most of the Bar of the time, succeeded in excluding at the inquest what amounted to a confession when de Ponthieu had admitted telling Dr Phillips he would take full responsibility for what had happened. He was also able to nullify the effect of the evidence of the *dum casta* clause, showing that Dr Phillips had told Ethel she would have a hard time during pregnancy and had scared the young woman so much that she had resorted to an abortion irrespective of the penal

---

[2] Lewis was undoubtedly the most fashionable solicitor of his day. His defences included that of Adelaide Bartlett, accused of killing her husband and acquitted.

clause of the separation agreement. D'Eyncourt declined to commit de Ponthieu for trial.

At the inquest at Westminster the jury, as it was entitled to do in those days, had returned a verdict of wilful murder against Laermann. He was tried at the Old Bailey where, defended by Abinger, he pleaded not guilty.[3] Convicted of manslaughter on the second day after the jury had retired for three hours, he was sentenced to the swingeing term of 15 years' penal servitude. The jury commented that de Ponthieu and Mrs Grandt should have been charged as well.

The *dum casta* clause was still being inserted in separation agreements – without, it is to be hoped, such disastrous consequences – until the 1960s.

---

[3] Abinger, an emotional man, was never really in the top flight of criminal defence advocates. In 1910 he unsuccessfully defended Steinie Morrison for the murder of Leon Beron. Considerable doubts still exist whether Morrison was guilty. Certainly Mr Justice Darling, the trial judge, thought he was not. Morrison's sentence was commuted to life imprisonment. He starved himself to death protesting his innocence.

6

The 1920s

Back in 1909 Lord Gorell had headed a Royal Commission on Divorce. It had been accepted for some time that the divorce laws were 'full of inconsistencies, anomalies, and inequalities, almost amounting to absurdities'.[1] Unfortunately, when it reported three years later the Commission was irrevocably split. With amazing foresight the majority of its members wished there to be far-ranging reform of the divorce laws. Their proposals included equality of access to divorce for men and women both rich and poor. They saw divorce as a cleaning-up operation after the spiritual death of the marriage, and argued that there was no correlation between an increase in divorce and an increase in immorality. They also wished to add desertion to adultery as a ground for divorce.

Unfortunately, a minority of three thought that all the important recommendations would simply serve to make divorce much easier, and that any extension of the causes for divorce beyond female adultery was against

[1] 5 Parl. Debates: Lords (1937) 105: 843.

the express teachings of Christ.[2] As a result nothing happened.

The First World War provided a striking example of how events can overwhelmingly change the *status quo*. The number of divorces had been increasing annually but slowly in the 70-odd years since 1858, but the rise in the years from 1913 – the last pre-War year – to 1921 was sixfold. The great increase was in petitions during the War years. Other reasons would include hasty weddings in the flush of excitement of the conflict – marriages which were doomed to failure. Some husbands must have made other attachments during the War and wanted to remarry, but unfaithfulness by wives was the significant factor. This is not to say there was not a significant amount of adultery by the soldiers, but theirs was more easily concealed.

In 1920 Lord Buckmaster introduced a Private Bill in the House of Lords seeking to add desertion to adultery as a ground for divorce, and lost by a mere ten votes. Undaunted, he shifted tack and tried again. Now he not only added desertion but suggested that a series of courts be set up throughout the country which would hear divorce cases. This time he was successful but the Government, with at least one ear on the horrified bishops who opposed any extension of the grounds for divorce, allowed the Bill to die. In 1921 Lord Gorell tried asking for equal access for women, but Lord Buckmaster again wanted desertion to be a ground and so the measure was lost. In 1923 at last women were to be granted a divorce on the grounds of their husband's adultery (Divorce Reform Act 1923). It was a Bill 'practically universally demanded by the women of this country'; after all, women over 30 had received the vote in 1917 (though it would be 1928 before they could vote on a parity with men at the age of 21).[3] There was still

[2] Royal Commission on Divorce 1912, 1: 171–85.
[3] 5 Parl. Debates: Commons (1923) 160: 2356–81.

a healthy minority who believed that a single act of adultery
by a husband – perhaps seduced, after a night's drinking, by
a harpy – should not count against him to the same extent as
a single act of adultery by a wife which would have a more
deleterious effect on an otherwise stable marriage. There
was also the fear that there would be a rise in collusive
divorces now that only a single act of adultery had to be
proved. And to that extent opponents of the Act were
correct. Collusion amongst those who could afford a divorce
was rife. This was the era of the heyday of the Brighton
divorce, where girls from clubs such as Mrs Meyrick's 43 off
Jermyn Street travelled down to the coast for the weekend,
not for any particularly pleasurable naughtiness but to be
seen by waiters and chambermaids who brought breakfast
to the room and so provide evidence that the husband had
committed adultery. The husband would then provide proof
to his wife's solicitor, who in turn would send a private
inquiry agent armed with a photograph of the husband and
wife to the hotel to establish that the lady in question was
not the real Mrs Smith. Of course, Brighton was not the
only seaside town which specialised in this service, but it
was the best known.[4] The fact that the whole expedition was
clearly arranged does not seem to have been regarded by the
Queen's Proctor as connivance. It did, however, upset Lord
Merrivale, who was the President of the Divorce Division.
In 1925 he decided that these visits to Brighton were not
sufficient proof of adultery:

> The woman may have been his aunt, for aught I know.
> The inference of adultery arises when there is proof of
> the disposition of parties to commit adultery together
> with the opportunity of committing it.

---

[4] There is a very entertaining account of one such dire weekend party spent by
a husband in these circumstances in Evelyn Waugh's *A Handful of Dust*.

All that happened was that the Brighton hotel trade profited, and for four years two nights in Brighton was deemed to be sufficient until Lord Merrivale once again threw out a petition. This time, however, he was overruled by the Court of Appeal and the practice continued until the 1970s with hotels throughout the country profiting, as did their staff who were tipped heavily first by the erring husband and then by the inquiry agent.

Throughout the 1930s, with legal aid available to the lower middle classes, divorce was now an option, albeit a limited one. There were now slightly under 4,000 divorces annually. The cost held the parties together if only in the strict legal sense; there were undoubtedly legal problems for those not willing to take the Brighton Belle, and there was also still a pervading sense of shame attached to a divorcee. This was not alleviated by the collective guilt felt by the abdication of King Edward following his relationship with Wallis Simpson. Steps still needed to be taken, and they were – by writer and wit Alan Patrick Herbert, to whom the credit for the change in the divorce laws largely belongs.[5] His 1936 Bill extended the grounds for divorce to desertion for three years, and cruelty, as well as habitual drunkenness and insanity. It was, he argued, better that divorces were granted on genuine grounds rather than by collusion. The old-fashioned action of judicial separation was now running at a mere hundred cases a year and he wanted this phased out completely. His argument was that, *dum casta* clauses or not, they merely encouraged illicit cohabitation. As a sop to conservatism, he threw in a clause which prevented divorce within the first five years of marriage save on the grounds of exceptional hardship or depravity – sleeping with the bridesmaid on the wedding night would qualify

---

[5] For accounts of the absurdities of the divorce laws which led to his move for reform and an account of the passing of the Bill, see his novels *Holy Deadlock* and *The Ayes Have It* respectively.

as the latter. Curiously, much of the opposition to his liberating Bill came from working-class women, with the half-million-strong Mothers' Union to the forefront.

Herbert's campaign, in which he managed to satisfy the Anglican clergy by exempting them from having to remarry divorcees, as well as traditionalists and Catholic members who feared reprisals at the next election, was masterly. He and his supporters repeatedly cited Scotland, where matters had been ordered differently from the sixteenth century when both desertion and adultery had been grounds for divorce, and only a fraction of marriages had been affected by it.

A decade and a half earlier, the Russell divorce of 1922, which so occupied the press and public, had ended the detailed reporting of divorce proceedings. This long-running divorce, as with all good stories, had romance, sex, the upper classes, high-quality counsel, indeed everything which sells newspapers. Over the decades it involved two trials, two appeals and finally a hearing before the Committee of Privileges in the House of Lords.

In October 1918 Christabel Hart married the 6′ 6″ John Russell, who in 1935 would become the third Baron Ampthill. She had already had something of a chequered romantic career. Russell, then an officer serving in the Royal Navy, had proposed to her when he was 19 and she two years older but, rejecting him, she had cantered off to Gretna Green with one of his friends and shipmates, Gilbert Bradley. There, despite the general simplicity of marriage requirements, they had fallen foul of the residency qualification and had returned to England unwed. Now she wrote to Russell agreeing to marry him. Things did not go well from the start. His parents did not attend the service at St Jude's Church, Kensington, and the day before the nuptials his bride had told Russell that she did not wish to have children 'to begin with'. The first night ended with

Russell turning over and going to sleep. At three in the morning they woke up, and she said, 'Is this all that marriage means?' They then did kiss after he had reminded her of her stated intention not to have children immediately.

Things went from bad to worse for Christabel, with the second part of the honeymoon spent with his parents at the family home. Her mother-in-law made little secret of the fact that she believed that her son could have done a great deal better than the daughter of a deceased colonel in the Leinster Regiment. Indeed, with a little luck, minor royalty might not have been out of the question.

As a proposition, provided the parties are suited in bed the husband may pick his nose at the breakfast table with his boiled eggs. It is only when there is discord between the sheets that the wife notices these things and comments adversely. Sex did not go well. Although there was kissing and cuddling on his Christmas leave, she could find little pleasure in the climax, which consisted of her husband ejaculating between her legs. She described this as 'Hunish'. He provided her with a copy of Marie Stopes's *Married Love*.

When Russell left the Navy he took a job with Vickers. Christabel and her mother opened a successful dress shop in Curzon Street. The Russells no longer shared a bedroom, nor did he share her passion for dancing and hunting. They dined together twice in two years. On one occasion she spent the night at Gilbert Bradley's flat and Bradley had to telephone Russell in the morning to bring round day clothes for his wife. She wrote to a friend: 'I have been so frightfully indiscreet all my life that he has enough evidence to divorce me about once a week.'

It is curious how manners change. If in the 1960s or the 1970s this conduct had taken place, intercourse would have been an almost irrebuttable presumption. As we approach the end of the 1990s this would not necessarily be so. It does

not appear to have been the case with Christabel Russell,
for things then took an extraordinary turn. She went to a
clairvoyant, who told her she was about to have a child;
then consulted a gynaecologist who confirmed that she was
seven and a half months pregnant, but also that she was a
virgin. Christabel told her husband the news on 23 June
1921, adding, 'I suppose I must be another Virgin Mary.'
Either the gynaecologist had things slightly wrong or it was
an extremely protracted pregnancy, for she gave birth on
15 October 1921 to a son, Geoffrey.

Russell petitioned for divorce, citing Bradley and Lieutenant George Cross (who had trained a horse for her) as
well as an unknown man. There were allegations of nights in
Salisbury and Paris. The case was heard by Lord Merrivale
and a jury, beginning on 7 July 1922. Sir John Simon led
a bevy of silks (including Mr Douglas Hogg, later Lord
Hailsham) for the petitioner, whilst Mrs Russell's line-up
included Sir Patrick Hastings. The dress shop was clearly
making good money.

Russell fell foul of Hastings almost immediately.

—If I proved in this Court that the child is yours, would
you be glad or sorry?
—You never could.
—Answer my question. Would you be glad or sorry?
—Supposing that I am able to prove that in June 1921
your wife was a virgin, would that affect your view?
—Not in the least.

Russell told the story of delivering clothes to Bradley's flat
and Hastings again rounded on him.

—When you found her in Mr Bradley's flat and you
brought her clothes, you did not accuse her of adultery.
—I believed my wife. But since she has had a child . . .
—Then it all comes back to the child. Would you

believe that she had committed adultery if she had not
had a child?
—I accepted her story at first. If she had a child and I
was not the father of it, it is quite obvious that she has
committed adultery.

Russell called no medical evidence to show that he was
not the father. There was no doubt that the Russells had
spent two nights together around Christmas in December
1920 and so, Hastings claimed, partial intercourse had
taken place. Medical evidence was that assuming there
had been relations at that time, then a birth date of 15
October was wholly consistent. *Fecundatio ab extra* was
quite possible.

In the witness box Christabel Russell admitted her
indiscreet behaviour but denied adultery. She had been
in Paris with Bradley, but they had stayed on separate
floors. She had been in his flat, but there had been no
improper behaviour. Bradley followed her into the witness
box and denied adultery, as did Cross.

Hastings now applied to have the jury inspect the baby
and it was taken to the jury room for examination during the
luncheon adjournment. It is doubtful if this would take place
now. In bastardy proceedings in the days before accurate
blood typing and DNA testing, magistrates were enjoined
'not to view' the baby.

After ten days the hearing – for the Russells at least –
ended in disaster. Both Cross and Bradley were exonerated,
but as to adultery with the unknown person the all-male
jury, after five hours, could not agree. Neither of the
Russells would accept a majority verdict. Retrial.

It began, this time before Mr Justice Hill, on 28 February
1923 and lasted one day longer than the first trial. Now
Edgar Mayer joined the list of the co-respondents; he
had helped her to set up the dress shop. Douglas Hogg

had become Attorney-General and so stood down. Sir John Simon had another brief. They both unhesitatingly recommended Marshall Hall. Apparently he did not want the brief, his *amour-propre* perhaps offended that he was a late substitute, and only accepted it after Lady Ampthill had called on his chambers begging him to do so. Apparently she reminded him of his own mother and he was touched by her pleading.[6]

This time there were three women on the jury, one of them unmarried, and the judge invited her to stand down: '. . . it would save her hearing very unpleasant details,' said Marshall Hall. 'I am inclined to agree,' said Ellis Hume-Williams for Mrs Russell. 'I think the details will be found rather shocking to an unmarried lady. For a married one it would be different.'

'It is for you to decide rather than me,' said Hill.

'I think I should be better employed elsewhere,' said the lady, to be greeted by an outstanding example of judicial wit.

'I am sure we all here think the same,' agreed Hill.

Then came the legal problem which put the case into the textbooks and thus provided generations of law students with the reason to study the intimate details of the case so closely. Russell started to give evidence that there had been no form of sexual relations between him and his wife after July 1920, so making it impossible that he could be the father. Hastings argued that the evidence was inadmissable. As the law stood in declarations for legitimacy, neither the husband nor the wife could prove the illegitimacy of a child born in wedlock and that marital relations had not taken

---

[6] Supplicants tended to visit Marshall Hall to press for his services. When in 1922 Alfie Solomons was on trial for the murder of Buck Emden, the racecourse gangleader Derby Sabini visited him in his rooms in Welbeck Street to ask him to appear for Solomons. This time, however, it was not tears which were offered but white banknotes. Hall took the brief and obtained a verdict of manslaughter.

place when it was admitted that there was the opportunity for intercourse. He argued that the same principle applied in divorce cases, but Hill ruled that the evidence was admissible.

This time Christabel Russell offered a curious explanation for her pregnancy when Marshall Hall threw at her something she had said to a friend shortly after she discovered she was pregnant:

> I have never done anything to be ashamed of in my life. I don't mind having an illegitimate child. I would rather it was anyone but John's, but as a matter of fact it is his. He behaved like a Hun. John walked in his sleep, and I found him in his pyjamas in the street sleep-walking. Is it not curious? That is how it happened.

She stood her ground against Marshall Hall in full flight.

> —You have heard Mr Russell say on oath that he does not believe he is the father of the child.
> —Doesn't believe it. He knows it.
> —You have indeed married a bad man?
> —I married a fool.

Mayer was dismissed from the suit and Christabel Russell was found to have committed adultery with a man unknown. A decree *nisi* was granted, and so began the long and ruinous proceedings towards the House of Lords. On 24 July 1923 the Court of Appeal unanimously dismissed Hastings' submission on the admissibility of Russell's evidence. Christabel Russell appealed. Hastings had now become Attorney-General and he was replaced by Stuart Bevan KC. Sir Douglas Hogg was back, leading Marshall Hall. By a verdict of 3:2, their Lordships ruled the evidence was inadmissible and ordered a new trial.

On 27 June 1924 Marshall Hall again appeared for Russell in front of Mr Justice Hill to say that, quite apart from being unable to give crucial evidence, his client could not afford a new trial. He had paid his wife's solicitors £8,640 as her taxed costs, and he still owed her the costs in the Lords and his own solicitor's fees estimated at around £30,000. Hill rescinded the decree *nisi* and, making the judgement of the House of Lords an order of the High Court, effectively legitimated Geoffrey Russell, something which was done formally on 29 July 1926 when Mr Justice Swift made a declaration of legitimacy.

John Russell took the title in 1935, two years before Christabel divorced him in an undefended suit. He remarried twice; by his second marriage he had a son John who, on his father's death in 1973, claimed the title.

In February 1976 the Committee of Privileges in the House of Lords heard the claim for succession to the title. Geoffrey Russell declined to make available blood tests carried out on himself and his mother, who by now had died. In April the Committee ruled in favour of Geoffrey Russell. It was, said Lord Russell of Killowen, in effect an appeal 50 years out of time against the ruling of Mr Justice Swift. Lord Wilberforce said:

Declared the lawful son of his parents in 1926, treated, as documents show, for the purpose of family settlements as legitimate, having married and founded his own family in the assumption of legitimacy, he is now after fifty years, when both his parents and probably other contemporaries of his birth, are dead, to have his status questioned, to be graded as some kind of fictional issue which cannot rank as lawful issue, or qualify as such under the terms of the barony. This cannot be the law. If ever there was a case for closing the chapter in a family's history, the case for closing this in 1926, after the distressing revelations over so many years, must be the one.[7]

The House of Lords' decision of 1924 became known as the rule in *Russell v Russell* and remained law until it was abolished by the Law Reform (Matrimonial Causes) Act 1949 – which, in turn, was re-enacted in the Matrimonial Causes Act 1950. From then on, evidence of sexual access or the lack of it became admissible.

There were, however, occasional benefits from being regarded as a chattel, as Mrs Owen Peel – or actually her lawyers – discovered in 1921. She and her husband the gallant Captain, down on their luck, had engaged in a racing fraud of the simplest but usually effective kind, backing known winners. Unfortunately, because the race was late off, Post Office workers became suspicious and the pair were prosecuted.

When the case came before Mr Justice Darling, the lawyers for Mrs Peel ingeniously ran the old defence that a married woman was irrebuttably presumed to be coerced into misdoing by her husband where they were acting in concert. This had stemmed from the time when, because they could not read and write, women were unable to claim the benefit of clergy at assizes. Now it did not matter that Mrs Peel had the money or that there was no possibility of this very striking and self-possessed woman kow-towing to her amiable but ineffectual husband. That

[7] At the time of the legitimacy hearing in 1926 Christabel Russell told the court that John Russell had never recognised nor even seen his son. After the Second World War she went to Ireland, becoming Joint Master of the Ballymacad Hunt in County Meath and continuing to hunt side-saddle until her seventies. At the age of 78 she rode across Australia and then drove home in a van which back in London she discovered had been unlicensed and uninsured. She died at the age of 80 in Galway on 16 February 1976. For an account of her life, see Eileen Hunter, *Christabel*. For accounts of the Russell case, see H. Montgomery Hyde, *A Tangled Web*, Chapter 7; H. Montgomery Hyde, *Sir Patrick Hastings: His Life and Cases*, pp. 87–94.

was the law as set out in cases from 1813 and 1814 – the last time the defence had apparently been raised – and try as the prosecution might it could not wriggle out of the problem. Mrs Peel had to be acquitted. Captain Peel then pleaded guilty and received a nine-month sentence. Members queued up in Parliament to denounce the iniquity of this particular exercise, and in time the Criminal Law Act 1925 blocked that little benefit.[8]

One of the long-standing grounds for divorce had been that one of the parties had failed to comply with an order for restitution of conjugal rights. This was an example of the husband's ownership of the wife's body. The court would make an order that the erring party return to the matrimonial home and perform her – or much more rarely his – marital duties, which did not necessarily include intercourse. Instead, the court saw the conjugal rights as 'the antithesis of that wilful separation without cause or reasonable cause which constitutes desertion'.[9]

In 1891 the Court of Appeal had the opportunity of considering the question of just how far a husband could go in his effort to enforce an order for the restoration of his conjugal rights. Earlier cases had established that he could confine his wife if she was about to 'be guilty of misconduct touching upon the husband's estate or honour'.

Edmund Haughton Jackson and his wife Emily Emma Maude had lived apart throughout the whole of their brief marriage. They married on 5 November 1877, he executed a settlement of his wife's property on 9 November and the next day left for New Zealand. The intention was that she would join him after about six months, and for the time being she went to live with her sisters and brother-in-law.

---

[8] *The Times*, 8, 9, 15 March 1922.
[9] *Russell v Russell* [1895] P.315. Yes, the same Russell who gets prosecuted for bigamy a few years later. Until 1884 the court had the power to attach or imprison the person who refused to comply with an order for restitution.

Rather than go out to him she wrote asking him to return
home but, curiously, when he did she refused to join him
in Clitheroe, Lancashire. He applied for and was granted
an order for the restitution of conjugal rights. She failed
to comply.

There followed what was a disgraceful incident. As she
was leaving church on Sunday, 8 March 1891, her husband
– accompanied by two young men, one of whom was a
solicitor's articled clerk – seized her in full view of the
congregation and bundled her into a waiting carriage. The
clerk then accompanied the husband and wife to Edmund
Jackson's home in Blackburn, where she was kept a prisoner
in the charge of his sister. It was the appearance of Emily's
relatives outside the house which the husband insisted
necessitated the clerk and others staying in the house to
prevent a forcible rescue. Warrants were taken out on a
charge of assaulting the wife's sister and the police were
called, but they withdrew when an undertaking was given
to appear before the local police court. In an affidavit to
the court, Jackson said he had treated his wife with every
courtesy. She had, lucky woman, the free run of the house,
and he had even offered to take her for a drive. There was,
however, other evidence that the blinds had been drawn to
prevent her exchanging signals with her relatives outside.

The first judge declined to make an order for her release,
but the Court of Appeal took the view that at the end of the
nineteenth century this really was overdoing things.[10]

---

[10] One of the more appalling examples of an application for restitution was in
the case of Cornelia Connelly, founder of the Society of the Holy Child Jesus.
This American nun married and had three children before her husband Pierce
decided to convert to Catholicism and become a priest. In 1846 she joined a
convent and began working with young mill-girls in Derby. Pierce Connelly
took against celibacy and reappeared in her life demanding his conjugal rights.
When she refused to see him, he kidnapped the children and began an action
for restitution. It was only when her case reached the Court of Appeal that
she succeeded. See Radegunde Flaxman, *A Woman Styled Bold: The Life of
Cornelia Connelly*.

I do not mean to lay it down as the law that there may not be some acts which might give the husband some right of physical interference with the wife's freedom – for instance if the wife were on the staircase about to join some person with whom she intended to elope, I could understand that there might be to some extent a right to restrain the wife.

The husband's contention is that, whereas the Court never had the power to imprison her as for a contempt for disobedience of the decree for restitution of conjugal rights, and even that power has now been taken away, the husband may himself of his own motion, if she withdraws from the conjugal consortium, seize and imprison her person until she consents to restore conjugal rights. I am of the opinion that no such right exists or ever did exist.[11]

Certainly the courts, in more recent times, never expected that an order for the restoration of conjugal rights actually meant what it said, and over the years it was used more as a step to a divorce.[12]

One of the last actions was brought by the singer Dorothy Squires, still passionately in love with her husband Roger Moore, who had in turn fallen in love with an Italian starlet.

---

[11] Lord Halsbury, L.C., *The Queen v Jackson* (1891) 1 Q.B. 679–80.

[12] Sometimes it was used for purely financial reasons and sometimes it appears out of spite, as illustrated by two cases from 1923. In October Alice Ada Parkes, who had married in 1899, brought a petition for the restitution of conjugal rights. The marriage had apparently never been consummated and in December 1922 a petition for nullity by her husband – who wished to exchange his wife for a newer and presumably more co-operative model – was rejected by Mr Justice Horrocks. Mr Parkes then offered his wife a £150 annuity. She countered with a petition for restitution and succeeded.
   The next month barrister Edward St Clair Harnett successfully resisted a petition for restitution by his authoress wife who had lampooned him in a novel. He had taken umbrage and left. She failed. (*Reynolds News*, 28 October and 18 November 1923.)

In 1972 Squires brought an action for restoration of conjugal rights and, although successful, never subsequently
presented the divorce petition to which the order would
have more or less automatically entitled her.

The A.P. Herbert Divorce Act of 1936 nearly doubled the
number of divorces to 8,200 in the two-year period to 1939
and, with the Second World War, for all the same reasons
as in the First, there was a rocketing number of divorces.
By 1947 the number of petitions had reached some 60,000.
Two-thirds of the immediate post-War divorce petitions
were brought by husbands, which suggests that there
had been a good deal of discovered infidelity on the
Home Front.

Thereafter the number of divorces shrank to a low of
28,000 in 1958. Two years before (1956) another Royal
Commission on Marriage and Divorce showed the general
trend of rising divorces in the Western world. These
included housing shortages which forced a young couple
to live with one of their parents, often creating unacceptable
tension. It was still a time when a pregnancy was followed
not by an abortion or an illegitimate birth but by a marriage,
however ill-suited the parents might be. The report also
suggested that the greater emancipation of women was an
influence in the increased divorce rate. As they entered the
labour market in increasing numbers, albeit in subservient
capacities, the fear of financial dependency was lessened.
From 1960 the Pill and penicillin were also contributing to
a greater sexual freedom. In the 20 years to 1970, 70 per cent
of divorces granted to husbands were on the grounds of their
wives' adultery. Such stigma as there was in society probably
came from being a cruel wife rather than an unfaithful one.
Without doubt, there was a readiness of both parties to cut
away from a stale and unhappy marriage.

By the end of 1960s the undefended divorce had become
something of a farce, with barristers taking bets on how

quickly they could push through increasingly weak petitions. There was usually a tame doctor (rather like abortionists) to whom the solicitor would refer the women –
or, less commonly, the men – for a medical report. No
one queried whether the patient was one of long standing
and no one cared. The *quid pro quo* was that the doctor
referred his genuine patients to the solicitor. There were
few queries from judges and, except in the most ludicrous of
cases, decrees could be expected in a matter of minutes.

However, there was still the Queen's Proctor with whom
to be reckoned, and many a helpful letter winged its way
from behind neighbourhood curtains to his office explaining
that the petitioner was not all she (mostly) might be. As a
result what were called discretion statements – elaborate
and very often lying documents which from the writer's
point of view would have been better called indiscretion
statements – were composed. The discretion, in fact, was
all his Lordship's. If suitable penitence was displayed,
then adultery by the petitioner could be pardoned. It
might read:

> After the shock of my husband's adultery I rarely
> socialised until on the — of — I went to a party
> at the Regent Palace Hotel (Piccadilly) where I met
> a man whose name I only knew as Nigel. Following
> too much to drink sexual intercourse took place. I have
> never seen the man since.
>
> Save as aforesaid I have never committed adultery
> and I humbly crave the discretion of this Honour-
> able Court.

Or:

> After my husband left me I met a young man Nigel
> Smith at the local tennis club. Following a social rela-
> tionship sexual intercourse took place on one occasion

on a weekend visit to his widowed mother's flat in Bognor Regis.

Save as aforesaid I have never committed adultery and I humbly crave the discretion of this Honourable Court.

Note that after this appalling lapse the misconduct was never repeated by the erring petitioner. That would be perfectly in order, and the judge would invariably be in a forgiving mood. Serial adultery was more difficult to deal with, but it was by no means impossible. A few selected instances would be listed in the hope that the hand behind the twitching curtains did not put pen to paper once more.[13]

In 1969 the Divorce Reform Act took away the concept of 'guilt' in a divorce suit. Now all the courts had to be satisfied about was that the marriage had 'irretrievably broken down'. The old grounds of adultery and cruelty – now disguised as unreasonable behaviour – remained the reasons for the breakdown. Cruelty was now watered down to 'grave and weighty conduct making a continuation of cohabitation intolerable, which has caused or is likely to cause injury to health'.

Much depended on the attitude of the barrister invited to draft the divorce petition. One might go through on the grounds that the wife tickled her husband too often in bed, whilst another might not on the grounds that a husband wished to watch his wife bath. 'My wife and I do it all the time,' one barrister told an unhappy petitioner. It is not clear why the behaviour of the upper classes should have been a bar to a divorce for those less socially adroit than themselves. This woman had probably grown up in a

---

[13] A most entertaining account of divorce cases of the period comes in Bill Mortlock's factional *Inadmissible Evidence*. Mortlock was the pseudonym for a divorce lawyer with a substantial South West London practice.

house where there was no bath, and the invasion of the small luxury of privacy in middle age probably was genuinely cruel to her. But there it was.

By 1993 any stigma attached to divorce had vanished. That year 165,000 couples were divorced; 350,000 had been married. The quarrels over conduct were transferred to disputes over children and financial matters.

7

Bigamy

The next way to deal with an unhappy marriage is to defy
Dr Johnson's belief that a second marriage is the triumph
of hope over experience and to marry bigamously: that is, in
the lifetime of a spouse the marriage to whom has not been
dissolved. It is an offence to which, it is said, the British as
a nation are particularly susceptible. In 1961, for example,
it was estimated that there were probably about 20,000
bigamists, with around 100 being prosecuted a year.[1]

It has always been a defence to show that the spouse
has been absent for seven years and is not known by the
bigamist to be alive. In the past the courts took a fairly
open-minded view of things. Even if the accused could have
put him or herself about and located the whereabouts of the
missing partner, they required actual knowledge before a
conviction. In 1888 Mrs Tolson was fortunate. She honestly
but mistakenly believed her husband was dead after she

[1] However adroit the British are at contracting bigamous marriages, they have
a long way to go to equal the achievements of Giovanni Vigliotto, who was
estimated at his trial for fraud and bigamy in Phoenix, Arizona to have married
105 times. He received 34 years and a $240,000 fine.

heard from his brother that the ship in which he had sailed to America had been sunk with the loss of all hands. She was prosecuted for bigamy at Carlisle Assizes and, after the jury added a rider to the conviction that they believed she had acted in good faith, she received one day's imprisonment. On appeal, the Queen's Bench Division held that despite the fact that she was wrong this would provide a good defence.[2] Now, with world-wide communication available at the press of a key, it is doubtful that courts would take such a liberal view.

One of the more unfortunate defendants of the time was Earl Russell, the elder brother of the philosopher Bertrand. In April 1900 he remarried in the United States, a month after obtaining a Nevada divorce not recognised by the English courts. His wife then petitioned for divorce on the grounds of bigamous adultery and on 17 June 1901 he was arrested. He elected trial by his fellow peers in the House of Lords and, pleading guilty, was the last peer to be convicted in such a trial.[3] His Lordship received three months as a First Division offender.

Until recently the English courts have always regarded this bit of bad behaviour as being cured by an immediate custodial sentence. Much would depend on whether the second wife was deceived, as in the case of John Burke in 1920 who received three months in the Second Division.[4] Sometimes the courts of those days could be merciful, as when Frank Mortimer had his sentence reduced in 1917 to

[2] *Tolson* (1889) 23 QBD 168.
[3] *Earl Russell* [1901] AC 446. Such trials of peers continued in a desultory fashion throughout this century. The last trial was in 1935 when Lord de Clifford was accused of 'feloniously killing and slaying' Douglas George Hopkins on the Kingston Bypass. Despite those grand words the case was what would now be called death by dangerous driving. His Lordship was acquitted. The right of trial by peers was abolished by the Criminal Justice Act 1948. See PRO/MEPO/3/839.
[4] 14 Cr App R 127. A sentence in the Second Division meant greater privileges for the prisoner.

avoid the loss of his pension. David Braidwood was not so fortunate; in 1921 he was given 12 months' hard labour.[5] On the other hand, minimal or no culpability could result in imprisonment. In 1917 George Stuart Ellis received six weeks in custody plus a day; he had believed his original marriage to be illegal, and in any event his first wife had died before his trial.[6] Two years later, John Thomas Williams received eight months when the court found there were extenuating circumstances.

Account was clearly taken of the Great War and the increase in the offence. The Court of Criminal Appeal had the right to increase sentences and took the opportunity to explain why in the 1917 case of Robert Spargo.[7] Repeat offenders could expect three years, as Henry William Brandon discovered in 1920.[8]

In recent years there have been few prosecutions for non-commercial bigamy and it is difficult to establish now what sentence the bigamist is likely to receive. It will all depend on the circumstances. As Waller LJ commented:

In many cases of bigamy it is possible to deal with the case by some sentence which does not involve deprivation of liberty. In other cases there may be a clear deception which has resulted in some injury to the woman concerned; in which an immediate custodial sentence must be passed, and the length of that sentence must depend greatly on the seriousness of the injury that has been done.

In the case he referred to, the bigamous marriage which lasted only a week was never consummated. Nevertheless,

[5] 13 Cr App R 146; 16 Cr App R 85.
[6] 13 Cr App R 194.
[7] 13 Cr App R 122.
[8] 15 Cr App R 131.

the woman had said she would not have married her husband had she known he was already married – she might otherwise have found herself on an aiding and abetting charge. It was held that 18 months was out of all proportion to the facts, and the sentence was reduced to one month.[9]

In fact, financial dishonesty by a solicitor was regarded as rather worse than his bigamous behaviour. In October 1993 Victor Harris, who had used both his wives to obtain mortgages, received six months for the marriage offences and two and a half years for false accounting.

In one of the most recent cases, Wayne Roberts managed his affairs both extremely badly and duplicitously and received just under two years for his pains. Married to a woman pregnant with their second child in July 1997, he then met Donna Harris, a personnel manager, and began spending time with her, telling his wife he was staying with a friend in Preston and assuring Miss Harris that he had obtained a divorce. He then took his family to Spain for a holiday, telling her he had gone to France for the World Cup. Two days later he borrowed divorce documents from a friend and scanned them through a computer, producing a decree absolute. He then diverted a telephone call from the court so that it would appear everything was in order.

Roberts told his wife he was going to Atlanta but instead, following his marriage at the Chester Register Office, had a wedding reception costing £7,500 and then flew to the Maldives. Rumours back in England led to the police being tipped off and he was forced to tell Miss Harris that their marriage was illegal.

The court was told that she had lost a stone in weight, could not sleep and felt she could never trust a man again. Roberts's wife also had difficulty in sleeping and

[9] *Crowhurst* (1978) CSP B9-43A01.

felt humiliated, bringing him well within the *Crowhurst* guidelines for sentencing. The cynical might suspect that the court also felt deceived and humiliated by Mr Roberts's manipulation of their documents.[10]

It might be thought that commercial bigamy is regarded much more seriously, as it is generally done to provide British citizenship otherwise unavailable to one of the parties, but this does not appear to be the case. It has been suggested that between 60 and 70 per cent of all marriages involving foreign nationals are a sham, with professional brides being paid up to £1,000 a time. In 1998 Samantha Parry was charged with marrying eight times in the previous eight years, with a record four marriages in 1996, whilst a former lap-dancer, Susan Coates, married seven illegal immigrants from West Africa in 14 months. Three men were each jailed for between seven and nine months. One schoolgirl bride borrowed her elder sister's birth certificate and married at Croydon Register Office at the age of 14. She was caught through the wedding photograph for which she posed after the ceremony, and later at the Old Bailey was ordered to do 120 hours' Community Service. Mark Charled and Sylvia Van Beest, who married 12 times over a decade, only received a year each for their pains.[11]

[10] See Russell Jenkins, 'Inventive bigamist jailed for 22 months' in *The Times*, 14 November 1998.
[11] *Daily Mail*, 2 January 1999; *Evening Standard*, 9 February 1999.

8

Death

The most socially undesirable and personally the riskiest way of ending a marriage is to kill one's partner.[1] Over the years the British courts, unlike their continental counterparts, have never really recognised the concept of the *crime passionnel*, perhaps believing it to be the invention of Marie Stopes. In France, if proved, a *crime passionnel* could reduce a murder charge to one of manslaughter, which, in turn, would often reduce the sentence to a matter of months or – if a really good tale was told – bring about an outright acquittal.[2]

---

[1] In more recent times, arranging contracts on one's no longer cherished husband or partner has come into vogue. Inevitably this has proved risky in that the person approached to dispose of the victim has *sometimes* turned out to be an undercover police officer, with long-lasting, unpleasant results for the commissioning party. For an account of some of the cases see Frank Jones, *Paid to Kill*.

[2] One of the best French *crimes passionnels* is that of Yvonne Chevalier, who on 12 August 1952 shot her unfaithful husband Pierre, a former Resistance hero and a rising political star. At first the public and press were firmly against her; but as she told of his series of infidelities, the flaunting of his mistress, his refusal to take her to receptions, a suggestion that she should take a lover and the final morning when he said he was leaving her and she should remain in her own filth, the tide turned. She told the court that she had threatened to kill herself with a 7.65 Mab automatic but that he had said, 'Go ahead. It will be the first sensible thing you've done in your life.' Instead she shot him. The prosecution asked for a sentence of two years, but she was triumphantly acquitted.

Probably to qualify as a genuine *crime passionnel*, the killing had to be in hot blood and the provocation so immediate that the ordinary person would lose self-control. Words were generally not enough, but the finding of a strange bare bottom peeping through the sheets undoubtedly would be.

Strictly speaking, therefore, Kitty Byron might not qualify. On 11 November 1902 she stabbed her lover Arthur Reginald Baker to death. He had been abusive to her over a lengthy period and when their landlady had threatened to evict the pair of them, he had asked if he could stay if Kitty went. When this little piece of betrayal was relayed to her she said, 'I'll kill him before the day is out.' Unfortunately it was several days before she stabbed him outside the Stock Exchange where he worked; she had sent him a message saying it was imperative she met him. She did not give evidence at her trial and, with her counsel not trying to argue insanity, suggested she had bought the knife to kill herself. Kitty was convicted of murder, with the jury adding a strong recommendation of mercy. She was reprieved following a huge wave of public opinion in her favour and eventually served ten years' imprisonment.[3]

In 1922, Mrs Edith Jessie Thompson was effectively tried for adultery. There is no doubt that her younger lover Frederick Bywaters intended to kill Percy, her husband. What is certainly not as clear-cut is the part she played when her husband was stabbed to death as he walked along Belgrave Road, Ilford, in the early minutes of 4 October.

The Thompson marriage had not been a happy one, with the attractive and vivacious Mrs Thompson smothered by her husband's behaviour. According to her, at best he was pernickety and at worst a wife-abuser. He was 32, she four years younger and Bywaters only 20 years of age.

[3] *Lord Darling and His Famous Trials*, pp. 125–8.

She was a great romantic and fantasist. Bywaters, a steward on the P. & O. liner *Morea*, had known Edith when he was at school with her brothers and in 1921 he took lodgings with the Thompsons. She fell deeply in love with the younger man, writing him a series of passionate letters which were to become her death sentence. Because of his job Bywaters was abroad for lengthy periods, and the letters Edith Thompson wrote him while he was away were to become a pivot of the prosecution's case at her trial. She destroyed his letters, and it is even possible that he kept hers with a view to blackmailing her at a later date.

On his last leave, the pair met in a café in Aldersgate Street on 3 October 1922. That night she went with her husband to the Criterion Theatre. As they reached home, Bywaters attacked and stabbed Percy Thompson. She was heard to cry, 'Oh, don't, oh don't!' and ran to help her husband. When a doctor arrived, she complained he had not come soon enough to save him. Both were arrested and taken to the police station, where, when she saw Bywaters by chance, she called out, 'Oh, God, what can I do? Why did he do it? I did not want him to do it.' She continually denied that she had known Bywaters's intentions. Unfortunately, in the past she had written in one of her letters to him that she had tried to poison Percy on three occasions by giving him powdered glass. When Sir Bernard Spilsbury examined Thompson's body, he found no trace of poison or of the powdered light bulbs of which she had written.

Mrs Thompson gave evidence much against the advice of her counsel, Sir Derek Curtis-Bennett, who later wrote:

> I know – I am convinced – that Mrs Thompson would be alive today if she had taken my advice. She spoiled her chances by her evidence and her demeanour. I had a perfect answer to everything, which I am sure would have won an acquittal if she had not been a witness.

She was a vain woman and an obstinate one. She had an idea that she could carry the jury. Also she realised the enormous public interest, and decided to play up to it by entering the witness-box. Her imagination was highly developed, but it failed to show her the mistake she was making. I could have saved her.

The judge, Mr Justice Shearman, was wholly against her – he ruled her love-letters to be admissible – and she made a terrible witness. Both she and Bywaters were condemned to death. Any reprieve for which she might have hoped was dismissed by the Home Secretary. Two things counted against her. First, the outcry there had been over the recent reprieve of Robert True, from a wealthy family, for the murder of prostitute Olive Young; and second, because of a newspaper campaign which suggested that she had led a younger and weak-willed man astray.

It is now generally accepted that Edith Thompson should not have been convicted on the evidence before the court, but that she was tried and convicted for what was seen to be her lack of morals.

Both were hanged on 9 January 1923, he at Pentonville and she at Holloway. It is possible that she was pregnant, but no examination of her by a Jury of Matrons took place.[4]

The sad Ruth Ellis is perhaps the best-known British example of the *crime passionnel*, but she was a great deal less fortunate than Kitty Byron. Part-Welsh, part-Belgian, model and part-time prostitute, Ruth Ellis was convicted of shooting her faithless lover and a passer-by on the evening of Easter Sunday, 10 April 1955, outside the Magdala public house in Hampstead. By no means was she a gangster's moll

[4] In fact the judge sentenced three women to death that week. Two were reprieved. For an account of the trial, see Rene Weiss, *Criminal Justice*. Of the other women who were convicted and reprieved, Daisy Wright had drowned her child at Tower Bridge and Ellen Jones had killed Florence Stevens, a widow, with whom her husband had been having an affair.

or proactive in crime, but she belonged in the twilight world of Mayfair and South Kensington drinking clubs and the Edgware Road and Paddington abortionists.

In 1946, after she had had a child by a Canadian soldier, she began to work for Morris Conley – the owner of a number of clubs including the Court Club in Duke Street and the late-night Hollywood in Welbeck Street. Shortly after the Ellis shooting, Duncan Webb named Conley as '. . . Britain's biggest vice boss and the chief source of the tainted money that nourishes the evils of London night life'. This was really rather going it a bit, since the Messina brothers still had part of their operations intact. Perhaps because they were Maltese this didn't count. Conley lasted another six years before the *News of the World* reported his conviction for keeping a brothel in Westbourne Terrace, Paddington. The police had seen 82 men go to the address over a three-day period and, best of all, there was 'the nature of various paraphernalia one associated with these types of premises'. There were four known prostitutes amongst the tenants. Conley, who initially said, 'I did not know what was going on,' had £400 in his pocket at the time of his arrest. He was fined £100 and ordered to pay 25 guineas costs.[5]

Ruth Ellis drifted from club to club and man to man, ending with racing-car driver David Blakely, with whom she had a relationship for two years. She still continued her work as the manageress of the Little Bottle Club, entertaining men in her flat above the premises, and Blakely had other girl-friends. In February 1955 they began to live together in a flat in Egerton Gardens. The relationship was stormy and Blakely left shortly before Ellis had a miscarriage at the beginning of April. There is some evidence that he hit her in the stomach, which led to the miscarriage. On Good Friday – driven by a man named Desmond Curren, described as

[5] *The People*, 11 December 1955; *News of the World*, 10 September 1961.

her alternative lover – she went to see him where he was staying with friends in Tanza Road, Hampstead, and the police were called twice to remove her. On Easter Sunday there was a party at the house. Blakely left with a friend about 9 p.m. to go to the Magdala. When he left the pub Ellis shot at him six times. One bullet hit a Mrs Gladys Kensington Yule in the hand, one missed and the other four hit Blakely. He died instantly. Ellis was immediately arrested.

There was no real defence proffered by Melford Stevenson QC, who appeared for her, and she was asked only one question by Christmas Humphreys for the prosecution:

—Mrs Ellis, when you fired that revolver at close range into the body of David Blakely, what did you intend to do?
—It is obvious that when I shot him I intended to kill him.

The judge, Mr Justice Havers, told the jury, 'Even if you accept every word of it [her story] it does not seem to me to establish any sort of defence to murder.' In view of the judge's ruling Melford Stevenson made no closing speech to the jury, who retired for only 14 minutes before returning a guilty verdict.

There was a very real campaign to save Ruth Ellis from the gallows. She was an attractive woman who by now had two young children. Her mother told her story to the *Woman's Sunday Mirror*, and the *Empire News* had a few words from Mrs Jackie Dyer, who had been a barmaid in the Little Bottle Club. Sidney Silverman, the campaigning MP, put together a petition for Ellis's reprieve which carried 50,000 signatures. It was in sharp contrast to the recent executions of two other women, both of them ugly and with whose crimes it was impossible to sympathise.

Grace Merrifield had poisoned her employer thinking she would be left money in her will and Styllou Christofi, a Cypriot lady who spoke little English, had strangled her daughter-in-law and set fire to her body in the garden. The brilliant journalist Robert Conner, writing as Cassandra in the *Daily Mirror* on 30 June 1955, had this to say:

> Ruth Ellis does not matter any more than her two recent female predecessors to the hangman's noose – Mrs Merrifield and Mrs Christofi.
> But what we do to her – you and I – matters very much, and if we continue to do it to her sad successors then we all bear the guilt of savagery untinged with mercy.

Mrs Yule certainly didn't feel that way. She wrote to the *Evening Standard*:

> Don't let us turn Ruth Ellis into a national heroine. I stood petrified and watched her kill David Blakely in cold blood, even putting two further bullets into him as he lay bleeding to death on the ground . . .

The efforts of Silverman and the others were to no avail. The fact that a passer-by had been injured is said to have influenced the Home Secretary against granting a reprieve. Ruth Ellis had taken little interest in the efforts to save her, regarding the matter much as a life for a life. She was hanged at Holloway Prison on 13 July 1955, the last woman to be hanged in this country. She was, said a prison officer to the *Daily Mirror*, '. . . the calmest woman who ever went to the gallows'.

Within two years the law was changed and the Homicide Act 1957 was passed. Now under s. 3 there was an extended defence of provocation by words as well as deeds. In 1958

Ernest Fantle – who had shot his wife's lover after verbal provocation – was sentenced to three years' imprisonment under the section. It is inconceivable that a jury would not have found the same provocation in the case of Ruth Ellis had the defence been available.

In fact, for years women have complained that they received more severe sentences when they disposed of disappointing spouses. They have continually urged that the law should take into account the 'battered spouse' defence, which at the beginning of the 1990s seems, in practice, to have been available to men only. In 1991 Sara Thornton was sentenced to life imprisonment for murdering her alcoholic husband, while Joseph McGrail was given probation for disposing of his bullying wife and a year later Bisla Rajinder Singh the same for killing his nagging wife who had berated him for two hours.

Over the next few years the Sara Thornton case, along with two or three others, became a rallying cry for feminists seeking to establish the 'battered wife syndrome'. Malcolm Thornton had been an alcoholic for some 15 years. He was either a peaceful one who slept off his drink, according to his first wife, or a violent bullying monster, according to Sara Thornton. She would maintain that there was a final brutal quarrel following which he went back to sleep; she found a knife in the kitchen and stabbed him while he slept. They had been married less than a year.

Eventually her supporters won her a further visit to the Court of Appeal, which ordered a retrial of her case. She pleaded guilty to a reduced charge, thereby rather spoiling things for those observers who wished to see how things worked out on the question of provocation.

The argument of women campaigners had centred on the man who kills in a fit of sudden temper whilst under provocation and can receive a seemingly nominal sentence, as compared with the woman who smoulders under years of torment and then without any apparent specific trigger kills her husband and receives life imprisonment for her pains. Things have improved, however, and although the Court of Appeal, noticeably in the case *Ahluwalia*, has regarded itself as incapable of redefining provocation so as to blur the distinction between a sudden loss of self-control and retribution, the courts have been more willing to accept that there now may be a period of time between the final straw and the defendant's reaction. However, this was not the case in 1981, when a period of seven days had elapsed and the Court of Appeal noted with approval that the trial judge had not allowed the defence of provocation to be put to the jury.[6]

The English courts lagged behind their American counterparts, which recognised the 'battered woman syndrome' in the early 1980s. On 20 May the previous year Gladys Kelly had stabbed her husband, Ernest, with a pair of scissors. She ran self-defence at her trial and tried to have expert evidence introduced to show that she had been the subject of emotional and physical abuse. The court ruled it was inadmissible, and she was convicted of reckless manslaughter. On appeal, the New Jersey Supreme Court ruled that she could, indeed, introduce that expert evidence and claim self-defence, even though at the time when she killed her abuser she was not actually under immediate threat.[7]

The extent to which things had changed for the better for women can be seen from two cases reported on the same day. In the first at Liverpool Crown Court, Jan Painter was cleared of the manslaughter – an earlier charge of murder

---

[6] *Ibrams* (1981) 74 Cr App R 154; *Thornton* [1992] 1 All ER 306; Thornton [1995] 1 Cr App R 578; *Thornton* (No 2) [1996] 2 All ER 1023; *Ahluwalia* [1992] 4 All E R 889.
[7] *State v Kelly* 478 A.2d 364 (N.J. 1984); Elizabeth L. Turk, 'Excuses or Justifications' in *Whittier Law Review*, Volume 18 1997.

had been dismissed by the judge – of her husband James, whom she had stabbed during a row over £1.20. She had suffered from premenstrual tension and they had quarrelled when she found he had taken the money to make some telephone calls.

Across the country at Truro Crown Court, Peter Care was jailed for life. His wife Lesley Ann had begun an affair and had written to her lover that her husband did not read her incoming mail. She was wrong. When Care returned from night shift he slipped into bed with his wife and, when she refused to have intercourse with him, stabbed her with an ornamental knife and then strangled her. His plea of manslaughter on the grounds of diminished responsibility was rejected by the prosecution.[8]

A marginally less extreme way of dealing with an abusive husband was one which earned American Lorene Bobbitt and her husband John world-wide fame if not fortune. Following a domestic quarrel, she cut off his penis and threw it in a field about a mile away from their home. It was found and packed in ice, and was reattached in what was the first successful operation of its kind. She was acquitted of causing him grievous bodily harm at her trial in September 1993. John later appeared in a sex show with the ingeniously named Long Dong Silver.

Nullity

A marriage is a nullity if it is bigamous; it was induced by duress or mistake; at the time of the ceremony one of the parties was insane or under age; it was not solemnised in due form; or it was between parties within the prohibited

---

[8] *Daily Express*, 17 December 1994.

degrees of affinity or consanguinity. The only ground on which a marriage is voidable is the inability to consummate the marriage.

The courts were always willing to give the non-consummating party a chance to put things in order, and it could be argued that the petitioner had accepted the non-consummation as part of life and had adopted the sexless marriage.

In one petition of the 1960s, in a variation on the old legal story, when a middle-aged petitioner was asked why she believed her husband to be incapable of consummating the marriage she blushed and replied, 'He masticates.'

Jactitation of marriage

If over the years someone falsely claimed they were married to you, a petition of jactitation could always be brought. The benefits lay in a release from liability for debts incurred by the *soi-disant* wife. The action was rare, and the last reported case seems to have been in 1922 when Israel Goldstone claimed that Leah Goldstone was falsely claiming to be his wife. They had gone through a ceremony of marriage in 1889 at Tscherevitz in Poland, then under Russian rule, and he claimed that not all the technical requirements had been fulfilled. They had lived together in Leeds and in 1909 she had brought proceedings for maintenance, but these had been dismissed when the pair were reconciled. Now he sought to rid himself of this turbulent wife. He failed.[9]

[9] *Goldstone v Goldstone*, 127 L.T. 32.

PART TWO

Extramarital Sex

9

Incest

In 1920 Mr Justice Darling, sentencing a brother and sister after they had pleaded guilty to incest, complained:

> When these people began cohabitation, their crime was not punishable. It had been punished by the Ecclesiastical Court long ago, but this had ceased in the 1850s, and in 1908, Parliament made it a criminal offence, punishable with seven years' penal servitude. These two particular people received no information that what they were doing was a crime. Many people – their relations – knew they were living this way.[1]

Darling, lately a much reviled judge, often (as on this occasion) had his heart in the right place. Later in the year he had something to say about the practice of holding incest cases in camera:

> I was certain myself that incest would be much less

[1] *The Times*, 23 January 1920.

frequent if people knew that since 1908 it is a crime
punishable in the ordinary criminal courts ... to be
to the public advantage that the system of trying these
cases in secret should be abolished.[2]

It was only an outbreak of late-Victorian and early-
Edwardian purity which had put incest on to the statute
book as a crime. Before that it had enjoyed a long, if not
respectable, life so far as the courts and society were
concerned.

The Lord, about the same time as He expatiated on
the subject of bestiality, had a word or two to say about
incest:

None of you shall approach to any that is near of kin
to him, to uncover their nakedness.

The Hebrews, along with their Assyrian and Hittite neighbours, took Him at His word and His remarks – which had
covered sisters, grandchildren and step-daughters – now
extended to the uncovering of maternal grandmother's
paternal brother's wife. The elders could get quite punitive
about the whole thing. Not only did this rule apply from
after marriage but also from courtship onwards. Penalties
ranged from the mild – flagellation, to the rather more final
– death.

Whatever the historical and literary significance of
Oedipus and the Egyptian King Akhenaten, whose fifth
marriage was to the third of his daughters – indeed incest
was almost *de rigueur* amongst Egyptian royalty – the English

---

[2] *The Times*, 19 November 1920. For Darling's unpopularity see amongst others
Martin Beales, *The Hay Poisoner* and Brian McConnell, 'Charlie is not my
Darling' in the *New Law Journal*. Despite this he certainly did what he could
to save Steinie Morrison (convicted of the murder of Leon Beron on Clapham
Common in 1911), from the gallows and, indeed, almost invited the jury to
acquit him.

courts, overall, did not take too stern a view of the matter. In its prayer books the Church prohibited sexual intercourse in the case of a close blood relationship or one defined by marriage. It was a popular concept, and it may well have been true, that a deceased wife's sisters were terribly attracted to the widower. Perhaps it was thought that the prohibition of a subsequent marriage kept a failing marriage (and the wife) alive a little longer.

Apart from a short spell of Puritanism, when incest became a felony and attracted the death penalty, punishment for the crime was in the hands of the 'feeble coercion of the spiritual court, according to the canon law'. The old punishment had been a spell of public confession in the church or market place. The penitent wore a white shirt, clutched a white wand and was barefoot. Richer penitents could escape this particular bit of unpleasantness with the more practical monetary retribution.

The truth is that by the 1800s no one cared very much about incest. Such cases as there were concerned incestuous marriages, and it remained 'the only form of immorality which in the case of the laity is still punished by Ecclesiastical Courts on the general ground of sinfulness'. Again, as with bestiality and wife-selling, the majority of people did not believe it took place. But it did and, according to the purity movements of the late-Victorian era, rather too often.

The Punishment of Incest Act 1908 was another of the symbolic crusades mounted so that the prestige of the proponents of the new law overrode the concern for those whom it was designed to protect. Homosexuality may have been the 'love that dares not speak its name', but incest was the love whose name others dared not speak. Beatrice Webb, the Fabian Society leader, had written in her diary of the sweatshops in the East End and of the prevalence of incest in one-room tenements, but she excised them from her published account. The *Lancet*, albeit not the prestigious journal of today, referred to 'things done in secret' and thought they should never be published. Hansard reports that the Parliamentary Bills published in 1903 (which failed) and 1908 (which led to the Act) referred to a 'very disagreeable subject' and 'a very painful subject'. No further explanation was given.

There was no real statistical evidence of the incidence of incest, and it was thought that admissions that such things did happen would tarnish the Victorian home and family as a 'repository of the highest Christian Virtues'.

That incest ever did reach the statute book as a crime is largely due to the crusading zeal of a number of societies set up in and from the 1880s. These included the National Vigilance Association (NVA) (not to be confused with the Vigilance Association for the Defence of Personal Rights)[3] and the National Society for the Prevention of Cruelty to Children. Under the Criminal Law Amendment Act 1885, fathers could be prosecuted for unlawful sexual intercourse with their daughters under the age of 16, and it was the self-appointed role of the NVA to ensure that they were. Was there, therefore, any need for further safeguards? 'Yes,' said the purity leagues with one breath.

The first stumbling block to the prosecution of a father was that parental consent had to be obtained before a medical examination of the child could take place. The second was that a prosecution had to be commenced within three months. If the first did not confound those seeking to protect children, the second certainly did.

Apart from the intention of protecting young girls, the Incest Act may have been a by-product of the quest for better housing for the working classes. 'Incest is common,'

---

[3] Its full title was the National Vigilance Association for the Repression of Criminal Vice and Immorality. Its leaders included Millicent Garret Fawcett, Josephine Butler and Ellice Hopkins.

said the Reverend Andrew Mears, with none of the reticence displayed by later politicians, in *The Bitter Cry of Outcast London*. The Reverend John Horsely believed that incest was common in London and that it was invariably due to overcrowding in one-room accommodation. William Booth, the Salvationist, said in 1890 that, 'Incest is so familiar as hardly to call for remark.'

Meanwhile Ellice Hopkins, who – funded by the Salvation Army – had helped to promote the Criminal Law Amendment Act 1885, was still stomping the country advising the working classes on how to avoid immorality in general, and incest in particular, whilst living in close and crowded conditions. The advice included hanging a curtain between the beds, using hammocks and, particularly, washing in shifts – by which she presumably meant both smocks and turn – so that brothers and sisters never saw each other naked. Additionally Ms Hopkins was to tell the ladies of her country associations to 'keep a watchful eye on the hayfields at mealtimes'. Incest was really only a tiny part of the larger 'immoral behaviour' from which the working classes, whom it was believed had exclusive rights to this sort of conduct, had to be protected. In 1893 the NSPCC promoted a draft Incest Bill. Morality was the keyword. No longer were they interested only in the protection of the young but also in the prohibition of incest between consenting adults. In this they had the support of Chief Constables of Police. Out of a poll of 177 senior officers by the NVA, almost all were in favour of legislation.

Ellice Hopkins was still hard at work. Mothers' Unions were now proliferating and Snowdrop Bands had spread through Sheffield and the North of England. The YMCA had talks on the 'fascinating sin of impurity', not specifically incest but embracing all forms of impurity.

In reality there had probably been a drop in urban incest,

but there was still bad behaviour in the cornfields. Indeed, one tract for agricultural workers was published under the title *Smut in the Wheat*.

When Colonel Amelius Lockwood moved the second reading of the Incest Bill in 1903, he explained that what had persuaded him to do so was the number of crimes being committed in the rural districts of England, and he did not think that Hon. Members would imagine that such crimes should not be severely punished. But he was wrong. The Hon. Members were not that concerned and the Bill was defeated, to be reintroduced five years later. This time it would be strongly supported by the Liberal MP for Bath, Donald McLean.

McLean was one of the founders of the NSPCC and the solicitor for both that society and the NVA. In late 1908 he had been paid £1,000 by the NVA to have *The Yoke*, a novel by Hubert Wales, suppressed. Ninety years later the theme of the novel – the self-sacrifice of a mother who gives herself to her son to save him from an unsuitable marriage – seems ludicrous. Now, in the Commons, McLean turned his attention to 'this grave moral offence which', he was sorry to say, 'is rife in certain parts of the country'.

The passage of the Bill was by no means smooth. Elder statesmen still thought such things did not happen and, even if they did, there was no point in publicising them. The Earl of Halsbury thought that 'the evil, though shocking, is of rare occurrence' and that legislation was not required. He believed the Bill was 'calculated to do an infinite amount of mischief'. It was he, in particular, who believed that press publicity would produce 'a crop of similar offences at other Assizes'. Rawlinson, the Member for Cambridge, said he thought that the level of incidence of incest had dropped in the past 30 years. It is not clear on what evidence he based this but he certainly feared that, just as the Criminal Law Amendment Act 1885 had been a Blackmailer's Charter with homosexuals as the targets, so the same would happen with an Incest Act.

The Bill was passed with two amendments. The first sensible; the second, with Lord Halsbury at the helm, rather less so. The more sensible suggestion was that prosecutions could be brought only with the sanction of the Attorney-General or the Director of Public Prosecutions. Lord Halsbury, fearful that others hearing of the crime at their local Assize Court might go out and do likewise, secured the amendment that the cases should be heard in camera; it was this amendment which Lord Darling criticised and which was removed in 1922.

Nearly half a century after its enactment, the Punishment of Incest Act 1908 was consolidated in the Sexual Offences Act 1956 S. 10 (1) and the relevant provision became:

> It is an offence for a man to have sexual intercourse with a woman whom he knows to be his grand-daughter, daughter, sister or mother.

The converse offence is under S. 11 (1):

> It is an offence for a woman of the age of sixteen or over to permit a man whom she knows to be her grandfather, father, brother or son to have intercourse with her by her consent.

The terms brother and sister included both the half-blood and illegitimate relationships.

From the fuss, it might be thought that incest was occurring day and night in every hovel and behind every stook of corn but, whilst this may be the so-called dark side – the unreported side of crime so beloved by sociologists – so far as prosecutions went it was not the case.

Scotland, which had an Incest Act as early as 1567 and

which carried capital punishment on a conviction until 1887, had an average of six convictions annually between 1896 and 1905.

As might be expected, there were rather more cases recorded in England and Wales after the Act came into force. In the period 1920–24, 89 cases were reported of which over 80 per cent were prosecuted; in the period 1950–54, some 235 (55 per cent); and 295 (40 per cent) in 1977. As might be expected, in recent years the severity of the punishment has usually, but not always, been linked to the age of the victim.

Two years after the Act came into force Mr and Miss Hall found themselves in the House of Lords and subsequently in prison. Before the passing of the Act they had had a child, and the birth was used as evidence of the commission of the offence. Their Lordships put it as follows:

> evidence of conduct at an earlier date tending to prove
> that the parties had gratified a mutual passion is admiss-
> ible as relevant to the issue raised in the indictment
> and to rebut the defence that the relations between the
> parties were innocent.

There was no question in their Lordships' minds that all passion might be spent. They considered sleeping in the same bed to be an act of passion.

Over the years it has usually been cases of the older man who commits incest with his daughter rather than offences between brother and sister which have been brought before the courts, although when the latter have appeared for sentence a spell of imprisonment has been thought to be a proper solution.

In 1922 at Leeds Assizes, Harold and Blanche Priestley received 12 and 15 months' hard labour; they were at the time of the offence 17 and 19 respectively. Presumably the

additional three months given to the girl was for leading her
younger brother astray. The Court of Appeal was merciful.
Swayed, no doubt, by G.D. 'Khaki' Roberts's plea in the
best of middle-class taste on their behalf that 'they offended
as the result of ignorance and defective training', the Lord
Chief Justice felt able to observe:

> It is obvious when we look at the circumstances in which
> these young people – not much more than children at
> the time of the offence – lived, that there were certain
> opportunities and temptation offered. They are certainly
> deserving of pity but of some punishment as well.

Sentence reduced to six months in the Second Division.
The housing situation always called for comment.

> I don't know how you can expect people to go straight
> under such circumstances, all herded together in a small
> house . . .

This was Mr Justice Sankey at Bedford Assizes, sentencing
Henry Cullip, who pleaded guilty to incest with his 14–
year-old sister. His Lordship was rather more merciful
than the Court of Appeal, putting the boy on probation
for two years.[4]

The judge was only expressing the general sociological view:

> It [incest] usually results from prosaic and obvious
> factors – overcrowding, alcoholism, poor intelligence,
> lack of opportunity for sexual outlets outside the family,
> adolescent ignorance and curiosity.

It is generally a far cry from Byron and Augusta and

[4] *News of the World*, 23 January 1928.

Lawrence Durrell's creation of Pursewarden and his blind sister, although in the latter case art may have been imitating life for there have been serious suggestions of a relationship between Durrell and his daughter, Sappho.

Not so fortunate were Frederick Ross and his sister Elizabeth Hart, who each picked up six months at the Old Bailey in 1944. The circumstances were tragic. Mrs Hart had been adopted by her uncle and grew up thinking he was her father. She therefore believed Ross was her cousin but, when the facts were known, she continued living with him.[5]

Times change. Now young men and adolescents are charged in less than a quarter of the cases each year. The sisters who are charged in consensual cases total a mere handful annually. Rarely prosecuted before they are 21, they almost invariably receive non-custodial sentences. Indeed this would seem to be the pattern of sentencing for all women in incest cases. In 1971 George – then 16 and from a family in which all the children shared the same bedroom – had his sentence of Borstal training varied to one of probation; and in 1974 when a brother and sister in their thirties were cohabiting a sentence of two years suspended for two years was varied to a conditional discharge.

It is the father-daughter relationships which are shown most public and judicial opprobrium, particularly if there has been a suggestion of intimidation, or where the offences have started when the daughter was young, or to whom a number of children have been born. '"Worst case," says Coroner' and 'My most shocking case' are typical headlines.

The Coroner quoted had been sitting at the inquest of Henry Virgo, then aged 63, who had eight children by his daughter, Lavinia. The matter had come to light through

[5] *News of the World*, 15 March 1944.

poison-pen letters and, rather than go to the police station, Virgo had cut his throat in Greenwich Park.[6]

Mr Justice Streatfield at Exeter Assizes thought while sentencing Cyril Sandford that:

> This, without exception, is the most shocking case of this kind with which it has been my misfortune to be concerned.

Judges tend to make comments like these, and a glance through the Sunday newspapers of the decade will produce a crop of such statements. In this case, however, Streatfield must surely have been right. Sandford had 15 children by his wife and another five by two of his daughters. His counsel had urged in mitigation

> . . . he should not be too hardly punished because he was a breadwinner of a large family and a first class workman and had not been in trouble before.

Sentencing him to a total of seven years, the judge indicated that he would have taken into account a plea regarding the overcrowded condition of the house but for the fact that the incidents had been in the daytime and, with one exception, they had not taken place in the bedroom. He commented: 'There are five children who in due course, if not now, will be able to call you both father and grandfather at the same moment.'[7]

But times change. The guidelines for sentencing in incest cases have now been clearly established in the *Attorney-General's Reference No. 1 of 1989*,[8] where, in father–daughter cases where the daughter was not far short

[6] *Reynold's News*, 6 September 1931.

[7] *News of the World*, 13 November 1949.

[8] *The Times*, 1 August 1989.

of her thirteenth birthday and there were no particularly adverse or unfavourable circumstances, on a not guilty plea a sentence of about six years would be appropriate; in cases involving girls between the ages of 13 and 16, somewhere between three and five years; and in the case of girls over 16, from three years down to a nominal penalty. In *Attorney-General's Reference No. 7 of 1989*,[9] the Court of Appeal substituted probation for an 18-month suspended sentence on a 42-year-old man who had admitted two charges of indecent assault and two of incest on his teenage daughter.

Admitting the offence has always been an essential for a defendant who wishes to obtain a reduction in his sentence or later parole. In *Harding*,[10] a sentence of three years' imprisonment was reduced to 18 months. He had contested the allegation but had been convicted on two counts, having admitted to the police intercourse on about 50 occasions when he was aged between 13 and 20; his sister was three years younger. A suggestion that he should be placed on probation after having served part of his sentence was rejected:

> . . . we have been told today on behalf of this appellant that he continues to deny having committed these offences. That, in our view, hardly bodes well for a period of probation. *per* Potts J.

A father who was given an 18-month suspended jail sentence for incest and indecent assault was put on probation for three years after the Attorney-General had applied to have his sentence increased under the terms of the Criminal Justice Act 1988. This was the fifth time the Attorney-General had effectively appealed, and it was his first loss.

---

[9] *The Times*, 11 November 1989.
[10] (1989) 11 Cr App R (S) 190.

The Lord Chief Justice on this occasion said that the trial judge, Mr Justice Hodgeson, had been right to treat the case as wholly exceptional. The 42-year-old man from Newquay had pleaded guilty at Truro Crown Court. Unfortunately, what was considered 'wholly exceptional' was never made public by the Court of Appeal.[11]

Is there any need for retaining incest as a crime? There are surely enough sanctions available for the father-young daughter cases. One argument is that there is a higher risk of abnormality, possibly as much as 28 per cent, in the offspring, but there is no prosecution of the uncle-niece union and there is a correspondingly higher risk of defects in children born to older mothers. There is no suggestion that the latter should be prohibited from giving birth; indeed, on the whole they receive a good press. In the 1990s there was a string of well-publicised cases of older mothers who had been given a fertility drug subsequently giving birth. The record holder for the oldest – a lady who may not have been completely frank about her age when she sought treatment – seems to be in her early sixties.

Indeed, in these instances whilst the child may not, as in the *Sandford* case, be able to call her mother grandmother, that is who she is more likely to resemble during the formative years. There will be no suggestion that the parent will be a likely winner of the mothers' race on school sports day. Paraphrasing Candida: 'When I am ten you will be sixty/seventy; when I am twenty-one you will be seventy/eighty-one.' Nor is intercourse prohibited in unions where one party suffers from, say, haemophilia or

---

[11] The Criminal Justice Act 1988 s. 36 gave the Attorney-General power in indictable cases – those which could only be tried before a judge and jury, for example manslaughter, death by dangerous driving, rape and incest – to apply to be allowed to proceed to the Court of Appeal with a view to an increase in the sentence. One effect of this has been to allow the Court of Appeal to set sentencing guidelines in such cases. See *Attorney-General's Ref. No. 5 of 1989. Daily Telegraph*, 11 November 1989.

Huntington's Chorea, both of which illnesses carry a high risk that the defect will be passed to the child.

The Criminal Law Revision Committee has recommended that incest between a brother and sister over the age of 20 years should no longer be a crime, and it has the support of a working party of the Howard League for Penal Reform, which argues against the prosecution of consensual acts for adults, as does the Sexual Law Reform Society.[12]

[12] The Report of a Howard League Working Party, *Unlawful Sex*, p. 26; see also 'Comment' in *New Law Journal*, 29 January 1988.

10

Contraception

Until the beginning of this century contraception in England took a variety of forms, including buggery, itself a capital offence until 1861, the condom, abortion and the destruction of the child after birth. So far as the condom is concerned one version of its creation is that, made of animal gut or fish bladder which was moistened and tied with a ribbon, it was first made by a Colonel Cundum or Condom. It was possibly a specifically English invention, and initially was used not to prevent conception, but as a protection against venereal disease.[1]

But in 1798 Thomas (the so-called 'Gloomy Parson') Malthus had published his essay raising the spectre of man-kind's multiplying with such vast rapidity that the demand

[1] Other versions such as Ivan Bloch, *A History of English Sexual Morals*, p. 312, have Dr Conton as the inventor during the reign of Charles II. Richard Davenport-Hines in *Sex, Death and Punishment*, p. 51, suggests that it is first described by Gabriello Fallopio in 1564, which rules out the good doctor, and that the earliest description in English is by John Marten in 1704. By the middle of the eighteenth century Casanova was using those 'little shields which the English have invented to keep the fair sex from worrying' (*Memoirs* Vol. XIII).

for food and other necessities might soon overwhelm the supply. In the previous three decades the population had increased by 25 per cent. There was the fear of bad harvests. A year earlier Jeremy Bentham had vaguely described the use of sponges, but abortion and coitus interruptus were the basic methods of contraception.

Francis Place, the self-educated London tailor who himself had 15 children, had begun to harangue labour and political leaders on the disastrous consequences of a large family. With a handbill given out at workers' meetings, *Illustrations and Proofs of the Principle of Population*, he became the first campaigner for contraceptive techniques. The condom was changing its use.

Over the years, one thing that the Government and the ruling classes – both here and in the United States – were unwilling to do was to allow the working classes to know about the benefits of contraception. There was a long-running battle between the authorities who wanted a large workforce to fight battles and populate the factories, and social reformers who saw large families as counter-productive and women as something more than breeding-machines.

Nevertheless, there was also over the years a considerable body who thought that not only was contraception for married women morally wrong, in that it promoted immorality, but that by limiting a family the mother became prone to nervous disorder at menopause. One propagator of this particular doctrine was Mary Scharlieb, who qualified at Madras Medical School and, although she was 40 before she undertook her first operation, was held in high regard for her abdominal surgery.

The proponents of contraception battled on, spinning seductive webs of the benefits. The publisher Richard Carlile offered practical hints on *How to Enjoy Life and Pleasure without Harm to Either Sex*, whilst Place went altogether too far when he produced three pamphlets. The first, *To the Married in Genteel Life*, suggested the introduction of a soft and moistened sponge in the shape of a small ball attached to a narrow ribbon and was aimed at the aristocracy. The middle classes were rewarded with *To the Married of both Sexes*, where it was suggested that a one-inch-square sponge attached to a double thread should be used; whilst the working classes had to make do with a sponge 'the size of a green walnut or small apple'. The first device was a 'cleanly and not indelicate method'. What really got up people's noses, so to speak, was the suggestion that 'neither does it diminish the enjoyment of either party'. Now since women were deemed to be incapable of sexual enjoyment, retribution followed in the shape of the magazine the *Bull Dog* – launched to harry and persecute both Carlile and, more particularly, Place.[2]

Six years later the American Charles Knowleton produced *The Fruits of Philosophy – An Essay on the Population Problem*, which contained details of how to effect a douche using alum and sulphate of zinc; the solution to be applied within five minutes of intercourse. It was a great success. By 1839 10,000 copies had been sold in America, and by 1876 42,000 sold in a variety of editions in this country. Untouched in its early days, it would become a *cause célèbre* by the time it was 50 years old. Soon after the decision in *Hicklin* became the standard test on how obscenity was to be defined, *The Fruits of Philosophy* now offended Victorian moral standards. Chastity and not birth control was the order of the day.

One of the early great champions of birth control, as well as equality in marriage, was Annie Besant. Born in 1847, she considered herself psychic and attended a

---

[2] For those interested in the technical details, an account of early versions of contraceptives can be found, for example, in Ronald Pearsall's *The Worm in the Bud*, pp. 273–7.

ritualistic church in Chelsea where she met Frank Besant, the curate. She flirted, he succumbed and asked permission of his beloved's mother – her father had died when she was five – for permission to marry. It was promptly refused, and just as promptly Annie defied her mother and married, saying, 'My ignorance of all that marriage meant was as profound as though I had been a child of four instead of twenty. My dreamy life . . . kept innocent of all questions of sex, was no preparation for married existence.' Living in Cheltenham, they had three children in quick succession. The marriage lasted six years before she obtained a judicial separation, something of which she would later write that '. . . the system of judicial separation should be swept away. Wherever divorce is granted at all, the divorce should be absolute.' The reasoning behind her thinking was that 'Judicial separation is a direct incentive to licentiousness and secret sexual intercourse.'

Nevertheless, she extracted £110 a year from her husband. For the time being her life seems to have been peripatetic. Her mother died and she obtained a job as a governess and later as a researcher at the British Museum. It was there that she learned of a magazine, the free-thinking *National Reformer*, and from this that there was to be a lecture in the Hall of Science in Hoxton. The lecturer would prove to be both her soul-mate and her nemesis, Charles Bradlaugh, whose critics have described him as a professional malcontent. In his early life he had held various clerical jobs – with a solicitor for 10 shillings, as a timekeeper for £1 a week. He was an indifferent lecturer, but his friend Austin Holyoake had funded a printing press. Bradlaugh with his *National Reformer* became a publisher.

The meeting at the Hall of Science was a great success. Annie Besant is described as a ravishing beauty, and it is clear that she captivated him and Bradlaugh her. Together they read pamphlets on the existence of God, and Bradlaugh employed her on the *National Reformer* at a guinea a week. Through him she gave her first lecture, "The Political Status of Women", in a Co-operative Society Hall; when he left England for a spell of lecturing in America, she was left behind as the star of the circuit.

In 1876 Bradlaugh persuaded the publisher Charles Watts to reissue *The Fruits of Philosophy*. The result was an immediate appearance at the Central Criminal Court the following January, when Watts pleaded guilty. Bradlaugh, who was rather sniffy about the fate of poor Watts – declaring that he himself would never have republished the book on grounds of style, not content, but 'If I had once published it, I would have defended it until the very last' – now decided he would after all republish it.

In the March of 1877 he and Annie Besant went to the Guildhall to say that they were republishing and would be out selling the book the following day. Just to make sure, they informed the police and the City Solicitor. When next day they appeared for the sale, they were promptly arrested. Their friend the bookseller Edward Truelove was found with 650 copies of the book. With some prescience Bradlaugh and Besant had hidden theirs under the floorboards in the lavatory in Bradlaugh's flat.

They came up for trial in June 1877 to determine, as Chief Justice Cockburn put it, 'whether it is a scientific production for legitimate purposes, or whether it is what the indictment alleged it to be, an obscene publication'.

Bradlaugh and Besant thought they had arranged a number of guns on their side but, as Radclyffe Hall found out some 35 years later, not everyone was willing to stand and be counted. Charles Darwin pleaded ill-health and Professor Henry Fawcett said he would send his wife abroad rather than see her in the witness-box.

Bradlaugh and Besant were convicted, the jury delivering

one of those curious verdicts which make people despair of the system:

> We are unanimously of the opinion that the book in question is calculated to deprave public morals, but at the same time we entirely exonerate the defendants from any corrupt motives in publishing it.

One juryman said that six of them did not agree with the verdict, and two donated their guinea fee to help with the defence fund.

Bradlaugh now leaped into action, protesting that the judgement be respited, that there be a new trial and the indictment be quashed. He and Annie Besant were out on the street selling again, but this time with more serious consequences: both were arrested and given a £200 fine and sent to prison for six months. In the end they did not serve their sentences, but Annie Besant's daughter Mabel was taken from her and returned to her clergyman husband. Poor Truelove, now nearly 70, was fined £50 and sent to prison for four months, where there was no question of serving his sentence in comfort as W.T. Stead and others would do. He picked oakum for his sins.

Bradlaugh went on to greater things. He was elected Member of Parliament for Northampton, but could not take his seat because he refused to take the oath of allegiance and was ejected from the House of Commons. Six years later he was re-elected and this time did take his seat. Karl Marx described him as a 'huge self-idolator'; Gladstone as 'A distinguished man and admirable member of this House . . .' Annie Besant went to the bad, dabbling first with Socialism – probably having an affair with the young Bernard Shaw – and in 1888, through her magazine *The Link*, championing the match-girls who were earning eight shillings a week and dying the while from 'fossy-jaw'.

So far so good, but then she began to dabble in the occult and took up with the dubious Madame Blavatsky, the leader of the Theosophist Movement. Annie Besant resigned from the Secular Society and became other-worldly.

But change was coming, and in 1895 a writer in the *Saturday Review* commented:

> The only woman at the present time who is willing to be regarded as a mere breeding machine is she who lacks the wit to adopt any other role, and now she is the exception rather than the rule . . .

Fine though they might be, the sentiments were not those with which women could necessarily agree for the better part of the next 100 years.

But the undoubted champion of birth control was Marie Stopes, born in 1880 and whose mother had been to university. She too went to Oxford, but after two years of marriage, at the age of 33 (according to some accounts of her life) she apparently discovered the union had not been consummated. She may not have consummated the marriage – indeed her husband seems to have been impotent – but it is difficult to believe that she did not *know* it had not been consummated. She had been involved with a married but estranged Japanese professor, Kuryo Fujii, whilst working in Munich; and following her marriage to her first husband, Dr Reginald Ruggles Gates, she had a close relationship with the author Aylmer Maude, and for some time they formed a platonic *ménage à trois* at the couple's home in Well Walk, Hampstead. More likely she did not know that non-consummation was a ground for annulment, which is not exactly the same thing.

In 1917 her marriage was annulled and she wrote *Married Love*. On 17 March 1921 she opened a birth control clinic at 61 Marlborough Road, Holloway, financed by her and her second husband, Humphrey Roe, whom she had met with a friend in the Lyons Popular Café in Piccadilly. Roe – a wealthy man who with his brother built Avro aeroplanes – was himself interested in birth control. He had tried to donate £1,000 a year for five years to a Manchester hospital, but this had been rejected on the grounds that it would offend people's religious and moral sensibilities.

Marie Stopes's clinic offered the fitting of contraceptives by trained nurses and was absolutely free. The only charge was for check pessaries supplied at cost price. Meanwhile she continued to write pamplets designed to teach the use of contraceptives; as a birth control *Early Days of Birth Control* (1922), and as a prevention against infection *Prevention of Venereal Disease* (1921).

News of her clinics spread, and with patients now in their thousands she had the idea of approaching the Government for financial help. Although Lloyd George, then Prime Minister, was privately sympathetic to her idea of a chain of clinics, he believed that public opinion was not yet ready for them to be state-financed.

Five years later she was accused by Halliday Gibson Sutherland, who held the clumsily titled office of Deputy Commissioner of Medical Services under the Ministry of Pensions, of taking advantage of the ignorance of the poor to subject them

. . . to experiments of a most harmful and dangerous nature . . . It is truly amazing that this monstrous campaign of birth control should be tolerated by the Home Secretary. Charles Bradlaugh was condemned to jail for a less serious crime.

His book *Birth Control* attacked her personally:

In the midst of a London slum a woman who is a

Doctor of *German* Philosophy (Munich) has opened
a Birth Control clinic, where working class women
are instructed in a method of contraception described
by Professor McIlroy as 'the most harmful method of
which I have had experience'.[3]

Marie Stopes issued a writ for libel and the case began
before the Lord Chief Justice and an all-male jury on 21
February 1923. It lasted nine days and with the Lord Chief
leading the way, at the end the all-male jury returned a
verdict that the libel was true in substance.

Some time later she heard that Dr McIlroy was herself
fitting check pessaries and, disguising herself as a char-
woman, she went to the Royal Free, which she left having
been fitted up by the doctor. Meanwhile she appealed the
decision and this time was successful by a 2:1 majority. The
five Law Lords gave the final decision in November 1924
when, on Sutherland's appeal, they found in his favour by
a 4:1 majority.

In fact, although she had to pay over £1,300 in costs
the loss of the action did her no harm. Her clinics gained
enormous publicity and her supporters increased by the
thousands.

By 1928 Stopes was the President of what, by the
standards of today, sounds rather odd: the Society for
Constructive Birth Control and Racial Progress. On 28
March that year she gave a speech at the Society's meeting
held at the Criterion Theatre, London, setting out her
future stall.

I am out for a much greater thing than birth control. I
am out to smash the tradition of organised Christianity
and to enforce Christ's own tradition of wholesome,

[3] Dr Anne Louise McIlroy was Professor of Obstetrics and Gynaecology of the
Royal Free Hospital. She objected to the rubber check pessary.

healthy, natural love towards sex life. The attitude of
unmarried bishops on the subject is insolence and I will
make it impossible for them to say the things they say.
Their unnatural and unhealthy attitude to sex should
be swept away.

Sir John Cockburn, who presided at the meeting, added a
trifle dubiously:

Only by carrying out the aims of the Society can we
ever expect to rear an imperial race.[4]

It was not until the Labour party conference in 1966
that Tom Braddock called on the Government to make
contraceptive advice freely available at family planning
clinics as part of the National Health Service.

England was not the only country where the authorities
were keen to suppress the sexual education which might lead
to increased appetites and so to unnecessary enjoyment on
the part of the working classes. In America, the leader of
the movement was the redoubtable Anthony Comstock.

Born on 7 March 1844 as one of ten children in New
Canaan, Connecticut, where his father owned a saw-mill,
Comstock was brought up a strict Congregationalist possessing a reforming zeal. At the age of 18 he shot and
killed a mad dog and then campaigned against its owner.
Later, he would refer to those he prosecuted as 'mad dogs
endangering the community'.

After the Civil War he undertook a number of clerkships
before, in 1868 – inspired by the YMCA campaign against
obscene literature – he secured the arrest of two publishers
one of whom, Charles Conroy, he pursued for many years.
The infuriated Conroy later attacked him with a knife,

---

[4] *Nottingham Journal*, 16 March 1928. Marie Stopes died of cancer on 2 October
1958; she was 78.

cutting his chin. Comstock concealed the scar behind divided whiskers.

In 1870, supported and financed by the YMCA, he formed the Committee for the Suppression of Vice; two years later he went to Washington, where he forced through the passage of new postal legislation preventing the communication of obscene material through the mails:

> That no obscene book, pamphlet, picture, print or other publication of a vulgar or indecent character, or any letter upon the envelope of which, or postal card upon which scurrilous epithets may have been written or printed or disloyal devices printed or engraved thereon, shall be carried in the mail.[5]

This was amended by the Act of 3 March 1873 (17 Stat. L. 559) to include the words 'intended for the prevention of contraception or procuring abortion'.

It was then that Comstock was appointed a special unpaid (until 1906) agent of the Post Office Department in New York and Secretary of the Society for the Suppression of Vice. During his years in these positions he campaigned tirelessly against 'quacks, abortionists, gamblers, managers of lotteries, dishonest advertisers, patent medicine vendors and artists in the nude'.

In April 1878 Mrs Abbie Dyke Lee was prosecuted for selling *Cupid Yokes; or the Binding Forces of Conjugal Love and Marriage, Wherein it is Asserted the Natural Right and Necessity of Sexual Self Government*. The jury disagreed and the case was dismissed, but two months later E.N. Heywood was convicted of sending the same work through the mails. He was sentenced to two years' hard labour, but President Hayes pardoned him in the December. In 1882

[5] 8 June 1872 (17 Stat. L. 302) S. 148.

he was again prosecuted over the book but, in view of that
earlier pardon, the judge instructed the jury to dismiss
the case.

Sometimes there were small triumphs for the campaigner
and the serious author. In 1881 Walt Whitman benefited
enormously from an attempt by the Boston District Attorney to attack *Leaves of Grass*, published 26 years earlier.
Whitman consented to changes in some poems, but baulked
when the District Attorney extended his list of proposed
cuts. The book was republished in Philadelphia and the
controversy ensured sufficient sales for Whitman to buy
a home in Camden.

But these were relatively isolated triumphs. The decisions
before 1900 show what a stranglehold Comstock and the
Post Office had on the mails:

> Persons publishing books, necessary for medical instruc-
> tion, may be liable for uttering obscene libels, if the effect
> is to debauch society or to make money by pandering to
> lascivious curiosity. That the object is philanthropic or
> scientific is no defense.[6]

And so Dr Clarke's *Treatise on Venereal, Sexual, Nervous
and Special Diseases* – a small pamphlet in a paper cover
and two circulars with lists of questions to be answered –
went into the burner. So did Dr Richard V. O'Neill's *A
Physician's Testimony*. He had written of 'abuses of women
in coercive co-habitations, unnatural intercourse between
man and beast'. He was allowed to give evidence that his
motives were to correct sexual abuses, but it did him no
good. The court ruled that 'it made no difference how pure
are the defendant's motives'.[7]

[6] *Commonwealth v Landis*, 8 Phila 453.
[7] *US v Harman* (DC) 38 Fed 827.

To create a defence, there must have already been an established doctor–patient relationship:

> These medical pamphlets are usually sent out promiscuously to the public for the purpose of advertising the medicines or appliances of those sending them out.[8]

There was also the question of whether a private sealed letter came within the meaning of the statute, and the court held that if it contained obscene material but only had a name and address on the envelope, into the bin it went as well.[9] For a time there had been some divergence of opinion in the courts. In *US v Lamkin*,[10] the Court said that the postman could handle it:

> if free from lewd and indecent language, expressions or words although they may have been free written for the purpose of seduction or to obtain meetings for immoral purpose.

Not so, said the Court in *Dunlop v US*. He had been advertising in elegant language the places where 'courtesans could be found'.[11]

Comstock's career was not without setbacks, however, and perhaps the most famous of these came when he tangled with the notorious Clafin sisters, Victoria Woodhull and Tennessee Clafin. Their mother was a fanatical devotee of

---

[8] *US v Smith* 45 Fed Rep 476.
[9] *Andrews v US* 162 US 420.
[10] *US v Lamkin* 73 Fed Rep 459.
[11] *Dunlop v US* 165 US 486. A Mr Martin also fell foul of the law. He had written a letter to an unmarried woman proposing a clandestine trip to a neighbourhood town, to return the next morning; he to pay expenses 'and $5 besides'. Quite how the letter came to be opened is not made clear. The court held that it was the content, rather than the words themselves, which was obscene.

spiritualism, and Victoria claimed to have had visions from
the age of three.

In 1853 she married Dr Canning Woodhull, by whom she
had two children, and for a time the whole family travelled
in a medicine show. She gave spiritualism exhibitions and
her sister's picture was on the labels of the 'Elixir of Life'
bottles sold at their booth, while brother Herbert posed as
a cancer doctor. In 1864, Victoria divorced Woodhull and
married a military gent named James Blood. Tennessee was
now signing herself 'Tennie C. Clafin'.

The girls travelled to New York in the late 1860s and met
Cornelius Vanderbilt through his interest in spiritualism.
Under his guidance they made a fortune on the stock
market and, always keen on feminism and suffrage, became
involved in the socialist movement the Pantarchy. In 1870
the sisters launched *Woodhull & Clafin's Weekly*, advocating
amongst other things free love, equal rights for women and
a single standard of morality. Now Victoria met Theodore
Tilton, devoted to evangelical Christianity and anti-slavery.
At the age of 20 he had married a schoolteacher and
equal rights campaigner, Elizabeth Richards. The ceremony
had been performed by the Congregational divine Henry
Ward Beecher, through whose influence Tilton obtained
editorship. Meanwhile Elizabeth, another suffragist, edited
Revolution.

At the beginning of the 1870s Elizabeth confessed to her
husband that there had been what were described as 'intimate relations' between her and Beecher. Unfortunately, at
the time, undue delicacy seems to have prevented the parties
from actually discovering what exactly she meant. Tilton
and his supporters believed it to be adultery, whilst Beecher
thought he was accused of making improper solicitations.
A committee of Congregationalists exonerated Beecher.
Tilton's wife left him. Beecher claimed he was being
blackmailed. The minister's supporters levelled allegations

of slander and Tilton was dismissed from his editorial positions.

Woodhull & Clafin's Weekly took up the cudgels for the man with whom the first half of the sisters had an affair. Victoria, whilst giving a talk on spiritualism, went into a trance and denounced Beecher. His sisters came to his defence and turned on the *Weekly*, complaining that Victoria lived in the same house as her former husband, Dr Woodhull, and her current one, the dashing Colonel James H. Blood, former Commander of the 6th Missouri and now managing editor of his wife's magazine. Her reply was that her former husband, the good doctor, was in ill-health and hers was an act of charity.

On 2 November 1872 she published details of Beecher's alleged intimacy as well as an attack on Luther C. Challis, a broker, saying that at the French Ball he had seduced two maidens and boasted of it.

They then engaged the Boston Music Hall on 23 December, and Victoria prepared a speech, 'Moral Cowardice and Modern Hypocrisy'. The Governor of Massachussetts, along with the city council and the chief of the police, prevented the meeting.[12] Now Comstock struck, prosecuting them under the amended legislation of 8 June 1872 for mailing an obscenity. The words complained of were 'token' and 'virginity'.

Blood was taken to Jefferson Market prison and whilst the sisters were given bail, despite having the funds raised for them they refused and also went to prison for a month

[12] Over the years the city of Boston had something of a reputation for banning controversial meetings. For example, in March 1925 Mayor Curley announced that he would close any hall where birth control was discussed. In August 1928 a meeting of shoe workers was banned, and the owners of halls were warned that any who allowed such meetings would have their taxes raised and their licences refused. The same month the Sacco-Vanzetti committee was refused the use of Fanueil Hall. The following year all halls were closed to them, and the meeting had to be held in New York.

before consenting to be released.[13] They were defended
by the talented if rogue lawyer William Howe, who for
three days, aided by his partner Abe Hummel, tormented
Comstock. Howe then produced one of his greatest examples of barnstorming oratory, ending:

> Verily the days of Republican institutions are drawing
> to a close. Must it be as the poet says:
>
> > Truth forever on the scaffold
> > Wrong forever on the throne?

After that sort of rubric, how could anyone convict the
sisters? Not a New York jury.[14]

Tilton formally lodged an action for criminal conversation, claiming $100,000. This also was delicately worded:
'an offence which he forbore to name'.

After a six-month hearing and nine days' deliberation
ending on 20 August 1874, much to the chagrin of the

---

[13] One of their supporters was the wealthy businessman with great influence in
shipping and railroads, the eccentric George Francis Train (1829-1904). In 1870
he had been expelled from France after joining the Communist party and that
year had travelled around the world in 80 days. In support of Victoria, his
magazine *The Train Ligne* published extracts from the Bible showing that her
language fell well within Biblical limits. For this impiety he also was arrested
for obscenity and went to prison – this time the Ludlow Street gaol – where
for several months he too refused to be released. Against his wishes, his counsel
entered a defence of insanity as a result of which he was discharged and
placed in an asylum. Now a Sheriff's Jury found him to be sane and he was
released. In later life he became a recluse living in the Mills Hotel and rarely
speaking to people.

[14] The Clafin sisters went from strength to strength. Blood was divorced and their
friendship with Vanderbilt prospered to the extent that when he died in 1877 his
children brought a suit to annul the will. The sisters sailed for Europe. In 1883,
after six years of opposition from his family, Victoria married the wealthy John
Biddulph Martin, whilst Tennessee married Francis Cook and thus into the
minor peerage. In July 1892 Victoria founded the *Humanitarian*, of which her
daughter was assistant editor. She had named the child Zulu Maud, thereby
setting a fashion in eccentricity to be followed over the years by politicians and
entertainers – of both of which, of course, she was a shining example. She died,
apparently now received in London society, on 10 June 1927. Lady Cook had
predeceased her by four years.

parties and certainly the public there was a hung jury, the final voting of which was said to be 9:3 in favour of Beecher. The case was not retried. It cost Beecher $118,000 and it ruined Tilton, who left the country and died in Paris, where he lived on the Ile St Louis, playing chess and scraping a living from journalism. It did not help him that four years after the case his wife confessed her adultery. Apart from the money, which he recouped by lecturing, Beecher did not suffer. In July 1875 he was acquitted again; this time by a committee appointed by Congregationalists, although the *New York Times* commented:

> Sensible men throughout the country will in their hearts be compelled to acknowledge Mr Beecher's management of his private friendships and affairs has been entirely unworthy of his name, position and sacred calling.[15]

After the Clafin disaster Comstock was regarded as something of a figure of fun. But this thick-set, bald, short-legged and bewhiskered man – who ate heavily, collected stamps and loved children – remained undaunted in his self-appointed task, travelled across America to do his duty and in 1876 inspired the formation of the Watch and Ward Society in Boston.

One of his problems was that to him 'liberal' seems to have been a synonym for quack or libertine, and he prosecuted De Robigne M. Bennett and Ezra Heywood for their advanced opinions as free thinkers. In 1894 he failed in his attempt to have the *Decameron*, *Tom Jones*, the works of Rabelais and *The Confessions of Jean-Jacques Rousseau* declared obscene.

But Comstock's failures mostly came when the forces of evil were represented by Howe and Hummel, and he lost

[15] *New York Times*, 3 July 1875.

another brush with Abe over the aggravating spectacle of a *Danse du Ventre* by three Philadelphian Egyptians, Zora, Fatima and Zelika. Hummel had argued that the dance was part of an ancient religious ceremony which devout Moslems, such as these girls, were bound by their faith to perform at regular intervals. The second point was that the dance was not, as Comstock had said, 'a lewd and lascivious contortion of the stomach'. Hummel explained that the stomach was a small sac whose contortions, if any – which was not admitted – could only be seen from inside the body.

The girls gave evidence, swearing on a copy of the Koran which Hummel had thoughtfully provided; when he regularly mentioned Allah during his speeches, the girls looked appropriately and 'reverently toward the East, as is the custom with members of their faith'.

The case was dismissed and Comstock reprimanded as an interfering busybody. He died in 1915 after catching a cold attending the International Purity Congress meeting in San Francisco to which he had been appointed by President Wilson.

His entry in the *Dictionary of American Biography* reads:

> It is clear that he did not know how to distinguish between good art and bad or indeed between art and morals. He was a notably unsubtle man and has rightly been called an enemy of much that is valuable in literature and life. But, as a prosecutor of frauds and quacks, he did useful work and as a censor of books and post-cards he removed from circulation many items which have not been missed.

Comstock lived on in spirit anyway. In 1922 came the prosecution of Mrs Dennett, a mother of two adolescent boys who, first for their benefit, wrote *The Sex Side of Life*

– An Explanation for Young People. It was then circulated amongst her friends, and the editor of the *Medical Review of Reviews* reprinted it. Finally – and this was her initial undoing – she sold copies of the pamphlet at 25 cents, making no profit; 25,000 were distributed before the Post Office prosecuted. They had sent her a warning notice in 1922, but she had ignored it and continued to send out the pamphlets by first-class mail. Eventually she was trapped by sending a copy to a fictitious Mrs Miles in Grottes, Virginia. The damage was in the posting, not the receipt.

At her trial she was not allowed to mention the non-profit-making aspect, nor that she had received bulk orders from the YMCA, the Union Theological Seminary and from no fewer than 400 welfare and religious organisations. She was fined $300, refused to pay and appealed. Of course the verdict was unsupportable.

Judge Augustus Hand felt bound by the decision in Hicklin, but was able to distinguish the case, pointing out that '. . . the circumstances of the publication may determine whether the statute has been violated'.[16]

The final form of contraception was buggery, a crime punishable by life imprisonment after 1861 and, on conviction, liable to have the man imprisoned for some time, even after the Sexual Offences Act 1967. Males might bugger one another happily in private, but a man could not do the same to a consenting woman. A short term of imprisonment was regarded as essential to protect women from themselves. In the years before the offence was abolished in 1994, sentences ran from three months suspended to 12 months' immediate imprisonment. Generally speaking, the longer terms were handed out to men who had a previous conviction for some

---

[16] *United States v Dennett* 39 F. (2) 564. For an account of the case see Mrs Dennett, *Who's Obscene?* For a critique of the case see Sidney A. Grant and S. E. Angoff, 'Recent Developments in Censorship' in *Boston University Law Journal*, Volume 10, 1931.

form of indecency. They mostly occurred when a complaint of rape and buggery had been made and the jury acquitted the man of rape but was obliged to convict him of buggery. The judge would then take the view that the verdict of acquittal on the rape charge meant that the buggery had been consensual. Had it not been, the sentence would have been of three to five years. It was not regarded as being as serious an offence as rape.[17]

[17] *Cawley (Thomas John)* (1988) 10 Cr App R (S) 465; *Gorecki (Edward John)* (1994) 15 Cr App R (S) 538. *Malik (Mohammed)* (1988) 10 Cr App R (S) 313 CA.

11

Abortion

If despite the variety of contraceptive devices on offer a pregnancy occurred, then there was always the possibility of abortion. Indeed by the beginning of the Napoleonic Wars not enough British women were providing potential cannon fodder for the country. They were not carrying their pregnancies to term and abortion was on the increase. The elimination of potential fighting men could not be tolerated, and in 1803 Lord Ellenborough introduced another of those ragbag Bills so beloved by Parliament. This one dealt with . . .

> heinous offences, committed with intent to destroy the lives of His Majesty's Subjects by Poison, or with intent to procure the miscarriage of Women . . . have been of late also frequently committed; but no adequate Means have been hitherto provided for the Prevention and Punishment of such Offences.[1]

---

[1] Ellenborough, son of the Bishop of Carlisle, an unyielding Attorney-General in the sedition trials of Englishmen who spoke in favour of the French Revolution, was himself the father of 13 children.

Such was the rate of child destruction in France that in 1811 Napoleon ordered foundling hospitals to be equipped with a turntable device so that parents would not be recognised when leaving their unwanted children.

Before then there is little reference to abortion in the English criminal law. For one thing, no one was too sure when 'life' began for there to be an abortion. That was initially left to the clerics. St Thomas Aquinas thought that life began after the foetus moved in the womb, and St Augustine distinguished between the embryo *formatus* and the embryo *informatus*. Following their teachings, abortion was regarded – along with incest – as an ecclesiastical rather than a secular offence. The reasoning behind this apparently was that abortion had its roots in sorcery and magic. It was therefore up to the Ecclesiastical Courts to deal with the matter by way of penance, sanction and, in the last resort, excommunication.

There was a great distinction between the time before the foetus moved, deemed to be half-way through pregnancy, and afterwards. A more severe view was taken of the later abortion.

In the thirteenth century, the eminent jurist Bracton thought that abortion after quickening was 'the equivalent of murder'. But not all agreed with him, and the great Lord Chief Justice Coke considered abortion before quickening as 'a great misprision and no murder', while the judicial cornerstone Blackstone called abortion 'a misdemeanour', placing it amongst 'smaller faults and omissions of less consequence'.

The year 1803 changed all that. People were not doing their duty for England. There were now laws and sanctions.

As a result of a conglomerate heritage of religious dogma, fetal rights, maternal protection, population policy and national growth and even an obsession with the suppression of sin, it is little wonder that the 1803 Act and the later United States laws modelled on it inflicted confusion and misery on society for at least a hundred years.[2]

Even if the poor girl turned out not to be pregnant the mischief, so far as the Act was concerned, was still done. The word 'intent' was sufficient, and now the means of punishment were more than adequate; they included whipping, the pillory and transportation for 14 years. But, following the ecclesiastical view, the punishment was considerably muted if the pregnancy had been terminated in the early stages. There remained the good Saint's distinction between embryo *formatus* and *informatus*.

To determine the exact status, a Jury of Matrons was called to examine the position. It seems that these 12 married women took such little interest in their deliberations that on occasion they had to be locked in the courtroom to ensure that they reached a conclusion. Although they continued to determine whether a woman was pregnant and therefore should not (for the time) be executed, the ladies last sat in the capacity to decide quickening in 1837.

In the 1870s it was believed that Juries of Matrons, empanelled on an *ad hoc* basis to determine the pregnancy or otherwise of women, originated in the reign of Mary Tudor, when, after a woman was burned at the stake in Guernsey, her unborn child sprang forth through the flames and was saved by the spectators.[3]

As is so often the case, this makes a good story but sadly it is not correct. Juries of Matrons can be traced back to the twelfth century in civil cases and to 1387 in criminal ones.[4] That year Elizabeth Walton was convicted of conspiracy to murder and her death sentence respited until she had

[2] Lawrence Lader, *Abortion*, p. 84.
[3] See Editorial, *Medical Times & Gazette*, 27 January 1872.
[4] See James C. Oldham, *Pleading the Belly in Criminal Justice History*, Vol. V, 1985.

given birth the following year.[5] In civil cases the Jury was used to determine for the purpose of inheritance whether a widow was with child by her late husband. A third use of such Juries was to search for suspicious witches' marks – usually extra nipples – on the bodies of suspects, and a fourth from 1803 to 1836 was to determine the length a pregnancy had lasted before an illegal abortion took place.

It was a practice which led to a good deal of fakery – juries could be packed; pregnancies could be contracted whilst in prison; in 1613, in the Countess of Essex's case in which she claimed that her husband was incapable of consummating the marriage, there was a Jury of ten matrons plus two midwives chosen from a panel of four. The Countess petitioned that, because of the embarrassment, she could appear in a veil; once this was granted, a young girl of the same size was substituted for her ladyship.

In his survey, Oldham stated that the Jury was empanelled on relatively few occasions, and when they were called they regularly found against the claimant. Between 1727 and 1800 he showed that in only 40 per cent of the cases were the women found to be pregnant.

Nor was there any enthusiasm for women to act as matrons. In March 1809 Mary Bateman 'pleaded the belly' at the York Assizes. She had been indicted with the murder in May 1808 of Rebecca Perigo of Bramley, whom she was said to have poisoned. The initial problem for Mary Bateman, however, was that she was well known locally as a witch, something which did not stand her in good stead. She was found guilty and then claimed she was 22 weeks pregnant.

On this plea the judge ordered the sheriff to empanel a jury of matrons: this order created a general consternation amongst the ladies, who hastened to quit the court

[5] G.O. Sayles (ed.), *Select Cases in the Court of Kings Bench*.

> to prevent the execution of so painful an office being imposed upon them. His Lordship, in consequence, ordered the doors to be closed and in about half an hour twelve married women being empanelled they were sworn in court . . .[6]

The jury was not happy and in quick time found Mary Bateman was not pregant. She was hanged, refusing – despite considerable efforts by a local clergyman – to admit her guilt.

Earlier the same year, on 22 February 1809, Margaret Barrington alias Grimes alias Graham was sentenced to death for taking a false oath to obtain letters of administration saying that she was the widow of a soldier entitled to prize money. She pleaded she was pregnant, but a Jury of Matrons decided she was not.[7]

Because of the limited medical knowledge of the times, it was always a bit hit-and-miss even when the Jury of Matrons conducted themselves properly and there was no trickery on the part of the prisoner. The matrons had not to decide on pregnancy but whether the woman was 'quick with child'. This stage in the pregnancy was deemed crucial, as it had formerly been the belief (medical as well as general) that the foetus only received life at the quickening.

In one case a pregnant woman was hanged because the Jury had ruled against her since, during her pregnancy, she was still menstruating. In 1832 at Norwich Assizes, in the case of a woman named Wright, it was only after medical men intervened that she was found 'quick with child', something the Jury of Matrons had failed to assess. In a third case in 1847, an Old Bailey Jury found that Mary Ann Hunt was not pregnant, but three months later she gave birth to a full-term child.

[6] Lord Birkett (ed.), *The New Newgate Calendar*.
[7] N. McLachlan (ed.), *The Memoirs of James Hardy Vaux*, p. 194.

In the 1870s three Juries of Matrons were empanelled in relatively quick successsion. There had been no such jury for 15 years until in 1871 Rachel Bushey was found guilty at Oxford Assizes of the murder of her child. The matrons there had found against her and it was only as a result of the intervention of 'philanthropic gentlemen' that she was reprieved. She later gave birth to a stillborn child in the county gaol.[8]

But it was the case of Christiana Edmunds, the Brighton poisoner, which attracted most attention. In 1870 Christiana, an attractive if fading 42–year–old spinster, conceived a hopeless passion for her general practitioner, Dr Beard, who practised from Grand Parade, Brighton. The doctor seems to have been unwise because, although there is no suggestion that he encouraged his patient, he certainly did not discourage her sufficiently, instead allowing her to send him a stream of romantic letters which he kept from his wife, Emily.

In September of that year Christiana had obtained poison and one evening when the doctor was out, on the pretext that the sweets were for the Beard children, she took chocolates which she had previously filled with strychnine to the Beard household. There she popped one into Emily Beard's mouth. Fortunately her supposed rival reacted quickly. Later she would say, 'It had a very unpleasant, cold, metallic taste and I spat it out directly. I experienced very unpleasant feelings after it and saliva ran out of my mouth all night. The next day I had an attack of diarrhoea and felt very unwell.'

For some curious reason Emily Beard did not tell her husband, and equally inexplicably – apart from the fact that she was clearly mad – Christiana Edmunds did. Beard went to see Mrs Edmunds and, after delivering a carefully

[8] *Medical Times & Gazette*, 16 March 1872.

couched message, left Brighton for three months; he had warned his wife to be on her utmost guard. When he returned, Christiana called round to seek reinstatement but he refused her.

This was probably the breaking point for her fragile mind. She then set about a system which would draw her to the attention of the public. Buying quantities of strychnine to dispose of 'unwanted cats', she also bought chocolates from Maynard's, the local confectioners, filled them with poison and gave them to small boys to return as the wrong sort. She had also some returned to the shop herself. Her convoluted thinking was that if Maynard's could be shown to have been selling poisoned chocolates, then she could only have poisoned Mrs Beard by accident; therefore she was entitled to be restored to the family bosom. It was only a matter of time. On 12 June 1871 four-year-old Sidney Alfred Barker died of convulsions within 20 minutes of eating a chocolate bought for him by his uncle. Unfortunately the inquest verdict was accidental death.

Christiana then began a campaign against Mr Maynard, the confectioner, sending poison-pen letters, writing to Sidney Barker's father suggesting he take proceedings and consigning a whole selection of poisoned cakes and fruit to selected beneficiaries, many of whom ate them and survived.

She had come to the notice of the police through her intervention at Sidney's inquest, and comparison of letters sent to the police, the father and the recipients of the poisoned gifts showed her to be the sender. She was arrested on 17 August 1871. At her trial on 15 January 1872 at the Old Bailey, her mother told the jury of the long history of insanity in the family. Her father had suffered acute mania, ending with general paralysis of the insane; her maternal grandfather had died of the same affliction at the age of 43; her brother was lodged in a mental institution

as 'an epileptic idiot'; her sister probably had schizophrenia
and had tried to kill herself. Christiana herself suffered from
hysterical paralysis. The catalogue did her no good; the jury
returned a verdict of guilty. It was the practice of the time
before sentence was passed for a dock officer to ask a woman
prisoner if she was pregnant, and the newspapers reported
a hushed silence when he announced, 'She says she is, my
Lord.' She claimed Dr Beard was the putative father.

A Jury of Matrons was empanelled on the spot from
members of the public gallery and, according to a report,
even in the face of Christiana having been in prison for five
months – all but three weeks of which she had been catatonic
– would not give a negative answer without medical advice.
They sent for Mr J. Beresford Ryley, an accoucheur who
in turn sent for a stethoscope. He pronounced she was not
pregnant and now the unfortunate woman 'looked from
one to another of her unwilling and weeping judges in
meek, unspeakable woe'. The death sentence was passed
but later was commuted by the Home Secretary. She died
in Broadmoor in 1907.[9]

The *Medical Times*, at least, was outraged. Pointing out
that in New York such matters were judged by a panel of
six physicians and in France bare proof of pregnancy was
sufficient, it called for legislation to abolish the Jury of
Matrons. 'We do not wish to see another instance of it.'
There was no support for the proposition, certainly not
from lawyers. *The Law Times*, writing about the same
trial, was concerned at misguided criticism of the judge,
Baron Martin, over his direction of the burden of proof in
insanity defences. It was pleased that at least there were
some restrictions on reporting.[10]

[9] It was reported that a policeman sent out for a stethoscope returned with a
pocket telescope (*Medical Times and Gazette*, 27 January 1872). There is a very
full account of the case and an anecdote of Christiana Edmunds in Broadmoor
in Richard and Molly Whittington-Egan's *The Bedside Book of Murder*.
[10] 24 January 1872.

Seven years after the Edmunds case, Kate Webster also pleaded the belly. Born in Killane, County Wexford, she had a string of convictions before she was employed as the cook-general of Julia Martha Thomas in Richmond, Surrey. Mrs Thomas, a widow, was on any account a difficult employer, but she was killed for her possessions as she returned from church on 2 March 1879. Kate Webster cut up her remains with a razor, meat-saw and carving knife, boiled the pieces on the kitchen copper and threw the head into the Thames. She was also said to have tried to sell the rendered-down Mrs Thomas as meat dripping before she fled back to Ireland from where she was retrieved. The 30-year-old was tried in July at the Old Bailey and her pleas rejected. She was hanged by William Marwood on the 29th of the same month, still pleading her innocence. In her case, the Jury of Matrons had ruled against her after hearing the prison matron.

Two twentieth-century cases followed hard on one another. Louie Calvert claimed she was pregnant when she appeared at Leeds Assizes. She had tired of her life of prostitution and in 1925 persuaded a Leeds watchman, Arthur Calvert, to employ her as a housekeeper; she then persuaded him into believing she was pregnant and married him. Although she showed no signs of pregnancy she managed to convince him that during her confinement she should go and stay with her sister in Dewsbury. In fact she had returned to work the red-light district of Leeds. She then offered to adopt a newborn baby and stayed with a Mrs Lily Waterhouse, from whom she began to steal. Mrs Waterhouse took out a summons for theft and when she did not appear at court to prosecute, enquiries began. She was found battered to death in her back bedroom. When she was traced, Louie Calvert was found wearing Mrs Waterhouse's clothes and boots.

Before the death sentence was passed she was asked if

she had anything to say and replied, 'Yes sir, I'm pregnant.'
It did nothing to avail her. She was hanged by Thomas
Pierrepoint in Manchester on 24 June 1926.

The case of Olive Wise was the first occasion at the
Central Criminal Court since women jurors had been
allowed to sit that a Jury of Matrons had been required.

Just after midday on 24 December 1930 Olive Wise, who
lived in East London, told a neighbour, 'I have done the baby
in, I have gassed him.' She had put her nine-month-old son
Reginald in the gas oven. At the time she had been in severe
financial trouble. Married in June 1916, after her husband
had left for service in the Far East, she had, on and off,
been associating with an Alfred John Wheatley and he was
Reginald's father. A report in the papers had said she had
been deserted, but 'A Watcher' helpfully wrote to the police
saying she had been divorced by her husband on the grounds
of her adultery.

On 13 January 1931 she was found guilty of murder, with
a strong recommendation for mercy by the jury. Now a
Jury of Matrons was empanelled to decide whether she
was *enceinte*. There was not much doubt since she was
eight months pregnant at the time and they returned
a verdict of 'about to become a mother'. This ensured
there would be a stay of execution of the capital sentence
until after the birth of the child. In the event she was
reprieved.[11]

This appears to have been the last time that a Jury of

---

[11] After her release from prison Olive Wise took up again with Alfred Wheatley,
but the relationship was not a success. On 26 July 1933 he went into the
police station at Lea Bridge Road, London, to say that his wife Olive and his
two-and-a-half-year-old daughter were missing. She had left after a quarrel the
day before, taking the children with her. He had traced them to the Central
Homes in Union Road, where they had been handed back to him, but on their
way back home she had once more gone off with her daughter. The police
noted that there appeared to be no suspicious circumstances, but in view of
the previous history of Mrs Wise made enquiries into the safety of the child.
PRO/MEPO/3/1661.

Matrons sat. It was abolished in the Sentence of Death (Expectant Mothers) Act 1931, which provided for a term of life imprisonment to be imposed on a pregnant woman instead of the death penalty. If the jury found against the woman she had a right of appeal to the Court of Appeal. The function of the Jury of Matrons ended with the abolition of capital punishment.

It was in 1837 that Lord John Russell introduced the Act bearing his name which abolished the *formatus-informatus* distinction and established the offence of abortion in its modern form. There was also some leavening of the penalties. By 1861, when the law was nearly 30 years old, the Offences Against the Persons Act ss. 58 and 59 consolidated the then existing legislation, bringing within the four corners of one enactment all the statute law bearing upon a particular class of offence and now scattered through many volumes. Now the penalty for abortion was life imprisonment, and as good measure it was added that the pregnant woman herself, as well as the abortionist, could be found guilty of the offence.

The methods used by the back-street abortionists were crude, unreliable and dangerous. Even into the 1960s a favoured method was the Higginson syringe, a tube with a bulb in the middle, used to push an irritant liquid into the womb so that air bubbles would be forced into the bloodstream. The danger was that the air embolism the patient would suffer might well kill her. The other favoured method was to force a rubber tube up through the vagina and into the womb – rather than use the piano wire, knitting needles and hooks of old wives' tales, which were in fact rarely tried. Various drugs and emetics were nineteenth-century favourites and one favoured – and if less dangerous but totally unreliable – method believed to 'bring you on' was the hot gin and steaming bath remedy used by Rachel Roberts in the film *Saturday Night and Sunday Morning*.

Much earlier, the great charlatan Casanova once deceived a girl into thinking that intercourse with his penis covered with honey would have the desired effect; an act which would surely have brought a charge of rape in England.

Then of course there were pills containing such things as quinine and pennyroyal, and apiol capsules. Quinine could cause blindness and did. Reports of court hearings over the decades are full of such cases.

The early years following the 1861 Act threw up some interesting decisions. A variety of tonics and substances were used by the poor to procure abortions, and decisions had to be made as to what could constitute a poison and who intended to use it or for what it was to be used.

Savin was a common abortifacient, and when a Mr Hillman supplied the drug he intended that only the woman involved should use it. She had no such thoughts and, indeed, did not do so. It is not clear how he came to be arrested, but in any event the argument did not help him. He was convicted of supplying the drug with the intention that it should be used to procure a miscarriage.

Can someone be convicted of supplying a mixture with intent to procure an abortion even if the woman is not pregnant? In other words, to attempt to do something impossible? Mr Titley found out to his cost that he could. He supplied a mixture of ergot of rye and perchloride of iron in the mistaken view that a girl was pregnant. The defence that she was not did not help him at all. The enactment applied 'whether there is a woman in a state fit to be the subject of the operation or not'.[12] It was, after all, just as Lord Ellenborough had wanted back in 1803.

---

[12] There was considerable debate in the Titley case over the use by the police of the wife of an officer pretending to be pregnant. Titley, a chemist, had long been thought to be an abortionist. It was one of the first cases in the Metropolitan Police where an *agent provocateur* had been used. The officers involved were subsequently charged but the indictment was quashed. See *The Times*, 14 March 1881.

If the 'drug' was useless, then there was a defence. Mr Perry offered the girl feverfew, a herb rather like camomile, and what appeared to the doctor called by the prosecution to be a mixture of fenugreek and savin. Fenugreek would do nothing, and the small quantity of savin would cause a mildly upset stomach. He was acquitted, but it seems the decision was a wrong one. There was certainly the intent, and although the substance savin was 'noxious' it was just not quite noxious enough. Lucky Mr Perry.

Not so lucky was the aptly named Mr Cramp, who administered half an ounce of juniper oil. It was proved that considerably larger quantities could be taken without ill-effect, but that half an ounce was dangerous to a pregnant woman, and he was convicted.

In 1864 the National Medical Association offered no fewer than 123 kinds of pessary, from a simple stopper to a patent trashing machine which could only be worn under the largest crinoline and looked like a water-wheel. Dr Buck, writing in the *New York Medical Journal*, fulminated:

> Pessaries, I suppose are sometimes useful, but there are more than there is any necessity for. I do think that this filling the vagina with such traps, making a Chinese toy-shop of it is outrageous . . . Nowadays even our young women must have their wombs shored up, and if a baby accidentally gets in by the side of the machinery and finds a lodgment in the uterus, it may, perchance, have a knitting needle stuck in its eyes before it has any.[13]

In 1922, when Stella Browne argued for the legalisation of abortion at the neo-Malthusian Birth Control Conference, part of her audience left. In the early 1930s, Dr Marie Stopes wrote to *The Times*:

[13] *New York Medical Journal*, Vol. V, p. 464.

> In three months I have had as many as twenty thousand
> requests for criminal abortion from women who did not
> apparently even know it was criminal.

She added:

> In a given number of days, one of our travelling clinics
> received only 13 applications for scientific instruction in
> the control of conception, but 80 demands for criminal
> abortion.

Once medical knowledge and technique improved towards
the end of the nineteenth century, the problem arose for
doctors as to whether a pregnancy could be terminated to
save a woman's life. No one was quite sure whether it was
legal, and counsel's opinion was sought.

The advice was that *bona fide* efforts to save the life of
a mother established a good defence to a prosecution for
artificial abortion.

In 1929 The Infant Life (Preservation) Act made it legal
to terminate a foetus (described as viable, that is one of 28
weeks or more) in order to save the woman's life. But what
was 'necessary to save a woman's life'?

Mr Justice McCardie was again in the forefront, saying
in a 1931 abortion case that he believed the law of abortion
as it existed ought to be substantially modified. 'It is out of
keeping with the conditions that prevail in the world around
us. I cannot think that a woman should be forced to bear
a child against her will.'

In 1934, the Annual Congress of Women's Co-operative
Guilds by a decisive 1,340–20 vote called for the Government to revise the abortion laws, making abortion a legal
operation which could be carried out under the same
conditions as any other operations. Two years later the
British Medical Association asked the Government for a

clarification of the existing laws, and the Abortion Law Reform Association (ALRA) was founded.

The case which was to set the standards from 1938 until the Abortion Act 1967 was that of Dr Aleck William Bourne, a member of the BMA's 1936 Committee on Abortion and of ALRA.

In the cavalry regiments there had long been a practice of taking girls outside during the intervals between dances under the pretence of showing them 'the green mare'. It was, of course, simply a device so that some form of sexual familiarity could take place; but on 27 April 1938 a girl often referred to as Milly, aged 14, who had gone to see the Trooping the Colour, was 'gang-raped' by three troopers from the Royal Horse Guards who lured her into Wellington Barracks to see this mythical horse. She became pregnant and some weeks later a Roman Catholic doctor at St Thomas's Hospital refused to terminate the pregnancy. Later Dr John Malleson, a founder member of ALRA, wrote that he took the conventional stand-point . . . the child might be a future Prime Minister of England. He also said that sometimes girls lead men on.

Bourne had already had difficulties with his staff. A short time earlier a registrar, also a Roman Catholic, had left the operating theatre with his agreement when Bourne had terminated a pregnancy in 1935.

In his autobiography,[14] Bourne details the steps he took to assure himself that the girl should have an abortion; this included keeping her under observation for a week. He also determined that the legality of his conduct should be established. He told the police of his intention to carry out the operation and they arrived at the hospital early on the morning of the abortion, no doubt in the hope of preventing it. 'I came to warn you,' said the inspector, but he was too

[14] Aleck Bourne, *A Doctor's Creed*.

late for Bourne had already terminated the girl's pregnancy. Bourne was arrested and charged.

He appeared at the Old Bailey in July, when an impressive array of eminent doctors – including Lord Horder, then the King's Physician – appeared to give evidence on his behalf. He was fortunate too in his judge, Mr Justice Macnaughten, who told the jury:

> You have heard a great deal of the difference between danger to life and danger to health. I confess I have had difficulty in understanding what the discussion really meant. Life depends on health and it may be that if health is gravely impaired, death results.

The circumstances could hardly have differed more from the other case at the Old Bailey during that session, when a woman was accused of procuring a miscarriage for the princely return of £1. 5s. Whatever good faith she had shown the girl, it was nothing like that of Dr Bourne:

> The question is not are you satisfied that he performed the operation in good faith for the purpose of preserving the life of the girl. The question is, has the Crown proved the negative of that?

After a retirement of 40 minutes the jury acquitted Bourne, to general acclaim and the thanks of the girl who had waited outside. The newspapers were generally pleased with the verdict, although it was clear that the Macnaughten direction was not a *carte blanche* to the medical profession. There was talk of a Private Member's Bill, but nothing came of it.

Some 25 years later, Bourne defected to the anti-abortion lobby; at the time of the Abortion Bill in 1967, he wrote repenting of his former conduct. There is nothing like a reformed alcoholic to denounce the evils of drink.

The problem for doctors was that Bourne was only a decision at first instance. The situation could arise where a doctor was convicted and the Court of Criminal Appeal could then jump all over the profession. In fact it never did so; and when ten years after Bourne two female doctors, Bergmann and Ferguson, were charged and acquitted, the trial judge ruled that their belief in the necessity of an operation did not have to be correct but merely honest. They had each received a few guineas for their advice and the operation. Clearly the amount paid could be regarded as significant by a jury.

In 1952 a Private Member's Bill was quickly talked out of the House of Commons, and in 1957 the Home Secretary declined to move things along, saying: 'Legislation for this purpose would be highly controversial and I have no reason to think there is any practical need for it.'

On 15 October 1957, Jean Smith was admitted to the National Temperance Hospital, where she was described as very ill and agitated. Nine days later she died of renal failure following an abortion. Dr Newton had given her a uterine injection following a referral to him by Dr Ellis Stungo, a Harley Street psychiatrist. In fact the poor woman, a nurse herself, had been passed from medical pillar to post. First she had seen a psychiatrist, then a West End doctor, then Dr Stungo and finally Dr Newton. She had paid Dr Stungo three guineas, but Dr Newton £50 cash. She had told the former that she felt like throwing herself in the river.

Both doctors were charged and, when questioning one of the expert witnesses for the Crown, Stungo's counsel read a letter to the *Lancet* which commented on the problems of assessing suicide threats by pregnant women. The expert agreed with all the points made before counsel told him it had been written by Stungo some seven years previously. When counsel for Dr Stungo made a submission that there was no case for his client to answer, the Bourne doctrine was upheld. The trial judge, J. Atkinson, reiterated the principles:

> Such use of an instrument is unlawful unless the use is made in good faith for the purpose of preserving the life or health of the woman. When I say health I mean not only her physical health but also her mental health. But although I have said that it is unlawful I must emphasise and add that the burden of proving it was not used in good faith is on the Crown.

Newton did not have such a happy result. He was convicted and received five years' imprisonment. He was struck off, but was later restored to the medical register.

There were really four types of abortion available. At the lowest end of the spectrum came the back-street abortionists operating with the coat-hanger and the Higginson syringe at a few pounds a time. They had existed from time immemorial and were seen by the working classes as an essential part of society.

> The abortionists didn't have to have protection. People were honest. If that was her game, then there was a need for it and so she didn't need protection. Husband maybe, but he wouldn't be there just for minding her. If anything she was looked on with respect but in a fearsome way. She did give a service. She saved many a girl's reputation or many a wife who couldn't afford another baby. Women were frightened because there were deaths. A woman died and somehow or other they'd cart her home and say she died in bed at her own home as if she'd tampered with herself. That would be one of the deals the abortionist would make with the woman's family. It would only be if someone screamed she'd be nicked or if the girl went into a hospital where they'd known what had happened and

might pressure her. We needed the abortionists more than the local money lender. Maybe the police now and again would raid them, looking for the utensils and nick them for conspiracy, but in a way they were just confirming things. The news of the raid would get round the district and frighten people off going to her. She'd have to move to another house, if possible in the same area, and start up again.[15]

The second category were general practitioners who performed abortions on the side and charged between £40 and £75 a time. Assuming that all went well the fee was for a dilatation and curettage but, with the quality of drugs now available, unless something really unfortunate happened he or she was safe from prosecution. Doctor had perhaps been a little heavy-handed.

The third category was the carriage trade of the West End abortionists who covered their tracks with psychiatric opinions and charged between £75 and £100. In the fourth category were the legitimate operators, the National Health Service doctors.

In 1961 Kenneth Robinson, comparing the ALRA proposals, pointed out that only 40 per cent of abortions allowed in Sweden would be permitted, and suggested abortions were better performed by skilled doctors under hygienic conditions. The Government was neutral, but the Bill was killed off in a matter of hours.

Hospitals were consequently extremely wary. When the thalidomide disaster occurred in 1962, few hospitals granted abortions on the grounds of possible defective babies. A *Daily Mail* poll then showed that 73 per cent of those questioned favoured legalising abortion.

The third Abortion Bill came up in June 1965, this

[15] Frank Fraser, *Mad Frank's Friends*, pp. 25–6.

time brought by Renée Short and killed off by a Catholic MP. However, some progress was made. She obtained the signatures of 144 MPs to a motion for more time to be granted. The same year Lord Silkin tried to introduce a Bill into the House of Lords. It was now estimated that there were some 17,000 medical as opposed to back-street abortions being performed annually in Britain at the time, of which 3–4,000 were being undertaken under the auspices of the National Health Service. It was thought the total was equal to the number being performed in the whole of the United States.[16]

It was not until David Steel – then the youngest MP at the age of 29 and later to become the leader of the Liberal Party – managed to get support for his Private Member's Bill which was passed by 167 votes to 83 in July 1967 that the law changed. It came on to the statute books the following April and allowed an abortion if two doctors signed a certificate that the continuation of a woman's pregnancy would involve risk to physical or mental health or to any previous children 'greater than if the pregnancy were terminated', and if there was a substantial risk that if the child be born it would be seriously handicapped by physical or mental abnormalities. The woman's environment both present and in the future could also be taken into account.

In the years before the Abortion Act, which restated the principles of the Bourne and Stungo cases, the rate of illegal operations known to the police in England and Wales varied only slightly. In 1963 there were 239, and 314 a year later. Convictions for procuring an illegal abortion over a similar period ranged from 52 to 63 in 1967.[17] Registered

---

[16] *Time*, 27 August 1956, p. 68.
[17] The figures in the early 1900s had been around 15 a year, with two-thirds convicted. It had risen in the 1930s to between 40 and 50, with three-quarters convicted. In 1961, of 40 brought to trial 19 were women; and in 1964 there were 32 men and 37 women.

and therapeutic abortions increased steadily from 2,280 (1961) to 4,530 in 1965, and then after the Act to 38,150 in 1969.[18]

The figures had not been very different. In that period there had been an average of little over one conviction a week. Even in a high year such as 1962 – when 82 out of 90 alleged abortionists were sent for trial, of whom 48 were imprisoned – the figures were tiny compared with the number of illegal abortions believed to have been performed. The National Opinion Polls thought some 30,000 and C.B. Goodhart, a noted anti-abortion law supporter, believed that as many as 100,000 may have been carried out. It was a crime which the police were not prosecuting with much enthusiasm. For the offences to come to light there really had to be a death or a report from a hospital of a botched job. In 1934 there were 100 inquests on death resulting from abortion, but once sulphonamides came into use the death rate fell significantly to below 50 in 1945, then to around 25 in the 1960s. It was perhaps because of the availability of drugs which made illegal operations safer that a Committee under the chairmanship of Norman Birkett reported just before the Second World War that these abortions were on the increase.

The sentencing of abortionists kept on at one pace. There was a three-tier scale for offenders: those who procured the abortion as a favour or kindness; the semi-professional; and finally and most heavily sentenced, the professional. In 1962 the Court of Appeal reduced the sentence on a Mrs Stolarska from seven to five years. She had pleaded guilty to two counts and asked for a further 38 offences to be taken into consideration; she had been charging between £3 and

---

[18] It was estimated that in 1967 there were about 30,000 illegal abortions a year and 20,000 legal ones. In his book *Lovelaw*, Professor Anthony Clare suggested that in the middle 1960s between 30 and 50 million abortions were being performed worldwide annually.

£4 a time for her services. The Court felt that she had to be 'given such a punishment as would not only punish her but be sufficient to deter others'.

This was at the upper end of the scale. In 1971 Ms Aubry (who had been a nurse and had a young child) had her sentence cut from 18 to nine months and the Massaquois, a husband-and-wife team who had 'well-equipped premises', had a year shaved off their four-year term. That same year in *Scrimaglia*,[19] the then Lord Chief Justice, Lord Parker, commented:

> Now that abortions can be performed legally either under the National Health Service or at the patient's own expense, operations such as yours, carried out at a cut price and in disgraceful, insanitary and even dangerous conditions, are totally unnecessary apart from being against the law.

Since the Abortion Act 1967, there have been a mere handful of prosecutions annually, dropping to nine in 1977.[20]

What the Abortion Act did for a time was to throw up a new form of unhelpful behaviour. Women who came to London to have their abortions were being hijacked by taxi-drivers at railway stations and taken not to the clinic to which they intended to go, but to one from whom the driver obtained a cut or – it was thought in some cases – in which he had a stake.

[19] (1971) 55 Cr App R 280.
[20] In 1968 there were 23,641 notified abortions.

12

Baby Farming

One of the by-products of Victorian prudery and the ban on abortion was the trade of baby farming or, as the French called it, angel making. The practice was for the mother to reply to an advertisement which offered to free her from an unwanted child. She would then pay a lump sum and/or a weekly payment to the carer.

On 26 October 1888 boys playing football with a bundle they had discovered lying on a green in Cheyne Street, Stockbridge in Edinburgh, found the 'ball' was in fact a dead baby wrapped in an old coat. The baby was traced to Jessie King, then aged 27, and her elderly lover Thomas Pearson. She cleared him by saying that she did not know what she was doing. In turn he repaid her kindness by giving evidence against her. She had murdered two children, drugging them with whisky and then strangling and suffocating them.

The profits, according to the journalist William Roughhead who observed the subsequent trial, were not high: £3 for the adoption and strangling of the year-old Alexander Gunn;

£2 for the six-week-old Violet Tomlinson. Another child to be killed was the five-month-old Walter Campbell; it is not recorded how much his mother paid to King.

Roughhead described her crouched in the dock in Edinburgh as 'a miserable creature, mean furtive, shabbily sinister like a cornered rat'. Always keen on purple prose, he described Pearson as her 'truculent, robust paramour, with his dirty-grey bearded face and his bald head upon which a monstrous wen, big as a hen's egg, rose eminent on the vertex of his naked scalp'.

Suspected of killing a number of other children, whilst in the death cell she tried twice to commit suicide before being hanged by James Berry at Edinburgh on 11 March 1889. She had apparently believed she would receive only a short sentence.

Curiously, baby farming appears to have been more practised in England than Scotland. Many laws worked in a way which was contrary to the intentions of Parliament, and the Act for the Amendment and Better Administration of the Laws Relating to the Poor in England and Wales 1834 was one of them. Instead of assisting young women, it made it difficult for the mother of an illegitimate child to obtain maintenance from the father. However, a down payment could be sought from the father and handed over to the baby farmer with the child. An illegitimate child was also an encumbrance to a girl who wished to pursue a career of prostitution, marry or even be set up as a mistress.

The result was twofold. Abortion and infanticide became an even more common practice and if this was not successful, or the mother would not dispose of the foetus or newborn child, then the unwanted baby was left to the care of the parish and approved individuals contracted with the parish for the weekly sum of 4/6d to care for the children.[1] There were other, more informal ways of placing the child. Advertisements placed in papers which would be read by millinery workshops hands were a common method; James Greenwood found 11 advertisements in one issue alone. On the surface they appear innocent enough:

> A person wishing a lasting and comfortable home for a young person will find this a good opportunity. Advertisers having no children of their own are about to proceed to America. Premium. Fifteen Pounds. Respectable references given and required.

Greenwood provides a crib: 'Any person possessed of a child he is anxious to be rid of, here is a good chance for him.'[2] Do not be deceived by the words, 'Respectable references given' . This simply meant 'mutual confidence'.

Of course, care was rarely a word in the vocabulary of the contractor, and the children – without proper clothing, food and medical attention – died in droves. In some mitigation, a visit from a doctor cost one shilling, a fee not easily met by the very poor, but that shilling was often paid to an insurance society against the child's death. Once the child could walk, if not talk, it could be taken into the country and abandoned. Technically, given the mores of the time, they may not have been murdered. Indeed, some survived. Those who certainly were murdered were those who passed into the hands of the baby farmers.

It is difficult to determine how many Jessie Kings there

[1] In 1849 a number of inquests were held into deaths at the Infant Pauper Asylum at Tooting run by a man named Drouet. He was in receipt of the 4/6d per head and also worked the older of his 1,400 charges, who were aged between two and 15. The older boys controlled the food supply and meals were eaten standing up; there was not enough drinking water. Complaints to guardians were met with beatings. Almost certainly the very considerable profits were shared with officials of the local authority.
[2] James Greenwood, *The Seven Curses of London*, p. 35 *et seq.*

were over the decades and up and down the country. Certainly hundreds, probably thousands. It was not as if the crime went unnoticed. In Britain in 1851 there were an estimated 42,000 illegitimate children born, and probably thousands more were killed at or shortly after birth. Finding the dead bodies of children in the Thames was such a common occurrence that, in general, little notice was taken of them. In 1867 the death rate amongst illegitimate children under a year old was eight times higher than that of legitimate babies.

As to farming children, in 1868 the *British Medical Journal* carried an article saying: 'There is not the slightest difficulty in disposing of any number of children, so that they may give no further trouble, and never be heard of, at £10 a head'.

The summer of the next year brought a rash of anony-mous letters to the editor of the *Lancet* and to Scotland Yard. These directed attention to a Mrs L. Martin, a certified *accoucheuse*, of 33 Dean Street, Soho. In a letter to the *Lancet* the writer gave his name as *Senex*.

> . . . this woman is the greatest criminal in London; her house is a house where abortion and child murder is openly carried on! this woman boasts of having murdered no less than 545 children during the past year. Should a child be born alive it is drowned in a pan of water! the woman's fee is £10 to £50 according to the position of her patient.

Writing to Scotland Yard on 20 July, he – or more probably she, because a third letter in the same writing was signed Sarah Tilson – was 'One who Knows'. The writer certainly did know. On 29 July Mrs Martin was named in proceedings at the Worship Street Police Court when a servant girl, Elizabeth Davis, brought bastardy proceedings against John Curtis. Giving evidence, she told the court that Curtis had introduced her to Mrs Martin, who had told her, 'If you are confined here you will never see the child. I place them in the Foundling, but most likely it will die.' She had instead gone to the Chelsea Workhouse for delivery of the baby.

Now the newspapers took matters up and an editorial in the *Standard* of 4 August spelled things out:

> Really such evidence as this ought to attract more than a passing notice. One cannot help thinking that the public is interested in learning somewhat more than it now knows about this skilful female practitioner, who has so much influence at the Foundling Hospital, who is so ready to prognosticate the death of an infant entrusted to her charge, and can so confidently assure her patients that they will never see their children again. Far be it from us to hint at any malpractice on her part, but there is a singularity in her vocabulary, and a mystery in her promises, which it would be well to have cleared up.

Scotland Yard did take more than a passing notice, but it was signally unsuccessful in obtaining evidence. Women who had passed through Mrs Martin's hands were, in law, equally guilty. Mrs Martin was also adroit. A Sergeant Gould enlisted the help of two women and Mrs Martin came to terms with one of them, but insisted that the girl come into her home for two weeks prior to delivery. A draught was offered, but it had to be taken in Mrs Martin's home; there was no question of pills or medicine being allowed out of the house. The sergeant tried again, this time with a 'foreign prostitute' who declined to give evidence 'even if she was offered £1,000'.

There the matter rested, much to the annoyance this time of *Senex* who wrote telling the police that Mrs Martin had moved the scene of her operations to a house in Tulse Hill and from there to the Railway Hotel in Woking. By the time the police inquired into the accuracy of this intelligence, which was always half a step ahead of them, they found the woman had died of apoplexy on 29 November.

There is a suggestion, but no more, that Mrs Morgan's formerly estranged husband had returned to Dean Street to take over the business but, with her death, Scotland Yard effectively closed its file.[3]

Two years later came the case of Margaret Waters, who had come from Newfoundland and had invested in a sewing machine enterprise which did not work out. She then fell into the hands of the moneylenders, and then a female lodger whose protector was 'rich and respectable', gave birth and left the child with Waters. It was the start of a short career, one in which it was thought over 40 babies died – given, it seems, an amount of laudanum. Charged with her was her sister Sarah Ellis, who indeed had a laudanum habit and who, after her discharge, confessed to her solicitor John Mayo that it was she who had administered the drug. Margaret Waters was hanged on 11 October 1870:

> Margaret Waters died upon the gallows yesterday morning, with resignation and fervent prayers; but she died denying the justice of her sentence.
>
> Mr Bruce [the Home Secretary] was 'sufficiently fortified in his course by the strong opinion everywhere prevailing that the terrible prevalence of infanticide had to be checked by an example of terror'.
>
> The hanging of Waters may not have been quite satisfactory according to the law of evidence, but it has certainly changed the trade of baby farming from one of easy profits and quick returns to a most hazardous speculation, which must answer to justice if the children die, and can offer but small advantages if they live.[4]

[3] PRO/MEPO/3/92.
[4] *Daily Telegraph*, 12 October 1870.

The case had produced an outcry, and W. T. Charley MP expressed his belief at a meeting held in the Adelphi that thousands of babies were either drugged or starved to death in this country and 'what is called baby-farming exists to a frightful extent in the Metropolis'. He recommended the founding of the Infant Life Preservation Society.

The Morning Advertiser was not at all happy with this suggestion.

> We should be sorry to see the benevolence of the country called into play in order to relieve parents of their responsibility. This would be an encouragement to immorality for which the people of England are not prepared.

That old friend of the police, *Senex*, took a great interest in the case and offered them a number of other addresses around London at which they might find bodies.[5]

Apart from Jessie King and Margaret Waters, five baby farmers were hanged in the 37 years from 1870. One was Annie Took in Exeter in 1879. Another, Amelia Elizabeth Dyer, was hanged on 10 June 1896; she was described as a 'stunted woman only five feet tall with scanty white hair scraped into a meagre bun'. At one time she had been a Salvationist. When she was questioned by the police she said, 'You'll know mine by the tape round their necks.' She had thrown the bodies into the Thames at Reading.

So had Ada Chard-Williams, the wife of a Barnet schoolmaster, in 1899. In the summer of that year, having placed a card in a shop window asking for a child to adopt, she was contacted by Florence Jones, an unmarried mother with a daughter Selina. Mrs Chard-Williams told the girl her name was Hewertson, giving an address in

Hammersmith. She told Florence that she was free to call and visit the child at any time. When Jones did so a few days after the farming, she found no one with knowledge of the child or Mrs Hewertson.

At the end of September the body of Selina was found floating in the Thames; she had been battered about the head and suffocated before being thrown into the water. Ada Chard-Williams and her husband William were arrested. Their defence was that the body was not that of Selina. He was acquitted, but she was hanged by James Billington on 6 March 1900; she was aged 24 at the time.

North London seems to have been something of a catchment area, for in 1903 came the case of the 'Finchley Baby Farmers' Amelia Sach, the 29-year-old red-haired proprietress of a nursing home in East Finchley, and her partner 54-year-old Annie Walters. Sach placed an advertisement in the local newspaper reading: 'Accouchement: Before and during, skilled nursing. Home comforts. Baby can remain.'

Mrs Sach would tell the mothers that she was in contact with a foster-parent service which would take the child. Her fee was between £20 and £50, depending on how much she could extract from the mother.

After she received the money she would place the baby with Annie Walters, who would kill the child, often by suffocation, and then throw the body into the Thames or on a rubbish tip. In 1902 Walters took a child home, saying she was looking after the little girl while her parents were on holiday. Her landlady, the wife of a policeman, helped her to change the nappies and discovered the child was a body. Within a few days Mrs Walters said the child had died and the body was returned to its parents for burial; she seemed to be genuinely upset. Some few months later, however, she endeavoured to repeat the procedure and this time the policeman became suspicious and questioned her.

Mrs Walters ran away but was soon traced, and further inquiries led to Mrs Sach.

The women both maintained their innocence throughout the trial. In the death cells, Mrs Sach still protested her innocence, whilst Mrs Walters 'attributed her misfortune to a lack of sufficient funds to pay for a good defence'. They were hanged in a double execution by William Billington at Holloway prison on 3 February 1903.

The last of the baby farmers to be hanged was Rhoda Willis, a 39-year-old alcoholic, in Cardiff on 14 August 1907.[6] In fact she may be seen as pathetic rather than evil. The daughter of a respectable businessman, she moved to Cardiff in 1889 and married. When her husband died, she began a series of unhappy and unsuccessful relationships which drained her of what money she had. She then set herself up as a baby farmer. On 3 June 1907 she was paid £6 by Maud Tresor to adopt her child. She maintained she smuggled the child back to her room and after drinking heavily she fell out of bed. Her landlady, arriving to investigate, found the child dead at the end of the bed. Willis claimed she had accidentally smothered the child while drunk. In the death cell she said that she had in fact killed the child on an impulse in the railway carriage on her way home.

The end of baby-farming murders can probably be attributed first to legislation and social help. The Infant Life Preservation Act 1872 was in force but, more importantly, 1884 had seen the founding of the National Society for the Prevention of Cruelty to Children. However, no doubt the most likely reason is that the more intelligent of the farmers took greater care not to be caught.

---

[6] Charlotte Winsor was convicted in 1865, but was reprieved following legal argument the next year. There was a question over the admissibility of the evidence of the mother of the dead child. She herself had been put on trial, but curiously had been neither convicted nor acquitted.

By the 1990s illegitimacy had become a cachet. Well, perhaps that is not the way to put it. To have an illegitimate child was a cachet for the mother. It was also as often as not a way out of an unhappy parental atmosphere and into a nice council flat of one's own. With it, however, came a rise in the number of children in care; in 1999 there were more than 3,500 children under the age of two in this situation. It was now the fashion to move away from adoption. In 1968 there had been nearly 25,000 adoptions, but now the figure has dropped to under 6,000. The Home Secretary Jack Straw blamed 'well meaning but misguided' social workers for overestimating the ability of many young women to cope with the financial and emotional burdens of motherhood. He called on these teenage girls to give up their babies for adoption, so bringing a storm of protest down on his shoulders. The British Pregnancy Advisory Service was not impressed with the idea: 'A public health campaign aimed at teenagers to promote the contraceptive pill would be a far more sensible measure.'[7]

How Francis Place and Marie Stopes would have approved!

---

[7] *The Times*, 26 January 1999; *Daily Express*, 26 January 1999.

13

Rape

One of the many problems which women have faced is the apparent intransigence of the judges in taking rape seriously. Even as late as 1997, the Lord Chief Justice in his speech at a dinner of the London Criminal Courts' Solicitors' Association posed the question, 'What does one give a man who rapes a girl in a punt?' The answer was 'A half-blue.' His Lordship's story was received with cries and shouts of disapproval. Pressed, he later explained the apparent gaffe by saying that he had intended to point up the difference between current and past judicial thought. This was not as many of the audience received it.

Given that the judiciary has until very recently been largely if not wholly composed of white, middle-class, public-school-educated middle-aged men, it is not wholly surprising that they have, on occasion, adopted a schoolboy attitude towards rape and the sentencing of those convicted.

This has not been the only problem. Issues of consent, corroboration, the exposure to press and public of the woman's intimate private life – coupled with the law which stated that a husband could not be guilty of raping his wife even if separated – have all contributed to the belief of many women that the trial of the defendant is itself a second rape. In theory the law of rape has been simply defined for the past 140 years following the Offences Against the Person Act 1861. In practice it was not defined until 1976, however.

In pre-Anglo-Saxon law, only a virgin could be raped, and rape included abduction. There was a sense of wronging not merely the woman but more particularly her kin. Provided the judge and the families agreed, the woman could save her attacker by agreeing to marry him. If not, then penalties varied and related as much to the social status of the parties as to the offence itself. In Anglo-Saxon law the punishment was death, which at the time of William the Conqueror was changed to castration and blinding. In the reign of Edward I, the First Statute of Westminster in 1275 fixed the penalty, which was substantially reduced to one of two years' imprisonment followed by a fine. Now, however, non-virgins could be raped and marriage could no longer save the offender. In 1285 the death penalty was restored by the Second Statute of Westminster.

Critics of Parliament will argue that there is too much in the way of compromise in the legislation, and it is possible to argue that the *quid pro quo* which runs throughout the centuries for the major change in the attitude to rape, by the inclusion of married women and the abolition of the saving marriage, was the relatively light sentence of imprisonment and a fine. When things had bedded down and the public had come to accept the extension of the law governing rape, then the full punishment was restored. The other view is that the initial reduction in the penalty had simply brought about an increase in the crime. This argument, of course, goes against that for the abolition of capital punishment.

In modern terms, the principles for contemporary rape came from the jurist Lord Hale. When the Advisory Group

on the Law of Rape reported in 1975 they acknow-
ledged Hale:

> the traditional common law definition, derived from a
> seventeenth-century writer and still in use is that rape
> consists in having unlawful sexual intercourse with a
> woman without her consent, by force, fear or fraud.

However, Hale is condemned for what many see as the
misogynist bias that 'has pervaded the law and practice
concerning . . . rape'. In particular, it was to him that the
vexed questions of character, behaviour at the time of the
offence and corroboration are attributed.

In 1841 the death penalty for rape was abolished.[1]

For there to be rape there has to be vaginal penetration,
however slight. Neither oral nor anal sex constituted the
offence until 1994, when forcible anal sex became rape for
men and women alike. There is no need for the hymen to
be ruptured, nor (unlike the old cases of buggery) has there
to be proof of emission. In recent years rape was established
after an initial consent to intercourse. So, when a fiancé who
had taken his girlfriend away for the weekend in an effort to
bolster up their failing relationship failed to withdraw on her
remark, 'That's enough. I want you to stop,' he received six
months' imprisonment.[2]

It may not have been fraud not to tell your partner you
have a venereal disease, but as a general proposition fraud
vitiated consent and when a singing teacher told his charge
that intercourse would improve her pitch this was held to
be rape.[3] As is usual with the English law, there are so
many anomalies. It is not rape to seduce a woman under

[1] In America it continued until 1964.
[2] Gaston (1981) 73 Cr App R 164; Stanton (1844) 1 Car & Kir 415; see also
Kaitamaki v The Queen [1985] AC 147; *Cooper* [1994] Crim LR 531. It must
surely be rape in an instance of what is initially consensual buggery where
consent but not the member is withdrawn.
[3] *Williams* [1923] 1 KB 340. See also *Flannery* (1877) 2 QBD 410; *Papadimitropoulos*
(1957) 98 CLR 249.

the pretence that the man will marry her or take her to
Paris for the weekend. It is, however, rape to impersonate
her husband.

One of the most curious of decisions on identity took
place after a case in October 1971 at Essex Assizes. 'The
appellant was a young man of nineteen and the complainant
a girl of eighteen.' One night he had a good deal to drink and,
as Lord Edmund Davies delicately put it, 'was desirous of
having intercourse'.

> Passing the complainant's house he saw a light on in
> an upstairs room which he knew was the complainant's
> bedroom. He fetched a ladder, put it up against the
> window and climbed up. He saw the complainant lying
> on her bed, which was just under the window, naked
> and asleep.
>
> He descended the ladder, stripped off his clothes,
> climbed back up and pulled himself onto the window-sill.
> As he did so the complainant awoke and saw a naked male
> form outlined against the window. She jumped to the
> conclusion it was her boy-friend with whom she was on
> terms of regular and frequent sexual intimacy.
>
> Assuming that he had come to pay her an ardent
> nocturnal visit she beckoned him in. In response the
> appellant descended from the sill and joined her in
> bed where they had full sexual intercourse. After the
> lapse of some time the complainant became aware of
> features of her companion which roused her suspicions.
> Switching on the bedside light she discovered that he
> was not her boyfriend but the appellant. She thereupon
> slapped him and went into the bathroom. The appellant
> promptly vanished.

The youth was convicted of burglary with intent to rape
and received 21 months. His appeal was decided in a way
which makes the law the ass which Pickwick described.

The pivotal point, said Lord Edmund Davies, was where was he standing when he was beckoned in? If he was outside on the sill, then he was not a trespasser. On the other hand, if he was inside he had already entered and therefore was. Since the judge had not told the jury of this salient feature, the conviction must be quashed.[4]

More recently, a self-styled exorcist, Kenneth Martin, pleaded guilty to persuading a 17-year-old girl he had met in a McDonald's in North London to have sex with him on the basis that it was necessary to get rid of evil spirits. (She had told him she was having a run of bad luck.) He received 18 months at the Old Bailey, where he was told by Judge Neil Dennison, 'This was on any view pretty disgraceful behaviour by a middle-aged man to an adolescent girl.'[5]

It is to the pronouncements of Lord Hale that women have directed their attacks on the system of the trials of rape cases. It has been the practice to warn a jury that although independent evidence to support the woman's story is not essential it is dangerous to convict on her uncorroborated word, something which is seen not only as making the prosecution of a complaint more difficult but also as an unnecessary slur on womanhood in general:[6]

---

[4] *Collins* (1973) QB 100.
[5] *Daily Telegraph*, 18 November 1997.
[6] If the law relating to corroboration is felt unnecessary, then some thought might be given to the plight of Hajera Begum, a 14-year-old girl in the poverty-stricken village of Baksh Para in Kurigam, western Bangladesh. She had claimed that on 24 September 1994 she had been raped by Abdul Hye, an 18-year-old from the same village, but unfortunately for her she was unable to produce not merely corroboration but a witness to the attack.

At first it seems that, provided she agreed to an abortion (which she underwent), she would be married off to Abdul Hye, but then one of his uncles demanded a trial following the Islamic Shariah law. Her trial in front of the village court, *gram salishi*, of five village headmen, including a cleric, was for having 'illicit sex'. Sentenced to be beaten, on 25 October she was tied to bamboo canes and struck 80 times with a broom. When she fell unconscious the beating stopped and she was taken to a nearby hospital, where, according to reports in the local daily paper, *Janakantha*, the doctor on duty refused to admit her. (*Herald*, Panjim, 24 November 1994).

> [it] must be remembered that [rape] is an accusation
> easily to be made and hard to be proved, and harder
> to be defended by the party accused, though never so
> innocent.

The other evidential complaint has been that of allowing
the complainant to be cross-examined about her previous
sexual life. Prior to 1898, the defendant was not allowed to
give evidence in any criminal trial. As a general rule, in a
criminal trial a defendant could not attack the character of a
witness without losing the so-called shield which protected
him from questions by the prosecution on his own previous
convictions.[7] This did not apply in rape cases and the
defence could show that the complainant was a woman of
notoriously bad character 'for want of chastity or common
decency', or was a prostitute. Previous sexual behaviour
was admissible in evidence as was a rather more general
'immoral' behaviour with other men.[8]

In 1976 the law changed. Robin Corbett, in his introduction to the Sexual Offences (Amendment) Bill, put it:

> a woman could often be subjected to hurtful and
> irrelevant cross-examination about her previous sex-
> ual history, on the seeming assumption that because
> the woman had had, for example, an abortion or an
> illegitimate baby, or was even held to be promiscuous,

---

[7] The situation is very different in America, where actual entry into a witness-box
is often deemed to be putting one's character before the court. So if a defendant
has a conviction for a felony, it is rare to see him give evidence unless it has
been agreed with the judge beforehand that he will not allow questioning as
to previous convictions.
[8] *Barker* (1829) 3 C&P 589; *Tissington* (1843) 1 Cox 48; *Greatbanks* (1959) Crim
L.R. 450; *Clarke*, (1817) 2 Stark 241; *Hodgson* (1812) R & R 221 CCR. More
recently in the celebrated Taylforth libel case, possibly one of the reasons
the jury turned against the plaintiff was evidence that she had been eating a
German sausage in public in a manner which perhaps suggested a proclivity
to oral sex.

that somehow excused the rape or, worse, suggested
that rape was not possible against such a woman.[9]

Now under s. 2 of the Sexual Offences (Amendment) Act
1976, such cross-examination was allowed only with the
leave of the judge, who must be satisfied that it would be
unfair to the defendant to refuse to allow the evidence to
be adduced or the question to be asked.

But was it enforced? There are allegations that women are
still being questioned along those lines on a regular basis. In
December 1998, during a conference held at the House of
Commons a speaker claimed that women who allege rape are
questioned in about 75 per cent of cases about their sex with
other men, the race of those men, any previous abortions and
whether they had sex before the age of 16. This brought an
angry riposte from a Crown Court judge, Andrew Geddes,
who found the statistic incredible and said that in his
experience the section which prevented a general roam
around the woman's private life was strictly construed.[10]

The organisation Women Against Rape replied that the
1998 Home Office survey *Speaking Up for Justice* found
that 75 per cent of judges allowed questioning about the
complainant's sexual history, saying:

> . . . seems to go far beyond that demanded in the interests
> of relevance and . . . fairness to the defendant . . . There
> is overwhelming evidence that the existing law is not
> serving its purpose.

Another requirement was that any complaint should be
recent, really at the first opportunity which reasonably
offered itself. Doctors examining complainants were particularly advised to be on the look-out for the possibility

[9] House of Commons Debates, vol. 905 col. 802, 1976.
[10] *New Law Journal*, 11 December 1998; 8 and 15 January 1999.

of a false allegation. Threats were often thought to be insufficient. The married woman was expected to have put up a struggle, and the absence of physical injury was thought to be a sign that the complaint was a false one. Virgins could, perhaps occasionally, be terrified into submission.

Amazingly it was Professor Keith Simpson, who did such pioneering work on child battering, who wrote:

> a girl out of her first decade is seldom capable of being raped against her will without mark of forcible restraint or injury.[11]

Perhaps the most appalling case of judges' inhumanity to women came in the trial of *Morgan* in 1975. An RAF airman invited three colleagues home, telling them they could have sexual intercourse with his wife. He said that, whilst she might appear not to consent, part of her sexual turn-on was the experience of seeming to be raped. It was all lies. She did not consent, but the airmen continued. At their trial the jury disbelieved their story, but the House of Lords said that the test was if the men genuinely believed she was play-acting that would have been an answer to the charge.[12] It was the next year in the Sexual Offences Act 1976 that rape was for the first time defined and the Act confirmed the House of Lords' decision. 'No' could be 'Yes' if the man genuinely believed it.

By the early 1990s slow progress was being made to the law, again propounded by Lord Hale, that men could be found guilty of raping their wives. In June 1991 a draft bill drawn up by Women Against Rape (WAR) and proposed by Harry Cohen, Labour MP for Leyton, foundered.

[11] K. Simpson, *A Doctor's Guide to Court*, p. 125.
[12] *Morgan* (1975) 1 All ER.

There were the usual arguments against the concept on
the grounds that women would make false allegations. The
remarks of Helena Kennedy QC when she said, 'There is
still the notion that marital rape is about wives queuing up
at the police station in their nighties because they'd got a
headache and didn't fancy it' were rather held against her
by WAR, who chastised her in a letter to the *Guardian*:

> Women are sometimes forced to run to police stations
> in their nighties in fear for their lives. The police
> should not be encouraged to dismiss or demean such
> women. It is vital that those with prestige, especially
> women, make it clear that they consider it rape if
> a woman says no and a man doesn't take no for an
> answer.[13]

In December 1982 the very experienced Judge Peter Stanley
Price, sitting at Leeds Crown Court, caused the second
furore of the year when he sentenced a man to what
amounted to 25 days in prison for the rape of a six-year-old
girl. Price had actually imposed a year's imprisonment with
eight months suspended, but the time spent on remand
meant that the man served less than four weeks as a
convicted prisoner. The girl then saw him on the street
and was bitterly distressed. Unsurprisingly, the judge was
castigated in the press and in Parliament, where Margaret
Thatcher called the sentence unbelievable.

Of course there were calls for Price's resignation even
after he explained that he had sentenced the man on the
basis that the real offence – there had only been minimal
penetration, he said – was one of indecent assault. Mrs
Thatcher climbed down – but not before Lord Hailsham,
then the Lord Chancellor, indicated that in future only

[13] *Guardian*, 24 October 1991; 8 November 1991.

designated judges would hear rape cases. Ironically, Stanley Price would be one of those judges. He retired a year early in February 1983. The retirement, said the Lord Chancellor's Office, had nothing to do with the case.

His was not the first problem case for the Lord Chancellor that year. Judge David Wild had already caused a great deal of grief by saying:

> Women who say no do not always mean no. It is not just a question of saying no, it is a question of how she says it, how she shows it and makes it clear. If she doesn't want it she only has to keep her legs shut and she would not get it without force and there will be marks of force being used.

He compounded his bad behaviour by fining the man £2,000. The victim, a hitchhiker, was described by the judge as having been contributorily negligent for choosing to hike on her own at night.

This 'contributory negligence' may well have its origin in the fifteenth century, when women were forbidden to walk after dark without an escort across barren, isolated or desolate land.[14]

Lord Hailsham was obliged to write confirming that:

> . . . contributory negligence does not, of course, constitute any defence to rape, nor in my view in the absence of actual sexual provocation should imprudence on the part of a victim operate as a factor of mitigation in the reduction of a sentence.[15]

Attitudes have not changed that much in a quarter of a

[14] See Susan S.M. Edwards 'Contributory Negligence in Compensation Claims by Victims of Sexual Assault' in *New Law Journal*, Volume 132 (1982) 1140.
[15] *The Times*, 6 and 12 January 1982.

century. In February 1999, albeit in Italy, a court ruled
that a woman wearing tight-fitting denim jeans could not
be raped. The thinking behind this variation of the old
schoolboy joke of women running faster with their skirts
up was based on the belief that jeans can only be removed
with the co-operation of the wearer. An 18-year-old girl
had complained that she had been raped by her 45-year-old
driving instructor. He claimed consensual sex. The judges
had apparently discarded the possibility that she might have
been so terrified by threats of violence that she did take her
jeans off. 'It was difficult' to imagine anything worse than
rape, said the judges.

Over the years Price has not been alone in handing
out an inappropriate sentence. Worse, in many cases the
trial judge has also handed out some wholly inappropriate
comments.[16]

In January 1988, when a 19-year-old youth was sentenced
at Lincoln Crown Court to three years' youth custody, Mr
Justice John Owen commented that the 12-year-old girl had
been 'asking for trouble' by going into the youth's room
alone. Mr Justice Melford Stevenson, one of the last of
the old-fashioned bullying school of judges, commented
that one attack was 'an anaemic rape as rapes go'. As he
passed an 18-month suspended sentence, Judge Michael
Argyle told a defendant who had stripped and tried to
rape a girl, 'You come from Derby, which is my part
of the world. Now off you go and don't come back to

[16] American judges have not always been noticeably better. In 1986 a judge in
Philadelphia was forced to apologise after his comments to a defendant that he
could not understand how the man, as an attractive fellow could '[do] something to
her which was stupid'. Outside court the judge helpfully elaborated to journalists,
telling them that the 31-year-old victim was 'the ugliest girl I have ever seen in
my entire life . . . in the top ten. She is coyote-ugly.' The 'coyote-ugly' is a
reference to the habit of the animal to bite off its leg if caught in a trap.
The implication is that the man would bite off his arm rather than disturb
the sleeping woman in the morning. Quoted by Fenton Bresler, *Sex and the
Law*, pp. 184–5; see *The Times*, 8 February 1986.

this court.' At Birmingham Crown Court, the elderly and kindly Mr Justice Bristow put a man on probation for three years after he had accosted a girl on the forecourt of a public house, bolted her in a lavatory cubicle and tried to rape her. He thought the defendant would probably be more emotionally scarred than the girl.

One might have hoped that these kinds of remarks were a thing of the past – but not so. In 1998 Mr Justice Rougier advised the 13-year-old victim of alleged rape how to take her Pimms in future:

> Take this from an experienced Pimms drinker like me. If you want to drink, wait until you're older. But if you can't wait, dilute the drink with one part Pimms to six parts of lemonade at least.

Nor has the Court of Appeal always taken rape as seriously as perhaps it should. In 1977, Guardsman Holdsworth was sentenced to a term of three years for causing grievous bodily harm to a young woman during an attempted rape. This would mean that he would be sacked from the Coldstream Guards, where he was said to have a promising career ahead. The leniency caused another public outcry, which was fuelled when after all the Army decided it was better off without his services.

The nadir was reached in early 1987 when the very experienced Mr Justice Leonard, who had long been a prosecutor and was now sitting at the Old Bailey, sentenced the defendant in what was known as the Ealing Vicarage Case to a lesser term for a particularly nasty rape than he handed out for the burglary which accompanied it. The rapist attracted three- and five-year sentences. The judge justified the leniency on the grounds that the 'trauma suffered by the victim was not great'.

The Ealing Vicarage Case was the final straw and the

Lord Chief Justice set about establishing once and for all a tariff for sentences in rape cases. He had made a half-hearted stab at it immediately after the hitchhiker trial, when he stated that unless there were exceptional circumstances immediate imprisonment was the keyword. He then set out the basic factors which could affect the individual sentence, but nowhere did he indicate how long the sentence should be.

Now, in what was called a guideline case, he stated that in a rape committed by an adult without aggravating or mitigating features a figure of five years should be the starting point in a contested case. Although sentence bargaining has been discouraged, and from time to time outlawed in this country, it has always been understood that time will be knocked off a sentence where the accused has admitted his guilt at an early stage in the proceedings, and particularly in cases where he has not subjected his victim to the trauma of giving evidence and being cross-examined.

In cases of rapes by two or more men acting together, or where the man has broken into the victim's home, or in cases of abduction, then the starting point was suggested as eight years. In cases where the victim was subjected to perversions or other indignities, or was very young or old, then again the starting point was to be substantially higher. If a series of rapes was committed by men acting in concert, then ten and 12 years was not to be regarded as out of the way.[17]

But things did not go too well. A matter of six days after the guidelines were produced Lord Justice Stocker, sitting in the Court of Appeal, reduced a sentence of eight years to six when an airman had broken into a house in Ipswich and subjected his victim, a middle-aged nurse, to what

[17] *Billam* [1986] 1 All ER 985 CA; *Cramer and Ors* [1988] 10 Cr App R (S) 483.

were described as 'appalling' sexual indignities. The man's previous good character and service record were regarded as the key factors.

However, the cases in which an immediate custodial sentence has not been imposed have been few and far between. In one case in which the victim was suffering from Down's Syndrome and the attacker was a mentally retarded man, the Court of Appeal substituted a probation order for a custodial sentence. The man was said to have had only a child-like understanding of the serious nature of what he was doing. However, their Lordships rather spoiled things by adding that 'the low level of protest she made because of her own circumstances' helped make the case 'wholly exceptional'.

But, of course it can be argued that these were sentences handed out in the unenlightened 1980s by the middle-aged, middle-class and untrained-in-the-way-of-modern-manners judges and such inappropriate behaviour is over. Sadly, it is not the case.

Sometimes, however, the sentencing is difficult to understand. In the case of Roy Charles Biggs, the Court of Appeal upheld a sentence of three years given a young man convicted of rape where the victim both before and more particularly after the rape had consensual sex with him. On the other hand, *S. (Balraj)*, who raped his infant daughter, received only double that.[18]

One of the common misconceptions over the years has been that prostitutes cannot be raped. However, they have an equal right to decline intercourse in both their social and professional lives. Nevertheless, the courts have subtly distinguished between them and those seen as ordinary decent women by imposing lesser sentences on their attackers. They may be allowed to say no, but their vocation does

[18] *Biggs* (1979) 1 Cr App R (S) 30; S *(Balraj)* [1997] Cr App R (S) 123.

not permit them to say no quite so loudly, or if they do for their cries to be heard.

One thing happening was that when during the 1990s the Crown Prosecution Service declined to prosecute, women began bringing civil actions for rape, claiming damages from their attackers. One attraction in this was that the burden of proof required was not the 'beyond reasonable doubt' in a criminal trial but only 'the balance of probabilities'. Another is that the cases are heard by a judge sitting alone and the complainant is not subject to the vagaries of a jury.

However what is puzzling, and distressing to women campaigning in rape cases, is the fact that, despite the curtailment of inquiry into the complainant's sexual habits; anonymity; a certain amount of protection whilst giving evidence and, without doubt, more sympathetic treatment from police officers, when complaints are made, the percentage of convictions obtained is steadily falling.

Are many of the accusations therefore false ones? Anecdotal evidence from police officers varies. One experienced woman police officer suggested in the mid-1980s that 90 per cent of allegations were false,[19] and set against this is another senior officer who in the same year wrote:

> There can be no credible basis for the suggestion that 70 per cent, 50 per cent or even 20 per cent of allegations of sexual assaults are false, in the sense of being untrue.[20]

Whatever that may mean.

One British research paper backs the woman officer and suggests that some 90 per cent of allegations are indeed false, while another states that the figure falls between 29 and 47

[19] *Daily Mail*, 17 June 1985.
[20] I. Blair, *Investigating Rape – A New Approach for Police*, p. 54.

per cent.[21] Sociologists have tended to question whether the criteria used could itself stand up to examination, on the grounds that these surveys were carried out by police surgeons on small samples of complainants and without a control group against which to test the findings.

However, a survey conducted amongst British police surgeons, involving 1,379 women, found that 31 per cent were laying the basis for false allegations. In fact, the more experienced surgeons in the survey thought the proportion of false complaints was lower, just under 25 per cent.[22]

The most common reasons for false complaints in the mid-1980s were young girls coming home late and deflecting for the time being the wrath of their parents; women in extramarital relationships, and prostitutes whose clients had refused to pay. Today, to these can be added spite or dissatisfaction with the relationship, remorse and a slight variant on women in extramarital relationships: women in regular relationships who have 'cheated' on their boyfriends or partners and have become pregnant or at least have missed a period.[23]

Of course feminists have a vested interest in discrediting such research, which tends to argue against their cause. It is argued that the only methodologically sound study is the one of the New York Sex Crimes Analysis Unit which found that over a period of two years the rate of false allegations in rape

[21] A small survey concluded that 16 out of 18 women examined had made a false allegation. C.H. Stewart, 'A retrospective survey of alleged sexual assault cases' in the *Police Surgeon*, November 1981, pp. 28–32. Another survey over a five-year period with a rather larger sample concluded that 29 per cent were definitely false allegations and a further 18 per cent probably so. N.M. MacLean 'Rape and false accusations of rape' in the *Police Surgeon*, 15, pp. 29–40.

[22] R. Geis and others, 'Police Surgeons and rape: A questionnaire survey' in the *Police Surgeon*, pp. 7–14.

[23] For comments on how decisions were taken about charging women making false complaints see Joshua Rozenberg, *The Case for the Crown*, p. 164. In recent years there have been a number of prosecutions of women making such allegations. They have been dealt with in a variety of ways, depending largely on their mental health at the time the complaints were made.

cases was around two per cent, which matched that of false
allegations in other crimes.[24] Feminist theory also argues
that there is a basic male assumption that women have a
tendency to lie in rape cases and make false allegations,
and in any event a deeply male suspicion of women in
such cases, a suspicion which has permeated and indeed
fouled the whole of the handling of such cases by the law
over the years.[25]

It was not until the 1990s that serious attempts were made
to overturn the law that a husband, separated or not, could
not be guilty of raping his wife. It stemmed back to 1888,
when Charles Clarence was charged with causing grievous
bodily harm to his wife; he had gonorrhoea and passed it
to her. He pleaded guilty, but the Recorder passed the case
to the Queen's Bench Division to determine whether he
could properly be found guilty. It was argued that, if the
conviction was upheld, any man accused by a prostitute
of having defrauded her could be prosecuted for indecent
assault or even rape, something which clearly did not appeal
to male Victorian England.

Mr Justice Wills did not like the argument at all:

> If a man meets a woman in the street and knowingly
> gives her bad money in order to procure her consent to
> intercourse with him he obtains consent by fraud, but
> it would be childish to say she does not consent.

In any event women were often the wrongdoers:

> The unmarried woman who solicits and tempts a perhaps
> reluctant man to intercourse which he would avoid like
> death itself if he knew the truth as to her health must

[24] Report of the New York Sex Crimes Analysis Unit quoted in P. Pattullo,
Judging Women.
[25] See for example Zsuzanna Adler, *Rape on Trial*, pp. 25–6.

surely, under some circumstances at least, come under
the same criminal liability as the man.

The conviction was quashed.[26]

By the middle 1980s there was a growing lobby for a
change in the law, and in 1984 the Criminal Law Revision
Committee recommended, by a majority, that the *status
quo* remain. Fifteen years later their arguments seem, at
best, woolly. One such argument was that marital rape
was not the same as a rape by a stranger, and that if the
woman was injured she could undoubtedly bring an action
for assault.

In this respect, paradoxically, a woman cohabiting with
a man was in a better position than a married woman. She
at least was able to bring a prosecution for rape. Another
paradox was that there was never any doubt that a husband
would be guilty as a party to the rape of his wife, and
that other sexual practices not amounting to rape (such
as fellatio) could, if forced on the wife, be an indecent
assault.[27]

A second argument was that such prosecutions would
be:

a bargaining counter in negotiations for maintenance
or custody, or as a basis of a charge of unreasonable
behaviour in a divorce petition.[28]

---

[26] *Clarence* (1888) 22 Q.B.23. Mrs Clarence was by no means the only one to
suffer. Mrs Belcher had fared even worse in 1835. He husband infected her
with venereal disease on no fewer than three occasions and when she sensibly
declined to live with him petitioned for the restitution of his conjugal rights.
She cross-petitioned for a legal separation on the grounds of cruelty, only to
be refused. His disease had been contracted before her marriage and so she
could not claim he had been adulterous. In those days there was no question
that her marriage could be annulled.

[27] Cogan [1976] QB 217; Kowalski (1987) 86 Cr App R 339.

[28] Criminal Law Revision Committee: Fifteenth Report on Sexual Offences,
London, (HMSO 1984), paras 2.69.

If wives were to be treated in relation to rape in the same
way as other women, that might lead to prosecutions
which some would think were not desirable in the
interest of the family or the public.[29]

Three years later Judge Richard Lowry jailed a man for
five years for raping his wife. The parties were not legally
separated and lived under the same roof, but there was a
County Court order for them not to molest each other.

In 1990 there was sufficient support for a Rape in
Marriage Bill to be introduced. At the time a wide variety
of countries including Poland, the Soviet Union, Sweden,
Denmark and Norway – as well as three Australian terri-
tories and at least 18 states in America – had provisions.

In October the next year, the House of Lords upheld the
decision of Mr Justice Simon Brown at Sheffield Crown
Court that a husband could be guilty of raping his wife.
The parties had been married in 1984 and separated
on 21 October 1989 when the wife went to live with
her parents. She left behind a letter indicating that she
was going to petition for divorce. Two days later in a
telephone conversation she also mentioned the question
of divorce, but had done nothing about filing a petition
when on 12 November the husband forced his way into
her parents' house and, squeezing her throat, attempted to
have intercourse with her. Later they divorced.

After the trial at the Crown Court R. appealed to the
Court of Appeal, who upheld the judge's ruling and granted
the husband leave to appeal to the House of Lords. The
question to be answered was, 'Is a husband criminally
liable for raping his wife?' With some fairly convoluted
thought process, their Lordships ruled that he could be
criminally liable.

[29] Criminal Law Revision Committee: Working Paper on Sexual Offences, London
(HMSO 1980), para. 42.

This was a decision which was welcomed as common
sense but dubious in law.[30]

A month later, in the first decision after the ruling a South
African pleaded guilty to raping his wife. He had tied her up
and threatened her with a knife. 'I did it the way I usually
do with her.' He was sentenced to five years.[31]

The Court of Appeal was clear that it should not be
thought that a rape by a husband should be treated more
lightly than other rapes, as set out in the guideline case
of *Billam*.[32] In *Stephen W.* the defendant had been living
with his wife for three years when, after an argument, he
raped her, forced her to have oral sex at knife-point and
then raped her again. He received five years' imprisonment.
Sentencing will depend on the conduct and the amount of
violence shown. If those elements are present, then the fact
that there has been a long-standing relationship will be of
little account.[33]

In the years since rape in marriage became a crime, there
have been only a handful of prosecutions, seemingly giving
the lie to the Criminal Law Revision Committee's fears that
allegations would be used for blackmailing purposes. On
the other hand, there is really no way of knowing whether
they are employed in the same way as children are used in
bargaining positions in divorce settlements.

The apparent increase in the incidence of the so-called
date rape has become prominent over more recent years.
What was seen perhaps 20 years ago as an unfortunate
experience has now become a burning issue:

[30] See R *v* R [1992] CLR 207; and also Glanville Williams, 'Rape is rape' in 142
New Law Journal, 11. Marianne Giles, 'Judicial Law-Making in the Criminal
Courts: the case of marital rape' in [1992] *Criminal Law Review*, p. 407.
[31] 15 November 1991.
[32] *Billam* [1986] 1 All ER 985. A guideline case is one where the Court of Appeal
hears an appeal or a number of appeals together and sets out, on the facts, what
it considers should be the appropriate sentence in a variety of circumstances.
[33] (1993) 14 Cr App R (S) 256; see also *Michael H* [1997] 2 Cr App
R (S) 339.

It is simply that more complaints are being made in situations where, in the old days, a woman might just have gone to a friend's to talk it over.[34]

I dare say that if I examined my memory closely enough I could claim that I have been raped. If the issue is consent – 'Did you consent to this act?' – then I believe most sexually active women could say that there have been times in their lives when they did not consent to the act of love. Either by bullying or threats, by pestering or cajoling or even, believably enough, yielding out of pity, women have been coerced into acts of sexual congress which they afterwards regretted thoroughly.[35]

By the mid-1990s Jessica Harris's Home Office survey found half of all rapes were date rape; but out of a sample of 309 cases some two-thirds never reached the Crown Prosecution Service's desk and only 74 reached court. In 1994 it was suggested that one in six women in England and Wales suffered date rape, and in 1995 that one in four between the ages of 16 and 19 – and in Scotland one in three women – were similarly attacked.[36]

Given the belief that rape is an easy allegation to make and a difficult one to rebut, and considering the rightly severe penalties which attach to a conviction – to which may be added the punishment which will be handed out to sex offenders by other prison inmates – it may be that juries acquit out of sympathy. There is therefore an argument that there should be a distinction between forms of rape, and that violent rape by strangers resulting in grievous bodily harm should be distinguished from what is seen as a lesser crime of non-consensual sex. In other words, the starting

[34] Baroness Mallalieu QC.
[35] Mary Kenny in the *Express*, 5 July 1998.
[36] *Cosmopolitan*, October 1994; *Evening Standard*, 14 July 1995.

tariff of five years is too long for a 'date rape'. Women's groups such as Women Against Rape, however, paraphrase Gertrude Stein: 'Rape is rape is rape . . .'

One of the more pathetic examples of the so-called date rape was that perpetrated by Angus Diggle, one of the relatively few people whose name has passed into the language. In 1993 this solicitor was jailed for three years for attempted rape. Having been to a Highland Ball at the Grosvenor House Hotel in London, he had been invited back to the flat of the girl with whom he had been at the ball, where he was expected to spend the night on the sofa. She woke in her bed to find him in his spectacles and wearing only Highland cuffs and a luminous green condom, trying to have sex with her. When the police were called he seemed impenitent, saying, 'I have spent £200 on her. Why can't I do what I want to her?' His sentence was reduced to two years by the Court of Appeal and he was suspended from practice for a year on his release. Later he was bound over to keep the peace; he had been harassing a woman on a train quoting Latin and Shakespeare to her. Finally, he was struck off the rolls of solicitors after being found drunk in Glebe Street, Bolton.

In the last few years much has been made of the drug Rohypnol, the so-called date-rape drug, nicknamed 'Roofie'. A 2mg dose tipped in a drink is sufficient to induce an almost complete blackout and, it is said, hundreds of women are attacked in this way every year, particularly by college students in America. By February 1999, however, while there were believed to have been over 1,000 attacks in Britain during the 1990s only three men had been arrested and no one had been charged.[37]

Unfortunately, since no identifiable academic research is permitted into the deliberations of juries it is impossible to

[37] *Daily Express*, 2 February 1999.

determine the grounds on which defendants are acquitted. In America, however, the harsh sentences do seem to be a deterrent; not to rapists but to juries convicting defendants.[38] There is also the danger that the attacker will kill his victim; often the only witness against him.

In recent years rape has begun to be seen not always in sexual terms, but as an act of violence. For this reason the often-repeated call that all rapists should be castrated is likely to go unheard. Apart from the fact that castration does not prevent either an erection or the sexual urge, research in America has shown that castrated rapists simply turn to sticks and other implements with which to attack their victims.

By the middle of the 1970s, the Penile Plesythograph (PPG) had been devised; this test detected minute changes to the penis blood supply, which may occur when men are shown scenes of naked children, consensual intercourse, rape and strangulation of women. Devised in Czechoslovakia as a means of weeding out homosexuals from the armed forces, tests using the device were now being carried out in British prisons to assess sex offenders. In May 1995 the *Observer* reported that it was being used by prison authorities to test prisoners who had no convictions for sexual offences but who were serving life sentences for other offences.

In two instances prisoners who failed the test were told that they must undergo the year-long Sex Offender Training Programme. The thinking behind this appears to be that whilst in some cases where a man had been sentenced to life imprisonment there was no hard evidence of a sexual motive, the victim might still have suffered genital bruising or might have been a teenage girl.

Dr Peter Thornton, the prison service psychologist in charge of the PPG programme, believed it would make

[38] Ray Wyre, *Women, Men and RAPE*, p. 55.

an important contribution to testing lifers whose cases had 'unresolved concern'. Prisoners would be tested without notice to prevent their masturbating and so defeating the experiment, which consisted of the placing of a 'Barlow gauge', a band around the shaft of the penis with a U-shaped part across the tip. The device is extremely sensitive and can measure a minute change in penile size. In the general prison population, around 5 per cent revealed a 'deviant' response. The leaflet handed out to prisoners read, 'It is important for us to know if you are aroused inappropriately, as it will best help us tailor the treatment to help you.'

One prison psychiatrist told the *Observer* that he considered the testing to be a gross abuse of human rights. 'If you treat people like animals, they will behave like animals on release.'[39]

In early 1999 it was proposed that violent offenders with personality problems and paedophiles would be given indeterminate sentences. Criminals convicted of violent and sexual offences who are not considered treatable under the current mental health laws would have a minimum jail sentence imposed by the judge, which could be extended indefinitely by doctors if they believed these individuals were a risk to the public.

[39] David Rose, 'Penis test for sexual deviancy keeps lifers behind bars' in the *Observer*, 28 May 1995.

14

Unlawful Sexual Intercourse

When in 1875 the Criminal Law Amendment Act raised the age of consent to 16, there was a saving clause that a man could – when charged the first time – raise a defence that he reasonably believed the girl to be over 16. In 1922 the defence was restricted to men under the age of 24. When Parliament reconsidered the whole question of sexual offence in 1956 and produced the Sexual Offences Act of that year, the offence remained the same. Practitioners from that and the next two decades will recall troops of lisping girls – now dressed in school uniform and with their hair in pigtails, rather than the lipsticked little harridans of the night before – traipsing through the witness-box telling their tales of undoing.

There were, however, cracks in the armour. The previous June Neil McKinnon, one of the senior and more robust judges at the Old Bailey, sentenced a 22-year-old carpenter for having intercourse with a 15-year-old boarding-school girl. 'She has no complaints at all,' he said, ordering the man to be conditionally discharged for twelve months. 'A thoroughly satisfactory experience as far as she is concerned.'

Afterwards he spoke to reporters about his decision. This in itself was unusual because, at the time, judges were not expected to make *ex cathedra* pronouncements. He speculated whether the public at large now required the branding as a criminal of a young man who was provoked into intercourse by a thoroughly mature young girl of 15. He thought that maturity rather than age should be the test. He had some support for the sentencing if not his proposition because shortly afterwards Lord Justice Stocker, sitting in the Court of Appeal, freed a 21-year-old who, after a party, had sex with a 13-year-old girl.

> It has been known for young people's sexual desires to be aroused at parties. This happens almost every Saturday night all over the country. The sentence on this man was not only too severe, it was wrong in principle.

And that seemed to be the end of the run-of-the-mill unlawful sexual intercourse offence. Now the judiciary had an example to show how much in touch it was with everyday life. Judge after judge followed Stocker's example, where possible putting the blame on the girl. Judge William Oppenshaw thought that a 14-year-old girl was more to blame than a 26-year-old lorry driver with five children.

More and more judges leaped on the bandwagon. These included the normally severe Judge Edward Clarke, who fined a man £20; he rejected a suggestion that the youth should have probation. The offender had pleaded guilty to four charges of unlawful sexual intercourse with girls of 15 and 13, and had asked for 23 similar offences to be taken into consideration.

But the sentence depended upon the defendant's luck in getting the 'right' judge. Not content with short jail sentences, three Nottingham miners (two married) appealed to the Court of Appeal and, for their pains, found Lord Justice Lawton in full flow; they had treated the 14-year-old girl, whom His Lordship described as 'a wanton', as 'the village whore'.

Lawton continued that there seemed to be confusion as to what was the correct sentence in such cases and went on to anticipate the present concept of responsibility by some 20 years.

There were categories of offence. The boy in a virtuous friendship who had fallen from grace should not have a sentence of a punitive nature passed on him. At the other end of the scale came the schoolmaster or social worker. Jail for him ought to be at or near the two-year maximum. And in between? The young man who picked up a girl of loose morals at a dance could expect a fine. The 20-year-old who did the same could expect a short period of detention, and the older man one of imprisonment. The tradition of punishing the older man more harshly has continued in the courts. In March 1999 the Chelsea football coach, Graham Rix, was sentenced to 12 months' imprisonment, part of which was suspended, for intercourse with a 15-year-old girl.

Nor did his Lordship think that judges should be the arbiters of changes of opinion. Indeed, they were not cut out for it.

> Their very lives and backgrounds usually would make it impossible for them to know what went on in offices and factories all over the land. Their duty is to apply the law of the land.
>
> It follows that the law which we are applying is not a law dating back to Victorian times; it is a law which a recent Parliament decided should be enforced. In our judgement, it is the duty of the courts to enforce it.[1]

[1] Lord Justice Lawton in *Taylor* (1977) 3 All ER 527.

But if Lord Justice Lawton was not on the bench, then defendants could still expect some leniency from the Court of Appeal. In 1979 a 29-year-old bachelor had been picked up by an '11-year-old nymphomaniac' who told him she had run away from home (in fact the care of the local authority). She ended up having intercourse with him at least twice, and he ended up with a 12-month sentence. In the Court of Appeal the worldly Lord Justice Shaw quashed the sentence and gave the man a conditional discharge.

In the 1980s came a campaign by the National Council for Civil Liberties and others to have the age of consent reduced to 14 years, something rejected by two Home Office Committees. The law was clear. Some ten years earlier, Ann Berger had correctly stated in an educational handbook for teenagers that:

> No one can give contraceptives to girls under sixteen because to do so could be taken as encouraging or enabling them to have sexual intercourse which would then be an offence.[2]

However, the Labour Government of the time had other perhaps clandestine ideas about dealing with potentially unwanted pregnancies. The DHSS, then with Barbara Castle holding the reins, issued guidance in May 1974 to National Health Service doctors and family planning clinics alike. The doctor now had to make the decision in good faith, and he was not acting unlawfully if he was protecting the under-age girl from the potentially harmful effects of intercourse. There was a little kicker to the instructions:

> The parents of a child of whatever age should not be contacted by any staff without the child's permission. It

[2] Ann Berger, *Rights*.

would always be prudent to seek the patient's consent
to tell the parents.

No one seems to have noticed – or if they did, no one seems
to have taken any great interest – that the law had effectively
been changed without any parliamentary debate.

That is until 1982, when Mrs Victoria Gillick, a Roman
Catholic mother of ten, began proceedings for a declaration
that the circular was unlawful. Her argument ran along
the lines that the doctor was aiding and abetting a man
in committing a criminal offence which would not have
taken place without contraceptive devices being in place.
Many legal commentators thought her argument to be
unanswerable.[3]

Unfortunately for her, she ran up against one of the
more progressive judges of the time, Mr Justice Woolf.
The next year, in an argument which Fenton Bresler
describes as specious, he ruled that providing the Pill to
avoid a generalised risk of pregnancy did not assist in a
specific act of unlawful sexual intercourse. And it is easy
to see how difficult it would be to prove a case against
a doctor.

Mrs Gillick may have been downhearted but she was not
defeated. Off she went to the Court of Appeal, where she
found the rather older-fashioned Lord Justice Parker on
her side.

It appears to me that it is wholly incongruous, when
the act of intercourse is criminal, when permitting it
to take place on one's premises is criminal and when,
if the girl were under thirteen, failing to report an act
of intercourse to the police would up to 1967 have been
criminal, that either the Department or the local health

---

[3] For example Fenton Bresler in *Sex and the Law*, p. 196. I am particularly
grateful to him for allowing me to quote extensively from his book.

area should provide facilities which would enable girls under the age of sixteen the more readily to commit such acts.

And off went the Secretary of State to the House of Lords, where in 1985 Mrs Gillick again fell foul of the luck of the draw. By a 3:2 majority led by the elderly but thoroughly progressive Lord Scarman, she lost.

Lord Scarman was sure that the judges should not be open 'to a justified criticism for failing to keep the law abreast of the society in which they live and work'.

What all this really meant was that the Government had to consider whether the age of consent should be lowered. The *Daily Telegraph* ran its editorial uncompromisingly, saying:

> . . . it is clearly a nonsense to make the Pill legal at age thirteen but forbid the activity to which it relates. If, however, it concludes that lowering the age of consent poses an unacceptable threat of increased illegitimacy, and further undermines the family in which, as an institution, it professes to believe, then it has no alternative but to overrule Lord Scarman and prevent DHSS issue of Pills by making new law. It is a painful dilemma.

In fact it did neither. The next year the Government issued a new circular making it easier for girls under the age of 16 to be put on the Pill. As for sex where both the parties were under age, there was now no such thing as prosecution.

In the end, however, the threat of increased illegitimacy ceased to be unacceptable. Indeed, led by film and rock stars and followed by sporting heroes and then the middle classes, it became both fashionable and a way for the poorer members of society to get away from loveless homes into the freedom of their own council flats.

No longer was an unmarried pregnancy a source of shame for the family but rather a potential source of income. Indeed, it was almost a question of which newspaper broadsheet or tabloid printed the greater details of Britain's youngest proud father, who was at the bedside of his girlfriend as she gave birth, or a mother aged 29 who lightly chastised her 14-year-old daughter for becoming pregnant at the same age as she had done.

By the middle of the 1990s attitudes were changing, both as to sex between under-age teenagers and also cases involving older men. The key phrase might well be breach of trust, although it still often depends on the luck of the draw in the composition of the Court of Appeal. Six months was the correct sentence for Lloyd Alston Asher for sex with a young teenage girl, but three years was substituted for a probation order in the case of Robert MacLennan for sex with a 12-year-old girl.[4] In other cases the court's sentences varied between three years for a man who, when aged about 18, had unlawful sex with two girls, to nine months for a schoolteacher who had one-off sex with a 15-year-old girl pupil who became pregnant. Indecent assault on young girls by men in a position of trust will also lead to imprisonment – as solicitor and part-time music teacher Simon Jackson discovered when, under the pretence of checking to see whether they had their bassoons and oboes held in the correct position, he undid their bras and fondled their breasts. He received 15 months' imprisonment.

Boys, too, have to be protected from themselves and the stirring of the seed too early in life. S.15 of the Sexual Offences Act 1956 made it an offence for 'a person to make an indecent assault on a man'. The section goes on to say that a boy under the age of 16 cannot consent to

[4] (1995) 16 Cr App R (S) 708; *Attorney-General's Reference No. 20 of 1994*, 16 Cr App R (S) 578.

indecent behaviour and the other partner will therefore be found guilty. Intercourse itself is not an offence, so in a case where a woman had intercourse with several boys aged between 14 and 16 she was found not guilty, for the interesting reason that by permitting intercourse her behaviour could never be sufficiently active to constitute an assault. The best, or worst, she could do was to 'passively permit sexual intercourse'. It really was a question of lying back and thinking of England. This did not stop the judge saying that she had '. . . behaved in a wholly disgraceful way and in a way . . . (of which) many harlots would be ashamed.[5]

In another reported S.15 case a woman was convicted on the ground that she had unwittingly given the boy VD. This seems to have been a sufficiently active role for a conviction. Again, in recent years the question of breach of trust seems to have been the all-pervading influence on prosecution and sentence, and in 1994 a schoolteacher was given 12 months' imprisonment for indecent assault by way of sexual intercourse on a 13-year-old schoolboy.

In July 1998, 30-year-old religious teacher Lucy Hayward received two years for the seduction of a 15-year-old boy; the affair had lasted some months. There was no suggestion that the boy had gone to her for religious instruction, but the fact that she was a teacher *per se* counted against her. Passing sentence, Judge Michael Mander commented:

Suppose you were a man and that youngster was a girl; there would be no question whatsoever that you would be going to jail. And in this day and age gender should make no difference.

You were a teacher and a trusted member of the community. People living near you would have been

[5] *McCormack* [1969] 3 All ER 371.

happy that their children were spending time at the home of a teacher. You encouraged children to come to your home and plied them with drugs. You indulged in highly inappropriate sexual behaviour with a young boy who was so traumatised by it all that he left home.[6]

In the most highly publicised case of 1998, however, the woman involved received probation. This highlighted yet another absurd anomaly of the law, this time with regard to the reporting of cases involving children. The woman was thought to have gone to America with the under-age boy. The media was enjoined to give as much publicity as possible to the pair so that the boy could be returned from his mistress to his loving parents. They were found in a motel in Florida and the woman was pictured in shackles as she entered the local court and jail. However, the moment she returned to face trial in England her name was not permitted to be printed or broadcast as this would have led to the identification of the young boy who had been plastered all over the pages of the newspapers and on the lips of every newscaster during the preceding weeks.[7]

By 1998 breach of trust rather than age was the key phrase, and the quid pro quo for the reduction of the homosexual age of consent to 16 was the proposal to criminalise sexual relations between older teenagers and adults in positions of responsibility. In this case the age was to remain at 18 for homosexual behaviour and be increased to that age for heterosexuals.

---

[6] *The Times*, 18 July 1998.
[7] The American courts have taken a much harsher view. Mary Kay Letourneau became the mother of two children by a boy in an affair beginning when he was 12. In August 1997 she was sentenced to seven years and five months for second-degree rape. She was given a suspended sentence after the birth of the first child, but continued the affair. See Bob Graham, 'Lessons in Love' in *Sunday Times*, 3 January 1999.

PART THREE

Commercial Sex

15

—

Prostitution

Just how much prostitution there was in London when Queen Victoria took the throne in 1837 is difficult to gauge, since those who propounded the figures all had agendas of their own. Figures from the recently founded Metropolitan Police – which of course were highly likely to be an underestimate – show that the prostitute population remained fairly steady. In 1839, 6,371 had become known to the police. In 1841 the figure was 9,409, and it had dropped slightly by 1857 to total 8,600.

The Society for the Suppression of Vice provided statistics, as did the London Society for the Protection of Young Females and Prevention of Prostitution founded in 1835. In Michael Ryan's *Prostitution in London* (1839), there was a conclusion that one in five women between 15 and 50 was a prostitute.[1] This, of course, did not mean they were employed full-time; it is more likely that many were

[1] In York it was suggested that in the 50 years from 1837 there were 1,400 prostitutes and brothel-keepers operating for a population which reached 49,530.

part-time working girls. Nothing changes. As we today are now looking at the early prevention of criminal behaviour by better education, so *The Times* was suggesting on 6 May 1857 that teaching girls household skills with a view to entering into domestic service was the way to deal with this 'great social evil'.

Six months later on 7 November the *Lancet* suggested '. . . on good authority that one house in sixty in London is a brothel, and one in every sixteen females (of all ages) is, *de facto*, a prostitute'.[2] This supposition, which would have put the female population in London at around 137,600, could not possibly match with the figures garnered by the Metropolitan Police.

The editorial went on to read:

> The typical paterfamilias, living in a grand house near the park, sees his sons lured into debauchery, dares not walk with his daughters through the streets after nightfall and is disturbed from his slumbers by the drunken screams and oaths of prostitutes reeling home with daylight.

Trevor Fisher says, 'These comments testify more to the fears and frustrations of the writer than to reality,'[3] but they are not that different from the inhabitants of areas of London which in more recent years have been taken over on a semi-permanent basis by prostitutes.

Arthur Harding recalls prostitution in the East End around the turn of the century:

> There were two kinds of girl. Those who went up West

---

[2] *The Times*, 6 May 1857; the *Lancet*, 7 November 1857.
[3] *Scandal*, p. 13.

mixed with the toffs. They would get as much as 10s a time or even £1 and they would ride home in hansom cabs. Some of them used to hang about Aldgate where the hansom cabs would pull up for them, or they would have their customers from the late buses out of the West End. They would meet them at the coffee stalls 1 or 2 or 3 in the morning [sic].

The girls who stayed in Spitalfields were very poor. That was what you called a 'fourpenny touch' or a 'knee trembler' – they wouldn't stay with you all night. Jack the Ripper's victims were fourpenny touches ... Even if you stayed all night with girls like that it was only a couple of shillings.[4]

In 1881 a senior police officer gave evidence to the Select Committee of the House of Lords on the Law relating to the Protection of Young Girls:

... the state of affairs which exists in this capital is such that from four o'clock, or one may say, from three o'clock in the afternoon it is impossible for any respectable woman to walk from the top of the Haymarket to Wellington Street, Strand. From 3 or 4 o'clock in the afternoon Villiers Street and Charing Cross Station are crowded with prostitutes who are there openly soliciting prostitution in broad daylight. At half past twelve at night a calculation was made a short time ago that there were 500 prostitutes between Piccadilly Circus and the bottom of Waterloo Place.

By 1894 the Haymarket may have been cleared of prostitutes, but this was apparently not the case in Regent

[4] Raphael Samuel, *East End Underworld*, p. 110.

Street, where, during the Empire Scandal, a man wrote to
The Times saying that while he was free from solicitation
in the promenade he could not walk down Regent Street
unless it was in the company of his daughter without being
accosted.[5]

The *cause célèbre* of 1894 was the closure of the Empire,
Leicester Square. It had been opened with the best of
intentions, but as the years had passed its productions of
theatre, spectacle, drama and grand opera had not produced
the profit expected by the shareholders (who included the
moneylender Lord Coleridge, owner of the Café Royal).
The management then had resorted to acrobats, performing
dogs and ballet girls, at which time it came to the attention of
Ormiston Chant (née Laura Ormiston Dibbin in Chepstow)
a woman concerned with temperance, suffrage and the
less easily defined 'social purity'. It was she who wrote
the verse:

> We are standing on the threshold, sisters
> Of the new and brighter day
> But the hideous night of savage customs
> Passes, with the dark, away.

What particularly worried Mrs Chant, a committed official
of the National Vigilance Association, was what went on in
the promenade area at the back of the circle, which, she
believed, amounted to little more than open prostitution.[6]
The Empire was warned that unless it cleaned up its act
– particularly at the back of the circle, where 'rigidity of
decorum is not, as a rule, insisted on by its patrons of either

---

[5] *The Times*, 15 October 1894. In 1921 the pattern had shifted slightly. Tottenham
Court Road and King's Cross were now favoured as well as Charing Cross.
[6] There are also suggestions that the closing of the Empire was not because of
heterosexual prostitution but rather of homosexual behaviour.

sex' – there would be an objection at the next licensing hearing of the Middlesex County Council on the grounds that the Empire was 'a habitual resort of prostitutes in pursuit of their traffic'.

There are certainly some grounds for thinking that Mrs Chant might have been right. Young men were enjoined not to go to the Empire. The young Winston Churchill received a letter from Anne Everest, his former nanny:

> I hope you will be kept from all evil and bad companions & not go to the Empire & not stay out at night, its too awful to think of, it can only lead to wickedness & everything bad.

Churchill did not heed her words, visiting the music hall the following week. In its turn, nor did the music hall heed Mrs Chant, who duly objected. She gave evidence that dressed in her 'prettiest evening frock . . . I myself was accosted by men'. She had also overheard one outraged Frenchman say to his (male) companion during the ballet in which the participants wore flesh-coloured tights '*C'est trop fort*' and they had both upped and left. Apparently the *trop fort* had been an extra high kick.[7] Two Americans had been upset by the vulgar coster songs of Albert Chevalier, and they also had walked out. There had also been some pretty outrageous cross-talk, with a young woman saying to a comedian playing the part of a shop-walker, 'I want to see your underwear.' Later George Edwardes, the manager, told the committee that whilst he excised such vulgar repartee sadly this line had been overlooked.

Perhaps Mrs Chant was fortunate in that of the more prominent members of the Licensing Committee (who totalled eight) one was a promised abstainer and two others

[7] *Daily Telegraph*, 11 October 1894.

were members of the NVA. The Committee recommended that the licence be refused unless the promenade area was abolished or fitted up with seats.

As might be expected, battle lines were now drawn, with some unexpected names announcing their support for the Empire. These included the Reverend Stewart Headlam, who perhaps was not such a surprise since he later stood bail for Oscar Wilde. The London Cab Drivers' Union and the Grand Order of Water Rats came out for the stage, whilst the Central Prayer Meeting Branch of the YMCA stood behind Mrs Chant; likewise Lady Burton, who had burned her husband's memoirs, and Josephine Butler, as might have been expected, supported her also. Our friend Victoria Clafin, now Mrs Woodhull Martin and editress of the *Humanitarian*, kept interest alive with a column 'Should the same standard of morality be required from men as from women'.[8] Which after all was what it was all about. However, not all the sisters rallied.

Miss Helen Matthews, the novelist, wrote: 'Nature by establishing a considerable excess of women over men, seems to say that males are at a premium and have special privileges', which was not at all what was hoped for, and W.T. Stead rallied to the flag, damning her words as 'a harlot's gospel'. The critic William Archer called the NVA 'a pudibund fraternity' and said of the debate 'The whole thing is so new to me that I have not yet considered its moral bearing.' Pudibund, presumably a combination of purity and moribund, seems not to have become part of the dictionary.

Before the full Council met on 26 October 1894, Mr Edwardes had tried to pre-empt matters. In an announcement in *The Times*, he told readers that if the licence was

---

[8] For the adventures of the redoubtable Clafin sisters, see E.N. Sachs, *The Terrible Siren* (1928).

refused there would be financial ruin for the owners. There then would be no alternative but to close, putting 643 employees out of work and affecting another 3,000 who depended 'for their daily bread' on the house. Girls would now be out on the street. It was pointed out that the same had been said some 30 years earlier when the Argyll Rooms and the Haymarket establishments had been closed. A protest meeting was organised and a Mrs Evans of the Strand Board of Governors proposed a motion objecting to the decision of the Licensing Committee.

Neither Mrs Evans's motion nor Mr Edwardes's threats carried any weight. By a majority of 43 (75–32) the Middlesex County Council refused to renew the licence. There was talk of writs of *certiorari* and *mandamus* but, when it came to it, with a chorus of 'Rule Britannia' and a tableau of weeping ballet-girls embracing each other, the Empire closed its doors.

The *Methodist Times* called it a 'Great Defeat of Lust and Lucre and Lying' and spoke of the Empire's supporters as 'the very epilepsy of licentiousness'.[9] The *Sporting Times* termed it 'The Triumph of Cant'; that paper had already had the greatest of fun with Mrs Chant.

> The comic song is to be abolished and the experiment of the Chant is to be tried in the Empire.
>
> A lot of meddling and nasty-minded busy-bodies have obtained sufficient power to be able to dictate to the sightseer what he shall and what he shall not look at.
>
> Shrieking sisterhood.
>
> A couple of women earnest and well-meaning, no doubt, go to the Empire. They see things that nobody else sees, hear things that nobody else hears. The ordinary

[9] *Methodist Times*, 8 November 1894.

man about town uses the lounge of the Empire as a
club where he is sure to meet his friends. It will be
shameful if one of the pleasantest clubs in London is
interfered with without good cause. To anybody who
knows the perfect organisation of the front of the house
at the Empire, the idea of women accosting men there
is absurd.[10]

What is the result of the present Government being
in office?
Why, the interests of the Empire are in danger all over
the world – from Afghanistan to Leicester Square.

What woman calling herself a lady would go to a night
promenade without an escort? (Letter)

Prudes on the prowl.[11]

The *Daily Telegraph*'s correspondence columns were filled
with letters from 'Britisher', 'Fallen Woman' and 'Lover
of Truth'. It was pointed out that the girls were charged 5
shillings entrance, or a levy of £70 a year. The management
responded by saying that the levy was not always enforced.
On 5 November Mrs Chant, cartooned by *Punch* as Pauline
Pry, was burned in effigy. There were suggestions of a mass
meeting in Hyde Park, while the ever-useful Stead secured
the Queen's Hall for a rival gathering where the afternoon
session, entitled 'If Christ came to London what would he
say?', found George Bernard Shaw leaving at the opening
prayer, while the evening session, 'If Christ came to London
what would he do?', produced the unhelpful response from
a Mr Anton: 'He would put a stop to the Temperance
Movement.'

Mrs Chant was as well received as she had been the
night before when she attended at the Princes Hall. She

10 *Sporting Times*, 13 October 1894.
11 *Sporting Times*, 20 October 1894.

was so moved by the proceedings as to disclose her age:
'I'm 47, (giggle) and I don't mind telling you (giggle) and
I'm proud of it (giggle).'[12]

If anything, however, the reception for John Burns – who
had made a powerful speech before the Licensing Committee – was even greater. The *Methodist Times* described his
words as having a 'Christ-like denunciation'.[13]

When it came to it, the quarrel over the Empire was really
not necessary except as a piece in a scheme of greater things.
Within a week the Empire reopened, and on the opening
night the crowd tore down the screen which separated the
bar from the promenade. One of those in the throng was
the young Winston Churchill, who, in his autobiography,
claimed that it was there that he made his maiden speech.

He wrote to his brother, 'Did you see the papers about
the riot at the Empire last Saturday? It was I who led
the rioters – and made a speech to the crowd.' His cry,
he said, had been, 'Ladies of the Empire, I stand for
Liberty!'

> You have seen us tear down these barricades tonight.
> See that you pull down those who are responsible for
> them at the coming election.[14]

He had already written to the *Westminster Gazette* argu-
ing that:

> the improvement in the standard of public decency is due
> rather to improved social conditions and to the spread of
> education than to the prowling of the prudes . . . Nature
> metes out great and terrible punishment to the roué and
> libertine – far greater punishments than it is in the power

[12] *Sporting Times*, 10 November 1894.
[13] *Methodist Times*, 8 November 1894.
[14] Martin Gilbert, *Churchill: A Life*, p. 47.

of any civilised state to award. These penalties have been
exacted since the world was young, and yet immorality
is still common. State intervention, whether in the form
of a Statute or by the decision of licensing committees,
will never eradicate the evil . . . whereas the Vigilante
Societies wish to abolish sin by Act of Parliament and
are willing to sacrifice much of the liberty of the subject
into the bargain, the 'anti-prudes' prefer a less coercive
and more moderate procedure.[15]

But was there that hidden agenda of the symbolic crusader
behind the closing of the Empire? In an editorial directly
below the paragraphs praising Mrs Chant, the *Methodist
Times* wrote:

We quite agree that indecency and open solicitation to
vice ought to be prohibited on the streets. But it is
impossible to take vigorous steps until the infamous
one-sidedness of the present laws is altered. Let us have
the same law for both sexes and the friends of Social
Purity as a whole, will not object to reasonable police
regulations. But so long as solicitation to vice is not a
crime on the part of the man we vehemently object to
treating it as a crime on the part of the less guilty woman.
Anything more cowardly or base than the existing law
is inconceivable. It is a deep disgrace to men that they
have been mean enough to keep it on the statute book
all this time.[16]

'Let us have the same law . . .' That was the rub of it all
along. If so, it was going to take a very long time before
solicitation to vice came on the statute books. Of course
there were double standards. For example, it was conclusive

[15] ibid., p. 46.
[16] *Methodist Times*, 25 October 1894.

evidence of adultery if a married woman went to a brothel with a man, but like conduct by a married man did not raise an irrebuttable presumption although the onus on him would 'scarcely be discharged by the denial of himself and the woman he was with alone'.[17]

Over the years many a respectable man and politician – for they are not always the same – might have fallen if that law had been in force. One of them was William Ewart Gladstone.

In 1925 a book of essays written by Captain Peter Wright, *Portraits and Criticisms*, appeared, in which in an essay on Lord Robert Cecil and the League of Nations he alleged that:

> Gladstone founded a great tradition since observed by many of his followers and successors with such pious fidelity in public to speak the language of the highest and strictest principle, and in private to pursue and possess every sort of woman.

Out of it came another of these backhanded libel cases which from time to time creep into the courts. Gladstone's sons had a number of potential courses of action. Clearly, since a libel action dies with the death of either party they could not bring a claim on behalf of their dead father. They could ignore the allegations, in which case there would be more credence given to the stories which had circulated for the past 50 years; they could try to bring an action for criminal libel, but since they would have to show that the remarks were intended to provoke a breach of the peace this was unlikely to succeed; or they could horsewhip the ungallant captain. Since Viscount Gladstone and Henry Gladstone were then both in their seventies, this was not a workable

[17] *Astley v Astley* (1928) 1 Hag ECC 714.

proposition either, even if they had been willing to face a subsequent prosecution for assault.

> We held that if we did nothing, we should fail in our duty as sons. Moreover, we have reason to know that the allegations were disturbing the minds of many of those who revered Mr Gladstone's memory. Doubts and apprehensions would grow in the course of time; we could see that the charges had impressed the minds of those without personal knowledge of him. My brother and I, being of advanced years, realised that when we were gone there would be no one to give evidence we alone could give.[18]

And so, as was the fashion, the matter was regulated through the doors of Clubland. The pair wrote to Wright through his publishers, who sent their letter to him at his club, the Bath Club:

> Mr Peter Wright
> Your garbage about Mr Gladstone in *Portraits and Criticisms* has come to our knowledge. You are a liar. Because you slander a dead man you are a coward. Because you think the public will accept invention from such as you, you are a fool.

At the time Wright thought that, since the original letter had been sent only to himself, there was no publication in the legal sense and therefore there was no actionable libel. His reply was equally offensive. In it he suggested that he had his information from the late Lord Milner, and that Gladstone's interests in loose women had turned the politician from being a friend of Turkey and an opponent of Russia to a reverse attitude. A phrase of Milner's which

[18] Viscount Gladstone, *After Thirty Years*.

he quoted was 'governed by his seraglio'. He went on to quote Labouchère's remark – '. . . that Gladstone might be caught playing cards with a fifth ace up his sleeve but he would only explain that God had put it there' – and for good measure added that Gladstone had connived at the Irish politician Parnell's relationship with Kitty O'Shea but then used them for his own political purposes.

It was all good fighting stuff. Wright sent a copy of his letter, written on Bath Club notepaper (bad form), to the *Daily Mail*, which published it on 27 July, and immediately his publishers backtracked. Sadly they had not noticed that when correcting the proofs Wright had inserted the objectionable words. Had they done so, of course, etc. etc. . . .

The same day Lord Gladstone wrote to the Bath Club, to which he and Wright both belonged, words such as 'coward' and 'liar' peppering the page, and suggested that the Committee should look into things. This was followed by a second letter four days later in which Lord Gladstone explained his conduct.

> I wrote to you because I was so indignant that the fellow
> was sheltering in my old club, which, for my brother,
> myself, and my wife becomes uninhabitable so long as
> it is polluted by his presence.

The Committee did the right thing, sacking the Captain, who retaliated by issuing a writ for £100 for loss of use of the club and £25 damages for injury to his reputation, something he obviously considered worth a quarter of the value of the amenities. A second writ for libel was issued and Gladstone ran the gamut of the available defences – no libel and no injury, privilege, justification and fair comment.

Wright had a hard time of it. The case was conducted

on the fallibility of his research and that he had libelled Gladstone and made the suggestion that a certain Cecil Gladstone was the illegitimate son of the great man. In the witness-box he withdrew the allegation and Mr Justice Avory then asked: 'When you saw the birth certificate, did it not occur to you that it was not usual for an illegitimate son to be registered in the name of the father?'

He would not have been able to pose the rhetorical question today.

Wright had also suggested that the actress Lily Langtry had been Gladstone's mistress and Norman Birkett, acting for the Gladstones, was allowed to put in a telegram purporting to come from Monte Carlo from the Prince of Wales's great friend: 'Strongly repudiate slanderous accusations by Peter Wright. *Lily Langtry*.'

The jury found for the Gladstones and, amidst enormous acclaim in the public gallery, the foreman added a rider:

> The jury wish to add that in their unanimous opinion the evidence that has been placed before them has completely vindicated the high moral character of the late Mr W.E. Gladstone.

Wright, who had to pay costs totalling £5,000, later wrote to Lord Gladstone apologising.[19] In the light of evidence as we now know it, however, Wright may have been unfortunate.

Just what were Gladstone's relations with prostitutes? There is no doubt whatsoever that his behaviour was risky so far as his political and social standing is concerned. There is also no doubt that, like so many of us, he entertained impure thoughts but, as his diary entries show, unlike so many of us he regularly took a whip to himself to cleanse himself

---

[19] For accounts of the trial see H. Montgomery Hyde, *United in Crime*, pp. 77–80, and the same author's *Norman Birkett*, pp. 176–204.

of them. The whip came from a continental convent via Dr
Pusey at Oxford, and was used after a conversation with
one of the girls.

But was his relationship more than one of reformation?
The mischievous Labouchère noted with some asperity that
Gladstone rarely ventured down to the East End to rescue
the really fallen, contenting himself with rescuing the rather
classier sisters around the Haymarket.

> Gladstone manages to combine his missionary meddling
> with a keen appreciation of a pretty face. He has never
> been known to rescue any of our East End whores, nor
> for that matter is it easy to contemplate his rescuing any
> ugly woman, and I am quite sure that his conception
> of the Magdalen is of an incomparable example of
> pulchritude with a superb figure and carriage.[20]

On the credit side as early as 1840 he and some friends
established the House of St Barnabas in Soho as a refuge.
Other institutions to be credited to him included the
Church Penitentiary Association for the Reclamation of
Fallen Women and the St Mary Magdalene Home in
Paddington; also he was on the management committee
of the Millbank Penitentiary, where arrested prostitutes
were kept.

In 1853, when he was Chancellor of the Exchequer,
he was seen on one of his travels in Long Acre, where
he was approached by a prostitute to whose lodgings he
went. William Wilson, the unemployed clerk who spotted
him, saw gold – or at least employment – before his eyes
and, following him and calling him a lecher, threatened to
expose him unless Gladstone either paid over 'a tidy sum
of money' or he, Wilson, was given a post in the Inland

[20] Quoted in Ronald Pearsall, *The Worm in the Bud*, p. 308.

Revenue. Gladstone was made of much too stern stuff to
fall for this little bit of blackmail and he gave the youth in
charge to a policeman in Sackville Street. Wilson received
12 months' hard labour, but Gladstone intervened and he
was released after serving six.

Nearly 30 years later Gladstone's conduct was still giving
cause for concern. He was seen talking with a prostitute
near the Athenaeum Club and again he joked off the
suggestion: 'It may be true that the gentleman saw me in
such conversation, but the object was not what he assumed,
or, as I am afraid, hoped for.'

Four years later he was warned again, this time by a
Church of England canon as well as Sir Edward Hamilton
(his private secretary) and Lord Rosebery. After this
occasion he promised to stop speaking with such ladies.

Shortly before he died Gladstone said, rather ambigu-
ously, that he had never 'been guilty of the act which is
known as that of infidelity to the marriage bed'. President Clinton used much the same phrase in early 1998
when discussing his 'non-sexual relationship' with Monica
Lewinsky.

En passant, it is curious how people – through either
ignorance or wilful blindness – see sex and adultery.
Quite apart from the old soughs that intercourse with a
virgin cured gonorrhoea and that swallowing semen was a
protection against the same disease, in 1986 some 70 per
cent of an American poll thought that it was not necessary
to have sexual intercourse to be unfaithful, while just over
20 per cent thought that 'thinking about it' amounted to
infidelity.

When the Wolfenden Committee reported on the second
leg of their inquiry, they could not bring themselves to deal
with kerb-crawling by men. As for prostitution itself:

From the evidence we have received there is no doubt

that the aspect of prostitution which causes the greatest public concern at the present time is the presence, and the visible and obvious presence of prostitutes in considerable numbers in the public streets of London and of a few provincial towns. In the West End Central Division 808 prostitutes were charged a total of 6,829 times.[21]

And again:

If it were the law's intention to punish prostitution *per se* on the ground that it is immoral conduct, then it would be right that it should provide for the punishment of the man as well as the woman. But that is not the function of the law. It should confine itself to those activities which offend against public order and decency or expose the ordinary citizen to what is offensive or injurious: and the simple fact is that prostitutes do parade themselves more habitually and openly than their prospective customers and do by their continual presence affront the sense of decency of the ordinary citizen. In doing so they create a nuisance which, in our view, the law is entitled to recognise and deal with.[22]

And on the problems of bringing prosecutions against men:

To meet the problem it would be necessary to frame an offence the essential ingredient of which would be driving a motor car for the purposes of immoral solicitation. Whilst we appreciate the reality of the problem, as we consider it should be kept under review the difficulties of proof would be considerable and the

---

[21] Sir J. Wolfenden, *Homosexual Offences and Prostitution* (1957) HMSO Chapter IX, para. 229.
[22] ibid., para. 257.

possibility of a damaging charge being levelled at an
innocent motorist must be borne in mind.[23]

In fact in February 1966 the police in Preston had, ingeniously, decided to bring a charge of persistently soliciting
for immoral purposes under s. 32 Sexual Offences Act 1956
against a motorist who had been seen in a parked car chatting
to a known prostitute at 11 p.m. one evening. This was a
reworking of the Vagrancy Act 1898, designed in the White
Slave panic of the time to prevent men touting the services
of women in public, and which had been steadfastly used
since then against homosexual men.[24]

It was just as well that no other force had tried to bring
such a charge, because in all probability it would have been
they who would have had their wrists slapped and not the
Preston officers. The Divisional Court was quite clear that
the act referred only to homosexual men soliciting other
homosexual men for immoral purposes.

On 17 September 1976, then aged 75, Lord Wigg, the
soi-disant spymaster in Harold Wilson's Government, was
arrested in the West End and charged with insulting
behaviour. He appeared before the stipendiary magistrate
Leonard Tobin and received what many thought was a
very rough deal indeed. The evidence was that he was
seen to approach six women and get out of his car on
five occasions in the Park Lane, Cumberland Street and
Marble Arch area.

The previous year, in similar circumstances, one of the
police officers had written in his notebook that Wigg had
been stopped in order to check possession of his car. Asked
why he had done that, PC McNulty replied, 'I was trying to
give Lord Wigg a message on that occasion.' Wigg's version
was that he was simply trying to buy a newspaper, something

[23] ibid., para. 267.
[24] *Crook v Edmondson* [1966] 1 All ER 833.

which he always did late at night because he could not bear to have to wait for them to be delivered the following day.

The charge did not entitle Wigg to elect trial by jury and the magistrate accepted the police version of events. However, he did not find the charge proved: 'Kerb-crawling is not an offence against the laws of this country – if it happened six or six hundred times.' There was no evidence that the women had been insulted or that his behaviour had caused a breach of the peace, and Wigg was acquitted. This was the worst of all possible worlds. He had been acquitted on a technicality but disbelieved on oath. Moreover, because of his acquittal he had no right of appeal. Given the magistrate found there was not sufficient to make out the offence, why did he not stop the case at the close of the prosecution's evidence? To the end of his life Wigg believed he had been set up on Wilson's instructions. There were many – including Chapman Pincher, the *Daily Express* columnist who had given evidence for him – who believed he was right. Others spoke of his known enthusiasm for light ladies.[25]

The law which women had sought for over 70 years, banning kerb-crawling by men in search of prostitutes, came into effect in January 1986. A Home Office circular enjoined the police that 'save in exceptional circumstances' there should be evidence from the woman herself and evidence apart from police officers. The first 'victim' was a Danish businessman, who pleaded guilty and was fined £50. Almost immediately a barrister and part-time Crown Court Recorder was convicted at Wells Street, the same court which had 'done for' Wigg. The prosecution's case was that he had been propositioning girls from a hire-car, while his defence was that he had been touring the Paddington area

---

[25] Chapman Pincher, 'Did Wilson frame Wigg?' in *Spectator*, 14 November 1998; Andrew Dickson, 'Dining with a girl who slept with Wigg' in *Spectator*, 28 November 1998.

seeking out directions to his father's grave. On appeal his conviction was quashed, thereby showing how two tribunals can have directly opposite views on the same set of facts.

It has now become the practice for police forces to take photographs of the number plates of cars whose drivers are suspected of cruising red-light districts and post them to the man's home, so letting him explain the situation to his family.

Prostitution may never have been an offence in England, but both living off immoral earnings and keeping a brothel certainly have, although it must be admitted first that the English have never seemingly been very good at it. Firstly, prostitutes have been controlled mainly by European groups such as the Messina brothers and more lately Russians, although one chain of brothels was controlled until her death in 1998 by Mary Daly, a North London woman who had contacts with the Messinas and who was thought to make some £7,000 a week from a string of establishments, far removed from the gilt chandeliers of the nineteenth-century brothel, in and around Paddington.[26]

Secondly, in this century at any rate, a brothel has rarely compared with the great houses in Paris and New Orleans with ladies in hooped stockings, piano players and champagne flowing. All that is needed to constitute a brothel in law is for two girls to be working from the same premises.

---

[26] See Nick Davies, *Dark Heart*. Over the years the Sunday newspapers have named a number of people in the headlines as vice or brothel kings. Closer inspection of the text shows that the men rarely did much more than let out rooms in one building to prostitutes. Licensed brothels were abolished first in Paris and then throughout France in 1945, under what was known as *la loi Marthe Richard* after the deputy who introduced the measure. Far from preventing protection against disease, it was suggested that in 1934 there were some 6,000 prostitutes working in Paris, of whom half were in some 200 houses. Seventy-five per cent were syphilitic, most had tuberculosis and 40 per cent died before they reached the age of 40. Social worker Maxim Blocq-Mascart quoted in *New Review*, 22 March 1945.

Although there has been no recent prosecution, in law a man does not have to pay for sex for there to be a brothel. In 1930 the King's Bench Division ruled that a house which was frequented mainly by Cambridge undergraduates and girls 'of the working class type' could constitute a brothel, although there was no evidence that the owner did better than to charge for cream teas. There had been a police observation on River Cottage, Fen Ditton, for some time and the officers had seen sex taking place on the premises as well as people in 'suggestive and indecent positions'. When they raided the house they found two women who had been cautioned for prostitution but had never been convicted. Neither of them had been involved in the suggestive behaviour. It all seems rather thin.[27]

And so, as Fenton Bresler points out in his entertaining *Sex and the Law*:

> The businessman who rents a small flat for use as a love-nest for himself and his friends to resort to with their extra-marital partners for sexual entertainment is technically guilty of brothel keeping.[28]

In fact Britain's most famous madam, Mrs Cynthia Payne – who, in late 1987, was acquitted of 'controlling prostitutes' – would have had more trouble on a charge of keeping a brothel. Neither Mrs Payne (who had a house in Streatham) nor the prostitutes who frequented her lunchtime parties for old-age pensioners made a charge for services.

What she had done was to have all the equipment for catering to different sexual tastes. Pornographic films were shown and there were demonstrations of sexual intercourse. As was proper, to ensure their eyes were not deceiving them, the police took some time to keep observation

[27] *Winter v Woolfe* (1931) K.B. 549.
[28] F. Bresler, *Sex and the Law*, p. 72.

and saw some 249 men and 50 women visit the house in Ambleside Avenue, Streatham, where on the day of the grand raid they found 53 men and 13 women. Mrs Payne's fame had spread far and wide for on that fateful 6 December, the day when the police raided her premises, there were visitors from Wales, Dorset and Gloucestershire mingling with the locals. The police had kept an eye on her home and – with Constable Stuart Taylor garnished with an artificial beard and a like suntan, posing as a country gentleman returned from Egypt, and his colleague Jack Jones as Harry, a bisexual hotel owner from Wales – the parties were infiltrated. They had undergone the humiliation of having to take off their clothes in the line of duty to preserve their under-cover status.

The court, however, was neither sympathetic nor amused. Nor was it impressed by the fact that the neighbours had not complained. That was the true British spirit.

> Decent citizens, by and large, are reluctant to complain to the police about their neighbours. But it does not follow that those living in Ambleside Avenue did not know what was going on and were not outraged by it.

She received an 18-month sentence at the Inner London Crown Court.

Then came the terrible disclosures. Apparently the clientele was mainly middle-aged to elderly men – businessmen, managing directors, accountants, barristers, solicitors, vicars, a member of the House of Lords and a Member of Parliament, albeit from Ireland. Once it heard a member of the Bar had been in a brothel, the Court of Appeal was outraged and decided, as best it could, to check the 49 names on the list on the day of the raid. There was no Peer. Or if there was, his name was not in *Who's Who*. Nor, fortunately, was any name in the Bar List.

In a striking example of verbal dexterity the Court of
Appeal reported:

> Mr Carroll [the Superintendent in charge] was not
> asked whether over a period of weeks, months or
> years this woman had had clients who belonged to
> those professions. He was asked specifically whether
> the men found on the premises on December 6 belonged
> to those professions.[29]

It now seemed as though the information was wrong.
The Court of Appeal happily latched on to the apparent
discrepancy. But, as with the case of all those homosexuals
clubs in the 1960s and 1970s, the members' signing-in book
can only have revealed a tiny proportion of the correct names
of the punters. If members of the Bar do not know that,
who does?

Nevertheless, the Court of Appeal reduced Payne's
sentence to one of six months, and she was released on
20 August.

Following her release Payne had determined to give up
her business and had accepted a job as adviser on sexual
problems for a men's soft porn magazine. However, the
lure of the party had proved too much.

Paul Bailey, the author of her biography, told the court
that 'The parties seemed to me to be deeply respectable.
It was rather like a vicarage tea party with sex thrown in
at the end.'

Payne was fortunate compared with one of her pre-
decessors, the unlucky Stephen Ward, whose case had
occupied the press and Parliament in 1963 and had led
to the end of the Macmillan Government. The story of
Ward's downfall had begun when – with Captain Eugene

---

[29] *Payne* (1980) 1 Cr App R (S) 162. For an account of her life and the case
see Paul Bailey, *An English Madam*.

Ivanov, the Russian Naval Attaché, and a nightclub dancer, the stunningly attractive Christine Keeler – he was using the swimming-pool at Lord Astor's house at Cliveden, in the July of 1961. There Keeler met John Profumo, then Secretary of State for War, who was captivated by her. She was also attracted to Ivanov and both began visiting her Wimpole Mews flat.

Whether it was wholly national security that was at risk or whether there was a large element of 'moral risk, lowering the standards of polite society' as the report by Lord Denning later put it, is open to question. In all events it was not something to be kept from newspaper reporters and on 22 March 1963 Profumo uttered the words in the House of Commons which would be fatal to his career and indirectly to Stephen Ward: 'There was no impropriety whatsoever in my acquaintance with Miss Keeler.'

Within two months he had admitted that the statement was not true and resigned, bringing a political storm and endless speculation about the Government, of whom it was rumoured that a good half practised sexual perversions. Lord Denning, who died in 1999 aged 100, was invited to conduct an inquiry. His report was a huge success, with a queue of 1,000 outside the bookshop in Kingsway at 12.30 a.m. on the day of publication. The *Daily Telegraph* bought the rights to reprint the report as a supplement, paying £3,000 for the privilege.

Denning began his report with a chapter on the players, starting with Ward.

The son of a clergyman, he was a highly successful osteopath with rooms in Devonshire Street and was a painter of some talent. He had a flat in Wimpole Mews and a cottage on the Cliveden Estate. 'He was,' said Denning, 'at the same time utterly immoral.' Ward picked up girls in night-clubs and procured them as mistresses to his fine friends. Worse, Denning found that he arranged whipping and sadistic performances, kept pornographic photographs and attended parties where there were sexual orgies of a revolting nature. Even worse, he admired the Soviet regime and sympathised with the Communists.[30]

Denning found that Ivanov went to the Wimpole Mews flat to discuss politics rather than to have sex with Christine Keeler. Profumo undoubtedly did.

Three days after Profumo's statement in the House of Commons, the police received information that Ward was living off immoral earnings and on 1 April the Commissioner authorised an investigation. Unsurprisingly, Ward was not pleased. He wrote to the Home Secretary saying that he had shielded Profumo and that the minister had been economical with the truth in his statement to Parliament. Denning saw this as an attempt by Ward to blackmail the Government; he was probably correct. In any event, Ward received a dusty reply from the Home Secretary saying that police investigations were not under his control.

Like Oscar Wilde before him, Ward delayed leaving the country and was arrested on 8 June 1963. He was remanded in custody and eventually was given his bail. His trial for living off the immoral earnings of Christine Keeler and another girl, Mandy Rice-Davies, began at the Old Bailey on 22 July. Ward knew the case was going against him and while the judge was still summing up he took a drug overdose. The jury convicted him in his absence and sentence was postponed until he was fit to appear. He never recovered consciousness and died on 3 August.

John Profumo remained with his wife, the actress Valerie Hobson. He has continued to devote himself to voluntary charitable work in the East End and is a much-loved and respected figure. Mandy Rice-Davies, who had been a friend of the property racketeer Peter Rachman, did well

[30] The Denning Report, *The Profumo Affair*, para. 10. HMSO Cmnd. 2152.

financially and went to live in Israel. Christine Keeler did not do so well.

Dozens of rumours flew about London, including the story that at one of Ward's orgies a Government minister appeared dressed in a waitress's square lace apron and a black mask. Some said that this was a bit of fun, others that the man was a sex slave and that general 'sexual activities of a vile and revolting nature' took place. When Lord Denning investigated the story – something which had been puzzling journalists for some time – the identity of the man was disclosed to him and he was pleased to say it was not a minister.

He also undertook an investigation into another long-running story which has involved one of Scotland's best-loved divorces. Who was Margaret, Duchess of Argyll – naked except for an identifying pearl necklace – fellating in a picture used against her? The picture did not show the man's head and there was intense speculation as to whom this could be.

This most famous picture formed the basis of the 1963 divorce petition. In German circles the man was said to be the brother of a prominent scientist. In English circles the most often named candidate was Duncan Sandys or (slightly less in the running) a Pan-Am executive.

Margaret was born Ethel Whigham in Newton Mearns outside Glasgow in 1912, the only child of a synthetics baron. Educated privately and then at Heathfield School in Ascot, she had a stutter brought about by being forced to suppress her left-handedness. She was cured, so she said, by homeopathic medicine, but she was also visiting the royal speech therapist.

She was not intelligent, nor had she any sense of humour, but she was lovely; she was voted 'Deb of the Year' in 1930. Her love life was an interesting one. She turned down Lord Beaverbrook's son, Max Aitken, and broke off an engagement with Prince Aly Khan in favour of the Earl of Warwick, whom she subsequently deserted for Charles Sweeney, the American golfer.

Cole Porter wrote of her:

> You're the nimble feet of Fred Astaire
> You're the Mussolini
> You're Mrs Sweeney
> You're Camembert

Sweeney was not keen on her going out during the War and she consoled herself with American servicemen. They had two children – Frances in 1936 and Brian in 1940 – and were divorced in 1947.

In 1951 she married Ian, 11th Duke of Argyll, whom she met on a train from Paris to London. Despite advice that he was marrying her for her money, she went ahead. At the time he owed a substantial sum in taxes.

In 1959 Argyll obtained one of her diaries and then burgled her house for further evidence. On 14 August that year she was put under an injunction for spreading rumours about the legitimacy of one of his sons from a previous marriage. A month later Argyll had her barred from Inverary Castle before beginning proceedings for divorce which she defended enthusiastically, naming both Argyll's secretary and her father's new young wife.

The first action cost her £7,000 in libel damages. Margaret committed perjury, incitement to perjury and forgery. At first 86 men were to be named, but in the end this was whittled down to four: the German candidate; Peter Combe – whom she later claimed to be homosexual, saying 'there was no more question of an affair with him than with the man in the moon'; a John Cohane was also cited; and an unnamed fourth man. Yet another name in the frame was the actor Douglas Fairbanks, Jnr.

The trial judge Lord Wheatley said of her that she
was a

> . . . highly-sexed woman who had ceased to be satisfied
> with normal relations and had started to indulge what
> can only be described as disgusting sexual activities to
> gratify a base sexual appetite.
>
> There is enough in her own admissions to establish
> that by 1960 she was a completely promiscuous woman
> whose sexual appetite could only be satisfied by a
> number of men and whose attitude to the sanctity of
> marriage was what moderns call enlightened, but in plain
> language can only be described as wholly immoral.

The Duchess was not the only one castigated. There was
good stuff from the judge about Cohane, 'A self confessed
wolf, brash, voluble. He had the morals of a tom-cat.' As for
allegations against the brother of the space scientist, 'I will
spare the duchess the embarrassment of quoting these in
full.' She had maintained the fellatee was her husband, but
a Harley Street specialist gave evidence that his pubic hair
was thin and gingery whereas the man in the photograph's
was dark and luxuriant. He also apparently had a physical
imperfection. The Government Minister Duncan Sandys
was also ruled out because in one of the pictures the
man's legs were shown unscarred, whereas Sandys had
been injured in the War.

The Duke was granted a divorce on 8 May 1963, and
had a celebration bonfire at his castle. Margaret was in
Paris when the verdict was announced.

She lost all her money, but in 1990 was still paying
a man from Aspreys to wind her clocks once a week.
Frances, her daughter, was estranged and, tapped on the
shoulder by Margaret, who said, 'I'm your mother,' replied,
'I remember.' In 1974 her ex-husband Charles Sweeney had

agreed to pay her debts and to give her an allowance of £12,000 a year. 'I have outlived my time,' she said.

In 1993 she revealed that the 'Headless Man' was not a one-night stand but a married man, her lover for six years, whose wife had threatened to commit suicide.

Margaret Argyll died on 26 July 1993 at the age of 80 after a drunken fall. She had wanted to be buried at Inverary, but the new Duke, whom she had tried to bastardise, said, 'Of course if somebody came past in a car and threw them [the ashes] out of the window there would be nothing I could do.'[31]

Back in 1963 Denning was asked by a Government minister to eliminate him from the list of candidates for the position of 'Headless Man', a copy of the photograph having been found in Stephen Ward's possession, and also to inquire into the story that he had paid a sum of money to the Duke to have his head snipped off, so to speak. Denning was pleased to be able to do this.

The modern low-key British equivalent of the brothel is the sauna or massage parlour, something which has sprung up in every inner-city suburb and is now almost actively encouraged by councils as a way of providing discreet prostitution and taking girls from the streets. Any thought that masturbation of clients in saunas did not constitute prostitution was swiftly disabused. Indeed, the law has never thought that prostitution required the full sexual act. Way back in 1918 a Mr de Munck was accused of using his 14-year-old daughter for the purposes of prostitution. He

---

[31] At the time of the divorce case the night-club singer Hutch parodied another Cole Porter song to finish his cabaret act:

> Cats on the Tiles do it
> Soon we'll read how the Argylls do it
> Let's do it, let's fall in love.

See Michael Thornton, *Argyll v Argyll*; Charles Castle, *The Duchess Who Dared: The Life of Margaret, Duchess of Argyll*.

countered this by proving she was a virgin, but the court would have nothing to do with the argument. Masturbation and oral sex could perfectly well amount to prostitution.[32]

Susan Pando was acquitted of controlling prostitutes at Southwark Crown Court in early February 1995. The judge, Eugene Cotran, found that there was no evidence that the prostitutes were subject to her 'control, direction or influence' as required by the Sexual Offences Act 1956. He ruled the prostitutes were self-employed.

Unsurprisingly, the police were unhappy. Said Detective Inspector Theo Dawson of the Metropolitan Police Clubs and Vice Unit:

> This [decision] is a real danger. We won't be able to deal with the real problem because we won't be able to get the men behind it. We never said the girls were not willing participants. But if they didn't do what they were told, they would be sacked. That is a financial sanction.
>
> One of our concerns is the message this decision sends to the vice industry: 'Put a woman in charge, have some notional contracts that the prostitutes are self-employed and there is no offence committed.'[33]

By the end of 1997 it was believed that prostitutes were leaving the London streets in numbers and moving to work from commercial premises. A survey for *The London Programme* suggested there were 5,000 prostitutes working every week, with 80,000 clients. The turnover from flats, massage parlours, saunas, clubs and bars with hostesses was some £250 million annually. By far the largest number of clients were those in massage parlours and saunas, with an

[32] *de Munck* (1918) 1 KB 635. In his book *The Lesbian in America*, D.W. Cory cites the case of a lesbian prostitute who would only allow her clients to have cunnilingus with her, so remaining *intacta*. She would also fall within the definition.
[33] *Police Review*, 10 February 1995.

estimated 46,000 serviced by 2,200 women. It was thought that about one in sixteen men in London between the ages of 20 and 40 years bought sex.[34]

Councils and residents may have been pleased that prostitution was coming off the streets and into saunas, but some of the sex workers may not have been quite as happy. By 1999 there was growing evidence that not only were Triad groups bringing in Thai girls to work in saunas as prostitutes throughout England and Scotland but that Russian *mafiya* groups were bringing in women from Lithuania and forcing them to work in brothels. Of prostitutes working in Soho, a survey showed that some 60 per cent were of East European origin.[35]

[34] Professor Roger Matthews, *Prostitution in London – An Audit*. See also Jason Bennetto, 'Sex trade booms as prostitutes move upmarket' in the *Independent*, 26 September 1997. There was also a very substantial income, up to £100 a day, to be made from placing cards advertising prostitutes in telephone boxes.
[35] Tony Thompson and Nicole Veash, 'Britain's sex slave trade booms' in the *Observer*, 14 March 1999.

16

The Mann Act:
An American Interlude

In the early part of the twentieth century the linked topics
of prostitution and White Slavery were high on the agenda
of any self-respecting puritan organisation. Both here and
particularly in America in the years before the First World
War, prostitution had become an obsessive topic. It was
thought that prostitutes, many driven out of their homes
by disease, were entering from Europe in their thousands.
It was suggested by the United States Senate's Immigration
Commission in 1909 that the French and the Jews (strongly
denied) were the principal controllers of prostitution but
then it was suggested that young Italians were taking up
the business.[1]

The shift of emphasis in courting came from the overcrowded working-class tenements where there was no
parlour in which a young girl could entertain her beau

---

[1] S. Doc No 196, 61st Cong., 2d Sess. 23 (1909); George Kibbe Turner, 'The
Daughters of the Poor' in *McClure's Magazine* 34 (November 1909). For
protests, see e.g. 'White Slave Story False, says Guide' in *New York Times*,
28 October 1909.

to a glass of lemonade. Now the man paid for the outing and expected a kiss or even sexual intercourse at the end. Girls who traded sex for the excitement of an outing, or shoes, clothing or other presents were known as charity girls. And, of course, the step from an unsupervised kiss to the pavement was seen by vigilant and watch societies as but half a step away.

Over the next few years, even after the passing of the so-called Mann Act, there was almost hysteria over the plight of young women kept in the degrading conditions of the brothel. Figures varied, but in 1910 the Illinois Training School for Girls warned:

> . . . some 65,000 daughters of American homes and 15,000 alien girls are the prey each year of procurers in this traffic . . ..They are hunted, trapped in a thousand ways . . .sold – sold for less than hogs! – and held in white slavery worse than death.[2]

Ice-cream parlours combined with fruit shops, naturally run by foreigners, were seen as one of the first potential steps to slavery. Books and films, including the highly successful 1913 *Traffic in Souls*, abounded.

Clearly, what was in the air was that curious cloud, Moral Panic, an intangible which blows around from time to time and place to place and is often accompanied by a highly successful symbolic crusade in which the exterior motives of the organisers are not always on all fours with the ulterior ones.

The promoters (in the wide sense) of the Act which would bear the name of Congressman James R. Mann included the United States Attorney in Chicago in 1929, Edwin W. Sims, who is thought to have at least partly drafted the Bill. The year before he had written:

[2] Superintendent Ophelia Amigh quoted by Representative Russell of Texas, 45 Congressional Record 821 (1910).

The legal evidence thus far collected establishes with complete moral certainty these awful facts: That the white slave trade is a system operated by a syndicate which has its ramifications from the Atlantic seaboard to the Pacific ocean, 'clearing houses' or 'distributing centres' in nearly all of the larger cities; that in this ghastly traffic the buying price of a young girl is from $15 up and that the selling price is from $200 to $600 . . . that this syndicate . . . is a definite organisation sending its hunters regularly to scour France, Germany, Hungary, Italy and Canada, for victims; that the man at the head of this unthinkable enterprise it [sic] known amongst his hunters as 'The Big Chief'.[3]

So far as young American girls who became White Slaves were concerned, they were 'enticed away from their homes in the country to large cities'.

The Bill was introduced on 6 December 1909 and – like so many bills, such as the Criminal Law Amendment Act 1885 in the UK, which do untold harm – it went through Congress with only minor amendments and was signed into law by President Taft on 25 June 1910. It was now an offence to transport a woman across a state line for the purpose of having sex.

One of the measure's by-products was that it expanded the power of the Bureau of Investigation (in time to be renamed the Federal Bureau of Investigation) run by Stanley W. Finch, in whose interest it certainly was that the Act should come into force. By 1912, White Slave investigations were by far the largest part of the Bureau's work.

The Act's first success came almost immediately when, on 8 July 1910, a madam was arrested at Chicago's Union Station for transporting five perfectly willing prostitutes

[3] Quoted in Stanley W. Finch, 'The White Slave Traffic' in *Light*, 12 July 1911, p. 17.

to her brothel in Michigan. Throughout the operation of the Act, most of the successful prosecutions have been of this nature.

The *New York Times* – which had been plumb against White Slavery – was overjoyed when on 30 April 1910 it was able to banner-headline 'White Slave Traffic Shown To Be Real'. It went on to recount the arrest of Belle Moore and another who had sold two girls to two female investigators. The girls were apparently little more than children, giving their ages as 17 and 18; one of them wept because she had to leave behind her teddy bear; the other clutched a tattered doll. This, the District Attorney claimed, had 'netted the leaders in the traffic in the city'.

Sadly, as is so often the case, the reality turned out to be quite different. The girls were in fact 25 and 23. Both admitted to being prostitutes of long standing and during the hearing one 'swung a patent-leather toe in the neighbourhood of the stenographer's left ear'. They had been given money for the trip to their new brothel in Seattle and had spent it on clothes for the train journey.

The *Times* was less than pleased, recording that the convictions were 'not a victory of which anybody connected with the prosecution can or should be very proud and there was not in it anything obviously relevant to the traffic in white slaves'. It turned its face away from the panic and by 1916 was writing that 'the myth of an international and interstate "syndicate" trafficking in women was merely a figment of imaginative fly-gobblers'.[4]

Between 1915 and 1932 women were prosecuted along with their boy-friends for conspiracy to arrange their own transportation by agreeing to go along on the state line trip. The men were prosecuted for transporting their 'weak' girl-friends, the victims, and the girls for conspiracy to

[4] *New York Times*, 2–3 May, 19–21 May 1910, 20 September 1916.

effect their own transportation. Usually, however, the threat of conspiracy was used to persuade the women to pony up the details of hotels, train tickets and so forth.[5]

Certainly, after its commencement it was not intended that the Act should be used to prosecute non-commercial transportation cases. An early example came when in October 1910 a woman of 24 was invited from St Paul to Chicago by a young man at his expense, and they spent three days eating drinking and having sex. They repeated the experience in the following June. Whether she hoped for marriage is not now clear, but a year later with some sisterly support she sought an arrest warrant against him for violation of the Act. The Minnesota United States Attorney was unhappy; but he wrote to the Attorney-General, George Wickersham, saying he did not believe the case was within the spirit and intent of the Act, but that the girl had 'enlisted certain club women . . .who are insisting on the arrest being made'. Wickersham wrote in reply that the facts did not bring the matter within the true intent of the Act and there should be no prosecution. Not so in a case the next year when two married men who had passed themselves off as single took a 17-year-old from Oklahoma to Arkansas, saying they had hired her to sell building lots. There was no evidence that they were slavers, but a decision was made by the Assistant Attorney-General, a career official named Will R. Harr, that there should be a prosecution.[6]

From 1914 to 1916 inclusive there were some 300-plus convictions annually, with around 100 dismissals or acquittals. Punishments ranged from a fine for a man who took

---

[5] In much the same way, in England in the 1960s and 1970s young women charged with cheque offences were threatened with a conspiracy charge at the Old Bailey or the Crown Court if they did not plead guilty to specific offences before magistrates.
[6] See Motion for Rehearing at 2–3 Transcript of Record, *Caminetti v US*, 242 US 470 (1917); Record Group 60, Class 31–1, Box 2620, National Archives, Washington National Records Center, Suitland, Maryland.

his girl-friend across the state line to five years in bad commercial cases.

Then in January 1917, so far as the ordinary fornicator or adulterer in the street was concerned, the blow fell. There had been a considerable divergence amongst the judiciary as to whether affairs of the heart constituted a breach of the Act. The case of Drew Caminetti (a clerk in the Californian capital, Sacramento) and his architect friend Maury I. Diggs settled things once and for all, and not for the better. Both were married men in their twenties; both from wealthy and prominent families, and both became involved with girls from respectable families: Caminetti with the 19-year-old Lola Norris and Diggs with Marsha Warrington, a year older. The affairs began in 1912 and involved trips to San Francisco and San Jose. Marsha Warrington became pregnant and Lola may or not have had intercourse on these trips.

In February 1913 they learned that an article was planned in the local paper, the *Sacramento Bee*, exposing what would later be called their 'champagne orgies'. There was certainly some home-town activity, with Marsha's father threatening to kill any married man who messed with his daughter. There were threats of arrest for the two girls, still minors, for delinquent behaviour both by their parents and Mrs Caminetti. Panic set in and the four of them took off in flight. It must have been a bundle of laughs for everyone because they agreed to meet at a local restaurant near the railway station. Caminetti appeared both late and drunk and they missed the train south. Instead, they committed their great act of folly and caught the next, which went east to Reno across the state line. On 14 March, two days after their flight, they were arrested by the Reno Chief of Police. The men were convicted in August 1913 and were sentenced on 17 September, with Judge Van Fleet delivering a splendid homily:

. . . the laxity of social conditions and the lack of parental control made it possible. All through this case there is evidence that drink had its paralysing influence upon the morals and minds of these men and the young girls with whom they went on that trip to Reno. The terrible debasing influence of the saloon and the road-house is too disgustingly apparent, and I make the observation here that society must pay the price for permitting the existence of these highly objectionable places.

The pair certainly paid a high price. Diggs received a two-year sentence and a fine of $2,000; Caminetti six months and $500 less.[7] Reporting of the case had been banned in Boston and when it was stated that a film of the affair was being made, the Mayor issued a statement that under no circumstances would he permit a showing.

Their appeals, based principally on the ground that the statute did not intend to punish non-commercial transportation, lasted four years. Delivering the majority judgement of the United States Supreme Court, Justice Day ruled that the statute was not ambiguous, the conduct charged was 'any other immoral conduct' and that included non-commercial immorality.[8]

In his masterly and highly entertaining assessment of the workings of the Mann Act, Donald Langum looks at the thinking of the Supreme Court. There was the worry that this sort of behaviour would lead free-loving girls into actual prostitution. It had been argued by the Government in the case that 'a girl indulging even infrequently in illicit sexual intercourse is a prostitute in the making'. There was

[7] 'Prison for Diggs and Caminetti' in *New York Times*, 18 September 1913.
[8] There was certainly a precedent. The Immigration Acts of 1875 and 1903 had forbidden the importation of women for prostitution, and an amendment of 1907 had added after prostitution 'or for any other immoral purpose'. This had worked against Violet Sterling, who had come from England to live as the court put it 'as the concubine' of a John Bitty. [*US v Bitty*, 208 US. 393 (1908)]. Efforts to distinguish *Bitty* failed.

the thought, actually voiced by a former member of the Bureau of Investigation, that had these girls been abandoned by Diggs and Caminetti: 'What was the way out other than the red light?' The answer to that would have been a call to their wealthy if exasperated parents. Langum also lists other potential policy factors – the motor-car culture with which police departments were finding difficulty in coping, the forthcoming war effort and the spread of venereal disease. When the offences occurred there was talk of epidemic levels of disease. Charity girls such as Lola and Marsha were regarded as even more dangerous than professional prostitutes.

Opinion was split over the decision and newspapers which feared the possibility of blackmail in non-commercial cases included the *New York Times* and *World* as well as the *Washington Post*. On the other side was the *Boston Journal*, which took the view that no law-abiding citizen had anything to fear.

After the decision lawyers, judges and ten of the jurors who had convicted the pair back in 1913 were amongst the thousands who wrote to President Wilson asking him to pardon the men. He wrote to Caminetti's mother that his heart went out to her and he wished that he could follow its dictates. Unfortunately, his 'imperative duty to look at the matter from a public point of view' prevented him. He could not tell her 'what it costs me to write you this'. He sent copies to the press.

As for the combatants in this little morality play – both men were released after serving around a third of their sentences. They were later pardoned so that their civil rights could be restored. Caminetti was divorced in 1927, his wife citing a long string of adulteries; he died in 1945. Lola Norris married a superintendent of a construction company. The happiest (if ironic) note of the whole unfortunate saga had been the marriage of Diggs to Marsha Warrington on 15

December 1915, after his 1914 divorce. So when he was sent to prison it was for transporting his future wife. The marriage lasted until his death in 1953.

Immediately after the case, guidelines were set out for prosecutions in non-commercial cases. Generally they suggested prosecution only where certain aggravating facts such as cases involving fraud, very young and previously sexually inexperienced women, and married women living with their husbands were revealed. But a flood of prosecutions followed, the Justice Department and local prosecutors were snowed under with letters from husbands, wives, fathers, neighbours and general busybodies denouncing wives, husbands, sons and neighbours. Often the guidelines were ignored, as in the 1924 case of Henry Delaney, who had filed a divorce petition. His lawyers told him it would be final by a certain date unless he was informed otherwise. Having not heard, he married his girl-friend Ida in Georgia and the pair went to live in Florida. He then discovered his had been a bigamous marriage and behaved completely honourably; he took Ida back to her parents, regularised his divorce petition and remarried. He was then prosecuted for the journey between Georgia and Florida. Despite the efforts of the Macon, Georgia prosecutor who listed the case for hearing on a number of occasions, it foundered with the natural reluctance of Ida Delaney to appear to give evidence against her husband.[9]

There is no doubt that the Mann Act was used to prosecute perfectly law-abiding and, in terms of morals, decent people. In November 1934 Maurice Shannon took his girl-friend Eleanor Becker south to Mobile in his Graham Paige sedan. Short of money, they camped outdoors, worked to pay for petrol and finally spent Christmas week outside Mobile in a tent, until the day after Boxing Day,

[9] Box 2627. The names have been changed.

when they were arrested and charged with three felonies, including conspiracy to transport a woman for carnal illicit sexual intercourse. They had no money for bail or a lawyer and Shannon received six months' imprisonment. Becker was better treated, receiving only six months' probation. As a result both were now felons, would be unable to vote and many jobs would be closed to them.

From the beginning there had been warnings that the Act – like the Criminal Law Amendment Act 1885 – would lead to blackmail, this time by women who would lure men across state lines with just that in mind. And again, the transporters were prosecuted while their blackmailers drove away. The Act could also be used by wives trying to obtain the best possible divorce settlement from their husbands. The best-known example is that of Frank Lloyd Wright, the architect, who in 1924 separated from his wife Miriam and took up with Olgivanna Milanoff, with whom he had a child. In the autumn of 1925 Miriam Wright filed for divorce and the next summer tried to break into the Wright house in Wisconsin. Olgivanna fled to a cottage on Lake Minnetonka, Minnesota, where she was joined by Wright. On 20 October 1926, in a blaze of publicity, they were arrested and jailed for adultery and violation of the Mann Act. It was six months before the charges were dropped.[10]

Wright had also been the subject of a previous complaint when in 1915 a dismissed housekeeper had complained to the Justice Department that he had been taking his girl-friend Miriam (later Mrs Wright) between Chicago and Spring Green, Wisconsin. Wright was never charged, but he was sufficiently worried to consult the great lawyer Clarence Darrow.

---

[10] For a full account of the case with its countless separate law suits involving Wright, his family, Olgivanna and her first husband, see Frank Lloyd Wright, *An Autobiography, Frank Lloyd Wright* (1937) and Robert C. Twombly, *Frank Lloyd Wright: His Life and His Architecture*, pp. 183–92.

Langum sees a shift in the attitude of prosecutors from around 1928. The Act had been under attack for years, but the increase in prostitution in American cities now caused prosecutors to devote their time to waging war on commercial vice rather than immorality. He suggests that other factors included the Depression, which was just beginning, causing people to tend their own gardens rather than those of their neighbours. There was also the fact that a new generation which had grown up was not so in thrall to the fear of sex.

By 1933 the Director of the FBI, J. Edgar Hoover, wrote that it required aggravating circumstances before non-commercial Mann Act cases were to be prosecuted.[11] Nevertheless the Act was continually used to prosecute those who had offended the Government or the Bureau in some way. They fell into four categories, the first of which was gangsters. Machine Gun Jack McGurn is a notable example. Apart from his other unsocial activities he had been strongly suspected of involvement in the St Valentine's Day Massacre in Chicago in 1929, but he had largely avoided prosecution. Now in 1928, separated from his wife, he took up with the unmarried Louise Rolfe, travelling to Florida and Mississippi. Each received six years, with four suspended, plus a period of probation.[12]

The second category was black men who travelled with white girl-friends. This included the black heavyweight Jack Johnson who had had the temerity to knock out Jim Jeffries,

---

[11] Two included the 1934 case of Bishop Grace of the engagingly named House of Prayer for all People, who impregnated one of his flock whilst being chauffeured across the New Jersey State Line. Well, perhaps not at that precise second. 73 F. 2d 294 (2d Cir. 1934).The second (more serious) was of a travelling salesman who in 1932 persuaded an 18-year-old girl that he could cure a non-existent disease which he said would leave her sterile by means of an electrode. Instead, after taking her across the state line, he gave her gonorrhoea. *US v Hart* 55 F.2d 1058 (10th Cir. 1932).

[12] Another was the 1960 case of Isadore Blumenfeld, who was known as Kid Cann and had been acquitted of murder in 1936.

the white former champion who came out of retirement
to 'remove that golden smile from Jack Johnson's face'.
The champion was now seen as a symbolic threat to white
America. There was an attempt to prosecute Johnson over
his involvement with the prostitute Lucille Cameron, who
had come to Chicago from Minneapolis, but she maintained
that her move had occurred before she met Johnson.
Her lack of co-operation earned her a spell in Rockford
prison. The Bureau of Investigation now tried another tack.
Johnson was known for his huge sexual appetite and his
predilection for white women, and the Bureau mounted a
targeting operation. Eventually they found Belle Schreiber,
who had been sacked from the Everleigh Club, then the
best Chicago brothel, for entertaining Johnson. She then
travelled with him to his training camps. In 1910 she was
again working in a brothel, this time in Pittsburgh, and
was sacked for rolling a customer. When she telegraphed
Johnson for help, he sent her train money, asking her to
meet him in Chicago. There he set her up with her own
establishment.

When agents found her, they put her in front of a
grand jury and obtained an indictment charging that he
had transported her from Pittsburgh to Chicago for personal
sexual use and for the purposes of prostitution. Governor
Cole Blease of South Carolina spoke for the white South,
and indeed much of America, when he said, '. . . the black
brute who lays his hands upon a white woman ought not
to have any trial'.[13]

The charge against him of the transportation of Lucille
Cameron was dismissed; she was released and now, much to
the fury of white America, he married her. Twice he tried to

---

[13] Proceedings of the Fifth Meeting of the Governors of the States of the Union,
Richmond, Virginia, 3–7 December 1912, quoted in Al-Tony Gilmore, 'Jack
Johnson and White Women: The National Impact', in *Journal of Negro History*
58 (January 1973) p. 20.

plea-bargain a fine rather than be imprisoned, but eventually in May 1913 he was convicted of the Belle Schreiber offence and sentenced to a year's imprisonment. It had not exactly been a fair trial, with the prosecution playing the race card throughout. Afterwards the federal prosecutor announced:

> . . . this negro, in the eyes of many, has been perse-
> cuted. Perhaps as an individual he was. But it was his
> misfortune to be the foremost example of the evil in
> permitting the intermarriage of whites and blacks.[14]

Johnson fled while the Supreme Court was considering his appeal. They allowed it in part, confirming it on 'other immoral purposes'. He lost his title in Cuba in 1915 and returned to serve his sentence in 1920; he died in a car accident in 1946.

Another prominent black to face harassment under the Mann Act was the rock and roller Chuck Berry, who faced two charges and three trials before he received a sentence. In the case of the first woman, Joan Mathis, she was not a minor when she was found in his car which had a flat tyre on a bridge in St Charles, Missouri, in June 1958. Berry told the police he had met her a year earlier and she was travelling with him from a concert in Topeka, Kansas. She consistently denied she had been molested, and initially charges were not brought.

Then in December 1959 Berry had the misfortune to pick up an Apache Indian girl, Janice Norine Escalante, in Juarez, Mexico. She was 14, but looked older and was already a prostitute. Berry offered her a job selling photos at concerts and then as a hat-check girl at his club in St Louis. They travelled together, had sex and he placed her in the club. Then, she maintained, he threw her out. Berry said it was

[14] *Chicago Tribune*, 14 May 1914.

because she had begun prostituting herself again. She called the police and he was charged under the Mann Act.

In January 1960 he was indicted for the transportation of Joan Mathis. In March he went on trial for the transportation of Escalante and was convicted. However, the judge peppered the case with racial slurs, and the conviction was reversed on appeal and a new trial ordered. When the Mathis case came for trial, she said she loved Berry and the prosecution threw in their hand. In the second Escalante trial again the race card was played, with Berry's white secretary being asked, 'Did you tell your people you work for a negro?' Berry was convicted again – indeed, it is difficult to see how he could not be on the facts – and was sentenced to three years' imprisonment and fined $5,000. He was paroled after 20 months.

In the third category were those who had unacceptable politics, which included men who went out with the wives of servicemen temporarily overseas. Into this category fell John Tilley, married and separated from his wife, who together with his girl-friend crossed the Mississippi River from Illinois to Iowa. Since the girl was an adult and Tilley was separated, it was not a case which came within the guidelines when he was prosecuted in March 1942. His problem was that he was thought to be a German sympathiser who had 'appeared bored' during the singing of the national anthem, remarking that Germany was not defeated yet. He was acquitted.

The actor Charles Chaplin, on the other hand, was regarded as a Communist sympathiser when he was charged with transporting the statuesque Joan Barry from California to New York. He had met her at a dinner party and for a period of six months she was undoubtedly his mistress; he was at the time separated from Paulette Goddard. He thought she had some acting ability and paid for lessons, putting her on a contract. Then in the spring of 1942 she started to appear at his home drunk, saying that if he gave her $5,000 and paid for a trip for her and her mother to New York she would release him from the contract. Chaplin did not travel with her and stayed at a different hotel; he did not pay her hotel bill in the city either. Later she would allege that they had sex on one occasion, something Chaplin denied. Back in California, she drank increasingly heavily and on 1 January 1943 she was arrested for vagrancy in Beverly Hills. Placed on probation with the condition that she leave Los Angeles, she went to Tulsa but in the spring was back, claiming she was pregnant by Chaplin. He then had her arrested and she was jailed for violating her probation.

Now she enlisted the help of the Hollywood gossip columnists Hedda Hopper and Floribel Muir. On 3 June 1943 she filed a paternity suit, claiming Chaplin was the father of her unborn child. Tests would show this was not the case, but with the help of Mesdames Hopper and Muir the affair now became public. On 24 June a Los Angeles Special Agent alerted Hoover about Chaplin and the New York trip. Hoover was interested, and on 20 August he told the Los Angeles Bureau to expedite its investigation.

It is difficult to see on what grounds the prosecution was justified. Joan Barry did not fall within any of the guidelines. In any event the evidence of sex was flimsy. Without doubt it was a political prosecution designed to embarrass Chaplin, who had first been noticed in 1922 when he hosted a reception for William Z. Foster, then the leader of the American Communist Party. More recently Chaplin had made speeches in what could be interpreted as pro-Communist terms, beginning one 'Dear Comrades'. Before the trial he was consistently vilified in the press. He was acquitted after a retirement by the jury of some seven hours, but his career and reputation were severely damaged.

In the fourth rag-bag category came such undesirables as Joseph Conforte, who ran a legal brothel in Storey County, Reno. He was accused of transporting prostitutes and, so weak was the evidence, he was acquitted in 1968 at the end of the prosecution's case.

Back in 1942 came Marco Reginelli, who, whilst on a trip to Miami, missed his girl-friend Louise, left back in Camden, New Jersey. Thoughtfully he contacted her, she flew from Philadelphia and they stayed together in a beach hotel. He was prosecuted for transporting her for the purpose of illicit sexual intercourse. Unlike Shannon (see p. 202) he had money to pay for a defence, but it did him no good; he was given six months and fined $1,500. When he appealed, his conviction was affirmed. His application for a review in the Supreme Court was refused, as also his application for a review of this decision. He was fortunate not to be deported.[15]

How on earth did he come to be prosecuted? He was wealthy; he and his girl-friend were single. They caused no embarrassment to anyone during their stay. Indeed they could be said to be contributing to Florida's economy. The answer is that he had gambling interests in New Jersey and was deemed an undesirable.

It would presumably be within this category that the defendants in the so-called Cleveland case fell.[16] Here the defendants were fundamentalist Utah Mormon adherents of polygamy, a practice generally abandoned after the 1890 Manifesto of President Wilford Woodruff of the Church of Jesus Christ of Latter-Day Saints. Five of the defendants had transported, or paid for the transportation of, one or

---

[15] *U.S. v Maurice Lorenzo Shannon and Eleanor Becker* No. 9362 and 9363, United States District Court, Southern District of Alabama, Record Group 21. *U.S. v Reginelli* 133 F.2d 595 etc. See Donald J. Langum, *Crossing Over the Line; Legislating Morality and the Mann Act.*

[16] *Cleveland v United States*, 67 Sup Ct. 13 (US 1946).

more 'celestial' wives across state lines; the sixth had assisted. On those stipulated facts all six were found guilty and given prison sentences ranging from three to four years. On appeal the convictions were upheld by a majority.

In 1940 Hans Pete Mortensen and his wife Lorraine also fell foul of the Mann Act simply by doing their employees a good turn.[17] They owned a boarding house-cum-brothel, Nifty (presumably in the American rather than the English sense or perhaps both) Rooms, in Grand Island, Nebraska. In the August they planned a trip to see Mrs Mortensen's relations in Salt Lake City and two of the girls – Margaret Smith and Doris McMahon – asked if they could come for the vacation. They had been working in the brothel, obviously as satisfactory employees, for a year. The good-natured Mortensens agreed and off they all motored. On the way they visited Yellowstone National Park and in Salt Lake City they visited Mrs Mortensen's parents. The girls took in the town in the sightseeing sense, but no acts of prostitution occurred. It was, after all, a holiday. They returned via Colorado, and once home the girls resumed work.

Mann Act, said the authorities. Yes, said the jury. Three years, said the judge, adding $1,000 fine to Hans Pete's sentence. Quite right, said the Eighth Circuit Court of Appeal, but then the Mortensen luck turned. By a 5:4 majority the Supreme Court agreed with the Eighth Circuit dissenting judge, who had written, 'I can discern only one intent . . . and that was to take a vacation. They went away with that intent and held on to it till they got back.'

After 1962, Mann Act prosecutions for consensual, non-commercial sexual activities virtually ceased, but prosecutions under the Act for forcible sex following interstate transportation continued.

[17] *Mortensen v United States*, 139 F. 2d 967 (8th Cir 1943).

Whether the Mann Act even worked against commercial sexual transportations is doubtful. For example, in the late 1970s it was estimated that there were approximately two million prostitutes in the United States and of that number 600,000 were teenagers. In November 1977 a Minneapolis policeman told a New York legislative committee that pimps were taking 300–400 women annually from Minneapolis to New York.[18]

Donald J. Langum argues that:

> Had the Mann Act stopped with actual 'white-slavers', were there any, few would criticise. But it did not stop there, and instead of fostering, it interfered with liberty. The Act covered consensual transportation of willing prostitutes and then it was judicially extended to non-commercial, boyfriend-girlfriend travel . . . One of the ironies of the Mann Act's evolution is that women, as the protected class of the state, in fact became its chief victims.[19]

---

[18] Kathleen Barry, 'The Underground Economic System of Pimping' in *Journal of International Affairs* 35 (Spring/Summer 1981) p. 118.
[19] Donald J. Langum, op. cit., pp. 9–10.

PART FOUR

Unpleasantness

17

Venereal Disease

Syphilis was probably brought to England at the end
of the fifteenth century by mercenaries who fought
under Charles VIII in Italy. Known (as are all unpleasant things) by the name of past or future enemies,
it was called the Spanish Pox and the French Pox;
and in Bristol, Morbus Burdigalensis, because it was
believed to have been introduced there from Bordeaux. In
part because of Britain's trading activities, with London
their hub, venereal diseases spread apace. Statistics vary
and cannot be regarded as completely accurate, but
in the 90-odd years from January 1747 nearly 45,000
patients were treated at the Lock Hospital in the Har-
row Road. In another survey it was suggested that in
the years between 1827 and 1835 some 2,700 children
between the ages of 11 and 16 were treated for venereal
diseases.

Then in 1850 the *Westminster Review* published an article,
reprinted as a pamphlet three years later as *The Great Sin of
Great Cities*, by William Rathbone Gregg. He was not out

to suppress prostitution but rather to control the spread of venereal disease.[1]

What Gregg wanted was the establishment of more Lock Hospitals where VD could be treated compulsorily. It was a cry taken up by the *Lancet* in 1852, and a call was made for the regulation of prostitution on 20 January 1855. Nine years later, in 1864, the first of the Contagious Diseases Acts was passed with the aim of reducing the spread of sexually transmitted diseases in the armed forces.

A. N. Wilson maintains this was the beginning of the establishment of state brothels for the naval and military. It also involved what was seen as a gross violation of the civil rights not only of prostitutes but, by implication, of every woman in Britain.[2] This is really an oversimplification; while perhaps it was wishful thinking on the part of the authorities that they might extend the law, it was never more than that.

As Alice observed a half-century later, a soldier's life was indeed terribly hard. Pay was still a shilling a day in the 1860s. Soldiers had between 300 and 400 cubic ft each, compared with convicts, who had 1,000 cubic ft living space per person. The death rate in barracks in 1857 was higher than that in the worst of slums.[3]

Until 1847 signing-on had to be for life, and even after that it was for 21 years. Public flogging was an intrinsic part of life and 100 lashes was a light sentence; 1,000 strokes was a death sentence which took four hours to administer.

The officers and establishment lived in constant fear of an uprising. 'I don't know if my men scare the enemy,' said Wellington, albeit in 1815, 'but by God they scare me.' Marriage in the ranks was, in effect, not permitted. The right to marry was only granted to soldiers of seven years' service,

[1] See K. Nield (ed.), *Prostitution in the Victorian Age*.
[2] A.N. Wilson, *Eminent Victorians*, p. 185.
[3] Alan Ereria, *The People's England*, p. 79.

Una, Lady Trowbridge, with Radcliffe Hall, at the French Bulldog show (1928)

Chuck Berry

Jack Johnson and his wife
(15 February 1924)

Christine Keeler (r) and
Mandy Rice-Davies, leave
the Old Bailey after the trial
of Stephen Ward

April Ashley appearing at the
Northern Sporting Club
(1962)

William Gladstone (c.1850)

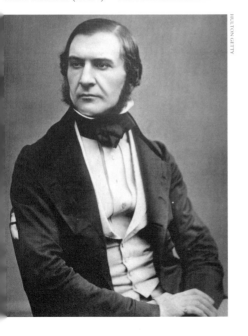

Mr Aleck William Bourne
leaves Marylebone Police Court
(1 July 1938)

The Duchess of Argyll leaves
London Airport, for Paris
(13 March 1955)

Tomorrow She Dies! said
the caption of this photo of
Ruth Ellis (12 July 1955)

Joyce McKinney, out on bail,
attends the premiere of the
appropriately named movie
'The Stud'

Marie Stopes, founder of the
first birth control clinic in
Holloway, London

The Marquess and Marchioness
of Winchester at their wedding

Liberace, with his
mother (August 1956)

Frederick Bywaters
and Edith Thompson,
murderers of her
husband (1922)

Lorena Bobbitt, at Manassas, Virginia, Courthouse, where she faced trial for cutting off her husband's penis (4 August 1993)

Maud Allan, dressed for her dance 'The Vision of Salome' (c.1910)

Mr. Justice Darling (l) talks to Mr. R. Roper Reeve K.C. at the Bar Point to Point, Northaw (April 1925)

who also had to be in possession of one good-conduct medal. Even then the establishments for married men were not allowed to exceed seven per cent of the total.

William John Acton, the writer and campaigner on venereal disease, may not today be regarded with the high esteem he enjoyed in his life, but he did strike a chord when he wrote:

> Considering that the men subject to the above restrictions are for the most part in the prime of life, in vigorous health, and exposed to circumstances particularly calculated to develop animal instincts, we may reasonably expect to find a large demand for prostitutes in all garrison towns, and may feel sure that there is always a supply in proportion to the demand. Our principal seaport towns are, of course, exposed to the same evil, from a similar cause.[4]

With the end of the Crimean War there was nothing to keep the troops occupied and not mutinying except drill and women. By the 1860s it was estimated that half the troops in Britain – which then included those stationed in Ireland – were suffering from some sort of venereal disease, but the more likely figure is around one in four. One possible reason was that the compulsory medical inspection for venereal disease was abandoned in the face of the men's hostility.

By the middle of the 1860s England had been at peace for some 15 years. The Crimean War was over and there was still little for the enlisted men to do in their barracks except to drill and parade. The devil made work for idle minds and

---

[4] William John Acton, *Prostitution*, p. 125. Acton (1813–75) was amongst the foremost pioneering sexologists. His attitude was that since prostitution was inevitable it should be regulated. His book *Functions and Disorders of the Reproductive Orders* ran to six editions over the 17 years following its publication in 1857. Amongst his less acceptable theories nowadays are that masturbation produced blindness; semen is so rare it must be hoarded; and that women 'are not very much troubled by sexual feeling of any kind'.

bodies. As a result sexual infection (260 per 1,000) increased in the garrison towns. It was estimated that one-fifth of the force spent 22 days a year in hospital being cured. The provision of clean women for the men was, to military eyes, a necessity. And out of this came a series of repressive Acts of Parliament, the Contagious Diseases Acts.

First had come the 1857 Royal Commission into the Health of the Army, which found that the physical health of both soldiers and sailors was poor. In 1860 a further inquiry into the state of the Army set up by Lord Herbert, Secretary of State for War, produced significant improvements in their conditions generally. Now there were day rooms, institutes and clubs. It was suggested that in six years the VD rate had been cut from 146 to 87 per 1,000.[5] This was not sufficient to appease the proponents of the Contagious Diseases Acts, however.

In 1861 Florence Nightingale wrote:

> The disease of vice is daily increasing in the Army . . .
> but it is to be feared that the present War Secretary, who
> is totally ignorant of his business, considers that there
> is no remedy for this but the French plan . . . a plan
> invented expressly to degrade the national character.[6]

The following year Palmerston's Government set up a committee to inquire into the prevalence of VD in the forces, but the result was not necessarily what the regulators wanted. Headed by Samuel Whitbread MP, it reported that compulsory inspections worked only in Malta, which, as a small island, was regarded as a special case. There were recommendations for more recreational facilities, which were promptly ignored on the grounds of expense. So too was marriage, on the same grounds. There was also

[5] Benjamin Scott, *A State Iniquity; Its Rise, Extension and Overthrow (1890–94)*.
[6] Quoted in Paul McHugh, *Prostitution and Victorian Social Reform*, p. 35.

a belief that marriage would weaken the resolve of men
in a conflict. 'Clean up the available women' became the
order of the day.

In the moral camp, there was hope that the Bill would fail.
Florence Nightingale rightly feared that, 'Any honest girl
might be locked up all night by mistake for it.'[7] She was right
to fear that, and indeed there were far worse consequences.
But she was wrong in her view: 'I don't believe any Ho of C
[sic] will pass this bill.' It did, with no debate or opposition.
Moved on 20 June 1864 by Lord Clarence Paget, Secretary
for the Admiralty, it was given Royal Assent on 29 July.

The Acts provided that prostitutes had to be registered
and allowed police supervision, periodical examination for
the detection of venereal disease and their compulsory
detention in special hospitals if found to be diseased.
The treatment was mercury ointment, which suppressed
the symptoms of syphilis but also led to kidney disease.
Of more immediacy, it caused painful burning. Any woman
suspected by a policeman of being a prostitute was liable
to arrest and forced medical examination. If she resisted,
she was imprisoned with hard labour. It was an offence to
house a prostitute suspected of having a venereal disease.

Middle-class women remained untouched by the police
in the garrison towns, but it has never been so for the
working classes – always regarded as fair game. The police
could not be prosecuted for wrongful arrest of a woman they
considered to be a prostitute. The burden of proof was on
the woman – almost invariably young, frightened and probably illiterate – to prove her innocence. The magistrates,
then as now, tended to accept the evidence of the police
as gospel and so it became the practice to denounce young,
sometimes quite innocent, women to them and watch as
they tried unsuccessfully to argue their way out of things.

[7] ibid., p. 37.

The first Act was operative in 11 garrison towns and naval bases in England (eight) and Ireland (three).[8] In 1866 the Skey Committee, set up to investigate how the Act was working, reported that all was in order and the system should cease to be an experiment. Windsor was the one addition by the Act of 1866, which also allowed periodical examination for up to a year of women who were suspected by the police of being common prostitutes, and the compulsory detention of infected women for six months.

A further six – Canterbury, Dover, Maidstone, Gravesend, Winchester and Southampton – were subsequently added, making a total of 17. In 1869, when the last of the Acts was passed, the so-called moral lobby now had its apron over its head as Acton and others campaigned to extend the scheme from the garrison towns to the whole nation. In 1867 the Harveian Medical Society of London decided to support a campaign to extend the Acts to the civilian population of the capital. On the books were 30 MPs as well as the Vice-Chancellors of Oxford and Cambridge. In May 1868, following a memorial presented to the House of Lords, a Select Committee was established.

Such lobbying as the moral lobby managed in its campaign against regulated prostitution for the military proved by 1869 to have been totally useless.[9] It was essential that

[8] In England the towns in the final list were Aldershot, Canterbury, Chatham, Colchester, Dover, Gravesend, Maidstone, Plymouth and Devonport, Portsmouth, Sheerness, Shorncliffe, Southampton, Winchester, Windsor and Woolwich. The three in Ireland were The Curragh, Cork and Queenstown.

The most degraded of the soldiers' women were those who lived in huts made of furze at the Curragh. They were the subject of an exposé by the *Pall Mall Gazette* in 1867 which described them as 'outcast wretches living in communities of fifty or sixty, making just enough money to keep body and soul together'. Many had followed lovers from distant towns. Their dislike of the workhouse was such that they preferred to be 'wrens'. If they overstepped prescribed boundaries, they could be fined or imprisoned.

[9] Not all feminists supported the abolition of the Acts. With the support of her male colleagues in placing the checking of the spread of disease before that of female liberty, Dr Elizabeth Garret, after whom the Garret Anderson Hospital was named, was a clear embarrassment to the movement.

tactics were changed, and so began a campaign to stop what was seen as an inexorable march to state-controlled prostitution. There had, however, been some success in stopping further inroads into the rights of the female civilian population as a whole. In 1868 the Rescue Society produced a report protesting against any further extension, and a conference was set up to protest when the Skey Committee's report was published on 2 July 1868.

There was an immediate success. Sir John Simon, Medical Officer to the Privy Council, rejected the idea of any extension. It was all right for the troops, but not for the rest. The progress halted, the campaigners now turned to repeal and it was to the trilingual Josephine Butler that they looked. Her father John Grey, a distant relative of the well-known politician and a man of reforming liberal sympathies, was an ardent campaigner against slavery and she equated his work with her own battle against the Contagious Diseases Acts, which she referred to as a 'slave code'.[10] She had assisted him in his long struggle against slavery and – regarded as a brilliant speaker – she was invited by the Ladies' National Association for the Repeal of the Contagious Diseases Acts to lead the movement shortly after its foundation in 1869.

The campaign opened on New Year's Day 1870 when the *Daily News* published a protest signed by 140 women including Florence Nightingale, her friend Harriet Martineau and,

[10] The position of Josephine Butler (1828–1906) as a Victorian feminist is slightly more ambiguous than her role as a campaigner. Her critics have claimed that she was not sufficiently interested in the suffrage movement or the question of the legal rights of married women to be in that exalted pantheon. She also fell from grace with her anti-Government stance to the Boer War, and was openly supportive of the imprisoned Oscar Wilde at a time when it was singularly unfashionable to be so. By the end of her life she was associated with almost every 'good cause' in the world, lending her name to such diverse campaigns as that of Russian Jews and Dreyfus. For contrasting views of her see Glen Petrie, *A Singular Iniquity: The Campaigns of Josephine Butler* and another Victorian feminist, Millicent Garret Fawcett, and E.M. Turner, *Josephine Butler: Her Work and Principles, and their Meaning for the Twentieth Century*. Probably the most complete biography is now E. Moberley Bell's *Josephine Butler: Flame of Fire*.

of course, Josephine Butler. To this may be traced the beginning of the feminist movement in Britain. It listed eight grievances. Three were complaints about the double standard of treatment for men and women; two disapproved of the state's approval of vice; two warned of the dangers of giving such powers to police, doctors and magistrates, and one disputed that the Acts did in fact contain the disease. The protest was republished and discussed endlessly, with some severe criticism of women for daring to intervene in this subject. The complaints did nothing to stop them and by the end of the year all major cities in England and Scotland had repeal societies, often coupled with ladies' committees. On 7 March Dr Hoopell, based in South Shields, who had challenged the extensionists at a meeting in Newcastle and to whom the formation of the repeal campaign can be credited, founded a weekly journal, the *Shield*.

The campaign sat well with neither the Conservative nor Liberal parties, who adopted the well-tried policy of ignoring it on the premise that it would peter out. It did not. The abolitionists scored a stunning victory in the Colchester by-election of 1870. The Liberals were defending the seat with a view to providing their candidate, Sir Henry Sorks, the ex-Governor of Malta, with entry to the House where, as an ex-military gent, his support for Army reforms was needed. As Governor he had enforced the Contagious Diseases Acts and is quoted as saying, 'I am of the opinion that very little benefit will result from the best devised means of prevention, until prostitution is recognised as a necessity.'[11]

As is often the case, Josephine Butler's work was part of a moral crusade in the strict sociological sense of the phrase. She was not specifically interested in the Contagious Diseases Acts, which provided a platform for

[11] Benjamin Scott, *A State Iniquity*, p. 11.

her apparent wider interests in prostitution generally and her longer-range attack on moral double standards, and in 1871 she joined the Vigilance Association for the Defence of Personal Rights.[12]

Addressing the Royal Commission, appointed in 1871 to inquire into the working of the Contagious Diseases Act, she told the members:

> This legislation is abhorred by the country as a tyranny of the upper classes against the lower classes, as an injustice practiced by men on women, and as an insult to the moral sense of the people.[13]

In 1880 the defeat of the Conservative Government saw the suspension of the Contagious Diseases Acts, and, in 1883 their abolition. The result was greeted with some joy. In his book *East of Aldgate* Horace Thorogood recalls talking to a barman who told him:

> I happened to be in Plymouth again on the night the Acts' repeal came through. Some friend of the women in the hospital got a telegram about it and gave them the news. There was an immediate riot, and I shall never forget the extraordinary sight of dozens of women climbing over the hospital walls and running off in their uniforms. Every one of them was diseased, and no doubt spread more disease that night. The police checked the mischief to some extent by arresting as many as they could for stealing the uniforms. The magistrates gave them six months for that – long enough, they said, to give them a chance of completing the cure.

---

[12] Her work in the Association, with its Committee for Amending the Law in Points where it is Injurious to Women, tends to give the lie to the suggestion that her field was a narrow one and that she was not interested in women's affairs generally.

[13] Quoted in E. Moberley Bell's *Josephine Butler: Flame of Fire*.

At the end of it all, the figures for venereal disease amongst forces garrisoned in Britain were 260 per 1,000; exactly the same percentage as in 1860. It is doubtful, however, whether the repeal of the Acts materially improved the lot of the prostitutes overall.[14] There were, however, other spin-offs from the campaign with the passing of the Law Reform Amendment Act 1885, which raised the age of consent for intercourse with girls.

In 1889 the Indecent Advertisements Act was designed to protect people who had received a 'smattering of education in our Board schools and factory and workshop workers who had nothing better to do than loaf around the streets in an evening' from handbills offering fake cures for both masturbation and venereal diseases.[15]

In 1913 a Royal Commission on Venereal Diseases was set up. It was not the first of such Commissions. There had been a previous one in Brussels in 1899 and another in the same city three years later. Both agreed that state regulation of prostitution would not prevent the spread of the disease, and after the first it was thought that 'public opinion was not sufficiently enlightened to make a Government inquiry useful'.

Five years later, after a Royal Commission on the Poor Laws reported, in part, on the infant mortality and childhood illness brought about by the disease, Colonel C.W. Long MP unsuccessfully tried to obtain a new governmental inquiry. A 1911 petition that venereally diseased paupers be detained came to nothing. Shortly before the First World

[14] See, for example, Judith Walkowitz, 'The Making of an outcast group: prostitutes and working women in nineteenth-century Plymouth and Southampton' in Vicinus (ed.), *A Widening Sphere*, pp. 72–93.
[15] The Act's proposer, the Earl of Meath, was a genuine if blinkered Christian philanthropist who deplored the pollution, bad housing and lack of recreational facilities of late-Victorian England. He was a mover behind both the installation of parks and playing grounds and compulsory physical training in schools. Unfortunately, he regarded condoms not as preventatives but as 'inducements to promiscuous sexual intercourse'.

War, the House of Commons voted to allot £50,000 to be spent on laboratories to diagnose and treat the diseases, but this was halved by the Treasury.[16] There was perhaps a thought that the moralists such as the National Vigilance Association were interfering – and anyway, that the wages of sin if not death were certainly disease. At a speech at the International Medical Congress in 1913, Lord Morley denounced the 'sheer moral cowardice in shrinking from a large and serious inquiry into the extent, causes and palliatives of this hideous scourge'. Two days later, the Government set up its Royal Commission.[17]

The final report was not a conclusive success. Some of the members – such as Louise Creighton, the widow of an Anglican bishop, and Sir Arthur Newsholme – had as their agenda the promotion of morality rather than the prevention of disease. Newsholme argued that 'non-personal and indiscriminate instruction' would 'increase the amount of promiscuity, which is the real enemy to be fought'.

The First World War proved a trial and torment for the authorities on the subject. There was, however, the problem that however the figures were glossed, the VD rate amongst the ranks was on the increase. Indeed, it was probably galloping away.

In November 1914 Sir Thomas Barlow, President of the Royal College of Physicians, recommended that the police

[16] PRO/MH/55/531.
[17] There was a curious rivalry between *The Times* and the *Morning Post* about the Commission. The former suggested that the support the *Post* was giving was merely an effort to build its circulation. Although it reported developments during the War, afterwards *The Times* was noticeably reluctant to support the medical campaign for prophylaxis or even publish correspondence on the subject. This, suggests Richard Davenport-Hines, may well have been because its proprietor Lord Northcliffe was reputed to have developed tertiary syphilis in 1916 and died of general paralysis of the insane seven years later. See *Sex, Death and Punishment*, p. 214; see also Hamilton Fyfe, *Northcliffe, an Intimate Biography* (1930), pp. 314–18. Davenport-Hines gives a detailed and entertaining account of the composition of the Commission and the attitudes of its members, ibid., p. 214 *et seq.*

be empowered to remove prostitutes from military areas. This was a suggestion which did not commend itself. The suffragette movement had gained in strength. There was, on the other hand, the almost irrefutable idea that a healthy soldier fights better than a sick one. A compromise was struck with the introduction of lectures, improved recreational facilities and volunteer female patrols whose aim was to shame and deter prostitutes.

In 1916 prostitutes had moved off the pavements into low cafés and cinemas. There was considerable correspondence between the Home Secretary and the police about whether cinemas should be better lit. If they were, this would lessen the opportunities for immoral acts, but it would give clients a better chance of selecting a prostitute.

There were suggestions at the time that of 60,000 prostitutes thought to be working in London, some 40,000 were foreign. This did not appear to be the case, however. In a sample of over 200, all but two were British. Of the others, one was Danish and the other Belgian.[18]

Also in 1916, an Army Order was issued directing soldiers to attend for treatment within 24 hours of infection. This again was a compromise. It would have been more relevant to impose the requirement on soldiers who had been exposed to infection.

The next year it was noted that of soldiers who visited Paris on leave who had no protection, some 20 per cent contracted venereal disease. Some deliberately sought out infected prostitutes so that they themselves could be infected and so for a time at least they could avoid the front line. There had also been a problem about soldiers from the colonies who were younger and naïve in the ways of the old world. The infection rate of Canadian soldiers was 22 per cent in 1915 and of Australians 17 per cent.

[18] PRO/MEPO/3 469.

Once prophylactic kits had been issued the rates dropped substantially.[19]

By 1917 Sir Robert Borden, the Canadian Prime Minister, was not, however, appeased. Not only was the flower of British manhood being slaughtered in France, venereal disease was being 'carried to every dominion of the Empire, and the future of our race damaged beyond any comprehension'.

That same year a clause was introduced into the Criminal Law Amendment Bill making it a criminal offence for a person with venereal disease in a communicable form to have sexual intercourse. The intention of Herbert Samuel, the Home Secretary, was to 'make the Statute law fit the moral sense of the community'.[20]

In the past there had been an unsuccessful prosecution of a man who had infected his wife. The court had decided that it was impossible to convict, on the basis that a man had rights over his wife.

In March 1918, clause 40D was added to the Defence of the Realm Act, making it an offence for any woman with communicable VD to have 'sexual intercourse with any member of the armed forces or any of His Majesty's allies, or solicit or invite any member to have sexual intercourse with her'.

It is clear that, at this stage, homosexual conduct did not enter the equation.

Any woman charged under the regulation could be remanded in custody for not less than a week for medical examination. It was the spirit rather than the enforcement that counted. By the July there had been fewer than 100 convictions under the Act. Now it was only a matter of

[19] Some thought that Colonial troops were also being picked up by prostitutes at Victoria Station and given dope before being robbed. The better thought was that the men were simply drunk. PRO/MEPO/3 471.
[20] House of Commons Debates, 19 February 1917; 90 col 1105.

time before women would be allowed the vote, and there was a great reluctance to inflame potential voters further. Nevertheless, an eye had to be kept on the desires of the Colonies, and a committee was set up to consider how the clause was working. It lasted a month and was disbanded following the Armistice. Nor was the clause making it an offence to have sexual intercourse whilst suffering from VD ever brought into force.

An Act which did make the statute books and was enforced for many years was the Prosecution of Venereal Diseases Act 1917, which prohibited unauthorised treatment and on conviction carried up to two years' imprisonment.

Just as in America Comstock had prosecuted those patent medicine vendors who advertised through the post on how to cure VD, so the Act was intended to stop advertising by quacks, many of whom were thought subsequently to blackmail their clients. As with much ill-thought-out legislation, the Act was riddled with anomalies. Pharmacists could not recommend decent self-disinfectants to customers who asked their advice, but they could sell the lotion if the customer specifically asked for it. This particular anomaly was one which was cured by a 1925 amendment.

Prosecutions were infrequent and Sir Archibald Bodkin, the Director of Public Prosecutions, claimed they were hard to prove. Although he was not a man with great liberal sensibility, he did have the decency to comment that:

> Section 2 somewhat remarkably forbids the advertisement of any preparations, even if they would be suitable and intended solely for prevention, although prevention would appear desirable to emphasize and make known.[21]

21 PRO/MH 55/182.

The first prosecution under the Venereal Diseases Act 1917 occurred in February the following year, when a naturalised Romanian, Adolphus Raymond of Lansdown Road, Clapham, was convicted. A Nickolas Kontides, suspecting he had VD, saw Raymond at his shop, The Family Drugs Stores, in Stepney, and was charged 10/6d for medicine which he and his wife said made him very ill.

Both Raymond and his business partner Annie Bunin, a Russian subject, were prosecuted. It seems the basis of the case against her was that the lease of the shop was in her name. He was fined £25 with two guineas costs; the summons against Bunin was dismissed. The police doctor who attended court wanted a fee of two guineas for his time, but the Secretary of State thought that anything more than one guinea and 2/9d for the certificate would create an undesirable precedent.

The fine imposed on Raymond seems to have been about the going rate, for in 1934 a pharmacist in Dudley was fined £20 for selling a useless cure for gonorrhoea.

Over the years the Act would be used for the suppression of information and for harassment. A Manchester magistrate with known sympathies towards the NCCVD convicted a man, sentencing him to six weeks' imprisonment for selling a leaflet advocating contraception. A Reading chemist was prosecuted in February 1930 for publishing a book on contraception. The intention of the local magistrates was to suppress the work before the local youth could obtain advice from it.[22]

In 1970 Richard Branson, now a mega-tycoon, was convicted under the Act. He had founded a Student Advisory Centre in Piccadilly which offered advice on sex and drug problems. Branson had probably brought himself unwelcome attention from the authorities by giving

[22] *Reading Standard*, 1 March 1930.

evidence for the defence a short time earlier in a case in which a youth was acquitted of a drugs charge.[23]

By the 1980s the Act was still in force. Another section forbade the advertising of private clinics, such advertising as there was about clinics being permitted only in public lavatories. An exception to the advertising was made in the case of Barbara Biding, who founded the Regent's Park Clinic. Nevertheless she found difficulty in having the copy accepted. When she was invited to speak at a 1986 conference organised by the Institute of Directors, her advertisement for her clinic was rejected as unsuitable for the conference programme. Asked if she would bowdlerise the copy by substituting 'personally transmitted' for 'sexually transmitted', she refused and withdrew from the conference. Nor did she have much luck with other magazines. *Punch* and *What's On* declined, as did the legal magazine *Counsel*. When questioned by the lawyer and writer Fenton Bresler as to why the last had declined acceptance, the then managing editor replied, at least with some honesty:

> There may be some people who have it, there may not. But it's not the kind of thing I'd like broadcast. Clap is not the sort of thing you go round declaring, especially at the Bar.[24]

For half a century from the 1920s onwards there have been both half-hearted and lunatic attempts to bring in a system of compulsory testing of prostitutes. In the early 1920s the then Metropolitan Chief Magistrate, Sir Chartres Biron, corresponded with the Commissioner of

[23] Mick Brown, *Richard Branson*, pp. 49–50.
[24] Fenton Bresler, *Sex and the Law*, p. 89.

Police on the subject of testing women who came before the court charged with soliciting. Biron thought it would not be possible to change the law:

> The law as it stands has been so long in operation that I am afraid it would be an almost hopeless task to endeavour to get it amended – especially when one takes into consideration the views expressed by many of the Women's Associations now in existence.[25]

An example of the lunatic fringe arises as a result of the researches of Dr Tyler Burke, the Venereal Diseases Officer of Salford. On the basis of the statistic that over 12 per cent of patients at the Salford Municipal Clinic were drivers, he became convinced that, since syphilis lowered perceptions, these people were a danger to life and limb in much the same way as a drunk driver only rather more so. He blamed this on the so-called lorry girl, recommending that the police and Ministry of Transport pay attention to these young women who travelled the countryside exchanging sex for a lift and a shilling. He had his recommendations published in the *News of the World* and found a sympathetic soul-mate in a Fulham lorry driver, Frank Bricknell. Modestly saying that his humble name could be used if it was thought to be of help, he proposed:

> Any person who is well versed in this matter, with a small car and a 'friend' armed with the necessary document to pick up a 'lorry girl' suspect and proceed with her to the nearest town's VD clinic would in a short time convince a dozen 'Ministry's' that this is something not to be scoffed at . . .[26]

[25] PRO/MEPO/3 471.
[26] Bricknell to Burke PRO/MH 55/1371; see also 'Symposium: the transport worker and the lorry girl' in *Health and Empire* 11 (1936), pp. 5–14.

During the Second World War the more reasonable suggestion was again made to empower the courts to order someone brought before them to be tested. It was sponsored by the Home Office and strongly supported by the Chief Magistrate. An addition to Defence Regulations 33B, it would avoid controversial legislation against prostitutes or the female sex because it was 'envisaged certain types of males' would come within the provisions.[27]

Other suggestions of the time included the routine testing for syphilis in pregnant women and a recommendation that the BBC be approached to broadcast information on the subject, preferably in the late evening.

From time to time the question of venereal disease entered the civil courts. If, unknown to the petitioner, the other spouse was suffering from a communicable venereal infection this was grounds for an annulment of the marriage. In England it would only be grounds for a judicial separation, until 1872 when it became grounds for annulment. But it had been grounds for divorce in Scotland for 300 years. In 1890 Lady Connemara obtained a divorce on the dual grounds required at the time. She claimed that her husband had committed adultery with her maid, and alleged cruelty in that he had infected her afterwards. In a fit of modesty *The Times*, contrary to its usual practice, refused to publish a detailed account on the grounds that 'the details of the cruelty charge . . . are unfit for publication'.[28] But could a claim be brought for damages by an innocent victim who contracted the disease from a lover?

The question was answered in 1878 when a Miss Hegarty brought an action in the Queen's Bench Division of the Irish Courts. Her claim – based on the fact that she would not have consented to intercourse with her lover, a Mr Shine,

[27] PRO/MEPO/3 471.
[28] *The Times*, 28 November 1890.

had he informed her of his condition – received short shrift from both the judge and later the Court of Appeal.[29]

Lord Justice Deasy summed up the general attitude of the judges:

> Since the time the disease in question was imported into Europe – as it is said to have been – we have never heard of such an action before. If we were to yield to the compassion which everyone must entertain for the serious injuries which this poor woman has incurred – if we were to make a precedent now; it would be one of very dangerous and wide application. The plaintiff led an immoral life for two years and if at the end of that period she can maintain an action against her comrade in sin for a common consequence of that sort of intercourse, we should have many such actions, and also, perhaps, verdicts obtained from motives of compassion. I think such actions are contrary to public policy and public decency, and that no Court should lend its aid to make a precedent for their institution.

He continued to fulminate for a little longer:

> The Lord Chancellor put a stronger example – the case of a woman seduced under promise of marriage. Has it ever been suggested that an action for assault could be maintained by her? Let me put an even stronger illustration – the case of a bigamous marriage, where a woman is induced, by the greatest fraud that can be practiced, to submit to the embraces of a man. Has it ever been suggested that she could bring an action against him for assault, though the woman in that instance would stand in a very different moral position from the Plaintiff here? Here she has led an immoral life for

[29] *Hegarty v Shine*, 4 B.C.P. & Ex Divisions.

two years, and one of the not uncommon consequences
of that is the disease which she has contracted. Therefore
she has no right to complain. The case affords an
instance of the mischiefs which would arise from the
Court's establishing the doctrine for which the Plaintiff
contends.

One problem faced by doctors was their rightful fear
that people would not come forward to be cured if the
confidentiality of the surgery was broken. In 1920 Mr
Justice McCardie more or less forced Sir Stanford Case,
of Westminster Hospital, to give evidence in a divorce suit
in which the wife was alleging cruelty by the transmission
of a venereal disease. Seven years later McCardie ordered
Dr Eric Assinder, then Director of the VD Department of
Birmingham General Hospital, to give evidence against a
husband whom he had earlier treated for venereal disease.[30]
It was a decision deplored by venereologists throughout the
country.

And there the matter rested until the 1980s and the
scourge of AIDS. Well, not quite until AIDS because
before that there was herpes, an infection which produces
clusters of watery blisters around the genital area and which
since it is a virus does not leave the body. One who fell foul
of a civil suit was a Hollywood actor, who, it was alleged by
a waitress, had an affair with her without telling her of his
condition and, as a result, left her infected. It was yet to
be a problem for the English courts.

AIDS surfaced in 1981 when the US Center for Disease Control published the first report of a rare type
of pneumonia, pneumocystis carinii, in five gay men in
Los Angeles. There have been many suggestions as to its

[30] *Garner v Garner* in *The Times*, 14 January 1920; PRO/MH 55/184; C.J.
McAlister, 'Law and Treatment of Venereal Diseases' in *Health and Empire*
7 (1932) pp. 38–54.

origins, including intercourse with llamas, but the latest research shows that it may have been initially contracted through eating chimpanzee meat. The following year the term AIDS (Acquired Immune Deficiency Syndrome) was coined, and in December 1982 the first documented case of AIDS transmitted through a blood transfusion was reported. Two months later, two women whose partners had AIDS contracted the disease.

In October 1984 Gaetan Dugas, a Canadian airline steward who was one of the first people in North America to be found to have the disease, died. It was estimated that during his lifetime he had some 2,500 homosexual encounters. In the initial AIDS panic there were reports that some pathologists had declined to carry out autopsies on AIDS victims, and that in America some judges had excused jurors who feared sitting in the same room as an AIDS sufferer. Litigants who had tested positive but had not developed the disease were required to wear surgical masks, gloves and gowns in courtrooms before they could conduct their cases. Police officers arresting homosexuals were issued with gloves to prevent contact. Britain adopted a more measured approach, although prison officers and policemen have been allowed to wear protective clothing and stand away from AIDS-infected prisoners in court.[31]

In 1985 AIDS was added to the list of notifiable diseases, to stand alongside cholera, smallpox and typhus together with a whole host of others. Within months the law swung into action. A 29-year-old AIDS victim who was bleeding badly wished to discharge himself from a Manchester hospital. A local magistrate made an order that he be detained for three weeks in an isolation unit. It was not

---

[31] There is also the case of an allegedly homosexual football referee thought to be carrying the virus protesting to the regional Football Association after players complained about being under his jurisdiction. He was then charged with bringing the game into disrepute.

a decision which met with universal approval, particularly by those working with AIDS victims.

Two years later, in November 1987, a 19-year-old caterer from Leeds who had been tested HIV-positive tried to donate his blood to a transfusion centre, in what he said was a cry for help. Although he was arrested, he was not prosecuted after the Crown Prosecution Service said there was no evidence of a particular criminal offence. This decision did not appeal to the local police, whose spokesman said:

> If there is no legislation to cover this sort of thing, then our view and that of the Blood Transfusion Service is that there ought to be.[32]

By 1991 it was reported that one million Americans were infected with HIV, and that half the 500,000 people in the Western Hemisphere with full-blown AIDS had died. By 1996 the death toll had reached 6.4 million, and a further 22.6 million worldwide were estimated to be infected with the virus.[33]

In 1995, what would have been a wonderful urban myth had it not had such serious connotations surfaced in Ireland. According to Father Michael Kennedy, a demented 25-year-old, promiscuous, tattooed, HIV-positive blonde had been scything her way through men in the village of Dungarvan near Cork. She had, according to the priest, infected up to 80 of them. In his sermon he reported that five of the men had tested positive for the disease and scores of others were in a state of panic should they prove positive.

The story was dismissed as incredible. Robin Gorna, health promotion officer with the Terrence Higgins Trust, said:

[32] Quoted in Fenton Bresler, *Sex and the Law*, pp. 269–70.
[33] 'The Battle Against AIDS' in *Time*, 30 December 1996.

The idea of the Aids avenger is an absolute fantasy.
But it is fascinating the ways AIDS and HIV pulls
together our greatest fears: sex and death, drugs and
homosexuality. None of the AIDS workers I know has
encountered anyone who intentionally used HIV as a
sexual weapon.[34]

In America there has been a spate of prosecutions of
men, and less commonly women, who have had sexual
intercourse without informing their partners that they had
tested HIV-positive. In Florida, for example, a person can
be convicted of a first-degree misdemeanour if he or she
knowingly exposes a person to a sexually transmitted disease
such as herpes, syphilis or AIDS (which was added to the
list in 1986). The maximum penalty is a year in prison,
something which did not appeal some years ago to an
assistant district attorney, David Peters:

> That's ridiculous. To my knowledge gonorrhoea is not
> deadly. It is hard to compare something that is deadly
> to something that is inconvenient.[35]

In June 1998, however, Judge Jonathan Crabtree called for
a change in the law at York Crown Court after he ruled that

[34] Mary Brady and Ian Mackinnon, 'Myth of the Aids Avenger' in the *Independent*,
13 September 1995.
[35] Quoted in Debbie Salamone, 'Exposing Someone to AIDS – is that a crime?'
in Orlando *Sentinel Tribune*, 12 May 1992. Peters went on to say the man had
exposed more than ten women to the virus, two of whom were now infected.
The man was sentenced to sexual abstinence for five years and house arrest for
six months; he was also ordered to stay out of bars. In 1987, when a prosecutor
had charged an Orange County (Florida) prostitute with having agreed to have
sex with two men without disclosing her condition, a circuit judge dismissed
the case for lack of evidence. The attitude of the American courts has varied
from state to state at different times since the disease became prevalent. By
1992 some ten states, including Michigan and Texas, had enacted specific laws
with felony penalties for exposing a person to the AIDS virus without his
or her knowledge. Other states relied on existing laws, and penalties ranged
from fines to ten years with hard labour in Louisiana. AIDS activists were
not impressed.

reckless sex was not an offence, and that a man identified only as R. who had given his pregnant girl-friend Hepatitis B as a result of unprotected sex could not be convicted of causing grievous bodily harm. In February 1998 a draft Bill designed to redefine the old Offences Against the Person Act 1861 did set out an offence of intentionally causing serious injury to another. 'Intentionally' would not mean 'recklessly', and so it would seem that R. would still escape prosecution.[36]

In the appeal of a rape case in 1987, Leslie Malcolm had a sentence of 12 years reduced to ten when infection of the victim with AIDS – which was taken into account in sentencing – did not actually occur.[37]

One thing which the onset of AIDS has done for the better is to change the attitude of homosexual men towards making wills. Without one, the surviving partner of a relationship would take nothing from the estate of his lover. In the United Kingdom, if there were no relatives to inherit, the estate would be forfeit to the Crown. Unfortunately, in America at least, it has also led to a spate of litigation. Bereaved relatives are not happy that the person they believe, rightly or wrongly, has infected their departed loved one, causing his death, should benefit from the estate. In America, one will which left half the deceased's estate to the gay lover – who, it was alleged, had infected the testator – was challenged by the man's relatives.

[36] In Cyprus in April 1998, however, a British woman was jailed for seven months for having unprotected sex with two men when she knew she was HIV-positive. In 1997 a Cypriot fisherman had been jailed for 15 months for knowingly infecting his British girl-friend.
[37] 9 Cr App R (S) 638.

18

Grievous Bodily Harm

The chastity belt, much loved in mediaeval continental literature, has never really had much of a place in English law, although Dorothy Baggerly (or Baggerley) might have welcomed one. At Leicester Assizes in 1737 her husband George was charged with causing grievous bodily harm to her. His work being five miles from home, he sewed up her private parts before he left one morning. She complained to her mother and Baggerly was arrested. He was fined 20 shillings and imprisoned for two years. As he left court he was scratched unmercifully by women in the crowd, not only because of the 'great damage done to the said Dorothy' but because 'his crime was a reflection on the moral uprightness of the whole of womankind'.[1]

Chastity belts were certainly in use in Europe in April 1882 when a man appeared before a court in León, Spain,[2] and were advertised in French magazines between 1860 and 1900. In 1910 the 'Affaire Parat' came before the Paris

[1] *Gentleman's Magazine and Historical Chronicle* 1737, Volume VII, p. 250.
[2] *El Liberal*, 20 April 1882.

courts; the husband had chained his wife's sexual parts while he was out, returning to unlock the belt at midday and 8 p.m.[3]

The use of the male equivalent of the chastity belt, infibulation, seems to have persisted until the end of the nineteenth century; there are also unprovable stories that Prince Albert wore a clasp or ring which prevented him from having an unwanted erection whilst wearing the tight trousers of the era. It was used as a means of sexual abstinence, and also as a supposed cure for mental disorders brought on by masturbation.

In 1827 Karl August Weinhold, Professor of Surgery at the University of Halle, proposed infibulation as a method of birth control. Those who were to be infibulated included beggars, unemployables and soldiers in the lower ranks between the ages of 14 and 30 years. The plan was that the prepuce would be drawn forward and two holes bored through with a metal piercer, through which four to five inches of wire were to be placed, the ends of which would be brought together and after being soldered, stamped with a metal seal to avoid tampering. From time to time doctors would examine the clasps; if they were found to have been tampered with, then a punishment depending on age would be administered. For those aged 14–17, there would be the birch; from 18 to 24 it was the treadmill, designed to dissipate surplus sexual energy; and 25–30-year-olds would receive a meagre diet of bread and water.[4]

For night-time use, a ring with spikes was to be inserted over the penis so that the skin was pierced and the sleeper awoken if an erection and potential emission occurred. As late as the years between the wars, boxers' trainers would

[3] *Daily Telegraph*, 'A wife in chains', 19 February 1910.
[4] *Von der Übervölkerung in Mittel-Europa und deren Folgen auf die Staaten und uhre Civilization.*

put a series of elastic bands around the base of their charges' penises so that nocturnal emissions did not weaken them. It is also said that the men were made to wear boxing gloves in bed.[5]

The 1920s and 1930s produced a hair-cutting mania which the courts in London dealt with as indecent assaults on females. They appear to have died out after the arrest of a Jack Boniel, who lived in Brook Green and would make raids on passing young girls. In 1938 he cut a girl's hair and then returned home. The police then arrested a William Alfred Wright and found in his possession photographs of women with long hair, an envelope with newspaper cuttings about girls with long hair and, unsurprisingly, a pair of scissors. He was put on a series of identification parades, when two girls thought their attacker was Wright and a third girl was definite in her identification. He was remanded in custody, and while he was in prison Boniel was caught in the act of cutting a girl's hair and confessed. On 8 February 1938 he was bound over to keep the peace and to provide a surety in the sum of £10; he was also ordered to attend a hospital as directed. Curiously, Wright too had numerous convictions for cutting girls' hair; they ran from 1921 to 1936, when he received 12 months' imprisonment at Tottenham Magistrates Court.[6]

Fetishists turn up in the courts from time to time. In 1991 Tony Daniel was convicted by Leicester magistrates of indecency and insulting behaviour, having stopped 50 women in the street and touched their shoes. In February 1993 a jury took only 20 minutes to find Karl Watkins guilty on five counts of outraging public decency. He had been found with his clothes off simulating intercourse with

---

[5] The belief in sexual abstinence before a major contest or match persists. In Australia the night before a Rules football game is known as 'bum to mum night'. See for example *Australian*, 17 April 1973.
[6] PRO/MEPO 3/904.

a paving stone. Another count in the indictment was that he had also had sex with an underpass.[7]

Mother of three, 35-year-old Julie Amiri, claimed to be the first person to have orgasms after being detained by police or security guards. Arrested for shoplifting, she said she only stole to get arrested so that she could have an orgasm, usually in the police cells. She has convinced doctors of her condition and although arrested 50 times had not been convicted between 1985 and 1993.[8]

In 1987, a prosecution began which effectively lasted ten years and trailed all the way to Europe and back. The police, quite by chance, discovered a collection of home-made videos showing gays participating in sado-masochistic acts. Forty-two people were arrested, and 16 prosecuted for offences of actual and grievous bodily harm.

The prosecution alleged that some of the acts were not consensual, but on any view the vast majority of them were. They included the nailing of foreskins to a piece of wood, branding with hot wires, being stung with nettles, having their buttocks and genitals cut with scalpels, and other really quite painful procedures. When Operation Spanner (as the police called their case) came before Judge Rant, sitting at the Old Bailey, he ruled that consent did not constitute a defence in law.[9] Substantial terms of imprisonment were handed out.

Judge Rant was really only following the well-established case law. On 8 March 1934, a Mr Donovan had arranged

[7] *Sun*, 20 February 1993. In Australia 30-year-old Mervyn Lilburne tried to have sex with a statue of Mercury at Ballarat near Melbourne. He was fined £200 and ordered to pay £50 for damage to flowers. Apparently he had tried to have oral sex, but was shouted at and fell off the statue. In his defence he said he had dropped his glasses. Rather more nastily, Douglas Clark, the so-called Sunset Slayer, kept the head of prostitute Exxie Wilson, which he used for sex in the shower. It was found with make-up applied and hair washed in a box in a Burbank driveway. He was given a life sentence in 1983.
[8] *Sunday Mirror*, 28 February 1993.
[9] *Brown* [1994] 1 AC 212; *Laskey v United Kingdom* Case No. 109/1995.

through a series of telephone calls to give Norah Harrison a caning. Independent evidence was clear that she consented but, whether she found it more painful than she thought or fell out with Donovan over some other matter, she complained to her mother. His conviction was quashed on a technicality by the Court of Appeal, but their Lordships were in no doubt that the fact that the girl apparently consented was no defence. In turn they had followed the old case of Coney, who was convicted of aiding and abetting a prize fight; the fact that the men Burke and Mitchell took a collection and were none the worse, short-term anyway, for the entertainment they provided was irrelevant. They could not consent to one causing the other grievous bodily harm.[10]

On the evening of 25 July 1968 Vincent Kelly, a park-keeper on Hampstead Heath, heard hammering and, going to investigate, found a Mr Joseph Richard de Havilland being nailed to a 12-foot cross. There were some thoughts that this was homosexual sado–masochism, and indeed one of the men involved had convictions for sex offences. There were also suggestions that it had to do with black magic, and de Havilland was reported as telling one of the men that by being crucified the world would be a better place with no sin and no racial discrimination, and his ordeal would enable him to gain complete supremacy over the Catholic world.

But, when it all shook out, it seems it was nothing more or less than a commercial enterprise. Photographs were to be taken and sold to newspapers. One of the participants received a 12-month prison sentence. De Havilland was not prosecuted, whereas in the *Brown* case some of the victims were.

When the *Operation Spanner* case went to the Court of Appeal the longest sentences were reduced, but the Court

[10] *Donovan* [1934] 2 KB 498; *Coney* (1881) 8 QBD 534.

unanimously upheld Judge Rant's ruling that consent was
no defence. As a warning, the court declared that the only
reason the sentences were being cut was that it was possible
the participants did not know they were doing wrong. No
other sado-masochists could expect leniency the next time
– but there again they might not want it.

> It is not in the public interest . . . that people should try
> to cause, or should cause, each other actual bodily harm
> for no good reason . . . what may be good reason it is
> not necessary for us to decide. It is sufficient to say . . .
> that sado-masochistic libido does not come within the
> category of 'good reason'.

Off to the House of Lords, where Lord Templeman listed
some of the enterprises which were legal. They included
male (but not female) circumcision,[11] tattooing, ear-piercing
and violent sports, including boxing. He concluded:

> I am not prepared to invent a defence of consent for
> sado-masochistic encounters which breed and glorify
> cruelty and result in offences . . .

---

[11] Genital mutilation, euphemistically referred to as female circumcision, involves
the cutting away of part or all of the external female genitalia, including the
clitoris. Only a small passage is left for urination and menstruation. It is practised
in England mainly by members of foreign communities, often by the females'
mothers. The operation is often carried out with unsterilised equipment such
as a piece of broken glass, and the pain for the recipient is extreme and can
be lifelong. The aim is to ensure virginity on marriage, but the practice is
also carried out on widows, divorcees and married women who will be apart
from their husbands for a long period. In the last century it was used in
England to treat psychological disorders, and until the Prohibition of Female
Circumcision Act 1985 was also practised by Harley Street doctors, but families
now travel abroad for the operation. In February 1999, Hawa Greou from Mali
was sentenced by a Parisian court to eight years' imprisonment for circumcising
48 girls. Twenty-six parents received sentences of up to two years' imprisonment.
Female circumcision was made illegal in France in 1984. A complaint had been
made by a law student after her sister had been circumcised. The practice
exists in at least 28 African countries and is thought to affect some 75 million
women and children worldwide.

Off to Europe to the Court of Human Rights went three of the men, Tony Brown, Roland Jaggard and Colin Laskey (who gave his name to the application but who died before the ruling). There they fared no better. Yes, it was fundamentally an interference with private lives, but that interference was justifiable on the grounds of protecting health and morals.

Before his death Laskey had been a mild-mannered rugby referee whose biggest regret over the case seems to have been that he was no longer invited to referee matches. Mel Davies, the appointments secretary for the Rhondda and East Glamorgan League, commented:

> It was the sado-masochism that shocked everyone, you see. You've got to realise that at the time down in the Valleys, even being gay was unheard of. Even now, we're still a bit behind.

As for Laskey, he regarded the experiences as being no worse than having one's nose or ears pierced and really rather the same as going pot-holing:

> Unless you've done it, you can't experience what the thrill of it is . . . We would go and stay with each other for the weekend, and then after the activity have a cup of tea or coffee together. Where was the hostile intent in that?[12]

In fact Messrs Laskey and Co. had not been wholly hard done by, as Mr Boyea found out when he and his girl-friend engaged in something approximating to what is now known as fist-fucking and she received some vaginal injuries. He received a six-month sentence.

[12] Andrew Walpole, 'A Welshman's ruling passion' in the *Independent*, 22 March 1995.

Although it tacitly accepted that the missionary position was no longer the only one to be undertaken during intercourse, the Court was in another of its pontificating moods:

> What is good for ordinary hetero-sexual intercourse will not necessarily be good for the practice of 'perversions' or what the Sexual Offences Act 1956 treats as 'unnatural intercourse'.[13]

The wranglings over *Brown* were followed almost immediately by the prosecution of a Mr Wilson, who branded his wife on her buttocks. This was apparently done at her request, and the complaint to the police over this piece of artwork came not from her but the hospital, just as complaints about abortions came from the medical profession rather than from the victim. With a little *legerdemain*, the Court of Appeal quashing Wilson's conviction was able to distinguish this conduct from the Spanner boys' bad behaviour. It was really more like a bit of tattooing, which was, of course, perfectly legal. On the other hand the Spanners had engaged in 'sado-masochism of the grossest kind involving physical torture and the danger of serious physical injury and blood infection'.

Quite possibly the *Wilson* case was one which the Crown Prosecution Service might have declined to prosecute on the grounds that it was not in the interests of the public. After all, it could be argued that the current fad of body-piercing is rather more than simple ear-piercing. But, there again, can you have husbands going around branding their wives with impunity? Yes, is the burning answer.

The dangers of bondage were never more clearly revealed than when PC Peter George Swindell – the policeman who

[13] *Boyea* (1992) CLR 574.

once guarded Mrs Thatcher and 10 Downing Street – stood in the dock at the Old Bailey charged with manslaughter. Over the years he had tied up ladies, including parking attendants, with, at first, pretty bows, and had photographed them, until he had progressed to an 18-stone lesbian prostitute who choked to death under the burden of leather, zips and manacles. Her fetters would not have mattered had she not been drunk at the time. He was charged with, and acquitted of, manslaughter but unfortunately when the lady passed away on his carpet he did not call the coroner's officer. Instead he cut up her body in the bath and then deposited the pieces in Epping Forest. He was convicted of hindering the coroner and sentenced to five years' imprisonment, but the sentence was reduced to three years when he found the Court of Appeal in one of its more amiable moods:

> First of all this man presents very little, if any, danger to the public. Secondly, this is an offence which ex hypothesi, is not likely to be repeated by this man. Thirdly, this is not the sort of offence from which it is necessary to deter others, again for obvious reasons.[14]

It is, no doubt, unprofitable to speculate as to whether if Mr Singh of Brick Lane or Mr Jones of Brixton had done this, he would have benefited in this way.

To bring things more or less up to date, the case of five of the Bolton Seven reached the Court of Appeal in February 1999. They were another collection of gay men who had also recorded their activities on videos, and as such had fallen foul of the law which prevents more than two men over 18 taking part in homosexual sex at a time. Also involved had been a 16-year-old youth; one of the handful

[14] *Swindell* (1981) 2 Cr App R (S) 255.

of youths under the age of 18 prosecuted for consensual
homosexual sex. The case, which was said to have cost
the taxpayer some £750,000, had become a focal point for
gay rights campaigners. The original sentences had been
probation or community service orders, and it was argued
on behalf of the men that the correct way of disposing of
them would be to grant absolute discharges – something
which indicates a technical breach of the law. The Court
of Appeal would have none of it. The sentences were too
severe, it said, and homosexual offences were not treated in
the way they once were. It did not matter that there was no
intention to distribute or sell the videos, but these offences
were worse than a single consensual act in a public lavatory
between two men.

One defendant, who (the court said) was the least
involved and had now settled down into a heterosexual
relationship, had his good sense rewarded by being given
a conditional discharge.

Afterwards the men's solicitor said that the result was:

> . . . at best a technical victory. The judgment shows
> homophobia is alive and well in the court of law. This
> was a missed opportunity to send a message that the
> police and the CPS should not pursue these cases.[15]

---

[15] Janet Cragg quoted in *The Times*, 12 February 1999.

19

Bestiality

It is impossible to estimate just how much buggery with animals takes place. After all, the recipients of attention, unless they are talking parrots with a large vocabulary, are not really in a position to complain. Indeed country people, as opposed to their urban counterparts, have rather taken bestiality as part of life in general and adolescence in particular.[1]

In *The Last Picture Show*, the American novelist Larry McMurtry describes life in a small town which he calls Thalia:

> The prospect of copulation with a blind heifer excited the younger boys almost to frenzy, but Duane and Sonny, being seniors, gave only tacit approval. They regarded such goings-on without distaste, but they were no longer as rabid about animals as they had been. Sensible youths, growing up in Thalia, soon

[1] Kinsey found that one in 20 young men in America had indulged in bestiality on an occasional basis. Alfred Kinsey et al., *Sexual Behaviour in the Human Male*.

learned to make do with what there was, and in the
course of their adolescence both boys had frequently had
recourse to bovine outlets. At that they were considered
over fastidious by the farm youth of the area who thought
only dandies restricted themselves to cows and heifers.
The farm kids did it with cows, mares, sheep, dogs,
whatever else they could catch. There were reports that
a boy from Scotland did it with domesticated geese but
no one had ever actually witnessed it.[2]

Later, in his *In a Narrow Grave, Essays on Texas*, he
defended himself:

When the book was published the passage involving
the blind heifer was apparently regarded as hyperbole,
another of my many unkind cuts against my hometown.
It was, however, sober realism. Masturbation excluded,
bestiality was the commonest and by far the safest
method of obtaining sexual release available to adolescent
boys in those days. Indeed, if adults were tolerant of
anything sexual, they were tolerant of bestiality – or
at least passive towards it. Less onus attached to it
than to masturbation, I would say. Incredible though
it seems, the belief that masturbation led to blindness
and insanity had not quite died out by the forties and
the campaign against the solitary vice was constant and
vigorous. Animals, on the other hand, were exempt from
the protection of God and man and, for all concerned,
a big mark in their favour was that they could not be
impregnated. That, come to think of it, was the only
mark in their favour.[3]

In his memoirs of life on the road in the Depression, Charles

[2] Larry McMurtry, *The Last Picture Show*. In the film of the same title the
calf is replaced by an overweight Mexican prostitute.
[3] Larry McMurtry, *In a Narrow Grave*, p. 67.

Willeford writes of a period in the McKinley Industrial School for Boys:

> The top job at McKinley was taking care of the cows, breeding them to the bull . . . This privileged work was reserved for boys of sixteen and older, and was much sought after because they could go to the dairy any time the supervisor wasn't around and fuck the calves.[4]

There is really little reason to suppose that attitudes have differed that much over the years in rural Wales or Somerset – or indeed anywhere else in the world. Speaking at Haifa University, Professor Arnon Sofer infuriated Israeli Arabs by asking his students the presumably rhetorical question, 'How can you explain the use of contraceptives to Egyptian or Iraqi peasants who mate with cows?'

Predictably there were calls for his resignation and a boycott of his classes but the professor appears to have been unrepentant: 'The phenomenon exists all over the world, in the Basque country, in the Alps, in Italy, you can't ignore it.'

Country people have always viewed animalism, or bestiality as it is otherwise called in law, 'intercourse by a man or woman carried out in any way with a beast or bird', with much less disfavour than urban dwellers. On the other hand, religion has taken against the sin or crime in a big way. The Lord, pontificating on sexual behaviour generally, was terminally against it:

> If a man lies with a beast, he shall be put to death and you shall kill the beast. If a woman approaches any beast and lies with it, you shall kill the woman and the beast.[5]

---

[4] Charles Willeford, *I Was Looking for a Street*, pp. 8–9.
[5] Leviticus 20.15 et seq.

Quite why the beast should suffer this double burden of assault and then death was not made clear. Perhaps it was thought that had it successfully tempted one person it might do so again.

The Hittites, the Mongols and Arab countries have all tolerated and often favoured bestiality. The Spanish, for example, generally believed that no pilgrimage to Mecca was complete spiritually for an Arab without the enjoyment of at least a camel boy, and probably a camel, *en route*. As a result of what they believed to be corrupt Moorish influence, they enforced anti-sodomy laws ruthlessly. In Spain the death penalty applied.

In his *Avisos*, the monk Jeronimo de Barrineuva recorded with some satisfaction the execution of two pilgrims in 1659. The first had fallen in love with his she-ass and the second had 'lain with his sow'. For the mystified de Barrineuva, the sin was compounded because – as he added in a mixture of righteousness and wonder – 'Yet all the while there are women around for three for a farthing.'

The French, always more urbane in sexual matters than other countries, considered the matter necessitated referral to the bishop. Under 20 years old the man could be dealt with by the parish priest, who was allowed to deal with all-aged 'manual pollution'. Adult zoophilia was far too grave to be dealt with at parish-pump level.

In England until the Middle Ages, the penalty for this crime – described as a *peccatum illud horrible, inter Christianos non nominandum* – was death. At the time of Richard I, the practice had been to hang a man and drown a woman found guilty of this offence. There was then a lightening of penalty for a period until the maximum punishment was restored by Henry VIII.

In 1793 John Hoyland was hanged at York after being found guilty of having intercourse with an ass in Sheffield. His was a remarkable case, since he was then aged 77. He was a man who was well thought of locally, and there was some suspicion that the evidence of his accusers, two labourers William Warburton and John Hurt, was perjured; but it did poor Hoyland no good at all.[6]

In point of fact, bestiality was one of the later crimes in the United Kingdom for which the death penalty was abolished. The Offences Against the Person Act 1861 reduced the penalty to a maximum of life imprisonment, and nearly a century later this was re-enacted in the Sexual Offences Act 1956 s.12.

There are some nineteenth-century cases which give examples of the court's attitudes. In 1888 a young man, Brown, appeared before Lord Coleridge, then the Lord Chief Justice, at Chelmsford Assizes and was sentenced by him to one year's hard labour after pleading guilty to an attempt to commit unnatural offences with domestic fowls. As his Lordship was leaving the Assizes, he was told of an unreported case in which it had been held that a duck was not an animal within 24 & 25 Vict. c 100 s. 61. His Lordship did the decent thing and referred his own decision to the Court of Crown Cases Reserved, over which he presided. There, fortunately, one of the other judges had heard of the unreported decision in the case of *Dodd* and informed his colleagues that the decision had been quashed on other grounds. All was well. Brown was left to serve his sentence, and his case went into the law books as one of the first to be read by students.[7]

In recent years, however, remarkably few cases concerning bestiality have reached the Court of Appeal. Most defendants have been satisfied with the punishment handed to them at the old Quarter Sessions or the Crown Court, but

---

[6] J.P. Bean, *Crime in Sheffield*, p. 24.
[7] 24 QBD 357. In fact, in 1812 a Mr Mulready had tried to commit the very same act but, fortunately for him, had been acquitted on the grounds that 'the bird's parts were so small'.

one of the earliest reported cases from the then newly set up Court of Criminal Appeal shows the severity of the Courts. In 1914 a 66-year-old man appealed against a sentence of seven years for an act with an unspecified animal. Because the offence had been committed in secrecy, and because of his advanced years, the Court was able to show clemency. The sentence was reduced to one of a year's hard labour.

In the last decades the practical aspect of sentencing has been more mild, aimed at helping the deviant rather than protecting the animal.

Perhaps the worst case to come before the courts was in 1949 after a Sydney Joseph Bourne, then aged about 28, thought it would provide entertainment to watch his wife being served by his dog. He received a sentence of nine years, but legally the interest was in whether the wife could be charged with aiding and be convicted. Her defence was that she had submitted under duress, and she was acquitted. His defence was that he could not be charged with aiding and abetting a crime of which she had been acquitted. Wrong, said the Court of Appeal very firmly, and so Mr Bourne also passed into the legal textbooks as one of the first cases to be sought out by first-year students.

In 1974 a man named Williams, together with a colleague, were found *in flagrante* with a sheep, by a man out walking his dog. Williams received a year's imprisonment and the trial judge – who did not take the tolerant view of the adults in Thalia – sentenced him in the following terms:

> I fully appreciate that this is going to be a matter of comment about you for years to come and I think the kindest thing I can visit upon you is the outrage which I think anybody with any decent feelings would feel about it so that nobody can say, in your village, that you haven't paid for it.

The Court of Appeal took a more merciful view. By the time the appeal was heard Williams had served some weeks in prison and the rest of the sentence was suspended. Professor David Thomas commented of the initial sentence:

> The case provides rare illustration of one of the oldest theoretical justifications of punishment – the view that the sentencer must inflict a penalty which will satisfy the feelings of other members of the community towards the offence so as to make it unlikely that they will take their own vengeance on the offender in an unauthorised and possibly uncivilised manner.[8]

The latest reported Court of Appeal case, again involving a dog, rather changed the principles on which the court will sentence. Colin Higson pleaded guilty to the attempted buggery of his pet. Whilst his wife was out for the evening, he had endeavoured to penetrate his Pyrenean Mountain bitch. She returned early. 'The dog was not receptive. His wife was understandably disgusted,' said the Court of Appeal. At first she telephoned the Samaritans, then next day she went to the police and left the marital home. By the time the court case was heard, she had returned to live with her husband.

He was sentenced at the Manchester Crown Court to two years' imprisonment. The trial judge, sitting with two lay justices, had used some harsh words:

> . . . in this country we now live in a society which is permissive and decadent, but that does not mean that the courts which act on behalf of ordinary decent people in this area will countenance the maligned depravity which causes a man to attempt to satisfy his sexual lust by having intercourse with a dog.

[8] [1974] Crim. L.R. 558.

The senior court was altogether more generous. Mr Justice Leggatt, giving the verdict of the Court of Appeal, began:

> In view of the sentence one might have supposed that a woman or young person, if not a child, was involved. In fact the object of the appellant's attention was a Pyrenean Mountain bitch ... Bestiality is repugnant to right thinking people. It cannot be condoned. But this kind of sentence leads a reasonable man to say with Mr. Bumble. If the law supposes that, the law is an ass.[9]

The sentence was changed to one of probation and his Lordship concluded with the words: 'When all is said and done, it is the appellant, and indeed his wife, and not the dog, who need help.' Not a view which would appeal to Mr Auberon Waugh – who, after the Jeremy Thorpe trial in which a Great Dane bitch, Rinka, featured prominently and fatally, stood for Parliament as Dog Lovers' candidate – but one more in keeping with the Thalians and certainly with the views of Professor Tony Honore.

Professor Honore takes the view, seemingly based on the fact that they cannot articulate for themselves, that animals have no rights; but, if they do, they have rights not to be killed as food for human beings and not to be treated with cruelty. They cannot claim not to be touched.[10] He argues that there is therefore no satisfactory reason for retaining the crime of buggery with animals. He was light-years – or at least a decade – ahead of the Court of Appeal when he wrote that in the case of *Bourne* the criminal conduct was an indecent assault and the wrong was to the wife and not to the dog. He goes on to argue, perhaps half humorously, that if a farmhand has sex with sheep when he should be tending

---

[9] (1984) 6 Cr App R (S) 20.
[10] Tony Honore, *Sex Law*, p. 176.

the pigs that conduct amounts to a breach of contract of employment rather than anything else. He maintains that if the animal is injured during the congress, then a charge under the Protection of Animals Act 1911 s. 1 would be appropriate.

In his novel *Native Tongue*, Carl Hiaasen has a girl television reporter resist (with some difficulty) the amorous attentions of a dolphin. In December 1991, animal rights activist Alan Cooper left Newcastle Crown Court to the cheers of the public gallery. He had been acquitted of indecency with Freddie the friendly dolphin, with whom he had been swimming. It had been alleged that whilst in the water with Freddie – who had lived around Amble Harbour, Northumberland for some five years – Mr Cooper had masturbated him to the disgust of watchers.

The case had (at least in part) been the culmination of a feud between Mr Cooper and the manager of a nearby dolphinarium. Mr Cooper had campaigned against keeping dolphins in captivity and alleged that the manager had encouraged people to make the complaint. He told the court that it was normal for a dolphin's penis to become exposed whilst swimming with humans, and they used it in the same way as an arm or a leg and would extend it so that swimmers could get a tow.[11]

The leniency shown to the owner of the Pyrenean Mountain bitch was a trend which has continued. 'By your actions, you have brought ridicule and contempt upon yourself,' Judge Giles Rooke told a defendant at what was described as a hushed Crown Court at Canterbury. 'It is very rare indeed to find this offence being committed with the defendant putting himself on the receiving end.'

[11] Sadly Freddie did not live long after the case. Six months later it was reported that he had perished in a transparent nylon net laid out from a boat in the Tyne Estuary. A radio ham recorded a conversation which ended, 'You stupid bastard, you've got Freddie the dolphin. If you get that back there'll be a lynching. Cut the bastard free and make sure it sinks.' *Independent*, 22 April 1992.

Earlier, prosecuting counsel Mr Oliver Saxby had described the events which led to the arrest of the 45-year-old man, on a charge of attempted buggery with his family's pet Alsatian:

> On the evening of the offence, when the defendant returned home from the pub, his two sons were in bed, and his wife was at work. At about 11. 30 p.m. the elder son heard the family dog, Bruno, yelping excitedly, so he went downstairs. There he saw his father, naked on his hands and knees, and the dog thrusting vigorously, its front paws on top of his father's back. Realising he had been observed, the defendant claimed it was all part of Bruno's training, and advised his son to say nothing to his mother. But next day the boy told a teacher and, when the police began making enquiries, the defendant eventually confessed the truth.

The man, who admitted similar previous offences, was bound over for 18 months. His barrister, Mr David Burles, told the court in mitigation that since his arrest his client had lost his job, been beaten up in his local pub and, worst of all, now lived alone in Margate.[12]

Other jurisdictions still take the offence rather more seriously.

'This is a despicable crime, just despicable . . .' said an enraged judge Kenneth Anderson of the Virgin Islands Territorial Court in passing sentence on Juan Hernandez. 'I order you to undergo psychiatric evaluation and, let me tell you, if the cow's milk had been adversely affected, it would have been prison.'

The court had earlier heard evidence from Andrew Joseph, the farmer who had brought allegations of bestiality against Hernandez:

[12] *Thanet Times*, June 1995.

I went to the field behind the old Carlton Hotel in Frederiksted just before midday, to check on my cows. Gerda was missing so I started looking for her. While I was passing the back of the hotel, I heard mooing, so I looked through an open window and saw Hernandez with my cow. He was naked from the waist down, and standing on two old tin trays with Gerda's tail in his left hand. His right hand was on her back and he was intercoursing her. I was so disgusted, I was sick all over a towel rack.'

Said Judge Anderson in his summing-up:

I will not accept Hernandez's claim in mitigation. However, I do accept that the accused had only been tempted to try sex with cows after hearing about a similar case. It is a disgrace that Victor Pinero, alias Billy Cruz, has not yet been apprehended. The man has become some sort of local hero in the twisted minds of the young, ever since the notorious incident with a Senepol calf at Melthorp Farm in April. He must be brought to justice.[13]

The question remains as to whether bestiality may lead the perpetrator to child abuse; as is often the case, psychiatrists appear to be divided. Dr Elliot Luby of Wayne State University's School of Medicine, commenting on the arrest of a ring of adults accused of molesting children and suspected of abusing dogs in Ypsilanti, Michigan, said that bestiality did not usually progess to child molestation; but Nancy Baum, a New York forensic psychiatrist, did not agree:

Some people start experimenting on animal victims and then move on to humans. Usually, it proceeds to

[13] St Croix *Avis*, 23 July 1994.

homicide, but there are rare cases where it can turn
into child molestation.

Carole J. Adams, a feminist writer on animal issues, believed
that bestiality

> . . . allows people to subvert consensual sex and lull
> themselves into believing it's 'affection'. What you see is
> power and that's confused with love. It doesn't surprise
> me if children are forced to participate. It's another way
> to abuse power.[14]

Just how common sexual activity is between adults and
animals will always remain dark because of the so-called
chiffre noir, the unreported crime figures. Some American
writers in the 1970s saw it as on the increase.

> Both males and females in Western society have engaged
> in ever more open erotic fondling of house pets, par-
> ticularly dogs, and veterinarians and psychiatrists report
> cases of the masturbating of dogs by humans, of dog
> bites on penis and female genitalia, and of other inju-
> ries caused by efforts to effect a human-canine sex
> relationship.[15]

However, those who argue that bestiality should not be a

---

[14] *Detroit News*, 30 May 1997.
[15] Donal E.J. MacNamara and Edward Sagarin, *Sex, Crime, and the Law*,
pp. 180–81. They too subscribe to Tony Honore's doctrine that 'human-infra-
human sex, particularly with a small pet, as subsumed under laws criminalizing
'cruelty to animals'. There are also stories, which may of course be urban legends,
of houses in the Hyde Park area of London where animals were especially trained
to provide sexual satisfaction for future owners.
  In Charles Willeford's detective novel *Sideswipe* the hero declines to take
on a house-sitting assignment when he finds he is required to masturbate the
owner's oversexed dog a number of times a day. For this piece of fastidiousness
he is chastised by the house agent, who points out that the only way for her
to obtain high-school dates was to masturbate her partners in the cinema.

crime had something of a setback to their hopes with the
news a little before Christmas 1998 that a Bradford man
had been sent to prison for a year for having sex with a
Staffordshire bull terrier confusingly named Badger. He
had been seen by a middle-aged couple by the roadside.
Later, he claimed that the dog had made the first approach.
He told the police, 'I can't help it if it took a liking to
me. He pulled my trousers down.' The sentence was
probably for the public nature of the offence rather than
the act itself.[16]

[16] 'Stop the Week' in the *Sunday Times*, 6 December 1998. In the same issue it was
reported that a television programme on bestiality was in the planning stage. It
would include a gentleman from Missouri, where sex with animals is not a crime
if conducted in private. Mark Mathews, a 47-year-old former electrician with
two children, 'married' a 22-year-old mare, Pixel. Nicholas Hellen and Trushar
Barot, 'Channel 4 breaks last sex taboo with bestiality film'.

20

Obscenity

> What is pornography to one man is the laughter
> of genius to another[1]

The case which is regularly suggested in the law books
and histories of pornography as being the first prosecution
for obscenity in England really cannot have been that at
all. It did, however, set a standard over the toleration of
public indecency. Sir Charles Sedley, a friend of King
Charles, was convicted following a night on the town
with his friends Lord Buckhurst and Sir Thomas Ogle
which had culminated in his stripping naked on a balcony
at Oxford Kate's the Cock Tavern in Bow Street, Covent
Garden, shouting profanities and pouring bottles of urine
on to the crowd below. Other accounts have him defecating
on the unfortunate crowd, who retaliated fiercely, pelting
him and his friends with the bottles they had thrown in the
first place. Sir Charles was convicted of a public indecency

---

[1] D. H. Lawrence, *Pornography and Obscenity*, p. 5.

offence, was fined, imprisoned for a week and bound over for a year to be of good behaviour.[2]

From the seventeenth century on there has been more than a rudimentary form of censorship. The Licensing Act 1662 was aimed at 'heretical, seditious, schismatical or offensive books or pamphlets' and undercover agents known as Messengers of the Press were employed to seek out and report undesirable literature. Where prosecutions took place penalties could be light. In 1677 an erotic bookshop in St Paul's Churchyard was closed for several hours following a raid. It had been selling *L'Ecole des Filles* imported from Amsterdam. Six years later in 1683 John Wickins, who had published a translation of Ferrante Pallavicino's *La Retorica delle Putane*, was fined 40 shillings.[3]

The works of the notorious rake Lord Rochester fared ill during the last decade of the century when his *Poems on Several Occasions* and his play *Sodom* were prosecuted on a regular basis. It is generally accepted that the first time magistrates had the power to seize and condemn what were deemed to be obscene publications came after Lord Campbell's Act of 1857, but there had been destruction orders in force from the end of the seventeenth century. On 12 October 1696 'about a cartload of obscene Books and Cards, tending to promote Debauchery, were burnt near the Gatehouse at Westminster by Mr Stephens,

[2] *Sedley*, 1 Keeble 620; 2d Wharton Cr Law, Sec 2545.

The Roman Catholic Church had long taken an interest in obscene literature. In 1559 Pope Paul IV sent the Inquisition a list of books he had banned, and five years later the Council of Trent issued its first comprehensive list of unacceptable books. At the beginning erotic books did not really feature. Qualification for the list was based on heresy or a satire on the Church of which *The Decameron* is an obvious example. Over the years, however, the rules changed and wider qualifications were introduced. In the 1948 list the works of Zola, Stendhal and both the Dumas were banned in their entirety. In 1952 the hugely successful novel by Alberto Moravia, *Woman of Rome*, was added. In the 1960s there was a world-wide total of around 4,000 titles.

[3] It was an old book published in 1642. In 1644 Pallavicino was executed in France, apparently for anti-clericism rather than for pornography.

Messenger of the Press'. Present were a justice of the peace and a constable. Apparently the books had belonged to an Italian named Bernardi.

Probably the first prosecution as we know it took place at the beginning of the eighteenth century when in 1708 James Read and Angelo Carter were indicted for libel for publishing *The Fifteen Plagues of Maidenhead*.[4] The Queen's Bench dismissed the indictment for obscene libel, saying that the book was not a reflection on government, church or any individual, and rejecting the concept that libel included obscenity. Said Mr Justice Powell:

> This is for printing bawdy stuff that reflects on no person and a libel must be against some particular person or persons or against the Government. It is stuff not fit to be mentioned in public. If there is no remedy in the Spiritual Court, it does not follow there must be a remedy here. There is no law to punish it: I wish there were: but we cannot make law.

It was, it seems, the usual problem of the Parliament and the judiciary. But if the latter was not willing to make the law in 1708, it had changed its mind less than 20 years later. The villain or victim on this occasion was Edmund Curll.[5]

[4] 11 Mod Rep 142 88 Eng Rep (1708) 953.

[5] Edmund Curll (1675–1747) may be regarded as the father of English pornographic publishing. Combining his trade with the sale of patent medicines, he also published the first English edition of Petronius' *Satyricon* as well as his most successful work, John Marten's *The Charitable Surgeon. Being a new way of Curing (without Mercury) the several degrees of the venereal Distemper on both Sexes.* Editions were published over several years before the author but not Curll was prosecuted after one edition was embellished with a good deal of pornographic material. He was acquitted after explaining that the book was a scientific one. Curll also published *Eunuchism Display'd*, which purported to include the tale of a young Lady who had fallen in love with the castrato Nicolini, who had been singing in opera at the Hay-Market. Curll is described by a contemporary as '. . . very tall and thin, an ungainly, awkward, white-faced man. His eyes were a light grey, large, projecting, goggle, and purblind. He was splay-footed and baker-kneed . . . .He was a debauchee.' See Ralph Strauss, *The Unspeakable Curll.*

This was not Curll's first brush with the law. In 1719 he had been acquitted of publishing an obscene libel after the death of Peter Motteux, a translator of Rabelais. Motteux had died in curious circumstances in a brothel near the Sign of the Dial and Bible in Fleet Street, where Curll had offices. The prosecution alleged murder against the brothel-keeper and her daughter, who were unexpectedly acquitted. The defence claimed Motteux had a fit, which may be true since he was undoubtedly indulging in a masochistic and flagellatory experiment at the time. Curll then published a translation of the seventeenth-century work by Johann Heinrich Meibom, who had held the chair of medicine at the University of Helmstedt. The translator was George Sewell – educated at Eton and Cambridge as well as having obtained a medical degree at Edinburgh – who was now seriously on the slide after his failure to establish a practice. The English title was *A Treatise of the use of Flogging in Venereal Affairs* (which was an almost exact translation from the original Latin). Ever mindful of the need to reach a wide audience, Curll had supplemented the work with a bonus in the form of a *Treatise of Hermaphrodites*. It was not a happy few weeks for the prosecution. Curll's defence that he had published the work with 'the least moral intent' was also accepted by another jury.

Then in 1727 Curll published *Venus in the Cloister or The Nun in her Smock*.[6] He had been engaged in a literary brawl with both Daniel Defoe and Alexander Pope, whom he accused of plagiarism. Defending himself in his *Curlicism Display'd*, he silenced his attackers and, now unchallenged, went on to publish *Cupid's Beehive, or the Sting of Love* – think of all the medicine he sold on its back – and *Pancharis, Queen of Love or the Art of Kissing in all its Varieties*.

[6] *Dominus Rex v Curll*, 2 Str 789; 93 Eng Rep (1727) 849.

Then the blow fell. He denied he was the publisher of *Venus* whilst admitting to selling one copy of this book which – written by the Abbé Du Prat under the pseudonym of the Abbé Barin – purported to recount behaviour in French convents. The Secretary of State, Lord Viscount Townshend, ordered his arrest and imprisonment. For good measure the *Treatise on Flogging* was also seized. Curll might have survived: he pleaded that *Venus* had appeared some 40 years earlier, published by a Henry Rhodes, and that no action had been taken against him. As for *Flogging*, well, that was a well-known medical treatise. In support of all this he cited Read's case. All might have been well. He was released on bail whilst the Court of King's Bench thought about things. Unfortunately, whilst their Lordships were thinking Curll was back publishing. One of the books was *The Case of Seduction* in which he reported the proceedings against the Abbé des Rues for the rape of 133 virgins; but, more seriously, in an early version of *Spycatcher* he also published the *Memoirs of John Ker*, a Government agent.

In November 1727 he was convicted, with Mr Justice Fortescue dissenting: 'There should be a breach of the peace, or something tending to it, of which there is nothing in this case' – finding corruption of morals to be a misdemeanour at common law. Curll was fined 50 marks, nowadays around £100, bound over to be of good behaviour, and so obscenity was accepted as a crime.

Worse, for the Ker memoirs' offence Curll was sentenced to a term in the pillory. He survived the ordeal, which could result in death, by having pamphlets distributed to the crowd saying he was being punished for defending the memory of Queen Anne.

With hindsight it is clear that his real offence was political, and he stayed out of that area of publishing for the remainder of his life. Translations of French 'classics' remained his stock-in-trade and he was left alone when shortly before his death he published *The Pleasures of Coition* and *The Secret Natural History of Both Sexes*.

Throughout the next 50 years, however, although obscenity was now a crime prosecutions were more often aimed at publications which coupled sedition or blasphemy with straightforward pornography. Although it would fall foul of nineteenth-century American laws and be seized in 1960 in England, for the time being John Cleland's *Fanny Hill* remained untouched.

Then in 1763 came *An Essay on Woman*, dedicated to a *demi-mondaine*, Fanny Murray, and a parody of Pope's *Essay on Man*.

> . . . life can little more supply
>   Than just a few good fucks and then we die.

All might have been well had not the author been the rebellious politician John Wilkes, described as the ugliest man in Middlesex but nevertheless one who could seduce a woman if she shared an umbrella with him. He was a member of the Medmenham Monks, one of those quasi-erotic, quasi-mystic clubs which have flourished over the years in the Thames Valley. He had written his *Essay* for private circulation for the twelve members, but the publisher ran off a thirteenth and possibly a fourteenth copy.

The House of Lords had great fun with the piece. Read to them by Lord Sandwich, an ancestor of the card player who gave his name to the fast food, he was interrupted by another member of the House suggesting that the reading had gone far enough. Just as some benches of lay magistrates in the twentieth century would volunteer *en masse* to be those who had the unpleasant task of viewing pornographic videos before condemning them, the interruption was greeted with cries of 'Go on! Go on!' To their credit their Lordships were resolved that the poem was 'a most scandalous, obscene and impious libel'. Wilkes was convicted, fined £500 and, refusing to pay, was banished.

Again the crime was sedition rather than pornography, which was being circulated quite freely in such magazines as Harris's *List of Covent Garden Ladies*, who advertised their attractions in the magazine. Not that Harris could not be critical. Of Mrs Howard of 14 Moors Place, Lambeth he wrote that she had contracted such an habit of intimacy with the gin bottle, 'that unless a person is particularly partial to it, it is almost intolerable to approach her'.[7]

Over the years Literature (with a capital L) has been bedevilled by societies, usually grandly titled to indicate their moral worthiness and domain over swathes of the public. By the late eighteenth century the 'mad' King George III, no doubt distressed by his son's profligacy, issued a suppression against vice. The aim of the proclamation was to . . .

> suppress all loose and licentious prints, books, and publications, dispensing poison to the minds of the young and unwary, and to punish the publishers and the vendors thereof.

And hard on the pronouncement came the formation of

---

[7] *Tempora mutantur*. In 1961, when a Mr Shaw published his *Ladies Directory*, something of a trade journal which was an up-to-date and sanitised if less critical version of Harris, he received nine months for conspiracy to pervert public morals. There were questions whether he could be convicted of living off immoral earnings since only a part of his income derived from prostitutes and fortunately solicitors, barristers and doctors do not fall into the trap. Secondly, the advertisements were couched in unerotic language. He was convicted on both those counts as well as the conspiracy. *Shaw v DPP* [192] A.C. 220. A visit to the telephone kiosks of the West End today shows that we are back in the times of Harris rather than Shaw.

the Proclamation Society by William Wilberforce MP, who later distinguished himself in his campaign against slavery. In 1802 the Society for the Suppression of Vice was founded, and it soon swallowed Wilberforce's child. Originally based in London, it soon expanded its branches to Bath, York and Wilberforce's home town of Hull. A noted name, Bowdler, was amongst the original subscribers; it was, however, John, brother of the more famous Robert, who would leave his name as a word in the language.

The Society had a field day and the Secretary reported in 1817 to the House of Commons that '. . . so little disguise and concealment were used by dealers of this class that with no great difficulty important discoveries were soon made as to its nature and extent'.

By 1820 the Society had instigated between 30 and 40 prosecutions, showing a 100 per cent conviction rate. Italian hawkers who worked the country from Maidstone to York and East Anglia were their principal victims, but the Secretary of the Society noted that snuff boxes with indecent engravings on the lids were very popular not only with undergraduates at Oxbridge but also with young ladies at boarding schools – 'the wholesome seminaries of female education are the scenes of pollution and vice'.[8]

The end of the Napoleonic Wars saw a flood in the importation of obscene literature and the Society was hard at work turning back the tide. In the seven years from 1817 20 prosecutions were brought and a clause in the Vagrancy Act 1824 made the exhibition of indecent pictures in a public place a criminal offence – carrying on conviction before a magistrate a fine or two years' imprisonment with hard labour. In 1838 the Act was amended to extend the exhibition to shop windows. By 1857 the Society had brought an average of three prosecutions a year of what

---

[8] The Police Committee of the House of Commons, 1 May 1817.

could fairly be described as hard-core pornography. There were five acquittals, including one of William Benbow – a bookseller who was acquitted after showing that a French novel he had published in sixpenny parts had been published 30 years earlier and could be obtained from circulating libraries.[9] Generally, however, to the satisfaction of the Society, pornography was driven underground. It was something of a struggle. In 1845 12,346 obscene prints, 393 books, 351 copper plates and 188 lithographic stones, along with 33.5 hundredweight of letterpress, were seized from one Aldwych dealer alone.

Aldwych and in particular Holywell Street – approximately where Australia House is today and where there were some 20 bookshops – was then the epicentre of pornography. The king was George Cannon, a lawyer's clerk who turned to this more profitable enterprise. He died in 1854 and his business was carried on by his widow, who was accidentally burned to death some ten years later.

After that William Dugdale assumed the mantle. He was a man of some parts. As a youth he had been implicated in the Cato Street Conspiracy to assassinate the Cabinet, and over the years was in and out of prison for trafficking in obscene publications. He merits his niche in legal history for his successful argument that intent to sell rather than mere possession was required for a conviction.[10] He died in the House of Corrections in Clerkenwell in 1868.

Then the Obscene Publications Act 1857, known as

[9] Benbow then published an account of his trial in the *Rambler*, June and August 1822. It is reprinted in Donald Thomas, *A Long Time Burning*.
[10] English Reports CXVIII 499,717; CLXIX 638, 716. Another very successful pornographer of the time but one who escaped conviction was James Camden Hotten. He published not only Swinburne's *Songs and Ballads* but probably more profitably the Rev. W.M. Cooper's *The History of the Rod*. Cooper was in fact James G. Bertram. For Hotten's life, see the *Dictionary of National Biography*.

Lord Campbell's Act after its sponsor, which was aimed at the French postcards which were flooding the market, gave magistrates the right to issue warrants to search for obscene materials, at the time mostly drawings, and have them destroyed. It was not, his Lordship told Parliament disarmingly, intended to apply to works of literary merit but instead . . .

> to apply exclusively to works written for the single purpose of corrupting the morals of youth and of a nature calculated to shock the common feelings of decency in a well regulated mind.

Lord Campbell did not have things all his own way. Lord Lydhurst pointed out that a print of Correggio's *Jupiter and Antiope*, the original of which hung in the Louvre, would be condemned. There were also fears for the Restoration dramatists and Ovid. Sydney Smith had earlier described the Vice Society as 'a society for suppressing the vices of those whose incomes do not exceed £500 per annum'. Now John Roebuck MP claimed that an attempt was being made to make people virtuous by Act of Parliament, and pointed out that a man who had a taste for the class of prints and publications in the Bill would get them in spite of all the laws which could be passed; an observation which over the years might well apply to many regulatory measures such as the recent ban on handguns.

But through the Bill went and now magistrates, subject to an appeal to Quarter Sessions, were the arbiters of artistic and literary morals and taste. Campbell was pleased to note that within a matter of months half the Holywell Street shops had closed. Dublin and even Paris had also been purged of much pornographic material. He was a contented man. But just what was obscenity?

The great definition came 11 years after the Obscene Publications Act became law when copies of an anti-Catholic pamphlet, *The Confessional Unmasked*, were published by a militant Protestant organisation. In accordance with the fashion for long explicatory titles it continued: *showing the Depravity of the Romish Priesthood, the Iniquity of the Confessional and the Questions put to Females in Confession.* The book, which had a tasteful cover of the Pope unleashing a dragon on Britannia and recounted in some detail the physical pleasures undergone by the confessor, was apparently sold without profit by Henry Scott in Wolverhampton. Two hundred and fifty copies were seized and the Wolverhampton magistrate Hicklin ordered they be destroyed on the grounds of references to intercourse and fellatio. Scott exercised his right to appeal to Quarter Sessions, where the Chairman ruled that he had acted not to corrupt public morals but to expose the iniquities of the Roman Church. The case was then referred to the Court of Queen's Bench, where Lord Chief Justice Cockburn presided, ruling:

> I think the test of obscenity is this, whether the tendency of the matter charged as obscenity is to deprave and corrupt those whose minds are open to such immoral influences, and into whose hands a publication of this sort might fall.[11]

The publication might fall on the strength of isolated passages, and literary or other merit was to be no defence.

Hicklin remained in force for nearly 100 years and also formed the basis of the American test. And down went the books one by one. The National Vigilance Association aimed its sights at Henry Vizetelly, who had introduced

[11] 3. Q.B. (1868) p. 360.

Poe and Longfellow to the British public. Unfortunately
he had also introduced the French realist school and he
was charged with 'uttering and publishing certain obscene
libels, to wit, certain books entitled *La Terre* by Emile Zola,
Madame Bovary by Gustave Flaubert, *Sappho* by Alphonse
Daudet, *Bel-Ami* by Guy de Maupassant and *Mademoiselle
de Maupin* by Théophile Gautier'. It did not matter a jot that
a fortnight before Vizetelly's trial, Zola had been appointed
to the French Legion of Honour. 'A voluminous French
author,' said Sir Edward Clarke, the Solicitor-General,
before he read out selected passages which had been
painstakingly cut and pasted by the future Liberal Prime
Minister Herbert Henry Asquith, then a junior barrister.
Vizetelly's fate was sealed when one juryman demanded
there be no further reading. On 31 October 1888 Vizetelly
pleaded guilty and was fined £100.

Unfortunately, this urbane connoisseur of literature and
good wine had not learned his lesson. First he published
*Extracts principally from English Classics showing the legal
suppression of M. Zola's novels would logically involve the
bowdlerising of the greatest Works in English literature* –
which, of course, did not go down too well with the
authorities. Then in early 1889 he republished Zola in a
slightly expurgated form. On 30 May on the advice of his
counsel, Arthur Cocks QC, he pleaded guilty, was fined
£200 and given three months as a first-class misdemeanant.
He was then almost 70 and although conditions for such a
prisoner were not that bad, his health was broken and he
died in 1894.[12]

The radical bookseller Bedborough was the only one

[12] In fact, for a first-class prisoner conditions were not too onerous. Former
Army officer Valentine Baker, imprisoned for indecent assault, had food sent
in from a restaurant, a furnished room and books and daily visits. It was noted
that about the same time the same judge had passed a stiff sentence, including
the treadmill and plank bed or skilly, on gas stokers who had been on strike
for better wages.

prepared to stock Havelock Ellis's *Sexual Inversion*. His prosecution duly followed and although his defence fund supported by Shaw and George Moore had lined up some experts to give evidence, he had learned from Vizetelly's experience and agreed to a bind-over. He was well advised for the Recorder, Sir Charles Hall, had some harsh words to say about the book:

> . . . you might at the first outset perhaps have been gulled into the belief that somebody might say that this was a scientific work. But it is impossible for anybody with a head on his shoulders to open the book without seeing it as a pretence and a sham.[13]

As Geoffrey Robertson QC points out in his engaging survey of Victorian repression, with the Vagrancy Act 1824, the Post Office Act 1853 and the Customs Consolidation Act 1876 the display, posting or importation of indecent material literary censorship was now complete.[14] Nor could newspapers report the obscene or blasphemous passages when read in court; the Law of Libel Amendment Act 1888 saw to that. There was also an informal social censorship, with the circulating libraries such as Charles Mudie and the railway bookstalls of W.H. Smith listening carefully to complaints from old ladies. With their commitment it was almost impossible to get a new novel published.[15]

Not that censorship did that much good at underground level. In the years following the Obscene Publications Act,

---

[13] C.H. Rolph, *Books in the Dock*, p. 59.
[14] Geoffrey Robertson, *Obscenity*, p. 32.
[15] In 1913 whilst agreeing that the article was admirable in many ways W.H. Smith refused to stock a pamphlet, *The Doctors and Venereal Disease*, which had been reprinted from the *English Review*. It did not think that it was suitable to be sold on railway bookstalls and further, most of its contracts with the railways prevented the sale of such books. Charles Wilson, *First with the News*, p. 379.

literacy had risen to around 95 per cent by 1893. By the 1880s Holywell Street was back in business. The new readership may not have been improving their minds with Zola and Flaubert but there was a thriving trade in pornography, the best and certainly most enduring of which were *My Secret Life* (1885) vying with *Lady Bumtickler's Revels* published 13 years earlier, *The Story of a Dildoe* (1880) and the splendidly titled *Raped on the Railway: A True Story of a Lady who was first ravished and then flagellated on the Scotch Express* (1894). This last title was presumably not on sale at the stations . . .

The first prosecution of the twentieth century was that of *Thompson*,[16] and in it the Common Serjeant pointed out that a book which sold at 1s 11d, would clearly tend to the corruption of morals:

> In the Middle Ages things were discussed which if put forward now for the reading of the general public would never be tolerated.

It was one more example of the beliefs, prevalent at the time, that if you paid ten guineas for a book you would not be corrupted by its contents and that the working classes had to be protected from themselves.

Efforts to rationalise the law came to nothing, despite a Joint Select Committee which in 1908 wanted an Act with graded penalties for a first offence, selling to a person under 16, and for second and subsequent offences. An exemption was recommended for a book of genuine merit. It came to nothing and when in 1915 D.H. Lawrence's *The Rainbow* was brought before Sir John Dickinson, the Bow Street magistrate, for a destruction order, Methuen & Co. simply apologised. The magistrate regretted that

[16] (1900) 64 J.P. 456.

the firm had allowed its reputation to be sullied by the publication.[17]

Radclyffe Hall 'from a deep sense of duty' wrote *The Well of Loneliness*. She was, by 1927, a novelist of some distinction. Her previous book, *Adam's Breed*, had won both the Prix Femina – defeating Liam O'Flaherty's *The Informer* in the process – and the James Tait Black prize. It was only the second time that a book had won both awards.[18]

The Well of Loneliness was highly autobiographical, recounting – with minor variations and a changed and (depending upon one's point of view) happy ending in which the younger woman is restored to heterosexuality – her love of Lady Troubridge. She persuaded the sexologist Havelock Ellis to write a foreword. He in turn was not persuaded that this was the correct course, and his preface Commentary was picked up by the *Sunday Express* of 19 August 1928 when the editor, James Douglas, described the book as an 'intolerable outrage'. Overall the book had mixed reviews but the *Sunday Times*, amongst others, recognised it as a serious plea for toleration. The *Sunday Express*, at its most crusading, was not to be deceived.

---

[17] Lawrence had no real luck with his work. Quite apart from the trials of *Lady Chatterley's Lover*, the DPP required the excision of 14 verses from his 1929 poetry book *Pansies*, and the same year 13 of his paintings were seized by the police. Some 60 years later I saw them in Taos, New Mexico, exhibited, if that is not too grand a word, in an office in an hotel on the main square. To get to them one had first to pass through another exhibition, this time of the clothes worn by Rudolph Valentino in the silent film *Blood and Sand*. The key to the room cost a dollar and the pictures were hung around three sides of the room, surrounded by signed photographs of long-forgotten boxers, baseball players, wrestlers and minor politicians. The pictures are possibly best described as sub-sub-Gauguin or more properly naïf. Nowadays they would not cause the flicker of an embarrassed eyelid. Were they not by Lawrence they probably would not sell outside a local art club. The proprietor of the exhibition also collected shoes. There at attention on the floor, like soldiers awaiting inspection, standing in rows were dozens of highly polished pairs. Indeed the proprietor also had a collection of the works of other Lawrences. Amidst the editions of *The Plumed Serpent* and *Sons and Lovers* could be seen copies of *The Mint* and *The Seven Pillars of Wisdom*.
[18] The previous double winner was E.M. Forster's *A Passage to India*.

It is a seductive and insidious piece of special pleading designed to display perverted decadence as a martyrdom inflicted upon those outcasts by a cruel society. It flings a veil of sentiment over their depravity. It even suggests that their self-made debasement is unavoidable because they cannot save themselves ... I would rather put a phial of prussic acid in the hands of a healthy girl or boy than the book in question ...What then is to be done? The book must be withdrawn at once.

Why it was not suitable for a boy is not immediately apparent, but Douglas was only echoing Canon Lambert's attack on H.G. Wells's *Ann Veronica*:

I would just as soon send a daughter of mine to a house infected with typhoid or diphtheria as put that book into her hands.

The then Home Secretary, the puritanical Joynson-Hicks, was asked by Jonathan Cape, the publisher, whether he should withdraw the book. There was no doubt in the mind of Jix as he was known. That was the best course and Cape followed it, arranging at the same time that it should be printed by the Pegasus Press in Paris and imported into England. Retribution was swift. The Director of Public Prosecutions applied for an order for its destruction and the case was heard before Sir Chartres Biron, then the Chief Stipendiary Magistrate at Bow Street.[19] Norman Birkett and J. B. Melville were briefed for the defence on behalf of Cape and the Pegasus Press.

The defence was marshalled by the solicitor Harold Rubinstein and he canvassed leading literary figures to give

[19] It is curious that in Biron's memoirs, *Without Prejudice*, there is no mention of the case. In his biography of *Norman Birkett*, H. Montgomery Hyde, writing in the thought-to-be more enlightened days of 1964, nevertheless described Radclyffe Hall as 'herself an invert'.

evidence on behalf of the book. Missing from the ranks
was Havelock Ellis. This was not altogether surprising. He
had earlier chickened out of appearing for the defence of
George Bedborough, who had been prosecuted for selling
Ellis's *Sexual Inversion*. Now Ellis wrote:

> I hope you will not misunderstand me if I say at once
> that I should not be willing to be a witness. I have
> never been in the witness box. There are two good
> reasons against it. The first is that I do not possess
> the personal qualities that make a good witness, and
> would probably make a bad impression, and certainly
> not a good impression. The second is that being the
> author of a book on this very same subject I am 'tarred
> with the same brush'. The less said about me the better
> for you.

Perhaps he was right. Another absentee was John Galsworthy
– then, with the publication of *The Forsyte Saga*, at the
height of his fame:

> I am not prepared to go into the witness box on behalf of
> Miss Radclyffe Hall's *Well of Loneliness*. I am too busy
> a man, and I am not sure that the freedom of letters is
> in question.

Nor was Hugh Walpole, the immensely popular author of
the *Rogue Herries* series of novels.

> I dislike intensely all the publicity given to abnormality,
> which ought, I think to be let lie on both sides.

Nevertheless, Rubinstein managed to collect a galaxy of
literary talent in support of the book when the summons
was heard on 9 November 1928. Amongst those said to be

prepared to give evidence were E. M. Forster, A.P. Herbert and Leonard and Virginia Woolf.

The case for the prosecution was simple. 'A person who chose an obscene theme could not but write an obscene book,' said Eustace Fulton for the Director of Public Prosecutions. Chief Inspector Prothero gave evidence that he had purchased a copy and paraphrased Fulton's words, saying, 'The book is indecent because it deals with an indecent theme.' He could hardly have said otherwise. Asked whether he considered the book to be sincere and courageous as well as being high-minded and beautiful, he conceded the former but not the high-minded and beautiful bit.

When Birkett began his defence he faced a singularly hostile Chartres Biron.

> Birkett: The book is concerned, not with perversion, but with what the medical profession calls inversion; that is emotions and desires which with most people are directed towards the opposite sex, but here are directed to their own sex.
>
> Biron: Do you mean to say it does not deal with unnatural offences at all?
>
> Birkett: I say not.

Much to the wrath of Radclyffe Hall, who explained the facts of life if not the law to her counsel over the luncheon adjournment. Before then there had been another disaster. In all, some thirty-nine people had been lined up for the defence and Birkett began his introduction with the words:

> People of every walk of life desire to go into the witness

box and to testify that this book is not obscene, and that it is a misuse of words for the prosecution to describe it as such.

Desmond MacCarthy, the literary critic, was the only one to make it as far as the witness-box:

> Birkett: In your view is it obscene?
>
> Biron: I shall disallow that question. It is quite clear the evidence is not admissible. A book may be a fine piece of literature and yet obscene. Art and obscenity are not disassociated at all. There is a room at Naples to which visitors are not admitted as a rule, which contains fine bronzes and statues, all admirable works of art, but all grossly obscene. It does not follow that because a work is a work of art it is not obscene. I shall not admit the evidence.

Birkett tried vainly to show the qualifications of his witnesses, including Sir Julius Huxley.

> Biron: I reject them all.

Birkett then asked Biron to state a case, which meant asking the Divisional Court to decide on the admissibility of the evidence, and was turned down. After the luncheon adjournment he asked for the summons to be dismissed and now both he and Melville, his junior, argued that there were no detailed descriptions of homosexual acts.

> Birkett: The theme deals with a disability laid up on certain members of humanity for which they are not responsible and shows the tragic unhappiness and tragic fate which might overtake such persons in their inversion.

Nothing either of them said impressed Chartres, who, when he gave his judgement a week later, was more interested in why Jonathan Cape had not been called to explain the withdrawal of the book in London and the surreptitious printing in Paris.

Here is Biron on the seduction of Angela:

> . . . who of course, I admit at once, is not described as a woman of any particular morality but that was not present to the mind of Stephen who seduced her and persuaded her reluctantly to indulge in these horrible practices . . . The mere fact that the book deals with unnatural offences between women does not make it obscene. It might even have a strong moral influence. But in the present case there is not one word which suggests that anyone with the horrible tendencies described is, in the least, blameworthy. All the characters are presented as attractive people and put forward with admiration. What is even more serious is that certain acts are described in alluring terms.

He had no hesitation in condemning the book and awarding a total of 40 guineas costs.

Before that he had dealt with an outburst by Radclyffe Hall. At the time Biron was reading out loud the passage about ambulance drivers at the front who were 'addicted to these practices'.

> —I protest. I emphatically protest.
> —I must ask you to be quiet.
> —I am the author of this book—
> —If you cannot behave yourself in court, I shall have you removed.
> —Shame.[20]

[20] *The Times*, 10, 17 November 1928.

Birkett, brought up as a strict Methodist, was probably not happy with the case in the first place. Geoffrey Robertson QC suggests that he made two blunders in his conduct of the defence; the first by denying in the teeth of the evidence that the book was about lesbianism. The second was that when he called MacCarthy he should not have asked him whether he found the book to be obscene – that question was for the magistrate alone – but whether it had merit.[21] Given the atmosphere of the time it is doubtful, however, whether there would have been any different verdict. Birkett was sacked and now Melville conducted the appeal at Quarter Sessions on 14 December 1928. There the Attorney-General prosecuting described the book as:

> . . . a missionary work, appealing for recognition of the status of people who engage in these practices, and there is not a word to suggest that people who do this are a pest to society and to their sex.

The Chairman, Sir Robert Wallace, dismissing the appeal, was certain of his moral ground:

> I might just say in a sentence what the view of the court is: that this book is a very subtle book; it is a book which is insinuating in the way in which it is propounded, and probably much the more dangerous because of that fact.

The Well of Loneliness was not republished in Britain until 1949.

Sometimes books never got further than their printers. The eccentric *soi-disant* Count Geoffrey Wladislas Vaile

---

Potocki de Montalk, who claimed the Polish throne and more prosaically could often be seen drinking in Soho swathed in a purple cloak, decided to publish 100 copies of *Here lies John Penis*, a parody of Verlaine, for his friends' amusement. The outraged printer passed them to the police, and in due course de Montalk passed from the Old Bailey to Wormwood Scrubs for six months in the Second Division.

He cannot have been helped by the fact that the Recorder, Sir Ernest Wild, was himself a poet *manqué*; nor by insisting that he swore on Apollo rather than taking one of the more conventional oaths.

> Are you going to allow a man, just because he calls himself a poet, to deflower our English language by popularizing those words? A man may not say he is a poet and be filthy, he has to obey the law just the same as ordinary citizens, and the sooner the highbrow school learns that, the better for the morality of our country.

Despite pleas by T.S. Eliot, Aldous Huxley and H.G. Wells, the Court of Criminal Appeal upheld the sentence.[22]

There were, however, some signs of enlightenment when the new Attorney-General, Sir Donald Somerville KC, declined to prosecute that much-talked-about if generally unread masterpiece *Ulysses*.

> In his [Somerville's] view the question of intention has to be taken into account as in the criminal law generally: the context has also to be considered. No one today would, he thought, be found to hold that such books as those of Havelock Ellis on sexual matters were obscene,

---

[22] Cr App R. (1932) 182.

nor any medical book dealing with sexual aberrations. Standards in these matters were constantly changing – as conventions and taste changed.

If he were challenged in the House of Commons his answer would be on a line that it was a well-established principle of law that the intention of a writer had to be taken into account as well as the general setting or context of the book. On applying these tests to *Ulysses* he was of the opinion that the book was not obscene and having regard, in addition, to its established position now in literature he had decided to take no action.[23]

Of course some books which invited prosecution went underground – or in reality to Paris, where from 1931 the Obelisk Press published Lawrence Durrell's *The Black Book*, the novels of his friend Henry Miller and Cyril Connolly's *The Rock Pool*. Those who stayed behind, as it were, found that prosecution might follow.

James Hanley's *Boy*, a novel which Alec Craig describes as an ''orrible warning tract'[24] about a young sailor who catches syphilis and is killed by the captain, was prosecuted the year the Obelisk Press was established, as was Wallace Smith's prostitution-in-Chicago steamer *Bessie Cotter* in 1935. The publishers pleaded guilty in both cases, so avoiding the possibility of imprisonment. Both the books had been well reviewed. In Cotter's case, the Attorney-General, Sir Thomas Inskip KC, took on the burden of the prosecution himself:

---

[23] PRO/MEPO/3/390. Geoffrey Robertson in *Obscenity* (p. 38) suggests that he may have been influenced by the fact that Lord Birkenhead, the former Lord Chancellor, had owned a sumptuously bound copy which was nearly auctioned on his death in 1930. In another case in 1949, Sir Hartley Shawcross explained his decision not to prosecute Norman Mailer's *The Naked and the Dead*, saying that, 'While there is much in this most tedious and lengthy book which is foul, lewd and revolting, looking at it as a whole I do not think its intent is to corrupt or deprave.'

[24] Alec Craig, *Banned Books of England*, p. 135.

The book deals with what everybody will recognise as
an unsavoury subject – gratification of sexual appetite.

The publishers were fined £100.

In the case of *Boy*, it was yet another example of the
belief that pornography is only dangerous if it is priced
so that the masses may be able to afford to purchase it.
The book originally published in 1931 had been through
two reprints, and it was only when a cheap 3s 6d edition
was launched that the ship sank.[25]

James Hadley Chase, whose literary career scaled the
heights with *No Orchids for Miss Blandish* – his rewrite
of Faulkner's *Sanctuary* said to have been completed in
four days on a houseboat at Maidenhead – probably had no
reviews at all when *Miss Callaghan Comes to Grief* perished
at the Central Criminal Court in 1942. Under his real
name of Rene Raymond he and his publishers Jarrolds
were prosecuted for publishing an obscene libel.[26]

Detective Sergeant Sidney Norman from Scotland Yard
had purchased a copy of the book on 26 March 1942, paying
7s 6d at a shop in Cecil Court off the Charing Cross
Road. Helped by the Director of Public Prosecutions
– not personally – he read the book and listed a large
number of passages which he found obscene. The officer
told the court:

[This is a] thin story about a gangster who, by shooting
a rival gangster obtains control of the brothels in an
American City where girls are kidnapped and beaten

[25] A period on the bookshelves was no guarantee that a prosecution or seizure
would not follow. Gervée Baronte's *Dying Flame* was in trouble in 1932 after
being in print for the previous five years. There was no destruction order
following an undertaking that the book would no longer be sold. In 1937 her
new book was rejected by publishers on the grounds that *Dying Flame* had
been banned. See *Reynold's News*, 17 November 1935.
[26] *Sleeveless Errand* had been prosecuted in 1929.

into submitting themselves to a life of prostitution, an excuse is made to describe (inter alia) the following episodes.

1. Three young men uncover and gloat over a body in a mortuary (pp. 9–10).
2. An elderly woman trying to seduce a young man in a motor car (pp. 16–17).
3. Sexual satisfaction obtained not by fornication but by strangulation (pp. 34–37).
4. Man who hears cracks of whips and screams of girls in brothel (p. 43).

Other offending passages included a detailed description of an electrocution at the end of which a girl spits in the face of the corpse and the stripping and castration of a man by several girls in a brothel. Even worse, a number of the scenes complained about 'featured negroes'.

On 13 May, Jarrolds entered a written plea of guilty.

What then changed the attitude of the authorities in Britain? Nothing other than the *Kinsey Report* of 1948.[27] The report offered the unpalatable suggestion that far from sexual knowledge being passed to young boys through the written word, over 90 per cent said they obtained it from their male friends. Worse, some 'perversions' were now so prominent that they could not be regarded as 'perverse'. After all, once 51 per cent of the population indulges in flagellation, those who do not become the peculiar minority.

However, it was too much for the Director of Public Prosecutions to stomach, and he applied for the destruction of the report in the Doncaster Magistrates Court, where, much to his and probably everyone else's surprise, the magistrates refused him the order.

[27] A.C. Kinsey et al., *Sexual Behaviour in the Human Male* (1948).

There was, however, a purge when – after an Interpol Conference which reported that pornography was one of the causes of sex crimes – the police stamped on seven novels of the American pulp writer Hank Jansen. This time there was a much happier outcome for the forces of good. The argument for Jansen's publisher was that his prose was no more explicit than that which could be found on the pages of decent books. The trial judge refused to allow the jury to read and compare the books, and the decision was upheld by the Court of Criminal Appeal with Lord Goddard in the chair.[28] Early during the judgement of the appeal, the publishers must have known their fate when Lord Goddard had expressed his disgust:

> ... the titles of which I refrain from mentioning because I have no desire to give any advertisement to this shocking literature ...
>
> There may be dirty-minded elderly people, no doubt, but it is not expected that many elderly people would read this stuff, but younger people might, and we are told that it circulates in the armed forces ...

His Lordship, who was alleged to ejaculate when passing the death sentence and so on those high days took a second pair of trousers with him to court – something denied by his friends and family – was so horrified that he suggested the Director look at the so-called decent novels and it was 'not an intimation which I can ignore'.[29] It led to a parade of reputable publishers before juries at the Old Bailey. But Lord Goddard, that keen supporter not only of the death

---

[28] *Reiter and ors* (1954) Cr App.R. 62. Julius Reiter and Reginald Carter were sentenced to six months' imprisonment apiece and the companies fined £2,000.

[29] Minutes of Evidence taken before the Select Committee, 16 December 1958, House of Commons, p. 122.

penalty but also flogging, had misjudged the mood of the public. By his words he had opened the sluice gates of pornography.

In the meantime into the dock went Secker & Warburg – well, in fact Frederick Warburg was not put in the dock but was allowed by Mr Justice Stable to sit with his solicitors – who had published *The Philanderer* by the Chicago film critic Stanley Kaufmann.[30] In fact this was probably the worst choice which could have been made for a prosecution. It contains no bad language, little in the way of sex and is the story of a happily married serial adulterer who knows his conduct is going to ruin his life, career and home. Mr Justice Stable pointed out that 'deprave and corrupt' did not mean 'shock and disgust' and the reader had to be seen as an intelligent adult and not a 14-year-old schoolgirl, otherwise literature would be confined to nursery rhymes.[31]

Next up to bat was Hutchinson, the publishers, who were unfortunate to run into the Recorder of London at his most formidable. He disagreed with Mr Justice Stable on nearly everything, pointing out that sex and marriage must be protected from being dragged into the mud and that the jury must consider whether the book might deprave or corrupt 'a callow youth or a girl just budding into womanhood'. They did, and Hutchinson were fined £1,000 and given a very severe ticking-off.

> I should have thought that any reader, however inexperi-
> enced, would have been repelled by a book of this sort,
> which is repugnant to every decent emotion which ever
> concerned man or woman . . . it is a comforting thought
> that juries from time to time take a very solid stand
> against this sort of thing and realise how important it

[30] Published in America as *The Tightrope Walker*.
[31] Even then that might not be too good an idea. Think of that early example of child sex abuse 'Ride a Cock Horse'.

is for the youth of this country to be protected and that
the fountain of our national blood should not be polluted
at its source.

In the galleries at all the cases were teams of well-known
literary figures who would not be allowed to give evidence
but whom it was hoped the jury would recognise as silent
supporters. Since research into the deliberations of juries is
not permitted, the success of the ruse will never be known,
but given that Graham Greene regarded the fact that he was
never recognised in restaurants as something of a triumph,
it is doubtful that it was of much help.

One-all – and the next match resulted in a draw when
two juries failed to come to a decision, which then had to
be unanimous, over Heinemann's *The Image and the Search*.
Now with Sir Alan Herbert, who 20 years earlier had done
so much to reform the divorce laws, at the helm, the Society
of Authors set up a committee which demanded a reform
of the law. In 1955 Roy Jenkins introduced a draft Bill with
all-party support, and in 1957 it was referred to a Select
Committee of the House of Commons. The criticism was
of the test in *Hicklin*, there was no evidence of literary merit
and prosecuting counsel only read out pieces, often out of
context, to support his case.

Robertson sees the resulting Obscene Publications Act
1959 as something of a horse-trade, and that a difference
could easily be drawn dividing sexual material into literature
(good) in one camp and pornography (bad) in the other. The
tendency to deprave and corrupt was to be judged in the
round and not on selected extracts, and as a general rule
the readership on which the book might have an effect
was to be the reading public overall. All pornography was
unjustifiable and obscene and therefore to be prosecuted.
Literature might be obscene, but its great significance might
outweigh the potential harm.

As a result:

> The old formulae broke down entirely in the following
> decade when confronted by *Playboy* magazine's modish
> appeal to both intellect and instinct, by 'soft-core'
> journals offering medical and psychiatric advice on
> sexual problems in a deliberately titillating but arguably
> therapeutic style, and by the underground press with its
> flamboyant revolutionary celebration of sex as a means
> of baiting a prudish political establishment. These pub-
> lications were neither 'pornography' nor 'literature', and
> whilst they did not particularly edify the public, there
> was not much evidence that they were prone to deprave
> or corrupt either. In consequence they flourished in this
> grey area between pornography and literature between
> public good and public corruption . . . Pornography of
> the hardest core slipped effortlessly through the thin
> blue line and took a stand in Soho, while much that
> was undoubtedly serious writing was harassed and
> persecuted at vast public expense.[32]

The first literary casualty of the new war was scheduled
to be *Lady Chatterley's Lover*. It seems there had been
an implied promise given by the police to the Select
Committee that as part of the horse-trade prosecutions
would be confined to pornography. But the police had
in fact only undertaken to refrain from prosecuting what
they saw as borderline stuff, and it was they who defined
the borders.

There had been a conviction of *Scanties*, against which
the publisher appealed on the grounds that the judge had
not told the jury that they should be sure the publication

---

[32] Geoffrey Robertson, *Obscenity*, p. 44. It should also be remembered that in the
years following the Obscene Publications Act senior officers in Scotland Yard's
Porn Squad were running a protection business for the Soho pornographers.
See James Morton, *Bent Coppers*, Chapter 5.

was 'something more than shocking or vulgar'. Again Lord Goddard did not listen. Anyone had only to pick up the offending book to feel 'quite certain that no jury could conceivably have failed to convict'.[33]

It is interesting to speculate why the Director chose to prosecute Penguin Books for their unexpurgated reissue of *Lady Chatterley's Lover* rather than go for a destruction order from magistrates, who could be regarded as more malleable than a jury. Perhaps, following Doncaster and Kinsey he no longer felt safe, but had he chosen Bow Street he would almost certainly have found that one of the austere stipendiaries who sat there at the time would have heard the case, as happened when *Fanny Hill* made her appearance in the dock some years later.

It appears that Sir Theobald Mathew was himself in two minds about prosecuting the book. He did not like his department being used, as some saw it, as a censor; but this, of course, is what the Director was. In those days there were few Mrs Whitehouses to bring a private prosecution. If the Director did not, then no one would. Eventually Mathew bent to what he thought was public opinion. To this end he was probably fortified by the usual financial argument. One officer commented:

> For if the prosecution fails the obscene version will be offered openly and persuasively to every child or teenager who has three and sixpence in his or her pocket. That is a fearsome thought.[34]

Lord Hailsham had similar thoughts, telling his fellow peers he would prefer the book between boards at 30 shillings.[35] The fear accompanying indiscriminate distribution

---

[33] *Clifford*; see C.H. Rolph, *Books in the Dock*.
[34] Sir Thomas Hetherington, Upjohn Lecture 1979, quoted in Joshua Rozenberg, *The Case for the Crown*, p. 56.
[35] House of Lords Debates, 15 December 1960, 227 col 572.

of knowledge to the newly literate masses has always been a thread which has run through both American and English prosecutions. *Fanny Hill* was safe to be read when she cost two guineas; when she was reduced to paperback price she became a corrupter. In more recent times, Lord Hattersley offered similar comments about a paperback version of Salman Rushdie's *The Satanic Verses*.[36]

The *Lady Chatterley* trial is memorable if only for the often quoted remark of the prosecutor Mervyn Griffith-Jones, later the Common Serjeant at the Old Bailey: 'Is this a book you would even wish your wife or servant to read?' The answer was surely that one would not mind one's maidservant but not one's gamekeeper reading it. The nine male members of the jury clearly did not mind their wives reading it, and the three women on the jury must have thought it suitable for their husbands, because they all voted for an acquittal. From then on literature was effectively safe from prosecution, so sparing Nabokov's *Lolita* and J.P. Donleavy's *The Ginger Man* from the ordeal of trial by jury.

Fanny Hill was also safe from prosecution, but not from an application for destruction. This came in 1964 when 171 copies were seized from a Mr Ralph Gold's The Magic Shop in Tottenham Court Road. Perhaps unfortunately, there was a notice in the shop reading:

Just out – FANNY HILL. Banned in America. 3s 6d.

Immediately the publishers wrote to the Director, asking him to prosecute them rather than go for a destruction order. This would, of course, have given them the right of trial by jury in what was a climate becoming more liberal

[36] When *Mein Kampf* was republished in English in 1972 it was priced intentionally high so that it could not be suggested it was catering to a mass market. The paperback was again priced above average.

by the day. Sensibly the DPP was having none of this. Verdicts for the prosecution (apart from aberrationists such as the Doncaster bench) were then, and now, far more likely in a magistrates' court. He wrote back, some may think speciously, that because the publishers had acted in good faith a prosecution under s.2 of the Act would be oppressive. The defence of literary merit was still available, plus an appeal could be made to Quarter Sessions. What could be fairer than that? And so on 20 January 1964, before Sir Robert Blundell, the Chief Magistrate, *Fanny Hill* was finally brought to book.

Jeremy Hutchinson QC argued in vain that the price was the cause of the prosecution, and that no one had been called by the prosecution as to the book's merits. Sir Robert may not have been so voluble as was Sir Chartres Biron or Lord Goddard, but the result was the same. 'Doing the best I can in the circumstances, I have no hesitation in saying that the order should be made.'

It would have been symmetrical that the earliest of books which could claim at least some literary merit should be one of the last to come before the courts, but there was a trickle still to come. In 1967 the court confirmed that in *Last Exit to Brooklyn*, Hubert Selby's novel of a homosexual prostitute, 'the essence of the matter is moral corruption'.

The Court of Appeal set aside the conviction on the grounds that the trial judge had not put the 'aversion' defence to the jury. It had been urged by counsel that readers of the descriptions of homosexuality and drug-taking would be so put off by the detail in the book that in fact it would deter rather than corrupt.

In the *Oz* magazine trial four years later, the Court of Appeal quashed the conviction after the judge, Michael Argyle, suggested that 'obscene' might include 'repulsive', 'filthy', 'loathsome', 'indecent' and 'lewd'. In his time Lord Goddard might have agreed, but now the Lord

Chief Justice ruled that this was 'a very substantial and serious misdirection'.[37]

Over the years, however, negotiations between publisher and prosecutor could sometimes take place over restricted publication. For example Sir Archibald Bodkin, one of the less enlightened Directors, a man who was annoyed by saucy seaside postcards and who described a book by Freud as 'filth', threatened to prosecute Allen & Unwin unless they restricted its sale to lawyers, doctors and dons who were prepared to give their names and addresses when they bought a copy.[38] Towards the end of the era of seizing single books, the Director of Public Prosecutions of the time contemplated the prosecution of a pornographic Henry Miller novel which the great man had churned out at $1 a page. After negotiations with the publisher, no prosecution was instituted following an undertaking that it would be displayed in a wrapper and placed on a high shelf at the booksellers.

In October 1998 Dame Barbara Mills QC, the DPP, announced that she would not be prosecuting a book containing the sado-masochistic photographs of Robert Mapplethorpe, which had been seized the previous year

---

[37] The 1971 *Oz* obscenity trial had a curious sequel. In an article published in the *Spectator* in May 1995, the trial judge, Mr Michael Argyle, suggested one of the defendants Felix Dennis had imported drugs and sold them to children, and implied that he and his co-defendants had been behind threats to his life during the trial. Mr Dennis had by now become a multi-millionaire international publisher. In 1991 he had received the Marcus Morris Award from the Periodical Publishers' Association for his long-standing contribution to the industry.

On 25 July 1995 the *Spectator* apologised. Mr Dennis had never sold drugs to anyone and the protection for Judge Argyle was because of threats from someone outside the *Oz* trial. The magazine paid a substantial sum to the National Library for the Blind and a Down's Syndrome charity.

[38] Bodkin, who described *Ulysses* as 'indescribable filth', ordered the police to investigate F.R. Leavis, who had asked to be allowed to import a copy. In 1923, when British delegate to a League of Nations conference on the international trade in pornography, he was adamant that there should be no definition of pornographic material. It was his proud boast that he had secured the imprisonment of two people who had exchanged pornographic material between each other.

by Oxford police. She had decided that there would be no real likelihood of obtaining a conviction. That the police seized the book in the first place was strange; it had been in many public libraries since its publication and was also available in the House of Commons library. Probably the most surprising thing was that it took almost a year for her to reach the decision.

PART FIVE

The Other Way

21

—

Homosexuality

The early Christian Church was none too keen on sexual activity of any kind. If it had to take place then it must only be for the procreation of children, an attitude which has lasted until today. After all, that reason for marriage is the first named in the wedding ceremony.

In the Middle Ages the Ecclesiastical Courts had the right to try cases of sodomy or buggery, and persons found guilty could be handed over to the civil courts for burning at the stake. In 1533 Henry VIII's reformation of the Church made 'the abominable Vice of Buggery committed with mankind or beast' a felony punishable by death. The act also went on to punish 'welshmen vagabonds'. The death penalty was, however, rarely carried out. In 1631 the Earl of Castlehaven was executed following, amongst other things, his participation in the rape of his wife by his catamite. There was also a problem of the inheritance of land and in 1640 the Bishop of Waterford was hanged for sodomy, but this case too had political undertones. He was convicted on the evidence of his accomplice John Childe, who, on the scaffold, confessed to having given false evidence against the

Bishop. The almost-contemporary Reverend John Wilson, Vicar of Arlington near Eastbourne, was altogether more fortunate. He was merely deprived of his benefice.

Between 1559 and 1625 there were only four indictments for sodomy in the combined counties of Essex, Hertfordshire, Kent and Sussex. During more or less the same period, some 15,000 of the citizens of Essex alone were summoned for sex offences. Either not much was going on or, more likely, no one took too much notice of it. It is likely that since for part of that time the homosexual James I was on the throne, a generally more tolerant attitude was in the air.

By the end of the century, however, there were stirrings in the Christian breast and the Society for the Reformation of Manners was formed. One of those who fell foul of the new morality was Charles Hitchin, a City of London Marshal, a shining example of those who lead a double life. He was also a receiver of stolen property who taught the so-called Thief Taker General, Jonathan Wild, his trade. He was tried for sodomy in 1728 but, acquitted of the capital offence, was convicted of a misdemeanour, fined, sentenced to six months' imprisonment and a spell in the pillory. Two years later the Warden of Wadham College, Oxford, fled to France to avoid a prosecution. This did represent a change in public attitude. In the previous century sexual relations between tutors and their charges were almost the norm.

It was then that Major Thomas Weir, who had founded a Guard of militia in Edinburgh and had been presented with a mare, was alleged to have been so fond of the animal that he had carnal knowledge of it. The woman who gave evidence that she had seen the act was disbelieved and whipped for her pains, but later remorse overtook the major and he confessed that not only was she correct but that he had performed the act also with a cow and 'three species more'. To compound matters, he confessed to incest with his sister.

He was strangled at a stake between Edinburgh and Leith, while his poor sister was hanged.[1]

In the summer of 1726 Margaret Clap – who was alleged to have kept a 'molly-house' in Field Lane off Holborn – was imprisoned for a year, whilst Will Griffin, who had frequented the premises, was hanged. Five were charged, including Griffin, and three of the four found guilty were executed.[2] This was about par for the course. Molly-houses – which flourished at the time, frequented by working-class men who aped marriage and childbirth – needed to be suppressed.

The great reformer Sir Robert Peel carried through the abolition of the death penalty for many crimes in 1825, but buggery was not included. Indeed, while a respite of the death penalty was becoming more common for crimes less than murder, unnatural behaviour was now considered beyond the pale.

Boxing Day 1833 saw the execution in Maidstone Gaol of a soldier named George Cropper who had been convicted at the previous Kent Assizes. Charles Pike had, fortunately for him, been acquitted. The *Maidstone Journal* reported with some relish that 'Cropper's offence and the clearness of the evidence at his trial precluded him from all hope of mercy'. The *Journal* was quite high-minded about him:

[He was] formerly a Catholic but some years since had abandoned himself to a most licentious course which commenced with Sabbath-breaking and drunkenness and ended in an ignominious death.

He was executed by William Chalcraft at 10 a.m. because

[1] William Roughead, *Twelve Scottish Trials*.
[2] *Select Trials of the Old Bailey 1720–1742* (1742) III, pp. 37–8.

it was feared there might be crowd trouble but in fact few turned out to watch, preferring to await the main event, which was the hanging of the 27-year-old labourer William Allen for rape. Now the crowd had grown to between seven and eight thousand and:

> Profane and obscene jokes were heard on every side and not a few persons were in a state of intoxication. Strange to say the greater part of the crowd consisted of women whose conduct evinced an utter want of feeling and decency; so much for the effect of example which it is alleged is intended to be produced by our frequent infliction of the penalty of Death![3]

Two years later John Smith and James Pratt must have passed a happy Christmas in Newgate awaiting their execution the next day. They were the only ones out of 17 men not reprieved earlier in the month. The others had committed a motley collection of crimes including theft, robbery and an attempted shooting.

> Yesterday John Smith (40) and James Pratt (30) expatiated their heinous offence by the forfeiture of their lives on the scaffold in front of Newgate. When sentenced to die at the last September Sessions the Recorder with his wonted zeal and humanity implored the prisoners to look for mercy only at a tribunal where upon sincere repentance all sins were forgiven since, in this country, mercy could not be expected to persons like them.
>
> Since their sentence both had been outwardly well

[3] *Maidstone Journal and Kentish Advertiser*, 31 December 1833.

behaved but they both, Pratt especially, seem to have had recourse to subterfuge instead of what God and their Country required – an open confession. So very fluctuating were they throughout that the Rev. Ordinary and his excellent assistant (Mr Baker) felt discouraged.[4]

On the eve of his execution Pratt was visited by a 'respectable Dissenting Minister who exhorted him to cover his sin'. Pratt was still apparently defiant, maintaining that 'not enough has been proved legally', but immediately after the man had left he confessed to a respited convict, Swan, that he had been lying. The good Swan had the minister called back and Pratt apparently made a full confession. It did him no good in this world.

Pratt and Smith must have been almost the last men to be executed for the crime because there are no records of any executions from 1836 onwards.

In fact after 1781, when both penetration and 'emission of seed' had to be proved, convictions let alone executions were on the decline with victims unwilling to admit the defendant had ejaculated inside them, preferring to give an account of a brave resistance.

This is a witness in the trial of George Duffus:

He forcibly entered my Body about an Inch, as near as I can guess but in struggling, I threw him off once more, before he made an Emission, and having thus forced him to withdraw he Emitted in his own Hand, and clapping it on the Tail of my Shirt, said 'Now you have it.'[5]

There is no doubt that the matter was taken seriously because when James Donally told the Honourable Charles

4 *Standard*, 27 November 1835; reprinted in *The Times*, 28 November 1835.
5 *Select Trials at the Old Bailey*, pp. 106–7, and see Richard Davenport-Hines, *Sex, Death and Punishment*, p. 79.

Fielding that unless he gave him a guinea he would bring him before the magistrates and accuse him of an unnatural offence, the court decided that this was the equivalent of highway robbery, which itself was a capital offence.

In 1817 the question arose as to whether oral sex constituted buggery and after Samuel Jacobs was convicted of forcing a seven-year-old boy to fellate him Lord Chief Baron Richards respited the execution so that the matter could be discussed with his fellow judges. Jacobs was fortunate. Their Lordships thought it could not, and he was pardoned.[6] In 1828 it was decided that it was no longer necessary to prove emission of seed during buggery to establish the offence.

The death penalty itself was abolished in 1861 (1889 in Scotland) being replaced by life imprisonment (with ten years' penal servitude for an attempt), but even this apparent leniency was causing some queasiness amongst regulators and worse there was no offence at all of sexual conduct between men short of sodomy. If there was any doubt that an offence needed to be created, this was dispelled by the case of Boulton and Park.

There were three great homosexual scandals, as well as a considerable number of lesser ones, in Victorian England. By the 1880s the Puritan brigade, wearing various cloaks, was out in force. Not only was heterosexual vice and particularly the trade in young girls to be suppressed, so was homosexual behaviour, which was becoming increasingly less discreet. The first of the scandals was that in 1870 of two homosexual transvestites, Ernest Boulton and Frederick William Park. Worse, it involved Lord Arthur Clinton, Member for Newark and third son of the fifth Duke of Newcastle.

Clinton lived in the same lodgings as Boulton and Park.

[6] *Samuel Jacobs* (1817) Russ & Ry. 331.

Unlike the two following scandals, there was no suggestion that these men were simply working-class prostitutes. Boulton, who had been encouraged by his mother from the age of six to dress as a girl and wait at their table as the maid, was the son of a stockbroker; Park, whose father was a Master in the Court of Common Pleas, was articled to a solicitor. Boulton, known as Stella and who had by accounts a fine soprano voice, was treated by Clinton as his wife – he had visiting cards printed 'Lady Arthur Clinton'. To show there was no jealousy, his Lordship was also on intimate terms with Park, who signed himself 'Fanny'.

Boulton and Park had been under police observation for some time when in April 1870 they were arrested leaving the Strand Theatre. Boulton was wearing a scarlet dress with white moiré antique petticoats and stays and false hair. Park was in dark green satin trimmed with black lace; he was wearing earrings. The police doctor, James Paul, was called and without waiting for a court order had them take their clothes off. Both had their bottoms examined and Paul found 'extreme dilation of the orifice' in Park's case and 'extreme dilation of the posterior and relaxed muscles' in that of Boulton. As is often the case, when the pair were examined by their own doctors no evidence of pedication was found and, perhaps more surprisingly since until recently prison doctors thought their duties lay more with the prosecution, J.R. Gibson, the surgeon to Newgate Gaol, examined them and found no evidence that they had been buggered.

Held in custody overnight, the next morning they appeared at Bow Street charged with frequenting the Strand Theatre with intent to commit a felony. Bail was refused. The preliminary evidence was that Clinton and Boulton had met a man named Cox in a City public house, where, after a champagne luncheon, Cox had kissed Boulton believing him to be a woman. Later Cox had been informed of Boulton's real sex and had met him in Evans's

Coffee House in Covent Garden, where he had, according to his evidence, exclaimed, 'You damned set of infernal scoundrels, you ought to be kicked out of this place.'[7]

Unfortunately the case produced a high mortality rate amongst its players. Cox never made it to the witness-box at the Old Bailey; nor did Lord Arthur Clinton, who died on 18 June 1870 following an attack of scarlet fever, reach the dock – by then he had been named in the indictment along with John Safford Fiske, the United States consular representative at Leith.

The trial commenced on 9 May 1871 before the Lord Chief Justice, Lord Cockburn, and unsurprisingly was the entertainment centre of London for the next six days. The defendants could not at the time go into the witness-box to give evidence on their own behalf but the prosecution had, of its own making, considerable difficulties. All the defendants were homosexuals, but there was no actual evidence that they had broken the law. The felony specified in the indictment was buggery but, despite affectionate letters between the accused, there was no evidence that it had taken place. Trotting round in drag was not evidence of a felony either and Louis Hurt, another in the indictment, had even written to Boulton disapproving of his cross-dressing and refusing to go to Derby with him if he persisted in appearing in women's clothing.

Cockburn did not like the way the indictment was drawn. The form it took, that of conspiracy, allowed evidence against one being used to the detriment of the others. He was of the opinion that if the evidence amounted to anything it amounted to the commission of the offence, and the defendants should have been tried separately.

I am clearly of opinion that where the proof is intended

[7] Evans's Coffee House is the model for the Cave of Harmony in H.W.M. Thackeray's *The Newcombes*.

to be submitted to a jury, it is not the proper course to charge the parties with conspiring to commit it, for that course manifestly operates unfairly and unjustly and oppressively against the parties concerned.

Despite his Lordship's thoughts on the subject, the practice of putting a conspiracy charge on the indictment in cases involving homosexual behaviour continued for the next hundred years.

It may have been as well that the defendants could not give evidence. The high water of many a defence case is the moment when the accused goes in the witness-box and so faces cross-examination. Boulton's mother and Park's father did, however, tell the court of their offsprings' interest in amateur dramatics. Cockburn had many a harsh word for the police, whom he believed had overstepped their authority. As for Dr Paul, had he examined 'two strong instead of effeminate men he might have met with summary punishment for such unwarrantable conduct'. The judge summed up in the defendants' favour. 'Was there not a solution consistent with innocence'? The jury thought so because they took less than an hour to acquit. The verdict was greeted by cries of 'Bravo!' Boulton fainted. *The Times* next day praised the verdict.

It was not without a certain sense of relief that we record this morning the failure of a prosecution which nothing but a strong conviction would have justified the Government in instituting. THE QUEEN v. BOULTON AND OTHERS is a case in which a verdict for the Crown would have been felt at home, and received abroad, as a reflection on our national morals, yet which, for that very reason, could not be hushed up after popular rumour had once invested it with so grave a complexion.

Now that justice has been satisfied and the whole

story thoroughly sifted, the verdict of the jury should be accepted as clearing all the defendants of the odious guilt imputed to them.

Not everyone felt quite that way, and one of the more inspired of limericks was soon doing the rounds:

> There was an old person of Sark
> Who buggered a pig in the dark;
> The swine in surprise
> Murmured 'God Blast your eyes,
> Do you take me for Boulton or Park?[8]

The enlightened Henry Labouchère provided the answer – if not to the pig's question, to the problem about male misbehaviour not amounting to sodomy. The amendment which bears his name was tucked into the Criminal Law Amendment Act 1885, an Act otherwise wholly devoted to the protection of girls and young women. For defilement – i.e. carnal knowledge not amounting to rape – of a girl under 13, the penalty was a maximum of life or penal servitude for not less than five years, or up to two years in prison with hard labour. Carnal knowledge of a girl above 13 but under 16 carried up to two years with or without hard labour. If a person under 16 was found guilty, the penalty was a whipping plus a spell in a reformatory for not less than two and no more than five years. Personation of a husband for sexual intercourse was made a specific offence, whilst in Part II brothel-keeping attracted £20 and/or up to three months for a first offence; £40 and/or six months for a second; and the additional requirement of the provision of recognisances and sureties for a third or subsequent offence.

---

[8] *The Times*, 16 May 1871; for an account of the case see William Roughead, 'Pretty Fanny's Way; or the Importance of Being Ernest' in *Bad Companions*, pp. 149–83.

Not, many might think, legislation designed to stamp hard on the classier brothel-keeper's toes, but one which might make the lesser fry think one and a half times.

Then at the end of the first Part of the Bill came the notorious s.11:

> Any male person who, in public or private, commits, or is a party to the commission of, or procures or attempts to procure the commission by any male person of, any act of gross indecency with another male person, shall be guilty of a misdemeanour, and being convicted of thereof shall be liable at the discretion of the court to be imprisoned for any term not exceeding two years, with or without hard labour.

Labouchère's amendment, from its early days regarded as a Blackmailer's Charter, was passed in a sparsely attended House in the early hours of an August morning on the eve of the summer recess; the implication is that it was slipped in when everyone was either out or dozing, but in fact this does not seem to be correct. Labouchère had taken soundings from on high. The 1861 Act was not being enforced with any regularity. It was just another example of the pious perjury by which judges and juries avoided convicting in cases which carried the death penalty for minor offences. What Labouchère did was to create a more acceptable penalty.[9]

He addressed the Commons on 6 August to move his amendment and immediately gave way to Mr Wharton, who wanted to know whether the clause was within the scope of the Bill as 'it dealt with a totally different class

---

[9] One example of a reluctance to convict was in a case of theft of an object valued at more than five shillings. Juries would return verdicts that the goods stolen were of a slightly lesser value, so avoiding the death penalty or transportation for the thief.

For an assessment of the causes and effects of the amendment see F.B. Smith, 'Labouchère's Amendment to the Criminal Law Amendment Act' in *Historical Studies* 17.

of offence to that with which the Bill is directed'. The Speaker ruled that, 'At this stage of the Bill, anything can be introduced into it by leave of the House.' Suggesting a penalty of one year, Labouchère then spoke for literally a few moments, concluding:

> I do not think it necessary to discuss the proposal at any length, as I understand Her Majesty's Government are willing to accept it. I therefore leave it for the House and Government to deal with as may be thought best.

It was Sir Henry James, the former Liberal Attorney-General, who moved the penalty be doubled to two years. From the time Labouchère rose the debate, if it can be called that, on the amendment is recorded in Hansard at slightly under 500 words, which at a speaking rate of 120 words a minute works out at around four minutes. The following day the Bill received a third reading in the Commons and was then sent to the Lords, where it was effectively rubber-stamped.

One school of thought regards the section as 'the weapon of persecution of Oscar Wilde and many others'.[10] Others, less charitably but perhaps more accurately, thought that in Wilde's case at any rate, given the state of the law, he was entirely the author of his own misfortunes.

Just who was Labouchère, and how did his amendment get through Parliament in the first place? He was the editor of the magazine *Truth* and the radical Member of Parliament for Northampton. Before their marriage he lived for some time with Henrietta Hodson, sometimes described as an actress but more properly as a burlesque artiste, whose father kept the Duke's Arms at Westminster. When addressing election meetings, some of the heckling

---

[10] For example Trevor Fisher, *Scandal*, p. 138.

at Labouchère would consist of "'ow's 'Enrietta?' Tiring of this, he opened his address one evening by saying, 'I wish to convey to you all the gratifying intelligence that Henrietta is quite well.' His premarital intimacy seems to have done him no harm at all. Indeed he was quite frank about his gambling, duelling, brothel visiting and general bad behaviour. *Truth* was a crusading magazine which is credited with 'exposing more schemes and scandals per hundred pages than any other organ'. It was also an extremely risky operation. In 1884 Labouchère was acquitted of criminal libel on a technicality after suggesting that the Duke of Vallombrosa had made his fortune by sending back the corpses of dead French soldiers to the French army as edible meat.

Said to be the finest wit since Sheridan, he was regarded as a powerful speaker, with his attack on the Government over the handling of the Cleveland Street Brothel Scandal thought to be 'one of the finest speeches ever delivered in the Commons, a masterpiece of eloquence and analysis which took him one hour precisely'.[11]

Labouchère was a man able to inspire the hatred of diametrically opposed personalities. 'That viper Labouchère,' said the Prince of Wales. 'That horrible lying Labouchère,' said the Prince's mother. This latter was not surprising; in his later political career Labouchère obtained a place on the Parliamentary Committee to vet royal expenditure – nothing is new – and proposed that Her Majesty could provide for her grandchildren by putting up Osborne, Balmoral or Sandringham for sale. The Government spokesman misguidedly suggested that since no one could afford the upkeep the properties were unsaleable. Labouchère responded by offering to write a cheque there and then for Osborne, the Queen's favourite residence. He considered it both a fair price and a sound investment.

[11] For an account of the speech and its ramifications, see Colin Simpson, Lewis Chester and David Leitch, *The Cleveland Street Affair*, p. 172 *et seq.*

When Gladstone was returned to power in the August of 1892, Labouchère hoped to obtain Cabinet rank. The antipathy shown to him by the Queen kept him from office and, while the Prime Minister, Gladstone, would have allowed him to head the Washington legation, which was his second choice, the Earl of Rosebery vetoed it. Labouchère made many powerful enemies.

It is recounted that as he lay dying in his villa outside Florence, Labouchère awoke to find that a small fire had broken out in the corner of his room. 'Surely not so soon,' he is alleged to have said.[12]

Why did Labouchère suddenly propose the amendment? One suggestion was made by the journalist Frank Harris, whose thoughts and views can never be regarded as wholly reliable but who was certainly *au courant* with the people and politics involved. He believed that by his amendment Labouchère intended to sabotage the whole Bill.

> . . . inflamed, it is said, with a desire to make the law ridiculous, gravely proposed that the section be extended so as to apply to people of the same sex who indulged in familiarities or indecencies. The Puritan faction had no logical objection to the extension and it became the law of the land.[13]

At the time of the Wilde and Taylor trial Labouchère explained why he had inserted his amendment into the Act, if that is a felicitous way of putting it:

> . . . in order to render it possible for the law to take cognisance of proceedings like theirs. I took the clause *mutatis mutandis* from the French Code. As I had drafted it the

---

[12] This and other stories about Labouchère appear in J.B. Booth, *Old Pink 'Un Days*.
[13] Quoted by F.B. Smith *supra*.

maximum sentence was seven years. The then Home
Secretary and Attorney General, both most experienced
men, suggested to me that in such cases convictions are
always difficult and that it would be better were the
maximum to be two years. Hence the insufficiency of
the severest sentence that the law allows.

Whatever is the case, seldom can such an amendment have
caused so much distress and pain over the years.

Five years after the amendment came the Cleveland
Street Brothel Scandal, stemming from the arrest of
Charles Thomas Swincow, Percival Wright, the appropriately named Henry Newlove, and Charles Thickbroom,
who worked in the Post Office at St Martin's-le-Grand –
who all supplemented their income from male prostitution.
It was thought at first that one of the boys had income from
the Receiver-General's Department, and Charles Swincow
was asked how he could have as much as 18 shillings in his
possession. Pressed for an explanation, he said it had not
been stolen but had been earned by going with men at
19 Cleveland Street. He had, he said, been persuaded by
Henry Newlove first to 'behave indecently' together and
then to go to the male brothel in Cleveland Street run by
Charles Hammond which catered for the nobility.

So far so vague, but when questioned Newlove said that
a visitor to the brothel was Lord Arthur Somerset, a Major
in the Blues and Extra Equerry to the Prince of Wales.
Somerset approached the up-and-coming and very suspect
solicitor Arthur Newton to act for him. The lawyer's part
in the affair was to try to get potential witnesses against
Somerset out of the country.

It is curious that a young man such as Newton should
have come to the notice of the high and the mighty so
early in his career. Some solicitors have, for good or bad
reasons, come to be the repository of secrets of their social

betters. Sir George Lewis was one and, a half-century later, Arnold Goodman was another. Just how Newton achieved his position is not clear, but he was definitely a man with whom to be reckoned. Early on in the inquiry, when things were escalating and it became apparent that it would be a far-ranging one, he went to the Assistant Director of Public Prosecutions, Hamilton Cuffe, to warn him that if Somerset were to be prosecuted another name would appear: it would be that of Prince Albert Victor, Duke of Clarence and Aviemore – known as Eddy – the eldest son of the Prince of Wales and grandson of Queen Victoria. It may be that Newton was exercising a spot of blackmail on behalf of his client – later in his career there were suggestions that he was not averse to the same for financial reasons. There may have been nothing in the suggestion, but it was sufficient for Cuffe to inform Sir Augustus Stephenson and so on up the chain to Lord Salisbury, the Prime Minister.

It was never clearly established that poor Eddy ever visited a homosexual brothel; he had enough problems already. He was engaged to Princess May of Teck, whose trousseau had already been delivered when her previous fiancé died of pneumonia, in 1892. He was already infected with both syphilis and gonorrhoea, both in a communicable stage.[14]

Even though he had offered substantial terms – £50 cash, a new suit of clothes and £1 a week to run for three years, as well as their passage to Australia – Newton failed

---

[14] The Duke of Clarence is one of the more exotic suspects for the mantle of Jack the Ripper. However, to fit him into the picture it must be assumed that he did not die in the flu epidemic of 1892, but was kept in an insane asylum by his family from which he either escaped or was released at strategic intervals during which he stalked Whitechapel. For those who wish to examine the theory, see Dr T.E.A. Stowell, 'Jack The Ripper – A Solution?' in the *Criminologist*, November 1970. Princess May did much better for herself; she changed her name to Mary and married George V. The gentry were an exotic collection in those days. The Marquess of Waterford, for example, whose wife was Lord Arthur Somerset's sister, was himself suspected, albeit without much evidence, of being the notorious attacker of women 'Spring-heeled Jack'. See M.J. Nye, 'Spring-heeled Jack' in *New Law Journal*, 16 September 1994.

in his efforts to get the boys who were to be prosecution witnesses to go abroad. What he was able to do was to warn Somerset that a warrant for his arrest was imminent. His Lordship left for France the next day and although he returned on 30 September 1889 and attended the funeral of his grandmother, his stay was short-lived. He left again on 18 October never to return, dying in Hyères on 26 May 1926.

As is often the case, it was the lower orders who suffered. Newlove received four months with hard labour in the House of Correction in September 1889; Swincow and Thickbroom were dismissed from the Post Office along with another boy, William Perkins. Hammond, the brothel-keeper, fled to America and settled in Seattle. The solicitor, Newton, received six weeks' imprisonment for conspiracy to corrupt, but he was not struck from the rolls and was soon back in legal society, popping up over the years acting for the famous and infamous and himself alike. Another who went to prison was Ernest Parke, editor of the evening paper the *North London Press*. He made the allegation that the Earl of Euston had patronised the brothel when in fact the noble lord had merely called in one day under the impression that he was to see some *poses plastiques* – not realising that the modelling, if any, would be carried out by young men. In January 1890, Parke drew 12 months for his mistake.

After the trials the mischievous Labouchère had a field day. On 28 February 1890, he alleged that the chief Government officers had conspired to defeat the course of justice by allowing Lord Arthur Somerset to escape to France; that the Government had helped Hammond flee to the United States; that Newlove and George Daniel Veck, another ex-Post Office employee who posed as a clergyman and who received nine months, had been given light sentences to buy their silence.

This brought the wrath of the Commons down on

Labouchère's head. In the ensuing row he called Lord
Rosebery a liar, refused to withdraw and was suspended.
With the suspension, such potential crisis for the Govern-
ment as there might have been blew away.[15]

At the time of the Wilde trial it was bruited that:

> A verdict of guilty would remove what appears to be a
> widespread impression that the judge and jury were got
> at in order to shield others of a higher status in life. –
> Sir Edward Hamilton.[16]

Lord Esher recorded that 'the Newmarket [horse racing]
scum say that . . . his insomnia was caused by terror of
being involved in the Wilde scandal.'[17]

There is some evidence that Lord Rosebery was bisexual, and he was said to have taken a great fancy to
Lord Alfred Douglas's eldest brother, Lord Drumlanrig,
whom he made his private secretary and then ennobled
in England so that he could represent the Government in
the Lords.

On 18 October 1894 Drumlanrig – then a guest at
a shooting party at Quantock Lodge near Bridgewater,
Somerset – was found dead from a gunshot wound. He
had, it appears, left the main shoot to look for a winged
bird. A single shot was heard and the other members of
the party found him killed by a shot which according to
the medical evidence

> . . . had entered the mouth, fracturing the lower side of
> the jaw on the right side, and passed through the roof

---

[15] The detailed answers of the Director of Public Prosecutions, Sir Augustus
Stephenson, to Labouchère's comments make for unconvincing reading. It is
the usual story of 'not knowing' and playing one department off against the
other. Public Records Office DPP 1/95/6.
[16] Quoted in R. Davenport-Hines, *Sex, Death and Punishment*, p. 263.
[17] ibid., 264.

of the mouth fracturing the lower jaw on the left hand
side. Death must have been instantaneous.[18]

The verdict at the inquest was 'accidental death', but there
were rumours that Drumlanrig killed himself rather than be
exposed in a homosexual affair with Lord Salisbury. Earlier
he had apparently proposed to Alix Ellis, his hostess's niece,
and had been accepted.

His father, Marquess of Queensbury, was distraught.
He had already sent letters to Rosebery, Gladstone and
the Queen and had followed Rosebery to Bad Homburg,
where he was taking the waters. After he had gone to
Rosebery's hotel and threatened to horsewhip him, and
the Prince of Wales – who was also there – had failed to
calm things down, the aid of the local police commissioner
was enlisted and '. . . in consequence of the entertainment
I had with him, found it advisable to part this morning with
the 7 o'clock train to Paris'.

Rosebery wrote to Queen Victoria that he was unhappy
at being 'pursued by a pugilist of unsound mind'.

Queensberry, convinced that what he regarded as the bad
blood in his sons was coming through his brother-in-law, Sir
Alfred Montgomery, wrote a letter which was the precursor
to his fateful card to Wilde. This time the semi-literate
and extremely wealthy Marquess penned one of those
letters you dread receiving because you know the writer
is unbalanced.

Sir,
Now that the first flush of this catastrophe and grief is
passed, I write to tell you it is a JUDGEMENT on the
whole LOT OF YOU. Montgomerys, The Snob Queers
like Roseberry [sic] and certainly Christian hypocrite

[18] B. Roberts, *The Mad, Bad Line*, pp. 256–7.

Gladstone the whole lot OF YOU. Set my son up
against me indeed and make bad blood BETWEEN us,
may it devil on your own heads that he is gone to his
REST and the quarrel not made up between him and
myself. It's a gruesome message: If you and his Mother
did not set up this business with that cur and Jew friend
[?] LIAR Rosebery as I always thought – At any rate she
[Lady Rosebery] acquiesced in it, which is just as bad . . .
I smell a Tragedy behind all this and have already GOT
WIND of a more STARTLING ONE . . . I am on the
right track to find out what happened. CHERCHEZ LA
FEME, when these things happen. I have already heard
something that quite accounts FOR IT ALL.
Queensberry.

Sensibly, Montgomery declined to be drawn.[19]

Oscar Wilde was not so sensible. His rise and fall has
been recorded countless times and so really needs only
the briefest outline. His supporters blame Labouchère,
but much of the blame must fall on his own shoulders.
Along with the sin of arrogance, more importantly he
would not listen to advice. He fell foul of the formidable
Marquess over his relationship with Lord Alfred Douglas.
On 28 February 1895 Queensberry left a calling card at
the Albemarle Club which described him as 'posing as a
somdomite' (sic) and ill-advisedly Wilde sued. It is not
clear whether the misspelling was another example of the
Marquess's illiteracy or whether he was trying to be clever

[19] John Sholto Douglas, Marquess of Queensberry, is also remembered for providing
the Queensberry Rules of professional boxing, the successor to bare-knuckle
fighting. Immensely wealthy, he quarrelled with all his sons, being brought to
Marlborough Street police court in 1895 for brawling with his son and heir
Percy, whom he referred to as 'this squirming skunk Percy'. Shortly before the
Wilde case he had been ejected from the stalls of the Globe Theatre, where he
was objecting to Tennyson's play *The Promise of May*. In the piece the villain
enters the heroine's bedroom. The ambiguous passage which upset the Marquis
was, 'She must be gone! Her bed has not been slept in. Her little chamber's
empty.' He died in 1899.

and lay down a technical defence to any action. In any event, it provoked Wilde into one of the most disastrous libel actions ever.

He abandoned his claim against Queensberry after he had been repeatedly trapped by the Marquess's Counsel, Sir Edward Carson, into damaging admissions, and faced a battery of witnesses against him. Despite advice and pleas from his friends to flee immediately to France, he stood his ground, and the result was ruin. A few hours later he was arrested at the Cadogan Hotel, Knightsbridge. The jury at his first criminal trial disagreed, but on his conviction after the second trial he was sentenced to two years' penal servitude. Immediately on his release he left for France, dying in Paris in 1900.

Douglas wrote in a French magazine in 1896 that, at the time of the second Wilde trial Rosebery – who had succeeded Gladstone as Prime Minister – had told Herbert Henry Asquith, then Home Secretary, that if the Wilde prosecution was dropped after the disagreement of the first jury this would create a damaging impression at the polls in the next election, almost ensuring a Liberal defeat. He also alleged that the Liberal party contained a number of other homosexuals and that the 'maniacs of virtue' threatened to launch further prosecutions.

Carson took no part in the prosecution of Wilde but after the jury disagreed he is said to have gone to Frank Lockwood, the Solicitor-General, and asked whether it was really necessary to have a retrial. The answer, apparently, was that the Government feared it could not stop one because it would be said that the prosecution had been abandoned in fear that prominent people were being protected.[20]

Over the years a number of politicians fell from grace,

[20] For an account of the Queensberry Trial see H. Montgomery Hyde, *Carson*, pp. 127–45.

resigning, fleeing or finding themselves in prison for homosexual offences, and usually in the latter case the trial judge was able to offer a few words of disapproval to send them on their way.

In May 1891, Edward Samuel Wesley de Cobain – who, as might be expected from his name, was the son of a Methodist minister – fled to Boulogne. He was the Member for East Belfast and had become involved with a forger and blackmailer named Heggie. He had been advised by a friend to go abroad for his health and when he was questioned he said he had taken the suggestion literally. A warrant was issued for his arrest and the Speaker demanded he return and explain his behaviour. Instead he went to America for 18 months, returning in 1893, when he was charged with ten counts of gross indecency with five people for which he received a year's hard labour.

The downfall of many a person – politician, actor and the common man alike – has come through the Vagrancy Act 1898, which made it an offence for a man 'persistently to solicit or importune in a public place for immoral purposes'. Originally only an offence which could be heard in a magistrates' court and carrying six months' imprisonment, it was upgraded by the Criminal Law Amendment Act 1912 to being one which could be heard at Quarter Sessions, later the Crown Court and now carrying a two-year penalty. The idea behind both Acts was an effort to control the spread of heterosexual prostitution. This was a time of the world-wide White Slave traffic paranoia and whilst (unlike the Labouchère amendment) there was considerable debate in both Houses, much of it was devoted to the rights and wrongs of flogging women. There was no apparent thought at the time that either of the Acts would be used to control homosexual men cottaging and cruising.

Just to what extent homosexuality was rife in the Liberal hierarchy of the time will never be known, but two contemporaries of Lord Rosebery, albeit some years later in 1922, bit the dust. Viscount Harcourt, known as Lulu, who improved the amenities of the House of Commons and who has a room named after him there, was found dead in his bed in Brook Street. He had taken an overdose. The verdict of the coroner's jury was misadventure, but it was generally thought that his arrest was imminent. The object of his attentions was said to be Edward James, whose mother was reputed to be the natural daughter of King Edward VII. According to James, the Viscount had tried to seduce him at Harcourt's country home. Foolishly he had told his mother, adding that the Viscount was a 'hideous and horrible old man'. His mother spread the story to polite society and after that it was only a matter of time.[21]

The other of Rosebery's contemporaries was William Lygon, Earl Beauchamp, then the Lord Warden of the Cinque Ports, who lived in Walmer Castle, where it was suggested he had been disporting himself too regularly with various local youths and fishermen. In 1931 he fled abroad rather than wait for the arrest which, it was said, was required by King George V.[22]

During the Second World War the only Member of Parliament to be prosecuted was Sir Paul Latham, the 36-year-old millionaire and Conservative MP for Scarborough and Whitby, who was court-martialled on charges of improper behaviour with three gunners and a civilian whilst he was serving with the 70th Searchlight Regiment, Royal Artillery. When he heard of the inquiries he threw himself off his motor-cycle and so added the charge of attempted suicide to his troubles. He served 18 months of a two-year sentence.

---

[21] Edward James, *Swans Reflecting Elephants*, pp. 26–8.
[22] He died in New York seven years later. On his flight his portrait – painted when he was Leader of the Liberal Party in the House of Lords – was removed from the walls of the National Liberal Club. It was restored, so it is said, on the instructions of Winston Churchill.

If prison was thought to be a cure, the authorities were sadly mistaken in Latham's case. The author James Lees-Milne remembers seeing him shortly after he was released from prison and being told by him that he was still obsessed by sex and was visiting the most dangerous place. Latham also told him that after his conviction he had never been insulted.

It may be that there was a change in the overall attitude of the British public. Certainly the War had altered attitudes to authority and to sex. Wives of servicemen had taken lovers during the War and divorce was on the increase. Perhaps this change also reflected itself in a slightly more tolerant attitude towards homosexuals. Perhaps the public was beginning to understand that social contact with homosexuals did not mean contamination and that pederasty did not necessarily equal paedophilia, although it must be admitted that the word was not in daily usage. However, it was not the same with politicians, led by the then Home Secretary, Sir David Maxwell-Fyffe, who conducted something of a witch-hunt in part on the ostensible grounds of national security.

In 1953 came the case which can actually mark the shift in public opinion and the long road to the reforming Sexual Offences Act 1957. Lord Montagu of Beaulieu, one time bit-part Hollywood actor and vintage car collector, together with his friend the film director Kenneth Hume, was charged with indecently assaulting Boy Scouts who acted as guides at Palace House, Beaulieu, when it was open to the public. The charges had come about following Montagu's report to the police of the loss of a camera.

He appeared at Winchester Assizes in December 1953 on charges of committing an unnatural offence and indecent assault. Much of the case turned on entries in Montagu's passport, which he said had been tampered with to assist the prosecution's case. The judge accepted that it had been altered, but it was never established who was responsible. In fact the jury seems to have regarded the passport as a red herring because Montagu was acquitted of the more serious charge and the jury disagreed on the count of indecent assault. The Director of Public Prosecutions decided that there should be a retrial of both defendants on the minor charge.

Three weeks later Michael Pitt-Rivers (Montagu's cousin) and the *Daily Mail* journalist Peter Wildeblood were arrested and charged with indecency offences with two RAF servicemen, Edward McNally and John Reynolds, at Beaulieu and also at the Pitt-Rivers estate in Dorset. They appeared with Montagu at Winchester Assizes in March 1954, when much of the evidence was that the three men had lavished hospitality on the lower orders in order to seduce them. If that is correct they were easily seduced. The 'lavish hospitality' seems to have been cider and meals cooked on the stove in the hall of Wildeblood's Kensington flat.

The airmen had not been 'corrupted' by the three defendants, said the Crown; they were already perverts. McNally had a friend, a male nurse, whom he described as 'my husband', and on their own confession they were involved in over 20 other homosexual affairs. Neither they nor the partners in these escapades were prosecuted, and it is impossible to see the case as anything but one designed to bring down Montagu and those who stood too close to him.

He had not stood trial again over the Boy Scouts but the prejudicial publicity – this was well before the days when a judge could order that there be no reporting of the case – must have been enormous. Montagu received 12 months and the others 18. But the crucial aspect of the case is what happened immediately after the trial. The crowd outside the court booed McNally and Reynolds and, crowding around the car in which the defendants were being taken to prison, began giving them the thumbs-up signs, clapping and calling out words of encouragement.[23]

Newspapers also began to question whether the verdict was in line with public opinion. In its editorial 'Law and Hypocrisy', the *Sunday Times* commented:

> The case for the reform of the law as to acts committed in private between adults is very strong. The case for an authoritative enquiry into it is overwhelming.[24]

Now politicians, led by the bisexual Sir Robert Boothby, took up the strain. The previous month he had urged that a Royal Commission be set up, claiming that the law was unevenly applied across the country, that it left men open to the misery of blackmail and it was unfair and ineffective. The Church of England Moral Welfare Committee's conclusion was that such behaviour was sinful but it should not be treated as a crime. Perhaps their support for a change in the law had at least to do with self-interest, since over the years the trickle of gay clergymen who had declared themselves has become, if not a torrent, at least a stream.[25]

---

[23] For an account of the case see Peter Wildeblood, *Against the Law*. Lord Montagu later married and became Chairman of the Historic Buildings and Monuments Commission.

[24] *Sunday Times*, 28 March 1954. See also for example *Sunday People*, 28 March 1954, and *Spectator*, 16 April 1954.

[25] The urbane and, for a time, influential Robert Boothby was a deeply flawed man. A committed gambler who resigned from the Food Ministry (where he had instituted a free milk ration for children) over allegations of impropriety in financial matters, he conducted a long-term affair with Dorothy Macmillan, the wife of Harold Macmillan, who would become the Prime Minister, and Boothby is thought to have fathered at least three children by the wives of other men. In the 1960s he was also in deep sexual hock to the East End gangsters the Kray Twins. He was able, however, with the assistance of the equally ambivalent Lord Goodman, to obtain a settlement of £40,000 from the *Daily Mirror* over allegations that he was consorting with the pair. It was yet another example of how the majesty and power of the law can be used to subvert the truth. For an account of his financial fall, see Matthew Parris, *Great Parliamentary Scandals*, pp. 111–17.

The Government prevaricated, suggesting that a Home Office departmental committee would be set up. It was too little, too late. On 19 May Earl Winterton initiated what was to be the first full-scale debate on the single issue of homosexuality.

If people thought that the noble Earl would be taking a liberal stance, they were immediately disabused. He spoke of 'this filthy, disgusting, unnatural vice'. All his 50 years in public life enabled him to dismiss the arguments for legalising homosexuality. He was not wholly supported by his colleagues. Lord Jowett pointed out that some 95 per cent of blackmail cases were the result of homosexual activity; but the Bishop of Southall, showing the dangers of speaking off the cuff, clearly did not recognise that deep down a goodly, if not Godly, number of the clergy were secret cassock-lifters.

> Once a people lets its ultimate convictions go, then there can be no stopping half way, and the whole moral bottom is in danger of falling out of a society.

It was perhaps ironic that the Government Committee on Homosexual Offences and Prostitution established in 1954 was chaired by Sir John Wolfenden, then Vice-Chancellor of Reading University, whose son Jeremy was a flagrant homosexual. Wolfenden *fils* claimed he received a letter from his father at the time informing him of the appointment, which included the lines:

> I have only two requests to make of you at the moment.
> 1) That we stay out of each other's way for the time being; 2) That you wear rather less make-up.[26]

Sir John having been approached by Maxwell-Fyffe, rather

---

[26] Quoted in Sebastian Faulks, *The Fatal Englishman*, p. 242.

appropriately the first meeting took place in the Home
Secretary's sleeping compartment on a London-bound train
with Maxwell-Fyffe wearing an overcoat over his underwear
or pyjamas – just the scenario which would appeal to an itinerant policeman and later court. Wolfenden's appointment,
along with those of his Committee members, was announced
four months later.

It was during their tenure that the prosecutions for
indecency between males reached their highest levels, with
the record of 2,331 being set in 1955, just under half of
whom went to prison. It was also during this time that
Wildeblood's account of his life as a homosexual and his
trial in particular was published to great acclaim. His thesis
was that the grinding down of homosexuals was a political
throwback to the anti-Communist campaign of Senator
McCarthy, and that the campaign against them was to weed
them out of Government positions. Three years earlier the
spies Guy Burgess and Donald Maclean had fled to Russia.
Homosexuals equalled potential blackmail victims.

> The problems of homosexuality amongst Government
> officials . . . is of growing magnitude. These people
> some of whom occupy important positions are obviously
> a target for blackmailers.[27]

The Committee reported in September 1957. One question
to be answered was exactly what was the homosexual
population of England and Wales. As for America, Kinsey
had found (para. 38) that four per cent of adult white males
were exclusively homosexual after the onset of adolescence,
10 per cent of the white male population were more or less
exclusively homosexual for three years between the ages of

[27] Lt-Col. Marcus Lipton, MP for Brixton, who would later raise the question
of the Krays and Lord Boothby, quoted in the Sydney *Sunday Telegraph*, 25
October 1953.

16 and 65 and 37 per cent of the whole male population had had some sort of homosexual experience to the point of orgasm between adolescence and old age. Sweden seemed to have been one per cent exclusively homosexual. The figures seemed both high and low to witnesses to Wolfenden.[28]

There is really no better example of the working of the Blackmailer's Charter than a case cited in the Wolfenden Report. A. (49) met B. (35) in a cinema. They went to A.'s flat and committed buggery and continued to do so for seven years. B. then began demanding money, and over a three-month period obtained £40. A. complained to the police and the Director of Public Prosecutions recommended no action over the demanding with menaces but that both be charged with buggery. Each was charged with two specimen counts. Neither asked for matters to be taken into consideration. Neither had previous convictions. Each received nine months' imprisonment.[29]

As part of a pathetic little statement to the police A. had written:

> I sent the money because I thought from his letters that if I did not do so he would tell the people at the shop and where I live that I had had sexual intercourse with him.

The tenor of the report may be summed up by one paragraph:

> We do not think that it is proper for the law to concern itself with what a man does in private unless it can be shown to be contrary to the public good that the law ought to intervene in its function as guardian of that public good.

---

[28] Sir John Wolfenden, Report of the Committee on Homosexual Offences and Prostitution [(1957) Cmnd 247, London, HMSO].
[29] ibid., para. 112.

The Committee dismissed a number of beliefs as myths. Gone went the corruption of young boys argument; certainly homosexuality would have a bad effect on marriage, but so would lesbianism and adultery; the potential collapse of the British Empire to follow that of Rome and Greece did not appear to trouble the Committee.

Then, having rejected the corruption argument, the Committee thought twice. Perhaps, after all, it would be better if young men were protected whilst they were still unsure of their sexuality. The age of consent for homosexual offences in private should remain at 21. Not all Committee members agreed with the overall recommendations and James Adair commented:

> No one interested in the moral, physical or spiritual welfare of public life wishes to see homosexuality extending in its scope, but rather reduced in extent, or at least kept effectively in check. Existing homosexual trends and tendencies are currently the cause of much public concern and disgust.[30]

He, along with Dr Whitley, rather took the view that, in many cases, homosexuality was curable.

This was a view which persisted into the 1960s. Those charged with homosexual offences who could afford it could generally find a consultant psychiatrist who would recommend treatment at their hospital. Magistrates and judges were often keen to follow their recommendations. Whether treatment took place in anything but a nominal fashion once the defendant was out of court is a different matter entirely.

It was another long and, for homosexual campaigners, hard, ten years before the Wolfenden Committee's report

[30] *ibid*, para. 118.

became law. First and foremost, the Government did not think the time to be right to decriminalise homosexuality. Certainly the public was not yet prepared to accept it. The Government were correct. In 1963 a survey of 2,500 people showed that only 16 per cent supported the decriminalisation.

Those caught in police traps in public lavatories or by park keepers faced disgrace if they were politicians. Down went Labour MP William Field, fined £15 for importuning in a public lavatory, and Ian Harvey found with a guardsman in Hyde Park. In a way Harvey was fortunate. He pleaded to a breach of the park regulations and was fined £5, as was the guardsman, of whom his barrister said that 'as far as could be traced he was not addicted in any way' and had merely been 'too curious' as he returned to barracks after a visit to his fiancée. Harvey paid his fine. He was socially ostracised and resigned from the Carlton Club, but the Junior Carlton allowed him to retain his membership provided he did not set foot in the place for two years.[31]

Some gay Members of Parliament, notably Tom Driberg and Robert Boothby, survived unscathed. Generally speaking, problems only arose when men consorted with what were seen as the lower orders. Provided one's homosexuality was kept discreetly within one's social class, not too much was done about it. But step into the realms of hotel waiters, soldiers and rent boys and the press and the world fell on your head. It is amazing that both of them – particularly Driberg, who approached almost everything that moved – survived so long without being outed.[32]

[31] Harvey divorced and some years later published his memoirs, *To Fall Like Lucifer*, after which he became honorary president of the Conservative Group for Homosexual Equality. He died, a broken man, in 1987.

[32] I have the humiliating distinction of being possibly the only person met in a lavatory that Driberg did not importune. The occasion was when we both attended an inquest in West London and had a drink together afterwards. It may well be that, in the words of Oscar Wilde, I was 'far too ugly'.

Nevertheless, progress was being made and it is impossible to underestimate the part that television and radio played in gaining ground for shifting the public perception towards the acceptability of homosexuality. Until 1958 the Lord Chamberlain had forbidden plays with homosexual themes and now, provided they were not overtly proselytising, 'sincere and serious' portrayals of homosexuality on the stage and screen were permitted. In the early stages, as a general rule the homosexual had to appear to be an ordinary, even superior, member of the public. One such was the 1961 portrayal by Dirk Bogarde, in real life himself the idol of schoolgirls, in *Victim*. In the film he played a pinstriped barrister whose marriage and professional reputation become at risk from blackmailers. In the same year, Murray Melvin played an overt homosexual in what was regarded at the time as a 'kitchen sink' drama, *A Taste of Honey*, when he befriended the pregnant and unwed (another scandal) Rita Tushingham. The year before we had two films with Peter Finch and Robert Morley respectively as Oscar Wilde, but since both adhered to history and the dramatist obtained his comeuppance there was little problem with them. It was like a Western that year: the Indian or the villain had to die or be arrested in the last reel.

Television played its part, with an episode in 1963 of the enormously popular *Z Cars* in which a homosexual couple were blackmailed. A little later, in the stage play and later film *Boys in the Band*, which portrayed a 'queers' party' in progress, the one decent, pipe-smoking, straight character, to whom the general public relate, is revealed in the denouement as being homosexual.

In the enormously popular radio programme *Round the Horn*, two overtly gay characters named Julian and Sandy were forerunners to show that homosexuals were not necessarily mere figures of fun or to be feared, but people with feelings and certainly not threatening to our wives and children.

There are two opposing views of the Sexual Offences Act 1967. The first is that it legalised gay male sexual activity. The other is that it decriminalised it to a limited extent, and it is certainly possible to have sympathy with that view. Gay male sex became a non-criminal offence provided it was committed in private by not more than two people and that both parties had attained the age of 18. What is private has always been a bone of contention. It is certainly not a locked cubicle of an otherwise empty lavatory provided the public have access. Gays also argue that a bandstand in the middle of a deserted park at midnight is about as private a place as could be found. It is a view which has not always been shared by the police and the courts. Privacy was not a subjective test.

To determine privacy, said one judge:

> You look at all the surrounding circumstances, the time of night, the nature of the place including such matters as lighting and you consider further the likelihood of a third person coming upon the scene.[33]

Two years after the Sexual Offences Act 1967, one of the key events in the long road to the general acceptance of homosexual activity came on 28 June 1969. Since it was a raid on the Stonewall Inn at 523 Christopher Street in Greenwich Village by the New York police, its immediate relevance to the U.K. was not immediately apparent. It was not an attractive bar. Morty Manford, a lawyer who subsequently worked in the New York State Attorney-General's office, recalled it as:

> A dive. It was shabby, and the glasses in it weren't

[33] *Reakes* [1974] Crim LR 615.

particularly clean. The place attracted a very eclectic crowd. Patrons included every type of person, some transvestites, a lot of students, younger people, older people, businessmen.[34]

It was owned by three Mafia figures – Mario, Zucchi and Fat Tony Luccia. It professed to be a bottle club and sported a doorman who controlled the incomers. Three dollars bought two vouchers for drinks at weekends. Sporadically there was a go-go boy dancing in a cage over the bar. Generally raids, which were telegraphed to the owners in advance, had taken place in a fairly stylised way with an early evening roust, a few arrests and then business as usual by the time trade really picked up about midnight.

This time, however, the raid took place a little after 1 a.m. when the bar was in full swing.

The raid was not a success. The late Sixties were the years of student protests over the Vietnam War in America and over civil rights there, in France and (to a lesser extent) in England, but it could never have been expected that homosexuals would take a stand. But take a stand they did. Five days later confrontations – which had included a chorus line of drag queens high-kicking in the style of the Radio City Rockettes singing a little quatrain which, whilst it may not have scanned terribly well, incensed what they saw as their oppressors – were still in progress.

> We are the Stonewall girls
> We wear our hair in curls
> We wear no underwear
> We show our pubic hair. . .
> We wear our dungarees
> Above our Nelly knees!

[34] Quoted by Martin Bowley in 'The Time has Come', The First Stonewall Lecture, London, 8 December 1994.

Later it was said of the raid and the subsequent riots that it was 'the hairpin drop heard around the world'.[35] Within six months, the first meeting of the British Gay Liberation Front took place at the London School of Economics. A year later it issued its manifesto for reform.

New York was, in any event, light-years ahead of Great Britain, where bars, masquerading as clubs, for homosexuals were constantly raided. One in the 1960s, and it was only one of many, was the Alphabet Club in D'Arblay Street, Soho, which allowed in men who wished to do nothing more on the premises than dance together. They would sign the members' book as 'C. Chaplin' and 'M. Mouse' – rather as print workers did in what was regarded as a struggle by the proletariat against capitalist control and, therefore, rather more heroic. In the 'club' would already be police officers who had perhaps signed themselves 'A.N. Other' and who were there gathering evidence. Prosecutions for keeping a disorderly house were the order of the day – not, in theory, for being meeting places for homosexuals but for breaches of the licensing laws.

It has been a practice which continued. The early 1990s showed an increase in the number of clubs, saunas and pubs which allowed sex on the premises. Known as backrooms, they fell into the 'private' trap and also the managers risked prosecutions for keeping disorderly houses. The cases could be tried either in the magistrates' court or at the option of the defence at the Crown Court and there were notable acquittals – namely those of the managers of the Pride of Stepney in 1994 and Attitude a year later. It was easier for the police to shift their line of attack and object to

---

[35] There are numerous accounts of the Stonewall Riot, including Dick Leitsch, 'The Hairpin Drop Heard Around the World' in *New York Mattachine Society Newsletter* 28 June–3 July 1969, and Donn Teal, 'Stonewall Anniversary: The Riots recalled' in *Village Voice*, 12 July 1979. See also John Loughery, *The Other Side of Silence*, Chapter 18.

the renewal of the liquor licence at the next Licensing Sessions; an objection that the licensee was not a fit and proper person and the premises were badly conducted resulted in the subsequent loss of the Attitude's licence.

To call someone homosexual was still regarded as libellous, although curiously few libel actions have been fought on the grounds that the plaintiff has been labelled a homosexual.[36] One of the great – and, wrongly decided – libel actions came in 1959, in which the complaint was brought by the entertainer-pianist Wladziu Valentini Liberace against Cassandra and the *Daily Mirror*. Liberace is nowadays largely forgotten, but in the 1960s he was immensely popular with television shows and appearances which drew huge audiences. He was not to everyone's taste; certainly not to that of Robert Conner, who wrote the trenchant Cassandra column in the *Daily Mirror*. Although the action was fought on the basis that the words complained of could not mean Liberace was a homosexual, the jury found that they were and that he was not. He was awarded £8,000. Liberace had already obtained damages from the music-hall comedian James Thompson, who appeared on television in a parody of the pianist and unwisely sang

> I get more and more
> They propose by the score
> And at least one or two are from girls.
> My fans all agree that I'm really mostly me
> When I play the sugar plum fairy.

Later Liberace was sued for $65 million palimony by Californian Scott Thoron, known as 'Boober'. Liberace had indeed employed Boober; but on the termination of his

---

[36] In September 1985 Claire Tomalin, the *Sunday Times* literary editor, obtained an agreed £2,500 and costs after Auberon Waugh wrongly accused her in *Private Eye* of having lesbian sympathies.

chauffeur's employment had generously given him $75,000, an interest in a house in Las Vegas, a Rolls Royce and another car as well as some furniture and two dogs.

What may well have been the last of the trials was brought by the Conservative MP David Ashby. But now, the complaint could not be that he had been called a homosexual – for in the 1990s that would not cause a person to be lowered in the minds of right-thinking people generally – but in the fact that he was a hypocrite and a liar for not 'coming out'.[37] The allegation in the *Sunday Times* in 1994 was that he had shared a bed with another man during a holiday in France. Ashby, whose wife gave evidence against him and his daughter for him during the 20-day trial, said that the reason had been both financial and as a result of a mistake made in the booking. Ashby lost on a majority decision after a journalist had told the court how he had run into Ashby in a known gay pub in Chelsea. It was a decision which would lose him his parliamentary seat and bring him close to financial ruin.[38]

Meanwhile progress was being made with obtaining equality for homosexuals. The Homosexual Law Reform Society became the Campaign for Homosexual Equality, and the Gay Liberation Front was formed in 1970. In 1975 a rally in Trafalgar Square produced what was seen as the largest public gathering of homosexuals of all time in this country. The attendance was 2,500. Twenty-two years later the Gay Pride rally would attract nearly 300,000. Progress was not always unchecked, however. In June 1972 the House

[37] Many would think that the action brought by Princess Youssopoff against MGM pictures was wrongly decided. The Princess secured some £35,000 on the grounds that the film falsely suggested she had been raped by the so-called 'Mad Monk' Rasputin. Given the test was that the plaintiff had been lowered in the minds of right-thinking people generally, she should surely have lost the action. Right-thinking people would evince horror and sadness, but surely she would not have been lowered in their estimation.

[38] For an account of the case and Ashby's reaction to the verdict, see Matthew Parris, *Great Parliamentary Scandals*, pp. 350–61.

of Lords upheld the *Gay Times*' conviction for conspiracy to
corrupt public morals. They had published advertisements
for gay men.

By the 1980s there was a gay culture with clubs, discos,
magazines and newspapers. But there was still the problem
of the age of consent being stuck obstinately at 21. The
issue was referred to the Criminal Law Revision Committee,
which after six years reported back suggesting a reduction
in the age to 18. The five women on the committee had
thought that 16 was the appropriate age.

One significant stage in the development of the gay movement as a community was the passage through Parliament
of the Local Government Act 1988. Section 28 prohibited
local authorities from 'promoting homosexuality' and 'the
teaching in any maintained school of the acceptability of
homosexuality as a purported family relationship'. Martin
Bowley in his *Advising Gay and Lesbian Handbook* adds,
'whatever that may mean', but the tabloid press had been
up in arms over what it perceived as unbridled promiscuity
in the gay community and worse the publication of a book,
apparently for use in schools, entitled *Jenny Lives with Eric
and Martin*, which depicted a homosexual couple in bed
with a five-year-old girl. With local councils perceived as
spending money, which could have been better directed
elsewhere, on gay causes; with AIDS rife, and a right-wing
Christian backlash against the propagation of the doctrine
of homosexuality in progress, this was seen as a page
too far.[39]

When it comes to it, however, the working of the section
has never been tested in the courts. From time to time there
have been rumbles and, as Bowley suggests, a result has been

[39] The book was never actually available generally in schools, but was recommended
by ILEA for use in individual cases. See for example *Sunday Mirror*, 3 May
1986, *Today*, 7 May 1986. There is a full account of the campaign against s.28
in Stephen Jeffrey-Poulter, *Peers, Queers & Commons*, pp. 206–7.

that teachers have been fearful of raising homosexual issues even in sex and education lessons. Just as there are stories that the BBC banned 'Rock of Ages' in a purge on Rock and Roll, and Anna Sewell's story of a horse *Black Beauty* was banned in South Africa, there is also the tale that one local authority banned children from seeing the film *Death in Venice* – thereby, perhaps, saving them a good deal of boredom.

What the section did, however unintentionally, was to radicalise the gay and lesbian community so that within two years *Outrage!* and *Stonewall*, in honour of the New York bar, had been formed.[40] Rallies with up to 30,000 present paraded to show their disapproval of the Section 38.

In the meantime, however, Members of Parliament who were 'outed' faced the wrath of their constituents and the possibility of an early retirement to the Chiltern Hundreds. It was this fear which in 1979 brought the then leader of the Liberal party Jeremy Thorpe to appear at the Old Bailey charged with conspiracy to murder Norman Scott.

There is still considerable disagreement on the facts of the allegations, but on any reading the dapper Thorpe behaved inadvisedly after he had befriended the mentally unstable 20-year-old groom Norman Josiffe at a friend's riding stables.[41] In 1961 Scott appeared at the House of Commons with his Jack Russell terrier Mrs Tish, asking for Thorpe's help over an accusation that he had stolen a horse. At the Thorpe trial, Scott then claimed that Thorpe had driven him to his (Thorpe's) other house in Oxfordshire.

---

[40] *Outrage!* was formed in May 1990 following the death of the homosexual Michael Booth, found dead in an area in West London popular with gay men. It was a time when gay bashing was in vogue, and the group focused attention on what it saw as a failure to take anti-gay violence seriously whilst resources were being wasted on gays themselves indulging in what were argued were victimless crimes.

[41] Born Norman Josiffe, he changed his name to Scott so that he could substantiate his claim to be a relative of Lord Eldon.

He went on to allege that Thorpe had arrived in the guest room where he was staying, had produced a tube of Vaseline, rolled him over, buggered him and left. The next morning he had returned to the room to ask whether Scott wanted his breakfast eggs fried or boiled.

Scott claims that Thorpe paid for clothes from his tailor and a pair of cufflinks from Cartier, but this Thorpe denies and Cartier accept they never sold cufflinks to Thorpe.

In his statement to the police – for he never gave evidence at the trial – Thorpe strenuously denied Scott's story. However, it is beyond doubt that he befriended the man, who was some ten years his junior and certainly his social inferior. Over the years he found him a succession of jobs and when Scott was accused of stealing a coat, he insisted the interview with the police should be at Westminster. At best he can be said to have behaved well if not wisely.

He then found Scott a job at stables in Somerset and committed to paper a phrase which would pass into popular culture. In reply to a letter from Scott, he wrote: 'Bunnies can (+will) go to France'.

Scott sensibly kept the letter and when in 1962 Thorpe, whose solicitor had been looking into Scott's stories of woe and finding them wanting, declined to assist him further he took it to Chelsea police station, where he made a complaint. Like Boulton and Park so many years earlier he was examined; only on this occasion it was with his consent, and again the doctor found that he had practised anal intercourse. The police, however, did nothing except file the letter. Meanwhile Scott's fantasies grew. He was not the Hon. Lianche-Hosiffe, a widower and son of a dead peer. Tragically, his wife had been killed in a car accident. In reality, he had never married and his father was working in a hospital. Then in 1964, with Thorpe's political star gleaming, Scott touched him for money to go to Switzerland, which he disliked so much that he left before his luggage arrived. Scott then wrote to Thorpe's mother saying that her son no longer cared for him but only used him sexually. The letter was sent to Thorpe, who contacted his fellow Member Peter Bessell, the outgoing and caddish Liberal MP for Bodmin. So began the last few miles on the road to the Old Bailey.

There are various accounts of the attempts by Bessell to buy off Scott, which portray the MP in an inept or heroic light depending on the teller. At least £700 was advanced by him over some months, which he alleged was repaid by Thorpe. The money went in one disastrous venture after another, and an effort to pack Scott off to America failed when he could not obtain a visa. Meanwhile Thorpe had married, as had Scott. The money dried up and Scott, now living in Wales with his wife and baby, told all to the sympathetic and horrified ear of the local postmistress. She wrote to her MP and an inquiry was set up under the Liberal MP Lord Byers which found no evidence of wrongdoing by the leader. Scott sold his story to the Mirror Group, who did not publish it. Thorpe's wife died in a car accident and in 1973 he married Marion, Countess of Harewood.

Scott, desolated that his story had never been published, was now living on Dartmoor, telling his version of events to anyone who would listen. Mrs Tish had long before been put down, following an incident with some livestock, and had been replaced by Rinka, a Great Dane. In 1975, so the prosecution alleged, a plot was made to kill Scott and the substantial sum of £5,000 up front was paid to an airline pilot, another less than stable man, to undertake the hit. He was to receive a further £5,000 on successful completion. If plot there was, then it demonstrated how unfit the Liberal hierarchy was for government at the time.

The pilot first went to Dunstable rather than Barnstaple, where he persuaded Scott and Rinka to get into his car. He had told Scott that he had been sent to protect him from a hit-man soon to arrive from Canada. On Exmoor, when he had stopped for Scott to take over the wheel, he shot the dog and then said, 'It's your turn next.' The gun either jammed or the pilot lacked the bottle to go through with the killing. He leaped into the car and drove off.

The case blew up in January 1976 when Scott told Barnstaple magistrates – before whom he was appearing on charges of defrauding the DHSS – that he had once enjoyed the sexual favours of the Liberal party leader. The revelation may have been a surprise to the magistrate, but it was not to the press who filled the public gallery. The House of Cards came tumbling down. David Steel suggested that Thorpe resign. The pilot was charged and sentenced to two years' imprisonment for a firearms offence. Bessell sold his story. Scott issued a summons against Sir Robert Mark as Commissioner for the Metropolitan Police for the return of his 'Bunny' letters, and succeeded.

Thorpe went to see the fixing solicitor Lord Goodman, who passed him on to the experienced criminal-law firm run by Sir David Napley. Goodman and Napley gleefully called each other Mulberry and Raspberry to throw potential office breakers off the scent if they should manage to penetrate the filing cabinets. On 10 May, with Bunny T-shirts on sale in Oxford Street, Thorpe resigned. After that things returned almost to normal. When Newton was released from prison in April 1977 he sold his version of events to the *Evening News*. Bessell, now in America, was given immunity to return and testify, at the same time making a deal with the *Sunday Telegraph* – £50,000 on Thorpe's conviction and only £8,000 on acquittal. Newton now received immunity from just about everything from murder to perjury. Arrests followed.

It was the *Telegraph* deal, along with a defence aided by a destructive cross-examination of Scott by George Carman QC and a sympathetic – some say overly-sympathetic –

judge Mr Justice Cantley, which did for the prosecution. There was no conspiracy to murder. Thorpe and the others who were alleged to have put up the money for the pilot were all acquitted.

After the hearing it was announced that there would be a service of Thanksgiving in Thorpe's constituency in north Devon. The Gay Liberation Front announced that it would be sending a coachload of supporters, and the event was criticised by the archdeacon. When it came to it, the congregation was composed mostly of locals and the press. It heard the vicar compare the acquittal with the resurrection – which may have been going it a bit.

'Outing' became the rage, and the name of the organisation, in the 1980s, when it was fashionable to disclose the sexual identity of those Members of Parliament and sporting and theatrical personalities who were regarded as being covert in their sexual preferences. To vote against a reduction in the age of consent and to be a homosexual qualified a member for this doubtful privilege, as did appearing in what was seen as an overtly masculine advertisement in the newspapers or on television. Nevertheless, by the time the Blair Parliament was constituted, while there was a significant number of Members who were quite prepared that their sexual preferences be known and indeed capitalised on, some still hid behind the curtain. One was notably Peter Mandelson, who was apparently 'outed' during an interview on BBC television with Jeremy Paxman and reacted adversely to the disclosure. That he did so is curious, because he had been 'outed' many years earlier by the *News of the World*.[42]

The fight for the reduction in the age of consent has continued. Eventually in 1994 the Criminal Justice and Public Order Act reduced the age to 18; but this was

[42] *News of the World*, 17 May 1987.

still not considered enough and, rightly, was certainly not regarded as equality, and in 1998 the House of Commons voted for the age to be reduced to 16 (17 in Northern Ireland, where that is the age for heterosexual consent). It was rejected by the House of Lords and in January 1999 the House of Commons tried again. The Members who voted against the reduction were themselves outed by the *Guardian*, which printed the dissenting names.

There are still other problems, particularly on discrimination aspects. The Sex Discrimination Act may ban discrimination on the grounds of sex, but it does not ban discrimination on the grounds of sexual orientation. So where it was alleged that there was sexual discrimination against a lesbian partner who was refused cheap travel on the trains to which a husband or even unmarried heterosexual partner would have been entitled, the European Court ruled against the woman. Similarly, where a man tried to take over his late partner's Rent Act tenancy – the Court said they had to all intents and purposes been living as husband and wife for 20 years – the Court of Appeal ruled against him.[43]

It remains to be seen what effect the Human Rights Act 1998 will have on future rulings.

---

[43] *Grant v South West Trains Ltd* Case C-249/96 [1998] All ER (ED) ECJ; *Fitzpatrick v Sterling Housing Association Ltd* [1997] 4 All ER 991, CA.

22

Lesbianism

It is said that the reason why lesbianism did not join homosexuality on the statute book of the Criminal Law Amendment Act 1885 was due entirely to the fact that no one in the Government could bring themselves to explain to the good Queen Victoria exactly what was meant by female homosexuality. It is probably just a good story. At least lesbians have not suffered under the criminal law as homosexuals have done. The perceived wisdom is that lesbianism is no crime, but since a woman can be convicted of an indecent assault on another woman it follows that a woman could be convicted of an indecent assault on a girl aged under 16 to which in law as opposed to fact she could not consent.[1]

It was the same in America. Kinsey reported:

Our search through several hundred sodomy opinions

[1] *Armstrong* (1985) 49 J.P. 745; A.N. Macksey, 'The Criminal Law and the Woman Seducer' [1956] Crim L.R. 446.

which have been reported in this country between 1696
and 1952 has failed to reveal a single case sustaining the
conviction of a female for homosexuality.

Buggery had, of course, been a capital offence until 1861
but, apart from the association of excessive female sexuality
with witchcraft, there had been no attempt to punish female
homosexual acts anywhere in Europe let alone in Britain
since the sixteenth century, when the Emperor Charles V
promulgated a short-lived and none-too-successful effort.
The thinking behind this *laisser-faire* attitude would seem
to be that procreation lay wholly in the male semen and
that women were mere receptacles and passive ones at
that. Given this, there was no way that their behaviour
with each other, however unmeritorious it might be, would
frustrate the increase of the populaton as would similar male
conduct.

The Han dynasty in China had set the tone. Lesbianism
was accepted as the natural consequence of herding wives
and concubines together. It was regarded as wasteful but
by no means harmful, except when dildos were used
to excess. In particular, a double version was regarded
as dangerous. Another popular variant was the so-called
Cantonese groin, a phallus-shaped plant which when soaked
in hot water swelled and hardened. The belief that the dildo
caused gynaecological problems has persisted throughout
the years. Here is Lovat Dickson on the troubles of
the twentieth-century novelist Radclyffe Hall and her
companion Una, Lady Troubridge:

Aside from the ills that plague all human beings, colds
and headaches and constipation and things of that sort,
it is clear that the sexual practices of lesbianism induced
some gynaecological woes of an unhappy kind for which
the medical treatment can be protracted and painful.

This may not actually have been the case. Una, Lady T. was undoubtedly a neurasthenic who told her friends her husband had syphilis and that her continual ill-health was a result of this. It appears from the prescription given to her that she suffered from a gynaecological irregularity.

Radclyffe – or John, as she preferred to be called – Hall had other troubles. She had an earlier relationship with Mabel Batten, whom she called 'Ladye'. Mabel, 22 years older than the novelist, had been displaced in Hall's favours and had collapsed over the dinner table to remain, like the Countess in Pushkin's short story, mute and watchful as her protégée and supplanter respectively blossomed. Her death brought about an interest for the pair of them in spiritualism, and messages came from the other side linked to Ladye's antipathy to the hunting field to which John had been so partial.

> She's so glad there are animals in the spirit world. She's not really afraid of horses and she knows now they can't hurt her but when she first passed over she was still a bit wary of them.

> Feda (the medium) sees a horse, how funny! He's looking over her shoulder, his is a brown, sleek horse, she says she is keeping it for when you come over.[2]

The pair rapidly became leading luminaries of the Society for Psychical Research. The meetings with Ladye were faithfully recorded and delivered as a paper in two parts, the first at the Society's rooms in Hanover Square and, because of its success, the second in public at the Steinway Hall. There was, however, one dissenter, George Fox-Pitt, who complained that the first paper was 'scientific rubbish' and did not bother to attend the second lecture. Worse,

[2] See H. Montgomery Hyde, *The Other Love*, p. 183 *et seq.*

he considered Radclyffe Hall abnormal and he was quite prepared to say so.

It is curious how things run in families. Fox-Pitt was the son-in-law of the Marquess of Queensberry, who, as it were, did for Oscar Wilde. When a Mrs Henrietta Sidgwick proposed Hall's nomination to the Committee of the Society for Psychical Research he blocked it. He knew Admiral Troubridge, and that he was currently campaigning for Una to leave Hall and to return to him. A meeting between him and Troubridge resulted in his visiting the secretary of the Society to tell her that Hall was a grossly immoral woman who had wrecked the Admiral's home. The next day he made the same allegations to Mrs Salter, who edited the Society's journal. This time, however, there were improvements and variations on the theme. Mabel Batten, the subject of the lauded paper, was also a thoroughly immoral woman who now spoke from the other side. If the Hall nomination was not withdrawn, Fox-Pitt would make the matter public at the next council meeting.

Queensberry may have done for Wilde, but Fox-Pitt was not so successful in his action with Radclyffe Hall. Nor, for that matter, was her action for slander an unmitigated triumph. But there again lawsuits rarely bring out the best in the protagonists.

Ellis Hume-Williams KC and St John Field appeared for Radclyffe Hall. Fox-Pitt, although he certainly had the money to instruct equally able counsel, followed the maxim that the man who acts for himself has a fool for a client. Early in the case he shifted his ground, saying his use of the word 'immoral' related not to her personal life but – and this was probably even more of a red rag – to Hall's scientific work, which he maintained was fraudulent and rubbish. Not only was she labelled a homosexual but a lunatic one at that. The award of £500 did not please her,

and there was worse to come. Fox-Pitt belatedly consulted
lawyers and an appeal was allowed on the basis that the judge
had not told the jury that the slanderous words might be
privileged between members of the society in the course of
that society's business. Hall went to see the astute solicitor
and adviser to the fashionable, Sir George Lewis, who told
her that her character had been 'more than cleared' and she
should leave well alone.

'Home Exhausted,' wrote Una, Lady T. in her diary,
'but it is all *over* and the vital issue attained, so early to
bed – both of us very pleased.' Which shows that many of
us have a great capacity for self-deception.

Lord Darling was the somewhat dubious star of the libel
trial of Pemberton Billing, the Independent Member for
East Herts, in 1918. It arose from the announcement of
two private performances by the celebrated actress Maud
Allen in *Salome* at the Prince of Wales Theatre. He had been
alerted to the announcement of the piece by the novelist
Marie Corelli and he seized on it.

Billing, amongst his many talents, was the editor of the
Vigilante – another of those magazines such as *Truth* and
the *Pall Mall Gazette* which existed to stir up a good deal
of trouble in the guise of reforming zeal. He was also anti-
Jewish, anti-German and an opponent of homosexuals and
lesbians. In the next edition of the journal there appeared
a short article, 'The Cult of the Clitoris'. The implication
was of lesbianism, and the producer Jack Grein and Maud
Allen issued a summons for obscene libel. Grein fell into
the first two categories and here he was producing a play
by a convicted homosexual for a private audience. Maud
Allen was, it was believed, a lesbian.

The trial displayed Darling at his worst. Billing sensibly
defended himself and was allowed any amount of latitude.
His opening questions in cross-examination of Maud Allen
included:

Was your brother executed in San Francisco for murdering two young girls and outraging them after death?
Were these bodies found in the belfry of a church?

Darling allowed this on the basis of Billing's argument
that since the brother was a necrophiliac murderer and
Salome was a sadistic play, there was a causal connection.
Nor did Darling stop Billing from giving evidence in the
form of questions. The protests of Ellis Hume-Williams,
who appeared for Maud, went unregarded by Darling.

The case was heard at a time when the German Army was
making some progress through the Allied lines and Billing
found he had a sympathetic audience for his patriotic ravings
amongst the jury. In an hour and a half they acquitted him
on one count in the indictment and the prosecution offered
no evidence on the others.

After the verdict Darling offered a few of those *bons mots*
of which judges are so fond:

Now it is perfectly plain that this play, as anyone who
has read it must see, is a play which never ought to be
produced either in public or in private.

He went on to talk about the role of women in politics:

. . . in a very short time women will be able to have their
influence on legislation, and then, at all events, I hope
they will make it their business to see that much more
purity is introduced into public representations than is
the case at present; and I hope this verdict may help to
bring about some reform in that respect.

Grein had a nervous breakdown. Maud Allen went abroad,
returning to England in 1928; she spent much of her
later life teaching children. Billing was later suspended

from Parliament and had to be carried out struggling.
He subsequently unsuccessfully ran a casino in Mexico
with the former boxer Jack Dempsey. In 1941 he wrote
a book, *The Aviation of Tomorrow*, explaining such things
as in-flight refuelling and the use of rockets for take-off.
He died in 1946, ten years before Maud Allen.[3]

In 1921 came the last serious attempt to raise the
status of lesbianism to that of criminality. The Criminal
Law Amendment Bill was passing quietly through the
House of Commons when a Scottish Tory MP, Frederick
McQuisten, woke things up. He moved a clause under the
heading 'Acts of Gross Indecency by females'. And he had
plenty of support, including Sir Ernest Wild, who later
became a judge at the Old Bailey:

> It stops childbirth because it is a well-known fact that
> any woman who indulges in this vice will have nothing
> to do with the other sex.

And the honourable and gallant Colonel J.T.C. Moore
Brabazon was quite clear what was the matter:

> We are dealing with abnormalities of the brain and
> we have got to look at these things from that point
> of view.

Lesbianism was clearly not understood, but it was being
written about. There had been a number of books which
had touched on the subject in recent years. They included
D.H. Lawrence's *The Rainbow* in which the relevant chapter

---

[3] Neither Darling nor Hume-Williams mentions the case in their memoirs.
There is, however, an attack on Darling's conduct in Travers Humphreys'
Criminal Days: Recollections and Reflections. See also Michael Kettle, *Salome's
Last Veil* and, for a shorter account, Christine Keeler and Robert Meadley,
Sex Scandals.

is entitled 'Shame', and A.T. Fitroy's *Despised and Rejected*, which dealt with both male and female homosexuality as well as conscientious objectors. None of the subjects pleased the authorities and his royalties (if any) suffered by the sum of £160, the amount he was fined.

Nevertheless, fortunately not too many people had heard of this disgusting word. In the debate in the Lords which followed the passing of the clause in the Commons, Lord Desart echoed the fears of Lord Halsbury in the punishment of incest debate:

> You are going to tell the whole world that there is such an offence, to bring it to the notice of women who have never heard of it, never thought of it, never dreamed of it.

The then Lord Chancellor adopted the same tack:

> I would be bold enough to say that of every thousand women, taken as a whole, 999 have never even heard a whisper of these practices. Among all these, in the homes of this country . . . the taint of this noxious and horrible suspicion is to be imparted.

And apart from corrupting women, it might frighten any horses who happened to be about.

Six years later the 999 women had, for a brief time anyway, the opportunity to actually read about these practices when Radclyffe Hall wrote *The Well of Loneliness* in 1927.

Described by the *Sunday Express* editor of the time as 'an intolerable outrage', this autobiographical account of Radclyffe Hall's love for Lady Troubridge received mixed reviews, though the *Sunday Times* among others recognised it as a serious plea for toleration.

The publisher Jonathan Cape agreed to withdraw the

book at the request of the then Home Secretary Joynson-Hicks, but promptly arranged for it to be printed in Paris and then imported into England. Retribution followed fast when the Director of Public Prosecutions applied for a destruction order and the case was heard before Sir Chartres Biron, then Chief Stipendiary Magistrate at Bow Street.*

The lesbian might not run foul of the criminal courts, but in civil matters she was seriously at risk. Not every woman found as sympathetic and perhaps as unworldly a judge as Mr Justice Davies, who in 1954 dismissed the part of a petition for judicial separation in which the Reverend Davis complained that his wife had either behaved in a lesbian manner or that her conduct was such as to give him grounds for thinking she was a lesbian.

> At the highest, the wife and Miss Purdon were seen hand in hand, used to call each other 'darling', kissed on the lips, spent a good number of holidays together, were constantly alone in the wife's bedroom at the vicarage and on two or three occasions, occupied the same bedroom at night . . . It was a very odd business, two grown-up women spending all this time together often in the same room and often in bed together but (the Court) is quite satisfied that that was perfectly innocent.[4]

It reads badly, but the evidence was that the wife (who was five years older than her husband) and Miss Purdon (who was a matron of a convalescent home) were both very High Church and tended to look down on the unfortunate vicar. It seems that when they were in bed together at the

[4] *Davis v Davis; The Times*, 1 June 1954. The vicar obtained his decree on other grounds.

* A full account of the case is given on pages 264–9 in Chapter 20: Obscenity.

convalescent home the judge found that it was in the nature
of an emergency, and when they had been in bed on another
occasion a third woman had been in the room. *Honi soit qui
mal y pense.*

Indeed the same year a persistent friendship between two
women had been held to constitute unreasonable behaviour.
It was the close friendship itself, not of what it consisted,
that was sufficient.

> So far as the precise nature of the relationship between
> the wife and the other woman is concerned I make
> no finding nor is it necessary for me, as I see it,
> to do so.[5]

By 1978 there had been few successes for lesbian mothers
in actions for custody or access to their children. From the
first the courts had never been that keen on ill-behaved
heterosexual women, let alone homosexual ones, having
custody.

> It will probably have a salutary effect on the interests of
> public morality that a woman if found guilty of adultery
> will forfeit, as far as this court is concerned, all rights
> to custody of, or any access to her child.[6]

And 20 years later, even quite well-behaved ones:

> The court holds this principle, that when, by birth, a
> child is subject to a father it is for the general interest
> of families and for the general interest of children and
> really for the interest of the particular infant that the
> court should not, except in very extreme cases, interfere
> with the discretion of the father, but leave to him the

[5] *Spicer v Spicer* [1954] 3 All E.R. 208.
[6] *Seddon v Seddon* (1862) 2 Sw. and Tr. 640.

responsibility of exercising that power which nature has given him by birth of the child.[7]

The authors of *The Law and Sexuality* wrote that they knew of only three cases where lesbians succeeded in claims for custody and access.[8] Indeed in the first, as they point out, success was perhaps not the correct word to use since the terms of the order in favour of the mother were so harsh.

The mother had been told that given her lesbianism there was no point in seeking custody, and obtained an order for access. However, she continued to sleep with her partner, and her former husband returned to the court to deny her access. The judge, expressing agreement with the husband's 'considerable concern', granted her access to her son on an undertaking that whilst her son was staying she would not sleep with the other woman, would keep all literature on homosexuality out of her son's sight and would never mention the subject in his presence.[9]

The second of their cases, this time for custody, was decided solely on the basis that the conditions for the children offered by the husband were even worse than the dangers of the contact with lesbianism. He had been planning to live in one house with his new wife, have the children in another and have them commute between the two for their meals. This was clearly unworkable, as, held the court, was the husband's request to vet the guest list so that the children would not be 'corrupted' by gay friends.

---

[7] *re Agar Ellis* (1883) 24 Ch.D. 317. In 1944 the sociologist John Bowlby produced a controversial study which purported to show that maternal deprivation was a possible generator of psychopathy. In his study *Fourty-four Juvenile Thieves: Their characters and home life*, he found that 40 per cent of his sample of delinquents had been maternally deprived in the first five years of their lives. From 1981 it has become recognised that it is the bonding experience in the early years, not necessarily with the biological mother, which is critical. See M. Rutter, *Maternal Deprivation Reassessed*.

[8] Steve Cohen and others, *The Law and Sexuality*, pp. 35–6

[9] *Guardian*, 7 August 1975.

The court nevertheless expressed sympathy for the husband in this difficult situation. It emphasised that its decision was based on 'bricks and mortar and nothing else'.[10]

The third of the cases was another access issue. The mother had been allowed access only when her lover was not present and she appealed against the decision. The court took the view that the children had to be protected against seeing a lesbian relationship because 'biologically the future of the human race is linked with heterosexual relationships'. Nevertheless, the reluctant decision was that it would be 'less dangerous' for the children if they learned of the relationship from the word go rather than if they learned the court had 'artificially cut it off'.[11]

Lesbians did not do well in the workplace, so far as rights were concerned at least. Whilst Louise Boychuck was working for a firm of insurance brokers she wore a badge with the legend 'Lesbians Unite'. She was dismissed and her employers argued successfully before the tribunal that she might put off Arab investors who were then the staple diet of the economy. The chairperson said Ms Boychuck was trying to introduce other women into 'the cult'.

In another case lesbianism was found to be a reason for diminution of damages when one woman who employed another as nanny fell in love with her. When the relationship broke up the nanny was dismissed. The Tribunal held the dismissal was unreasonable, but it considered that she had contributed to her sacking. Her conduct was described as objectionable, dangerous and reprehensible and she received only 60 per cent of the award.[12]

By the 1990s a slightly more liberal attitude had prevailed towards custody by lesbian couples as well as to adoption by them. The trend can be seen from the end of the 1970s and

[10] *Guardian*, 5 November 1976; *Spare Rib*, January 1977.
[11] *Marcovics v Marcovics* [unreported] 11 and 12 July 1977.
[12] *Wood v Freeloader* (1977) I.R.L.R. 455.

both are now regular occurrences. It has not been, however, a victory without a struggle.

For example, the routine policy of the official solicitor, in cases where he was acting as the guardian of the child, to require lesbian applicants wishing to adopt a child to undergo a psychiatric examination, ended.[13] The lesbian mother or co-parent was no longer perceived as the danger a gay father might be. The onus was still on the gay father to show that the child was not at risk. In *Re G* the Court of Appeal decided that a father's homosexuality alone was not a reason for refusing access. In that case the decision went against him partly because originally access had ceased at an earlier date and also because the mother was soon to remarry.[14]

Even if access is granted the court has powers to restrict the activities of the father by, for example, making an order that he should not share his bedroom with a male partner during the access, a variation on the belief that intercourse can take place only between the hours of sunset and sunrise.

---

[13] *Re W* [1997] 2 FLR 406.
[14] (23 March 1980, unreported), CA.

23

Transvestites, Transsexuals and Same-Sex Marriages

Whilst we are all prepared to be amused by the antics of Cherubino, have admired Sarah Bernhardt (wooden leg and all) as Hamlet, and envied and laughed with Danny La Rue and Barry Humphries, society as a whole has not been over-tolerant to the transvestite. It has been even more unkind to the transsexual. Our admiration of the representation on the stage has rarely spilled over into an admiration or even toleration in daily life.

The pages of social history are spattered with men and women who have gone through much of their life in drag, living their lives as the other sex, sometimes in secret and sometimes with at least a degree of openness. A look through a scrapbook of newspaper cuttings compiled by an eccentric Englishman, George Ives, produces a healthy crop of such cases from the 1930s, proving that the androgynous society of today is not the reason for such pretence. The headlines themselves tell the story.

'Two Sisters turn into Brothers' was the tale of Margorie and Daisy Ferrow, who reappeared in Yarmouth after some years of absence as Mark and David. 'Were Once Sisters' is the sadder story of Mark Weston, who until 1936 had been Mary and a member of the British Olympic team as a javelin thrower. The paper reported the death of her brother Harry, who had been brought up as Hilda.[1]

In the nineteenth century the transvestite often joined the Army, the Navy or took up piracy, and it appears his or her colleagues had been none the wiser or else too polite to mention the subject. Some 400 women were thought to have fought, dressed as men, in the American Civil War. Amongst them was Mary Edward Walker, who was awarded the Congressional Medal of Honor.[2] Sometimes it was a way for women to join their lovers or husbands on campaigns. Cross-dressing was a means of avoiding rape in these situations.

Sometimes, perhaps, it was the way to a small fortune, as when in 1695 a woman in Southwark offered a dowry of £200 for her daughter. Unsurprisingly there were several takers and the daughter chose an Irish boy, Mr K. The marriage took place and the bridal night was spent with some kisses and nothing more. The mother explained male shyness to her daughter, but on the second night apparently the girl felt for what she thought was rightfully hers. Her 'husband' lacking in these parts leaped from the bed and disappeared (with the dowry) from her life.

One of the earliest of the known cases is that of the Chevalier D'Eon de Beaumont, who gave her name to Eonism as a synonym for transvestism. She was a great duellist and soldier who ended her days as a ward of the English Courts following a particularly gross libel on the French Ambassador. Born in France on 5 October 1728,

---

[1] The music goes around and around. See 'Twins Go from This to This', the story of twin sisters Marilyn and Carolyn Vittitow, who became twin brothers. *Daily Star*, 31 October 1994.
[2] Dell Richards, *Superstars*.

D'Eon died in London, where at the autopsy the doctors
found that he was formed as a male. He had lived for the
past 15 years with a woman who said she did not know
of the Chevalier's real sex, something which had been of
enormous speculation amongst the English gentry with
whom he mixed. It was said that £20,000 was wagered on
the Stock Market as to his sex. There have been a variety of
suggestions as to why the Chevalier became the Chevalière,
including one that he was found disguised as a woman in
the Royal apartments of Queen Charlotte by George III,
and the deception took place to defeat suggestions that he
was the father of the Prince of Wales.

A contemporary of the Chevalier was Maria van Antwerpen,
prosecuted on 23 February 1769 and condemned by a court
in Gouda. She had changed into men's clothing, married
and enlisted as a soldier. She had also done exactly the
same thing, including marriage, two decades earlier and had
been charged in 1751. Hannah Snell, deserted by her Dutch
husband, joined the Army and was wounded in the Siege
of Pondicherry in 1749. Although during her service her
identity was never discovered, she later reverted to dressing
as a woman and performing a music-hall act as a soldier. She
married three times and had a number of children before she
ended her days in Bedlam Asylum, where she died in 1792.
Charley Wilson was born in 1833 and was married under
her real name of Catherine Coombe, at the age of 16. She
left her husband after three years and went to sea for the
next 17 years. She married three times more, living with
her second wife for over 20 years.

Hardly less remarkable is the case of James Miranda
Barry MD. In 1813 this seemingly effeminate teenager took
his MD at Edinburgh University. He then began life in the
Army Medical Service as a hospital assistant in 1813. He was
promoted through the ranks and was twice court-martialled
for insubordination; on both occasions he was acquitted. In

1865 he died from influenza, probably caused by London's drainage system, in rooms at Down Street, Piccadilly, when it was discovered that Dr Barry was indeed a lady who had probably once had a child.

In the seventeenth and eighteenth centuries, the researchers R. Dekker and Lotte C. Van der Pol found that there were authenticated cases of 119 women living as men in the Netherlands; also that there were some 50 in Britain, with others scattered around Germany, Spain and France.[3]

Another known case was when in 1746 Mary Hamilton 'marrid' 14 women under the aliases of William, George and Charles Hamilton. The fourteenth bride, Mary Price of Taunton, told the Quarter Sessions she believed herself to be well and truly married until she began comparing notes with neighbours and so became 'mistrustful'.[4]

Mary Hamilton was found guilty of being a common notorious cheat. The sentence was six months' imprisonment with whippings in Taunton, Glastonbury, Wells and Shepton Mallet. All were carried out in the winter of 1746.[5]

One of the most curious cases was that of Annie Birkett – a widow in her thirties with an 11-year-old son, Harry – who in 1912 was courted by Harry Crawford, the coachman to a doctor in Wahroonga, Sydney. It was not an ideal courtship so far as Mrs Birkett was concerned. Harry Crawford was uncouth and she was hoping for better things. There was,

---

[3] R. Dekker and Lotte C. Van der Pol, *The Tradition of Female Transvestism in Early Modern Europe*.

[4] She is celebrated in Henry Fielding's novel *The Female Husband*.

[5] Two same-sex marriages were actually recorded in the parish of Prestbury in 1707 and 1708 when Hannah Wright and Ane (sic) Norton married Anne Gaskill and Alice Pickford respectively. It was nevertheless more common for women to live together with one adopting the male role, and Mary East as James How lived with a woman for some 20 years, during which time they owned a public house together. They were blackmailed and had the bravery to prosecute their oppressor, who received four years. They were forced to give up the tavern but continued to live together.

however, little opportunity for socialising and so she would go with him to local amateur dramatic performances and drive with him to town.

Also a thrifty woman who wished to work her way out of the drudgery of being a cook-housekeeper, she saved her money and bought a sweetshop in the industrial suburb of Balmain. Crawford followed her and, three years later, began to live with her. Their relationship was not a success and although the business prospered, Crawford drank and did not work. He also produced a daughter from a previous marriage, the 16-year-old Josephine, who came to live with them. Annie Birkett decided to leave. She sold the shop and moved to Kogarah, but Crawford followed. Later they moved together to a slightly smarter suburb, Drummoyne.

On 28 September 1917 Harry Birkett went to the beach for the day and, on his return, was surprised to find that his mother had gone. Crawford reassured him; there had been a tiff and she had left to stay with friends in North Sydney.

Soon afterwards Crawford sold the furniture, Josephine went to live in the city and he and Harry Birkett took lodgings in Woolloomooloo. Crawford's drinking habits continued and Harry was sent to live with his aunt, who began to question him about his mother. Not satisfied with the boy's replies, she reported her sister missing. But, by now, Harry Crawford had disappeared. His landlady, in a device to get rid of him, had said that detectives had called. Crawford had promptly packed his bags.

Meanwhile, although so far unidentified, Annie Birkett's charred body had been found in Lane Cove. It would later be identified by a greenstone pendant still on the body and a dental plate. The search for Crawford continued, complicated enormously by the revelation by Josephine that Harry Crawford was not her father but her mother. The relationship with Mrs Birkett had been maintained by the use of a wooden phallus. Possibly the reason for the murder was the discovery by her of the truth; she had to be silenced to prevent disclosure. The police now feared that Crawford had switched sexes once more, making it almost impossible to trace him.

For two years Harry Crawford eluded them until he married again, this time at the register office in Canterbury. Some months afterwards he was arrested – the 'marriage' had again been maintained by mechanical means – and at the trial the true story, or at any rate something approaching it, emerged.

Crawford had been born Eugenie Fellini (sometimes Falleni) in Florence, Italy on 25 July 1886. Her parents emigrated to New Zealand, where, at the age of 16, she signed on as cabin boy on a trading barge in the Pacific Islands. On board was another Italian and by the end of the trip Fellini was pregnant. The daughter, Josephine, was boarded out and Fellini continued to find work as a man.

Crawford's defence at the trial at Darlinghurst Central Criminal Court in October 1920 was that there had been no quarrel with Annie Birkett and, so far as she knew, the woman was still alive. Crawford was found guilty, sentenced to death and reprieved. She served more than ten years in prison until in 1931 she was released. Under the name of Mrs Ford, she then ran a boarding house in Paddington, in central Sydney. On 10 June 1938 she was knocked down by a car and fatally injured.

At approximately the same time in London, Colonel Leslie Ivor Victor Gauntlett Bligh Barker ran a restaurant, hunted and boxed whilst having some spare time to be a leading light in the National Fascist party. It was only after the good Colonel's arrest at the Regent Palace Hotel on bankruptcy charges and his subsequent examination in the reception area of Brixton prison that he was hastily shuffled off to Holloway, where he was released after a day. Unfortunately the damage was done and he now appeared at the Old Bailey charged with causing a false entry to be made in a marriage register. She had been married as a woman and had then, towards the end of the First World War, had two children by an Australian who had left her. She then adopted men's clothing, gazetted herself and took a title. Thinking it better for her son Tony, to whom she was devoted, to have a woman's influence she married a chemist's daughter, Elfrieda Hayward. A lack of sexual intercourse was explained away by war injuries.

At the Old Bailey she found Sir Ernest Wild in intransigent mood, sentencing her to nine months' imprisonment before he took her counsel, Henry Curtis-Bennett, back to his room, where he explained his reasoning behind the sentence:

> I sentenced her for the profanation of holy matrimony and for her unfeminine conduct. She outraged the decency of nature and broke the law of man.[6]

He then read her some of his poetry.

Her son was killed in the War without knowing that his father was indeed his mother and she went to live, again as a man, in a village in Suffolk, where she died in 1960.

In court she had offered the sad explanation that 'the world offers more opportunities for advancement to a man than it does to a woman'. Some 50 years later, that lament is still true. Certainly it was when it was discovered in 1989

---

[6] C.G.L. DuCann, 'The Great Cases of the Curtis-Bennetts' in the *Star*, 18 November 1958. Wild could manage some splendid gaffes whilst on the bench. The article quotes him as saying, 'As long as I sit in this exalted seat I will cleanse the public urinals of our great Metropolis with the utmost vigour and determination.'

that the celebrated American saxophonist Billy Tipton was in fact a woman who had cross-dressed to obtain work.

It had also been true at the turn of the century when the Spanish woman bullfighter La Reverte, who achieved enormous success, was suspected of being a man. In 1908 the authorities banned women from fighting. Now she, La Reverte, fought as a man; he was indeed third-rate and had no success whatsoever. It seems that the bullfight historian Muriel Feiner's researches show that she was indeed a woman who was highly regarded in her own right, but the public turned against her when she fought as a man. Something about Samuel Johnson's dogs and women preachers.[7]

The question of logistics is something which must puzzle the non-long-term transvestite, and probably the long-term one too. How do they manage to lead lives as the opposite sex without discovery? How do they manage to explain away breasts, menstruation or the lack of a penis? The first may be explained because the women are flat-chested. In Colonel Barker's case, war injuries were to blame for heavy chest bandaging and his inability to have sex; he spent a period in hospital apparently without discovery. Tipton explained away her chest bandaging as the result of a car accident, and menstrual spotting with a claim to long-standing piles. She had lifts built into her shoes to give her extra height and probably had a jockstrap filled with a sock. As for sex, amazingly she had a succession of wives who spoke of deep sexual satisfaction and one, it seems, even thought she had become pregnant. One can only speculate if Tipton thought her wife had perhaps been unfaithful.[8] However, in many cases there must be the lingering suspicion of complicity by the partner.

[7] John Cornwell, 'Beauty and the Beastly' in the *Sunday Times Magazine*, 18 May 1997.
[8] Diane Wood Middlebrook, *Suits Me: The Double Life of Billy Tipton*.

Survival may have been the reason for the cross-dressing by Jack Lemmon and Tony Curtis in the Billy Wilder comedy *Some Like It Hot*, but a real counterpart seems to have been the case of Paul Grappes, who had lived in Paris as a woman after the First World War to avoid the possible death penalty after being accused of shooting himself to avoid combat.[9] It has also been an attractive form of disguise for bank robbers. The Bonnot Gang in France, which operated before the First World War, and the Ashley-Mobley Gang in Florida, who robbed banks a few years later, often dressed up in women's clothing – first, to allay suspicion and secondly, to prevent recognition. It is a practice which has continued over the years.

Until recently one of the principal fears of the transvestite has been that of being arrested in drag. The more serious charge which can be brought against the transvestite is under s.32 Sexual Offences Act, which makes it an offence for a man 'persistently to solicit or importune in a public place for immoral purposes'. The fact that the man is in drag has constituted a powerful piece of evidence against him.

The usual evidence in importuning cases has been that of police officers, often used in a stake-out of a particular public lavatory, who see the defendant 'nodding and smiling' at them. The clinching evidence is that whilst so doing the defendant is 'masturbating his exposed and erect penis'.

In one old case, *Horton v Mead*, the evidence was only that the defendant had smiled at people; there was no evidence of touching or even conversation. The crucial and damning piece of evidence was, according to the judge:

[9] Paul Grappes, 'My ten years as a Woman' in *Reynolds News*, 22 February 1925. He deserted in 1915 after he had been wounded at Anderlect on 4 November 1914 when a shell fragment took off two joints on one hand. However, he was charged with self-mutilation, which carried the death penalty. Grappes became Mlle Suzanne Landgard and was known in Montmartre – where, for part of the time, he lived with his wife – as La Garçonne.

his face and lips appeared to have been artificially reddened and in his pocket a powder puff with pink powder upon it was found, something not unimportant in an offence of this kind.

How much more damaging if the man was found in *décolletage*?

Fortunately the penalties are no longer those which Robert Trevelyan suffered in 1917. He was charged at the old London Sessions with 'loitering' and received 21 months' hard labour and 15 lashes with the cat. The *Star*, reporting the case under the banner 'The Cat for Street Pest', described him as 'wearing a fur hat over his long curly hair, a long coat trimmed with fur, and the bottoms of his trousers were concealed with spats. His face was powdered, his eyebrows blacked and his lips rouged.'[10]

The other criminal charges which a transvestite may face are those under the Public Order Act 1936 s.5, brought in originally to deal with anti-Fascist street fighting in the 1930s. The section is something of a catch-all.

... to distribute any writing, sign or visible representation which is threatening, abusive or insulting with intent to provoke a breach of the peace, or whereby a breach of the peace is likely to be provoked.

Now it is used principally against football hooligans and men wearing drag on their way to a club or pub. It is also used against men who are found in women's lavatories, whether wearing women's clothes or not.

It is only the last words which apply, and perhaps a

---

[10] Judges were in those days quite keen on imposing 'the cat'. One contemporary report from the Leeds Assizes reads: 'There was a happy day at Leeds on Saturday. His Lordship had a case of robbery with violence before him, and the law permitted him to order "the cat". He ordered forty lashes; and who will grudge his Lordship his little innocent pleasure.'

brave and wealthy transvestite will offer the Divisional Court the dubious pleasure of deciding whether this is a visible representation.

The lesser offence with which the transvestite could be charged is an offence under the bye-law, for which the penalty on conviction is a modest fine. It is brought as an incentive not to contest the matter, as a conviction does not qualify as a criminal record. Over the years it has therefore been a powerful inducement to plead guilty and get the case over with the least embarrassment and expense possible.

On the civil side of things, the married transvestite whose partner neither understands nor accepts his or her behaviour has provided grounds for divorce. The old cases where the behaviour had to be intentionally unreasonable no longer apply, although the courts would surely have considered cross-dressing as intentionally unreasonable behaviour.

All that is now expected is that the spouse cannot reasonably be expected to put up with the other partner's behaviour. In truth it is, of course, the old ground of cruelty wrapped up in modern cosmetic terms. People will accept that they have behaved unreasonably, whereas they will not accept they have been cruel.

In one case the wife's conduct was held unreasonable because:

> the wife refused to wear skirts and wore slacks. Shortly afterwards she bought a complete outfit of men's clothes and from that time afterwards she dressed as a man. She smoked a pipe. When the husband bought her a bicycle she insisted on a man's bicycle.

The old case of *Bohnel v Bohnel* – where it was held that cross-dressing by a husband was not a ground for divorce because it was not intentionally cruel – has gone out of the window with the Matrimonial Causes Act 1983.

However, the transvestite who thinks he or she is hard done by under the law should look more closely at the position of the transsexual – whose lot, like that of the policeman, has not until recently been a happy one at all.

But what, first of all, is a transsexual?

The lawyer David Pannick sets out the definition as:

> [an] individual anatomically of one sex but who believes that he or she belongs to another sex. This belief is so strong that transsexuals want their bodily appearance and social status altered to conform to what they perceive to be their true identity. It is neither a sexual preference nor a mode of sexual conduct. The transsexual is distinct from the transvestite (who obtains gratification from dressing in the clothes of the opposite sex) and from the homosexual (who enjoys sexual relations with persons of the same sex).[11]

It is worth describing, in brief, the basic details of the surgery because certainly in the male-to-female operations one of the requirements of a marriage cannot, according to law, be fulfilled and contracted.

Basically there are two principal types of male-to-female reassignment surgery. The first is often favoured by the older transsexual and is really cosmetic. The testes and penis are removed and labia formed. The urethra will now exit lower down. In the second operation, where the testes are removed, the penis and its bed are dissected and the scrotal skin retained whilst attached. The skin of the penis is inverted and inserted into the space created between the prostate and the bladder on the one hand and the rectum on the other. This creates most of the vagina. The rest is made from scrotum and the remaining genital tissue.

---

[11] David Pannick, 'Homosexuals, Transsexuals and the Sex Discrimination Act' in *Public Law*, Summer 1983.

It also creates the labia. It is possible to have further surgery if only the cosmetic operation has been undergone initially, but this is extremely complicated and involves either a splitskin graft from the thigh, or disconnection of the colon. Both are difficult, painful and dangerous. The first is rarely successful and the second, whilst it provides an excellent result if successful, cannot be guaranteed.

Anyone prepared to undergo the pain involved might seem to be deserving of a good deal of sympathy. Curiously this is not necessarily forthcoming from those perhaps in closest association with the transsexual. It is not uncommon for the transvestite to believe that the transsexual is in love with the knife and associated pain. Why, they argue, should they undergo such torture when they can have it both ways – a man when you want to be and a woman when the fancy takes you. Their lack of charity is reflected in the opposite attitude taken by the transsexual that the transvestite is little more than a drag queen who lacks the courage of his convictions. This attitude fails to take into account that many transvestites are heterosexual.

The first gender-changing operation took place in Europe in 1930, but no one seems to have paid any close attention until the former GI George Jorgensen became Christine. In England a former racing driver changed sex to become Roberta Cowell and from then on the newspapers and public took a prurient interest in the subject, with stories of Army officers, and even better Regimental Sergeant Majors, who had changed sex; the potential unfairness of male-to-female transsexuals playing in women's golf tournaments; men who had become female, had then taken up wrestling and now wished to change back; those who had entered Miss World contests, and the news that Princess Grace of Monaco's brother might be dating a sex-change man.[12]

[12] See as an example *News of the World*, 23 December 1973.

The legal starting point of the transsexual is the case of *Corbett v Corbett*. It is from that decision of Lord Justice Ormrod that all the legal woes of the transsexual begin to flow. The simple – if that is the correct word – question in the case was whether George Jamieson, now April Ashley, was a man or a woman. Jamieson had been born in April 1935 in humble circumstances in Liverpool. He had become a merchant seaman, graduated through the clubs in London to working at the Carousel night-club in Nice, and in 1960 had a sex-change operation in Casablanca. Six months later, whilst 'dislodging a sole meunière from its skeleton' on a blind date at the Caprice in London she was introduced by a transsexual friend, Louise, to the Honourable Arthur Cameron Corbett, 40, married with children, and son of Lord Rowallan, from whom he would inherit the title. Corbett was a visitor to male brothels and a transvestite. The judgement of Mr Justice Ormrod, himself a doctor, makes sad reading.[13]

Referring to Corbett, he commented:

> When he first saw her he could not believe it. He said he was mesmerised by her. 'This was so much more than I could ever hope to be' (a reference to his own transvestism in which he thought he had failed to create an acceptable fantasy). In examination he put the same thought into these words: 'This was so much more than I could ever hope to be. The reality was far greater than my fantasy.' In cross-examination he put the same thought into these words: 'It far outstripped any fantasy I could ever have contemplated for myself.'

Corbett was at first fascinated, later infatuated and finally besotted by April Ashley. He was jealous of her as an

---

[13] *Corbett v Corbett (otherwise Ashley)* [1970] All ER 33-51.

outstandingly attractive woman – a status to which he
could aspire but not achieve. He was also jealous of her
relations with other men. Soon he was seeing her daily,
and then twice daily.

> As a further indication of the unreality of his feelings for
> the respondent it is common ground that he introduced
> her to his wife and family and quite frequently took her
> to his house or on outings with them.

Corbett obtained a divorce from his wife and bought the
Jacaranda Club in Marbella. Sexual relations between him
and April Ashley were non-existent.

> At the most, their relationship went no further than
> kissing and some very mild petting. At no time did the
> respondent permit the petitioner to handle her naked
> breasts or any part of her body.

There was one single incident when in an apparent fit of
sexual jealousy Corbett 'attempted to assault her sexually',
but of that the judge made light:

> His description of the incident did not suggest to me
> that there was anything particularly sexual about it.

By this time Ashley had a passport in her name changed
by deed poll, and soon the Ministry of National Insurance
would issue her with a woman's insurance card and treat
her as a woman for National Insurance purposes. What
she could not have, as distinct from French and German
counterparts – and this has been the bone of contention for
British transsexuals – was a new birth certificate.

Even allowing for her transsexuality and Corbett's pen-
chant for transvestism, their relationship was an odd one.

She thought he 'both worshipped and resented me with a pathetic vengeance. Arthur often needed uncloying.'

One of the reasons for his jealousy was the numerous affairs and one-afternoon stands undertaken by Ashley:

> My disappearance now and again on one of the roads out of Marbella in the company of a beautiful young man nearer my age, sometimes below it, usually did the trick.[14]

The uncloying of Arthur, that is.

After Corbett's divorce the pair still remained separate a good deal of the time. They slept in separate houses, their engagement was continually on and off. His letters to her were:

> affectionate, quite passionless with continual emphasis on marriage and the pleasure which the petitioner felt in thinking of the respondent as the future Lady Rowallan.[15]

In July 1965 Corbett consulted a lawyer in Gibraltar about arranging a marriage. April Ashley continued to have doubts. The date of 10 September was set for the wedding but she still vacillated.

Then on that morning

> [she] suddenly agreed to go through with it and they

---

[14] Duncan Fallowell and April Ashley, *April Ashley's Odyssey*, p. 127.
[15] Corbett was by no means the only member of the aristocracy to fall in love with a transsexual. Roberta Cowell, the former racing driver, claimed she had received 400 proposals after it was disclosed she had undergone surgery. 'Some of them of marriage, I could have had titles, money, the lot,' *Sunday Times*, 12 March 1974. In May 1964 Sir John Waller proposed to the 20-year-old Brigitte Bond, whom he had met in Soho before he realised she was born a boy. 'He proposed to me before I had a chance to tell him all sorts of things. But I love him and I'm sure things will turn out all right,' *News of the World*, 24 May 1964.

rushed off to Gibraltar. I think that there can be little
doubt that the petitioner was still in the grip of his
fantasies and that the respondent had much more sense
of reality.

Once back from Gibraltar, there is a divergence of opinion
on what happened on that and subsequent nights. April
Ashley's version is simple:

> We went straight back to Marbella and I was feeling
> so foul I went straight to bed. The reception at the
> Jacaranda for which invitations had been printed had
> to be cancelled.

Ormrod's judgement is prosaic and cruel. It has the contempt of the medical man for those who tamper with
nature.

> After the ceremony they returned to the villa at Marbella
> where some sexual approach was made by the petitioner.
> It is, however, common ground that the respondent then
> said she was suffering from 'abscesses in her so-called
> vagina' and the subject was dropped and they continued
> to sleep apart.

Both returned to London, where Corbett's version is that
she was still complaining of 'abscesses' and April Ashley's
version is that they had cleared up, there was penetration
but that her husband withdrew before ejaculation saying,
'I can't, I can't.' He then burst into tears.

It was two and a half years later that Terrence Walton,
acting on behalf of April Ashley, issued an originating
summons claiming maintenance. By the time the hearing
of the suit for nullity took place in November 1969, April's
sexual parts had been examined extensively and one suspects

with some admiration for the technical craft of Dr Burou, who had performed the operation.[16]

> The vagina is of ample size to admit a normal and erect penis. The walls are skin covered and moist. There is no impediment on 'her part' to sexual intercourse. Rectal examination does not reveal any uterus or ovaries or testicles.

The supplementary report contained the encomium to Dr Burou:

> The surgical result was remarkably good. It may be noted that the normal vagina is lined by skin which is moistened by mucoid secretion from the cervic uteri. The artificial vagina in this case also appeared to be lined with skin and it was moist presumably owing to the presence of sweat glands in the skin used to line the artificial vagina.

Ormrod found against April Ashley in her account of the subsequent consummation, but it did not matter. The first and only problem for the judge was whether she was a woman. All the rest was entertainment for the press and public.

April Ashley's lawyers relied on a case *SY v SY* in which the Court of Appeal held that where the woman had a malformed vagina which did not allow complete and ordinary intercourse it would still count as consummation if, as had been the case, the vagina was artificially enlarged to permit penetration. It had even indicated that consummation might be possible by means of a wholly artificially constructed vagina.

---

[16] The urbane Burou commented, 'I don't change men into women. I transform male genitals into genitals that have a female aspect. All the rest is in the patient's mind.' 'Prisoners of Sex' in *Time*, 21 January 1974.

Ormrod had no trouble in distinguishing the facts of the Ashley case from *SY*:

> My conclusion, therefore, is that the respondent is not a woman for the purposes of marriage but is a biological male and has been since birth. It follows that the so-called marriage of 10 September 1963 is void.

He went on to explain things further:

> If the assignment to the female sex is made after the operation, then the operation has changed the sex. From this it would follow that if a 50-year-old male transsexual, married and the father of children, underwent an operation he would then have to be regarded in law as a female and capable of marrying a man! The results would be nothing if not bizarre.

A medical man himself, he was somewhat scathing about the technical details of the operation:

> I do not think that sexual intercourse using the artificial cavity constructed by Dr Burou can possibly be described as 'ordinary' and complete intercourse, or as 'vera coupla' of the natural sort of coitus. When such a cavity is constructed in a male, the difference between sexual intercourse using it, and anal or intracrural intercourse is, in my judgement, to be measured in centimetres.

In her book *April Ashley's Odyssey*, the eponymous heroine tells in some detail the physical trauma she underwent after her operation in the clinic at Casablanca where the celebrated Dr Burou carried out his operations. In retrospect she would probably agree that it was nothing compared with her Court case which settled the present law on transsexuality in the United Kingdom and which is so bitterly criticised by the post-operative transsexual.

> I felt Ormrod didn't like me, a gut reaction. I mentioned this to Terry and Professor Mills [a witness] over lunch in the basement of the court and they laughed it off. But I knew Ormrod was disconcerted by me. He never once looked me straight in the eye but glanced furtively in my direction and mumbled his references to me as if they were distasteful to him. His behaviour to me was contemptuous.

April Ashley was right when she feared that Judge Ormrod was unsympathetic to her. One witness for Arthur Corbett, a Professor Denham, had described her as a 'pastiche of femininity' and the judge agreed:

> Her outward appearance at first sight was convincingly feminine but on closer and longer examination in the witness box it was much less so. The voice, manner, gestures and attitude became increasingly reminiscent of the accomplished female impersonator.

Terrence Walton, the solicitor for Ashley, wrote:

> The case itself – it must be remembered – was not some gentle proceeding in Chancery for a declaration, but a bitter and protracted dispute arising out of a marriage settlement and an application for maintenance where it was the respondent husband who had at all times known the full facts, who raised the point of transsexualism by way of answer and commenced proceedings for nullity.

The result did for not only April Ashley but for the transsexual in general. As Terrence Walton wrote, 'Sadly and overnight thousands of happily "married" couples who had been living together for years with a good sex life were shattered.'[17]

And so after Ashley the matter rested for a decade and more until, for the transsexual, came an opportunity to redress matters. Gloria Greaves, a transsexual of 20 years' standing, was accused of offences under the Sexual Offences Act 1956 S.30, namely living off the immoral earnings of women.

The short point was that if she was a woman the charge could not stand. And of course the Court of Appeal, superior to Ormrod J., was by no means bound to follow his judgement. Anyway, we were now in the more liberated and understanding 1980s.

The Crown Court had rejected the argument that Gloria Greaves was a woman, but she was remanded to a women's prison. This of itself was, indeed, unusual and some progress. Homosexual rape is by no means uncommon in prison, and transsexuals can expect sexual abuse if remanded to a prison of their birth sex. There was also the question of whether she could continue to receive hormonal treatment, a decision in the hands of the prison doctor and not subject to any appeal.

---

[17] By the middle of the 1990s April Ashley was living in San Diego making ends meet by having two jobs working in a paste jewellery shop and clerking. From the interview with Margot Sheehan, she does not appear to have lost her spirit. Margot Sheehan, 'April Ashley' in *Oldie*, September 1996. Sadly not all sex-change 'marriages' work out. Author Gordon Langley Hall, who had an operation in September 1968, had her marriage blessed in November 1969 and claimed she had become pregnant. The adopted son of actress Margaret Rutherford, she then claimed she had a baby girl, Natasha, after she had become Dawn Pepita Hall.

A Harley Street gynaecologist had declared in 1969 that she was probably wrongly sexed at birth and could have a baby. However, after the birth in 1972 he said, 'I would be extremely doubtful that she has delivered a baby within the last year.'

In 1981, her husband John Paul Simmons, alleged to be a cross-dresser, was arrested in America for attempted kidnapping, burglary, arson and homosexual activities. Later she became engaged to Lemuel Smith, then on Death Row. See Dawn Langley Simmons, *Man into Woman*.

Hopes that the Court of Appeal would effectively over-rule the decision in *Corbett* were swiftly dispelled. 'Common sense and consistency demanded Corbett should apply.' Greaves's conviction was upheld.

Another major breakthrough came when in March 1999 the National Health Service announced that it would pay for gender reassignment surgery for six prisoners serving a variety of sentences. The change of heart came after a kidnapper, John Pilley, now known as Jane Anne, had campaigned for surgery for eight years. Prison Governors were given new guidelines on how to deal with trans-sexual inmates. The prison service has come a long way since *Tan*.[18]

So far as the criminal law is concerned, the dysphoric (one with a sense of unease about their birth sex) has been in an invidious position. A post-operative male-to-female transsexual could not be raped. No doubt a charge of indecent assault would lie against the attacked, but it would not reflect the gravity of the charge. If, for example, the transsexual submitted to the assault from fear, then possibly the most minor of the charges under the Offences Against the Person Act 1861 could be brought. Another of the great grievances, in the London magistrates' courts at any rate, is that the transsexual can be arrested and charged under the Sexual Offences Act 1956 S.32, i.e. as a man soliciting persistently in a public place for immoral purposes. This section is regarded by them as all the more unfair because the defendant has often been arrested only a few days earlier and charged as a female for soliciting for the purposes of prostitution.

Finally, on the subject of the criminal law and the transsexual, one academic[19] has come up with the ingenious

---

[18] *Tan* (1983) 76 Cr App R 300.
[19] P.J. Pace, Principal Lecturer in Law at what was then the Manchester Polytechnic.

theory that a married transsexual who nevertheless contracts a second marriage would be guilty of bigamy, despite the fact that the marriage is void because of the *Corbett* decision. It may be somewhat abstruse theory, but there seems to have been an unreported case of a transsexual and his partner who were charged with the offence of misleading a public registrar under S.2 of the Perjury Act 1911 when they went through a civil ceremony of marriage.

The transsexual is at a similar disadvantage in the civil law. If an operation is sought under the National Health Service, then the transsexual must not only have lived as a woman for two years prior to the gender reassignment – and working in a gay bar or club does not count – but she must either be single or have obtained a divorce. The wealthier transsexual is in a happier position. All the surgeon will require is a letter from the spouse absolving him from any civil liability for the operation on her husband. Towards the end of 1998 there was some hope for transsexuals when Mr Justice Hidden held that three claimants could have surgery, which now costs between £7,000 and £9,000 on the National Health Service. They had been refused gender reassignment surgery after it was decided they had not shown a demonstrable 'overriding clinical need' for treatment. The North West Lancashire Health Authority had argued that psychotherapy was available to assist them in reconciling themselves with their biological nature.

This was clearly progress from the 1970s, when there was one National Health sex-change a month and the *Sunday Mirror* expressed some surprise that these operations costing £300 and £350 were going ahead.[20] By September 1972 some 370 men and women had changed their sex.

---

[20] *Sunday Mirror*, 20 December 1971. The *Sunday Times* reported that sex-change operations were being undertaken at £1,000 a time by Harley Street surgeons without asking for a previous psychiatric opinion. They were described as backstreet operations, 25 May 1965.

In daily terms, however, it is the birth certificate which has caused the lasting trouble. S.29(3) of the Births and Deaths Regulations Registration Act only permits an error of facts which existed at birth to be corrected. X, who challenged a ruling by the Sheriff Court of Perth and Angus that it had only power to correct an entry erroneous at the date of birth, met with no success.

In this the British transsexual is less fortunate than his or her counterpart in many provinces of Canada, Germany and France. In Germany, for example, as the patient leaves the hospital her parting gift is the precious new and improved birth certificate.

So far as divorce is concerned, although in the only recorded case of a transsexual awaiting a sex-change his conduct was not intended to be cruel, now this has been abolished as a ground for divorce. There is, as with transvestism, little doubt that the conduct would be regarded as unreasonable.

The position regarding custody and access to children has also militated against the transsexual, and there seems to be no English case in which a transsexual parent has been awarded custody. In one access case the judge is reported as saying, 'She forfeited her rights as a parent the day she had the operation.'

Clearly, if the courts didn't hear about it not all men forfeited their rights.

This morning as a nine-year-old boy wakes up he will see beside his bed a photograph of his father in RAF uniform. He believes that he has never seen the man in the picture. For the person he calls Mummy has told him 'Daddy has gone away.' The little blond boy accepts that lie without question. But it is a lie.

When he gets older his 'mother' will tell him the truth. She will tell him an almost incredible story.

He will then hear that the woman he has called mother
for years is in fact his father.

He will learn that after he was born his real mother
went away and his father who has brought him up since
he was four days old, began to change sex.[21]

This is contrary to the views of some American courts,
where it has been ruled

the fact that the former wife was going through a
transsexual change from female to male, had changed
her name, had married a woman and had earlier suffered
financial reverses, did not justify change of custody to
the father in view of the high quality of environment
and home life of the former wife and children and, in
the absence of showing that the mother's relationship
with the children had been adversely affected or that
their emotional development had been impaired.

In the question of sex discrimination cases, the transsexual
has hardly fared better. In *E.A. White v British Sugar
Corporation*, the dysphoric, a female-to-male transsexual,
had been offered the job before it was known that she had
had a sex-change operation. In ruling that the claimant was
a woman and therefore there was no discrimination, the
tribunal followed the *Corbett* decision.

In America there appears to have been something of a
breakthrough for the transsexual. U.S. appellate courts
have consistently ruled that the Civil Rights Act 1964,
as amended by the Equal Opportunities Act 1972, does
not apply to transsexuals; but in *Ulane v Eastern Airlines*,
Judge John Grady held that the decision to fire Karen

[21] David Mertens, 'Terrible secret she dare not tell her son' in *News of the World*,
17 May 1970.

Ulane, a male-to-female dysphoric, was not for legitimate safety reasons but because Eastern Airlines were concerned about the image of having a transsexual flying their aeroplanes. 'Ignorance, prejudice, discrimination and hatred have throughout history been justified by, "I don't know. We can't take a chance," he said. He found that the medical witnesses for Eastern were "contemptuous of transsexuals with an intolerance and prejudice that's culpable".'

Karen Ulane was reinstated with back pay.[22]

Where does the transsexual go in his or her fight for justice? At present the answer is to the European Court in Strasbourg, where from start to finish the case will take about as long as it does to become a transsexual from commitment to post-operation.

Unfortunately, so far those dysphorics who have gone down the European Court route have been bitterly disappointed. Although in one instance the West German Government changed the law before a decision was reached in Europe, in a second case it was held that a Belgian female-to-male transsexual had not exhausted all his legal remedies in Belgium and the Court would not consider the merits of his arguments.

In 1986 Mark Rees, an applicant who had become a man, failed before the European Court; and in 1990 the model Caroline Cossey, Tula, a male-to-female model who had featured in vodka commercials, challenged the decision of the Registrar General not to allow her to marry. Nicholas Mason, a female-to-male transsexual, applied to have his birth certificate altered. Initially there was a small success: the Commission held that Mason's application would be examined and it would establish whether a friendly settlement of the matter could be achieved.

In fact, given the decision in *Rees*, the Cossey application

[22] *Ulane v Eastern Airlines*, 28 F.E.P. Cases 1438 (1982).

was really doomed to failure from the start. When it came
to it, there had been no settlement in the Mason case and
the Court of Human Rights dismissed both applications.

Then in 1996 G. and P. went to the High Court to seek a
change in their birth certificates at the same time as Kristina
Sheffield and Mark Rees (again) went to Strasbourg. The
High Court was told that there were now between 8,000
and 9,000 transsexuals in Britain. In March 1997 Stephen
Whittle, a lecturer at Manchester University, also went
before the European Courts. He had been registered at
birth as a woman and had lived with his partner Sarah for
18 years. They had four children by artificial insemination
and he now wished to register himself as their biological
father. Again he ran into the same stone wall. The United
Kingdom authorities were not in breach of the Human
Rights Convention by refusing him permission.

At least there has been some improvement legally. In
July 1997, the Employment Appeal Tribunal held that
the Sex Discrimination Act, which makes discrimination
on the grounds of sex unlawful, also protects transsexuals
from unfair treatment because of their sex change. C., who
had announced that she was changing sex in 1991 after
working in an amusement park for three years, found she
was ostracised and suffered serious and lengthy harassment
by some of her male colleagues. This followed a decision in
the European Court of Justice the previous summer which
gave public employees who were transsexuals protection
from discrimination.

Now, given the changing nature of conception and with
many children being conceived artificially, Whittle points
out his lack of rights. He cannot adopt the children, he
does not have the right to authorise medical treatment, he
is not entitled to receive confidential information from the
children's school. If Sarah dies, he has no automatic right
to bring them up.

In recent years, the attitude of the British courts under the influence of a series of more liberal judges has become much more open to change. In February 1998 the Court of Appeal held that a young woman, who had been deceived by a transsexual, Michael J., into believing him to be a man and marrying him, did not have to pay him maintenance after the marriage was declared a nullity. The woman was extremely naïve and had never been allowed to see her 'husband' naked. Intercourse, she discovered later, had been with an artificial phallus, and the two children had been conceived by artificial insemination. The key part of the decision was, however, that two of the judges said that where a party had knowingly married a transsexual, although the marriage was a nullity that person might still be able to obtain a financial order. April Ashley, after all these years you may have been vindicated.

Social attitudes have certainly altered and now sex-change has become almost fashionable. By and large over the last decade transsexuals have had a good press and this in turn has made them more acceptable in the public light. Public opinion has swung in their favour, the more so since in 1995 almost in a flash of light came news which could be used to upgrade the image of transsexualism to that of gender dysphoria once and for all. Researchers in the Netherlands discovered that a region of the hypothalamus, located at the floor of the brain, is about 50 per cent larger in men than in women, and almost 60 per cent larger in men than in male-to-female transsexuals. Now it could be argued that gender dysphoria was a genuine medical as opposed to a psychological problem. The 'woman locked in the body of a man' was, at last, a medical condition. Robust common-sense scepticism was led by the journalist Nigella Lawson. Allowing that if it were true it would be staggering evidence, she was not convinced. The 'vague unscientific nature of its reporting hardly makes it sound,

so far, conclusive', she wrote.[23] Nevertheless, it was a peg
on which outsiders could hang their hats of acceptance.

Now, at the turn of the century, instead of being
regarded as accomplished female impersonators, as a rule
those schoolteachers and lawyers who over the school-break
or a weekend announce that they will be seeking gender reassignment suffer no discrimination. When solicitor Richard
Bowden-Dan, of the well-known law firm Kidd Rapinet,
announced that he was having gender reassignment or 'to
adopt the argot of the gutter press I am having a sex change',
he took the trouble to write to all his clients explaining the
reasons: 'It is due to the nature of the formation of a small
part of the hypothalamus in the person's brain [that] a
person's gender does not match their chromosomal sex',
and he enclosed a leaflet. The Queen's surgeon has also
announced her change. Although sceptics thought this
might be the beginning of a defence such as those run
by Ernest Saunders and Judge Richard Gee, who would
respectively be found unfit to serve a prison sentence and
stand trial because of medical conditions from which they
recovered with remarkable rapidity, a defendant in a major
fraud trial made his first highly publicised appearance
before the court in a frock. A transsexual has become
the star of a television fly-on-the-wall series, *Paddington
Green*, something which a decade ago would have been
socially inconceivable.

The transsexual is still not appreciably nearer obtaining
the magic birth certificate. Nor, even under the pater-
nalistic and socially correct guidance of New Labour, is
discrimination wholly *passé*. Rosalind Mitchell, who had
been elected a Bristol Labour councillor as David Spry

---

[23] *Nature*, November 1995; Natalie Angier, 'Study Links Brain to Transsexuality'
in the *New York Times*, 2 November 1995; Nigella Lawson, 'Sex change operations
don't work' in *The Times*, 6 February 1996.

in May 1997, was thrown out of a women-only meeting because – as Graham Manuel, Labour's regional secretary, explained – 'The majority opinion at the women's meeting was that she was still a man.'[24]

[24] *Daily Telegraph*, 20 March 1999.

24

Children

The sexual abuse of children is nothing new. One of the principal trades in the Victorian sexual underworld was in under-age children – until 1875 the age of consent was 12 – partly because it was believed that intercourse with a virgin cured gonorrhoea.[1]

After the repeal of the Contagious Diseases Acts, Josephine Butler had been busying herself with the question of English children in European brothels and reported emotively in May 1880:

> In some houses in Belgium there are immured little children, English girls of some twelve to fifteen years, lovely creatures (for they do not care to take any who are not beautiful) innocent creatures who, stolen, kidnapped, betrayed, got from English country villages by artifice are sold to these human shambles . . .[2]

It was this trade which prompted the crusading journalist

---

[1] There is a similar trade nowadays in African countries, not as a cure for AIDS but as a precaution against the disease.
[2] A letter in the *Shield*.

W.T. Stead, editor of the *Pall Mall Gazette*, in tandem with
the Salvation Army, to expose the ease with which a child
could be bought and shipped out of the country.

In 1885 Stead was approached to see if he would stir
up opinion on behalf of these girls and to his credit he
went to see the Archbishop of Canterbury, the Bishop of
London and Cardinal Manning with a view to obtaining
their support for raising the age of consent. He also believed
that a Member of Parliament was in the market for buying
virgins at £25 a hymen.

To this end he purchased a child from its mother. At this
remove, it is difficult to say that Stead's motives were wholly
altruistic. He almost certainly had an eye on the magazine's
circulation. What he undoubtedly did was to make just about
every mistake possible. It was not as if he had no notice
of the problems which lay ahead. He had explained his
plans to the worldly Henry Labouchère, who had warned
him both to make sure his case was cast-iron and that he
should not believe all he was told when drinking champagne
with doubtful characters. They were words which fell on
deaf ears.

Stead was also introduced to a former prostitute, Rebecca
Jarrett, who had been seduced at the age of 12. Now, using
her as his agent, he bought a young girl named Elizabeth
Armstrong. The girl arrived in London with her mother –
the man said to be her father had objected to the scheme
– and was taken to a procuress, Madame Mourez, who
examined her. Stead then went to rooms in Poland Street,
where drinks were ordered; this was to let the landlord know
just how young Elizabeth was. Rebecca put her to bed after
chloroforming her. Stead then came into the room. This was
to be the final proof that young girls could be purchased for
as little as £5. Unfortunately the poor child woke up; she
must have been terrified.

After another examination, this time by a doctor to prove

she was still intact, the child was shipped off to Paris while Stead wrote up the events for the *Gazette*. The story duly appeared with some splendidly circulation-improving head-lines and sub-titles: 'The Violation of Virgins'; 'Strapping Girls Down'; 'Confessions of a Brothel Keeper'. Who could ask for more? The next issue had 'Where Maids are Picked Up' and more.[3]

Stead believed in his triumph, but others were not so sure. There was a suggestion that he should be prosecuted for obscenity, but the issues sold. Mrs Armstrong read the articles and found herself thinly and unattractively disguised as a 'poor, dissolute woman indifferent to everything but drink'. Elizabeth, still in Paris, had become Lily. She went to Marylebone Magistrates' Court, where she was advised to contact Scotland Yard. On the way she contacted a reporter from *Lloyd's Newspaper*. It was no great journalistic feat to unravel the plot, the denouement of which was finding Stead and the returned Elizabeth together in a garden in Wimbledon.

Stead had problems. He had neglected to obtain the permission of Mr Armstrong, and Mrs A. was under the clear impression that her daughter was going into service. Had he taken her 'fraudulently' from her parents? Yes, was the resounding answer of the Bow Street magistrate, and he received three months. The unfortunate Rebecca Jarrett and Madame Mourez picked up double that. Stead, ever the martyr, spent his time as a first-class prisoner with a table and fire in his cell. It was not the lot of the two women. He wrote that he had never been happier.

Nevertheless, to him must go a good deal of credit for the raising of the age of consent, which in 1885 was again raised and this time it became 16.

Given that it was not until the middle of the 1940s that

[3] *Pall Mall Gazette*, 6 and 13 July 1885.

doctors were prepared to believe that children with broken bones had actually been assaulted by their parents rather than having fallen downstairs, it is not surprising that sexual abuse has only recently been recognised.

Research shows that, on average, before an abuser is caught he will have attempted or committed 238 offences, said Michele Elliott of Kidscape. She provided figures from a survey of abusers who between them had committed 55,000 offences on a total of 16,400 children.

DI Bob McLachlan of the Metropolitan Police Paedophile and Child Pornography Squad describes three patterns of offenders and behaviour.

The first is the seduction pattern. Offenders court children with affection, attention and gifts, seducing them over a period of time to lower their sexual inhibitions. 'He frequently targets children who are victims of emotional or physical neglect. The child abuser is most likely to use threats, blackmail and physical violence to avoid identification and disclosure.'

The second pattern relates to the introverted offender who lacks communication skills to seduce children. 'He is most likely to abuse strangers or very young children – fitting the stereotype of a person hanging around playgrounds. He is most likely to be married, have children of his own, and to abuse them from a very young age.'

The third pattern is that of the sadistic offender. 'These are highly dangerous individuals who have a sexual preference for children but who, in order to be aroused, must inflict pain or suffering on the child victim. It is fortunate that these individuals do not appear to be large in number.'

An analysis by McLachlan's unit shows most offenders to be male, over 25, single, never having been married, lived alone or with parents, had limited involvement with adults in a relationship, if married had a 'special relationship' with his wife which existed without high sexual expectations, had an excessive interest in children and possessed an age and gender preference, and some had access to children.[4]

Female sex abuse of children has really only been recognised since the middle 1980s.[5] Virtually the first time when heads were publicly poked above the parapets came in 1991 when Dr Fred Matthews (speaking at a conference in Toronto) argued that approximately 10 per cent of child molesters are female:

> ... if one in seven Canadian men and women were sexually abused as a child, as a study has indicated, that works out to about five million people. Ten per cent of that figure would mean about 500,000 Canadians have been abused by girls or women; 1 per cent would mean about 50,000. I don't know about you, but that doesn't seem like a minor number.[6]

In his 1989 article, 'Adult male report of childhood sexual abuse by mothers: case descriptions, motivations and long-term consequences', Ronald Krug suggests some reasons – some of which parallel the reticence in the earlier failure to recognise the battered baby syndrome – why until the 1990s there has been little recognition of the abused male child.

1. Males do not get pregnant, and the evidence of sexual abuse has not been present.
2. A double standard in belief systems in which all fathers have the potential for evil and mothers are 'all good'.
3. Adult males are too embarrassed to reveal their sexual activity with, and arousal by, their mothers.

---

[4] Sarah Gibbons, 'The Risk File' in *Police Review*, 13 October 1995.
[5] The influential book of the time, E. Bass and L. Davis, *The Courage to Heal: A Guide for Women Survivors of Child Sexual Abuse*, devotes only three of 495 pages to the topic.
[6] Reported in the *Globe and Mail*, 30 October 1991, A1–A2.

4. Patients and therapists alike have been unaware of the connection between the sexual abuse of males by mothers and later interpersonal relationship problems.[7]

It is not as though child sex abusers have hidden their lights under bushels. In September 1977 the Paedophile Information Exchange held a meeting in the Conway Hall, that home of spiritualism and jazz concerts in Red Lion Square, Holborn. Unsurprisingly the meeting did not go unchallenged and a near-riot ensued, with those attending showered with flour, fruit and vegetables and kicked and spat on by the crowd.

The PIE had been formed in Edinburgh as a study group within the Scottish Minorities Group, which later became the Scottish Homosexual Rights Group. The group moved to London as a separate entity, where it linked with the more militant Paedophile Action for Liberty. PAL was destroyed after a number of articles in the tabloids, and its members – including Tom O'Carroll, who would take a leading part in the amalgamated group – regrouped within PIE, which had the seductively sounding objects of 'dispelling ignorance' and to 'clear away the myths' and (rather more dangerously) 'campaign for the legal and social acceptance of paedophile love'. For some time the group was even regarded as semi-respectable, and *Time Out* as well as the gay press allowed them to insert advertisements in the classified section. It even made submissions to the Criminal Law Revision Committee at the end of 1975, advocating the abolition of the age of consent. It suggested that from the age of four to nine years no action could be taken to stop a sexual relationship with a child unless the parent or guardian indicated the child was unable to communicate 'assent'.

The group also visited paedophiles in prison, providing

[7] *Child Abuse and Neglect* 13, pp. 111–19.

comfort and support in their travails. One who benefited was Peter Deathman, who was serving ten years for child-stealing. On 13 March 1981, O'Carroll and five others were jailed for conspiracy to corrupt public morals.

However, this was not the end of the organisation, which flourished until a further clamp-down in 1984. The organisation was in contact with paedophile groups in Holland and the United States and when a further round-up was made some leading members fled abroad. At the beginning of 1999 there were suggestions that the group was re-forming. It was a matter of conjecture whether paedophiles actually needed to go abroad to find under-age prostitutes. In the past decade there has been an increasing body of evidence that girls as young as 12 were acting as prostitutes, but there was disagreement as to its extent, with charities being accused of exaggerating the problem in order to obtain more donations.

Even given the cases of the PIE which had been heard in the previous years, the courts have not always registered sufficient disapproval of child pornography. In 1987 Lord Lane seriously blotted his copybook when he dealt with the case of the 46-year-old paediatrician Oliver Brooke. The good professor had amassed a collection of child pornography which he kept carefully indexed in 23 bound albums. He had apparently become hooked on child pornography in 1978 and had been buying in Copenhagen and Amsterdam, contacting dealers who supplied him, as did a dealer in Spain. The photographs and films were expensive and explicit. In December 1986 he pleaded guilty at Kingston Crown Court to six counts of procuring and distributing child pornography and received what many would think was a merciful 12 months.

He appealed and was fortunate to find the Lord Chief Justice in excellent humour. After paying tribute to Brooke's skills as a paediatrician, he said of the pornography:

It emerged ... that for reasons which it is hard to gauge this man over the years had amassed a huge and minutely documented and indexed collection of this type of photograph ...

The possession needs no further explanation. The distribution was on a very limited scale. It is not inappropriate, perhaps, in view of the puerility of this type of behaviour, to compare it rather to a schoolboy collecting cigarette cards in olden times, because the duplicates were handed on to other adults – three or four of them only – who were likewise minded to indulge in this sort of puerility.[8]

Brooke's sentence was halved, which meant his immediate release.

This case came at about the same time as the use of computers for communication between paedophiles began to develop, replacing video cassettes of the previous decade as the way forward for child pornographers.

By 1990 British police, in collaboration with other agencies, had begun searching the Internet for paedophiles with, in 1994, a major operation in which they recovered some 900 pornographic images of children.

One of the present dangers is the spread of what is known as 'encryption' software which encodes text or images before transmitting them along telephone lines and cannot be decoded by the police. In turn the police want keys to new encryption systems to be held by an independent agency which, given suitable safeguards, would make them available for surveillance.

[8] *Brooke* (Oliver Gilbert). Transcript of judgement of Lord Lane, LCJ. 11 May 1987.

Conclusion

Times have changed. I first toyed with the idea of this book in the 1980s. Since that time there has been a sexual revolution. Alvin Tofler once wrote that there is only so much change that may be absorbed in a lifetime, and we are possibly approaching that limit.

The acquisition by a woman of a younger man is no longer regarded as a sad reluctance to grow old but as a demonstration of her vibrancy, and is rather the cause of envy. Contrary to the belief of one's children, sex does not stop at 40 nowadays. There have even been cases where men allege they have been sexually harassed by their women bosses. Thirty years ago there were no women bosses, let alone those who might sexually harass their staff. Cybersex was unthought of.

Whilst Rinka, the Great Dane, would not have survived until today, it is likely he would have lived much longer instead of perishing one cold night on Exmoor and so with his death destroying Jeremy Thorpe. When in February 1999 it was discovered that a Tory Euro-MP was bisexual, it was not this revelation to the public – for his wife and family seemed quite content with his mode of life – but the fact that he was found to have illegal drugs which caused him to stand down at the May elections.

Homosexuality has indeed become accepted and even fashionable. There is a very powerful lobby and a considerable number of Members of Parliament are openly gay. Nowadays a case of defamation in which the words alleged that a man or woman was gay or lesbian would surely fail if it was argued that their sexual orientation diminished them in the minds of right-thinking people generally. The spite in the words would be that the person was a hypocrite.

In America in 1999 a gay defendant in a murder case was allowed to argue that he was the equivalent of a 'battered spouse'. There is no logical reason, given the appropriate facts, why this defence should not succeed here.

Most would agree that, whilst there is still considerable room for improvement, things have changed for the better since Queen Victoria and even since her great-granddaughter ascended the throne. Well, perhaps not everyone would agree with everything. When it was announced that a consortium of 12 London authorities was putting up nearly £300,000 to promote safe-sex awareness in the gay community, the right-wing papers were outraged. The money was to fund a sado-masochism course during which workshops instructors would show the men how to tie each other up correctly and how to construct a mobile S & M dungeon on the cheap.

'That's just a little fun thing,' said Jamie Taylor of Gay Men Fighting Aids, explaining that much of the course was designed to promote confidence amongst gays. 'We have to lighten the day a little.'

On the other hand, there is now no real question why homosexual behaviour is an absolute bar to taking a full part in parenting. By 1980 Mr Justice Ormrod, that slayer of transsexuals, ruled:

The mere fact of this homosexual way of life on the part of the mother is not in itself a reason for refusing to give her control of her children. There is no rule or principle that a lesbian mother or homosexual father cannot be granted custody of a child.[1]

In practice, however, things have not always been so straightforward and the courts have made it clear that a lesbian household is by no means ideal. Gay fathers also have a problem when matters are contested. Even though the following House of Lords comments are getting on for 20 years old, they are still being followed and it is the fathers who must show that they are not a risk to their children.

. . . the vigilance and severity with which they should regard the risk of children at critical ages being exposed or introduced to ways of life which, as this case illustrates, may lead to severance from normal society, to psychological stresses and unhappiness and possibly even physical experiences which may scar them for life.[2]

Scientific advances have also ensured that donor insemination has steadily increased and lesbians no longer have to have sexual intercourse with a man to become pregnant. Efforts at the committee stage of the Human Fertilisation and Embryology Bill in 1989 to prohibit lesbian and indeed heterosexual single women having access to clinics providing donor insemination were unsuccessful. The donor is not regarded as the child's legal father and a child has no legal claim against the donor, who is also exempt from the predations of the Child Support Agency.

[1] *E v E* (unreported) 27 November 1980.
[2] *re D (an infant)* [1977] AC 602; *AMT (known as AC (petitioner for authority to adopt) SR)*[1997] Fam Law 8.

The Sex Discrimination Act 1975 has revolutionised the attitude towards women in society. Complaint may be made of direct and indirect discrimination and victimization to either an Employment Tribunal or to the County Court. It does not matter that the transgressor may have had perfectly good motives, an instance of which was when the boxer Jane Couch was at first denied a licence by the British Boxing Board of Control. This is a far cry from the time when the GLC's ban on women wrestling professionally was upheld.

More problematical has been the application of the Sex Discrimination Act to gays and lesbians. The view has long been that they are not protected by the Act. If an employer treats them less favourably than heterosexuals, it is because of their sexuality and not because of their sex. Nevertheless, there is a certain amount of protection. If a gay or lesbian is dismissed, then the proper procedures must have been adopted. It is not sufficient for an employer to sack a gay or lesbian or someone who is HIV-positive simply because others did not wish to work alongside them. Education of the workforce, not dismissal of the perceived outsider, is the order of the day.

By the end of the millennium it seemed as though the debate about contraception had been irrelevant. Now conception out of wedlock occurred in 50 per cent of pregnancies, having risen from 37 per cent in 1986. The proportion of women who married before their children were born dropped from 20 to 10 per cent over the same period. The number of couples who cohabited was thought likely to rise from one and a half million to three million. Those who married would become a minority by 2021.

There are still anomalies which discriminate against the gay population, however. A girl under 16 who has intercourse commits no offence; young boys who do so can still be prosecuted. Even though they did not result in custodial sentences, there were some seven cases in 1997. Heterosexual commercial prostitution and kerb-crawling attract a relatively small level-three fine in magistrates' courts. Soliciting for an immoral purpose by a man can – but it should be said, rarely does – attract a two-year maximum.

It has, however, now been recognised that there can be such a thing as a female paedophile. In a study of some 836 victims, in more than 70 per cent of the cases the woman was acting alone. Previously it had been thought that women only acted under the influence of men. In 1996 38 women were prosecuted for sexual offences against children.[3]

The problem of male paedophile rings in prison was also being examined. At the end of 1998 it was estimated that there might be up to 240 such rings in British prisons with members organising themselves in the event of their release. A report suggested:

> The concentration of child sex offenders in prison has allowed a number of paedophile rings to form among people who were previously unknown to each other.
>
> On the release of the members of one group a large number of offences were committed against children both in Britain and abroad.[4]

In June 1998 Alun Michael, then Minister of State at the Home Office, announced that there would be a comprehensive review of the current legislation and penalties for sexual

[3] Ian Burrell and Lynene Wallis, 'New unit to treat female paedophiles' in the *Independent*, 22 February 1999.
[4] Bernard Gallagher, 'Grappling with Smoke', NSPCC: *Daily Express*, 30 September 1998.

offences. The review teams started work on 5 February 1999
with the following terms of reference:

> to review the sex offences in statute and common law
> in England and Wales and to make recommendations
> that will:
> (i)   provide coherent and clear sex offences which pro-
>   tect the individual, particularly the most vulnerable,
>   from abuse and exploitation;
> (ii) enable abusers to be appropriately punished;
> (iii) be fair and non-discriminatory in accordance with
>   the ECHR and Human Rights Act.

A Steering Group was made up of 'officials, experts and
advisers from a variety of backgrounds', along with a
separate External Reference Group comprising 'individuals
and organisations with experience, expertise and opinions
on a range of issues relevant to the consideration of sex
offences'.

It was envisaged that there would be the fullest account
of the widest range of public opinion, and 'seminars,
conferences and electronic access' will be used to facilitate
that process. It was thought likely to last a year, and so will
coincide with the publication of this little book.

Martin Bowley, a judge who was 'outed' when a newspaper was sent letters to his young lover and who is the
President of the Bar Gay and Lesbian Group, writing in
the *New Law Journal* commented:

> What is needed is an entirely new approach to sex-
> ual offences law incorporating the concepts of sexual
> equality and equality of sexuality across the board.
> Against that background a new Sexual Offences Act
> must provide protection and penalties against all sexual

assaults, however minor, however grave. It must protect
the vulnerable and those under the age of consent
whenever it is set. The law must also, of necessity,
provide adequate protection for members of the public
against public indecency.[5]

We shall have to see which of the recommendations the
Government thinks fit to enact. Past experience of the dis-
regard of the often staggeringly obvious recommendations
of the Law Commission – which advises on changes in the
law on a wide variety of legal topics, including sex – does
not lend encouragement to the belief that much will change
over the next ten years.

Since I began this treatise with the claim that it would
cover sexual behaviour from the womb to the tomb, perhaps
I may close with what many call the last taboo – necrophilia:
intercourse with the dead – a sport said to be the favourite
of many mortuary attendants. Other claimants for the title of
the last taboo have included incest and bestiality, but there
is something peculiarly final about this particular one. It
has never been a crime of statute in England, although it
is possible that a charge of indecency with a corpse could
be brought under common law. In America, various states
such as Kentucky and Georgia have legislation against the
practice. In the latter, the Georgia Supreme Court has held
that a killer who has intercourse with his victim is guilty
of rape and that necrophilia only occurs where the man
'happens upon' a dead body and has sexual intercourse with
it. In a relatively recent case in California, on 19 September
1995 two men broke into the Forest Lawn Memorial Park
and had sex with two female corpses. Given the tolerance
displayed to sexual attitudes in California, it is no great
surprise that sex with the dead is no crime and the only

[5] M. Bowley, *Advising Gay and Lesbian Clients*, p. 181.

charges the men faced were theft of computer chips and breaking into the building.[6]

The relatives of victims of this crime at least have the satisfaction of knowing that the funeral home owes them a duty of care for the molestation of their loved ones.

Gerhard Mueller argued:

> I simply cannot conceive of a psychiatrist who would succeed in this second half of the twentieth century in establishing that a person who engages in such conduct is perfectly mentally healthy . . . There is absolutely no justification for continuing such offenses on the statute books. Such matter must be taken care of by the mental health laws, but not by criminal law.[7]

Finally, not a sex crime but perhaps a fitting end. A devoted son took his father on a last motor-cycle ride through Copenhagen, bought him a drink and a cigar and then delivered him to the police station in Frederikssund. At one time in the journey, the bike had stalled and Femming Petersen had to ask for help from passers-by. He explained that his father had had a few drinks and was 'dead tired'. It was the adjective which was apposite. Petersen was charged with the illicit handling of a corpse. Some weeks later he was fined the equivalent of around £150.

---

[6] Frank B. Williams, 'Two Valley Men Arrested in Sex Assault on Corpses' in *Los Angeles Times*, 20 September 1995. A number of serial killers have had sex with their victims, including Edmund Emil Kemper in California and Jeffrey Dahmer in Milwaukee.

[7] Gerhard O.W. Mueller, *Legal Regulation of Sexual Conduct*, p. 26.

Bibliography

Acton W.J., *Prostitution: Considered in its Moral, Social and Sanitary Aspects, in London and other Large Cities: with proposals for the Mitigation and Prevention of its Attendant Evils* (1856); ed. Peter Fryer (1968) London, MacGibbon and Kee.

Adler, Z., *Rape on Trial* (1987) London, Routledge & Kegan Paul.

Andrews, W., *Bygone England* (1892) London, Hutchinson & Co.

Aronson, T., *Prince Eddy and the Homosexual Underworld* (1994) London, John Murray Publishers.

Bailey, D.S. (ed.), *Sexual Offences and Social Punishment* (1956) London, Church Information Board.

Bailey, P., *An English Madam* (1983) London, Fontana.

Barret-Ducrocq, F., *Love in the time of Victoria* (1989) Harmondsworth, Penguin.

Bass, E. and Davis, L., *The Courage to Heal: A Guide for Women Survivors of Child Sexual Abuse* (1989) London, Harper & Row.

Bean, J.P., *Crime in Sheffield* (1987) Sheffield, Sheffield

City Libraries.

Bell, E.A. (ed.), *Fighting the Traffic in Young Girls, or War on the White Slave Trade* (1909).

Bell, E.M., *Josephine Butler: Flame of Fire* (1962) London, Constable.

Berger, A., *Rights* (1974) Harmondsworth, Penguin.

Besant, A. and Bradlaugh, C., *The Legalisation of Female Slavery in England* (1885) London, reprinted from *National Reformer*.

Bessell, P., *Cover-up: The Jeremy Thorpe Affair* (1980) London, Simons Books.

Birkett, N., *The New Newgate Calendar* (1960) London, The Folio Society.

Blackstone, W., *Commentaries on the Laws of England* (1775) Oxford, Clarendon.

Blair, I., *Investigating Rape – A New Approach for Police* (1985) London, Croom Helm.

Bloch, I., *Sexual Life in England* (1958) London, Arco Publications.

Booth, J.B., *Old Pink 'Un Days* (1924) London, The Richards Press.

Boswell, J., *Same sex unions in pre-modern Europe* (1994) New York, Villan Books.

Bourne, A., *A Doctor's Creed* (1962) London, Gollancz.

Bowley, M., *Advising Gay and Lesbian Clients: A Guide for Lawyers* (1999) London, Butterworth.

Box, M., *Libel: The Trial of Marie Stopes* (1967) London, Femina Books.

Boyle, T., *Black Swine in the Sewers of Hampstead* (1989) New York, Viking Penguin.

Bresler, F., *Sex and the Law* (1988) London, Frederick Muller.

Brodie, J.F., *Contraception and Abortion in 19th Century America* (1994) Ithaca, NY, Cornell University Press.

Broun H. and Leech, M., *Anthony Comstock, Roundsman of*

the Lord (1927) New York, A. & C. Boni.

Browder, C., *The Wickedest Woman in New York* (1988) Hamden, Conn., Archon Books.

Brown, M., *Richard Branson* (1988) London, Michael Joseph.

Brownmiller, S., *Against Our Will: Men, Women and Rape* (1975) London, Secker & Warburg.

Butler, A.S.G., *Portrait of Josephine Butler* (1954) London, Faber & Faber.

Butler, J., *Personal Reminiscences of a Great Crusade* (1896) London, H. Marshall.

——*An Autobiographical Memoir* (1909) Bristol, J. W. Arrowsmith.

Cain, B., *Victorian Feminists* (1992) Oxford, Oxford University Press.

Castle, C., *The Duchess Who Dared: The Life of Margaret, Duchess of Argyll* (1994) London, Sidgwick & Jackson.

Chaplin, C., *My Autobiography* (1964) New York, Simon & Schuster.

Chase, J. H., *Miss Callaghan Comes to Grief* (1941) London, Jarrold.

Chesney, K., *The Victorian Underworld* (1972) Harmondsworth, Penguin.

Chesser, E., *Live and Let Live, the Moral of the Wolfenden Report* (1958) London, Heinemann.

Chester, L., Linklater, M. and May, D., *Jeremy Thorpe: A Secret Life* (1979) London, Fontana.

Close, R., *Love Me Sailor* (1959) London, Pan Books.

Cohen, S. and others, *The Law and Sexuality* (1978) Manchester, Grass Roots Books and Manchester Law Centre.

Collier, R., *Masculinity, Law and the Family* (1995) London, Routledge.

Cory, D.W., *The Lesbian in America* (1964) New York, Citadel Press.

Craig, A., *Banned Books of England* (1937) London, Allen & Unwin.

——*Suppressed Books: a history of the conception of literary obscenity* (1963) Cleveland, Ohio, World Pub. Co.

Davenport-Hines, R., *Sex, Death and Punishment* (1990) London, Collins.

Davies, N., *Dark Heart* (1997) London, Chatto & Windus.

Dekker, R. and Lotte C. Van der Pol, *The Tradition of Female Transvestism in Early Modern Europe* (1989) Basingstoke, Macmillan.

Delacoste, F. and Alexander P. (eds.), *Sex Work: Writings by Women in the Sex Industry* (1988) London, Virago.

Dennett, M.W., *Who's Obscene?* (1930) New York, The Vanguard Press.

Dershowitz, A.M., *The Best Defense* (1983) New York, Vintage Books.

Dingwall, E.J., *Male Infibulation* (1925) London, John Bale, Sons and Danielsson.

——*The Girdle of Chastity* (1931) London, George Routledge & Sons.

Driberg, T., *Ruling Passions* (1977) London, Jonathan Cape.

Dudley, D., *Forgotten Frontiers* (1932)

Edwardes, A. and Martin, R.E.L., *The Cradle of Erotica* (1962) New York, Julian Press.

Elliott, M. (ed.), *Female Sexual Abuse of Children* (1993) London, Longman.

Ellman, R., *Oscar Wilde* (1987) London, Hamish Hamilton.

Ereria, A., *The People's England* (1981) London, Routledge & Kegan Paul.

Ernst, M.L. and Schwartz, A.U., *Censorship: The Search for the Obscene* (1964) New York, Macmillan.

Fallowell D. and Ashley, A., *April Ashley's Odyssey* (1982) London, Jonathan Cape.

Faulks, S., *The Fatal Englishman* (1997) London, Vintage.

Fawcett, M.G. and Turner, E.M., *Josephine Butler: Her*

Work and Principles, and Their Meaning for the Twentieth Century (1927) London, Association for Moral and Social Hygiene.

Ferris, P., *The Nameless* (1967) Harmondsworth, Pelican.

——*Sex and the British* (1993) London, Michael Joseph.

Filene, P.G., *Him/Her/Self: Sex Roles in Modern America*, 2nd ed. (1974) New York, Harcourt Brace Jovanovich.

Finch, B.F. and Green, H., *Contraception through the Ages* (1963) Springfield, Ill., Charles C. Thomas.

Fisher, T., *Scandal* (1995) Stroud, Alan Sutton Publishing.

Flaxman, R., *A Woman Styled Bold: The Life of Cornelia Connelly* (1991) Darton, Longman and Todd.

Fyfe, H.H., *Northcliffe, an Intimate Biography* (1930) London, George Allen & Unwin.

Gaillardet, F. (trans. Antonia White), *The Memoirs of the Chevalier D'Eon* (1970) London, Blond.

Gibson, P.C. and Gibson R. (eds.), *Dirty Books: women, pornography, power* (1993) London, BFI Publishing.

Gilbert, M., *Churchill: A Life* (1991) London, Heinemann.

Gosling J. and Warner, D., *The Shame of a City: Vices of London* (1961) London, W.H. Allen.

Greenwood, J., *The Seven Curses of London* (1869) London, Chatto & Windus.

Guilfoyle, T.J., *City of Eros* (1992) New York, W.W. Norton & Co.

Gurr, T. and Cox, H.H., *Famous Australian Crimes* (1957) Letchworth, Frederick Muller.

Hall, R., *The Well of Loneliness* (1927) London, Jonathan Cape.

Harris, N., *Medical History of Contraception* (1936) Baltimore, Williams and Williams.

Harvey, I., *To Fall Like Lucifer* (1971) London, Sidgwick & Jackson.

Herbert, A.P., *Holy Deadlock* (1934) London, Methuen.

——*The Ayes Have It: The Story of the Marriage Bill* (1937) London, Methuen.

Higgins, P., *Heterosexual Dictatorship* (1996) London, Fourth Estate.

Hines, N.E., *Medical History of Contraception* (1970) New York, Schocken.

Honore, T., *Sex Law* (1978) London, Duckworth.

Hopkins, F., *Formation and Annulment of Marriage* (1976) London, Oyez.

Howard League Working Party, *Unlawful Sex* (1985) London, Waterlow.

Howe, W.J. and Hummel, A.H., *In danger, or, Life in New York: a true history* (1886) New York, J. S. Ogilvie.

Hunter, E., *Christabel, the Russell Case and After* (1973) London, André Deutsch.

Hunter, I., Saunders, D. and Dugald, W., *On Pornography: Literature, Sexuality and Obscenity Law* (1993) New York, St Martin's Press.

Hyde, H.M., *United in Crime* (1955) London, Heinemann.
——*A History of Pornography* (1996) New English Library.
——*Norman Birkett* (1964) London, Hamish Hamilton.
——*Sir Patrick Hastings: His Life and Cases* (1960) London, Heinemann.
——*Their Good Names* (1970) London, Hamish Hamilton.
——*The Other Love* (1970) London, Heinemann.
——*The Cleveland Street Scandal* (1976) London, W.H. Allen.

James, E. (ed. G. Melly), *Swans reflecting Elephants* (1982) London, Weidenfeld & Nicolson.

Jenkins, R., *Gladstone* (1995) London, Macmillan.

Jones, F., *Paid to Kill* (1995) London, Headline.

Karlson, E., *The Homosexual Uprising* (1967) San Diego, Adult Books.

Kellogg, J.H., *Plain Facts for Old and Young* (1880) Burlington, Iowa, Segner & Condit.

Kinsey, A.C., Pomery, W.B. and Martin, C.E., *Sexual Behaviour in the Human Male* (1948) Philadelphia, Saunders.

Kinsey, A.C., Pomery, W.B., Math, L.E. and Gebhard, P.H., *Sexual Behaviour in the Human Female* (1953) Philadelphia, Saunders.

Kinsman, G., *The Regulation of Desire: Sexuality in Canada* (1987) Montreal, Black Rose Books.

Kuh, R.H., *Foolish Figleaves?* (1968) New York, The Macmillan Company.

Lader, L., *Abortion* (1966) Indianapolis, The Bobbs-Merrill Co Inc.

Lawrence, D.H., *Pornography and Obscenity* (1929) London, Faber & Faber.

Levine, P., *Victorian Feminism 1850-1900* (1987) London, Hutchinson.

Lockhart, William B., *United States Commission on Obscenity and Pornography* (1970) Washington D.C., US Government Printing Office.

Loughery, J., *The Other Side of Silence* (1998) New York, Henry Holt.

Macnamara, D.E.J. and Sagarin, S., *Sex, Crime, and the Law* (1974) New York, The Free Press.

McHugh, P., *Prostitution and Victorian Social Reform* (1980) London, Croom Helm.

McLachlan, N. (ed.), *The Memoirs of James Hardy Vaux* (1964) London, Heinemann.

McMurtry, L., *In a Narrow Grave* (1968) Albuquerque, University of New Mexico Press.

Marjoribanks, E., *The Life of Sir Edward Marshall Hall* (1929) London, Victor Gollancz.

Marlow, J., *The Uncrowned Queen of Ireland: The Life of Kitty O'Shea* (1975) London, Weidenfeld & Nicolson.

Menefee, S. P., *Wives for Sale* (1981) Oxford, Basil Blackwell.

Middlebrook, D., *Suits Me: The Double Life of Billy Tipton* (1999) London, Virago.

Milton, J.L., *On the Pathology and Treatment of Spermatorrhea* (1887) London, H. Renshaw.

Moran, L., *The Homosexual(ity) of the Law* (1996) London, Routledge.

Mueller, G.O.W., *Legal Regulation of Sexual Conduct* (1961) New York, Oceana.

Nash, T.A., *The Life of Richard, Lord Westbury* (1888) London, R. Bentley & Son.

Nicholson, R., *Rogue's Progress* (1860) London, George Vickers.

Nield, K. (ed.), *Prostitution in the Victorian Age* (1973) London, Gregg International Publishers.

Nixon, E., *Royal Spy* (1965) New York, Reynal & Co.

Noonan, J.T. jnr., *Contraception: A History of its Treatment by Catholic Theologians and Canonists* (1965) Cambridge, Mass., Harvard University Press.

Norton, R., *Mother Clap's Molly House* (1992) London, Gay Men's Press.

Pannick, D., *Judges* (1987) Oxford, Oxford University Press.

Patullo, P., *Judging Women* (1983) London, National Council for Civil Liberties.

Pearl, C., *The Girl with the Swansdown Seat* (1955) London, Robin Clark.

Pearsall, R., *The Worm in the Bud* (1969) London, Weidenfeld & Nicolson.

——*Night's Black Angels* (1975) London, Hodder & Stoughton.

Pearson, H., *Labby: the Life of Henry Labouchère* (1936) London, Hamish Hamilton.

Perkin, J., *Victorian Women* (1993) London, John Murray.

Petrie, G., *A Singular Iniquity: The Campaigns of Josephine Butler* (1965) London, Macmillan.

Playfair, G., *Six Studies in Hypocrisy* (1969) London, Secker & Warburg.

Rae, I., *The Strange Story of Dr James Barry* (1958) London, Longman, Green & Co.

Reed, J., *From Private Vice to Public Virtue: The Birth Control Movement and American Society since 1830* (1978) New York, Basic Books.

Rees, John Tudor, *They Stand Apart* (1975) London, Heinemann.

Richards, D., *Superstars* (1993) New York, Carroll & Graf.

Roberts, B., *The Mad, Bad Line* (1981) London, Hamish Hamilton.

Robertson, G., *Obscenity* (1979) London, Weidenfeld & Nicolson.

Robinson, J.M., *The Dukes of Norfolk* (1982) Oxford, Oxford University Press.

Rolph, C.H. (ed.), *Women of the Streets* (1955) London, Secker & Warburg.

——*The Trial of Lady Chatterley* (1961) Harmondsworth, Penguin.

Rose, L., *Massacre of the Innocents* (1986) London, Routledge & Kegan Paul.

Roughead, W., *Twelve Scottish Trials* (1913) Edinburgh and London, William Green & Son.

——*Bad Companions* (1930) Edinburgh and London, William Green & Son.

——*Knave's Looking Glass* (1935) London, Cassell.

Rouse, A.L., *Homosexuals in History* (1977) London, Weidenfeld & Nicolson.

Rubinstein, William B. (ed.), *Lesbians, gay men, and the law* (1993) New York, New Press.

Rutter, M., *Maternal Deprivation Reassessed* (1981) Harmondsworth, Penguin.

Sachs, E.N., *The Terrible Siren* (1928) New York, Harper and Bass.

Samuel, R., *East End Underworld* (1981) London, Routledge & Kegan Paul.

Scott, Benjamin, *A State Iniquity; Its Rise, Extension and Overthrow (1890–94)*, Kegan Paul, Trench Trubner & Co., reprinted 1968 New York, Augustus M. Kelly.

Sharpe, A., *Crimes That Shocked Australia* (1982) Crows Nest, NSW, Atrand Pty Ltd.

Sherman, A., *The Rape of the Ape* (1973) New York, Playboy Press.

Simmons, D.L., *Man into Woman* (1971) London, Icon Books.

Simpson, K., *A Doctor's Guide to Court* (1962) London, Butterworth.

——*Forty Years of Murder* (1980) London, Granada.

Simpson, R., *From the Closet to the Courts: the lesbian transition* (1976) New York, Viking Press.

Simpson, S., Chester, L. and Leitch, D., *The Cleveland Street Affair* (1976) Boston, Little, Brown.

Sorokin, P.A., *The American Sex Revolution* (1956) Boston, P. Sargent.

Spencer, C., *Homosexuality: A History* (1997) London, Fourth Estate.

Stone, L., *The Road To Divorce: England 1530 to 1987* (1990) Oxford, Oxford University Press.

Strachey, L. and Fulford, R. (eds.), *The Greville Memoirs 1814–1860* (1938) London, Macmillan.

Strauss, R., *The Unspeakable Curll* (1927) London, Chapman & Hall.

Stychin, C. F., *Law's Desire: sexuality and the limits of justice* (1995) New York, Routledge.

Sullivan, A., *Virtually Normal; an argument about homosexuality* (1995) New York, Alfred A. Knopf.

Tate, T., *Child Pornography* (1990) London, Methuen.

Thomas, D., *A Long Time Burning* (1969) London, Praeger.

Thomas, J.L., *Law of Lotteries, fraud and obscenity in the mails* (1980) Littleton, Colo., F.B. Rothman.

Thompson, C.J.S., *Mysteries of Sex; Women who posed as Men and Men who impersonated Women* (1938) London, Hutchinson & Co.

Thornton, M., *Argyll v Argyll* (1995) London, Michael Joseph.

Thorogood, H., *East of Aldgate* (1935) London, Allen & Unwin.

Tomalin, C., *Mrs Jordan's Profession* (1995) London, Penguin Books.

Vizetelly, E.A., *The True Story of the Chevalier D'Eon* (1895) London, Tilston & Edwards.

Walkowitz, J., *Prostitution and Victorian Society* (1980) Cambridge, Cambridge University Press.

——*City of Dreadful Delight* (1992) London, Virago.

Weeks, J., *Sex, Politics and Society* (1989) London, Longman.

Weiss, R., *Criminal Justice* (1990) London, Penguin Books.

Westwood, G., *Society and the Homosexual* (1952) London, Gollancz.

Whittington-Egan, R., *William Roughead's Chronicles of Murder* (1991) Moffat, Lochar Publishing.

Whittington-Egan, R. and M., *The Bedside Book of Murder* (1987) Newton Abbot, David & Charles.

Wildeblood, P., *Against the Law* (1995) London, Weidenfeld & Nicolson.

Willeford, C., *I was looking for a Street* (1991) Edinburgh, Polygon.

Williams, G., *The Sanctity of Life and the Criminal Law* (1958) London, Faber.

Wilson, A., *The Naughty Nineties* (1976) London, Eyre Methuen.

Wilson, A.N., *Eminent Victorians* (1989) London, BBC Books.

Wolfenden, Sir J., *Homosexual Offences and Prostitution* (1957) London, HMSO.

Woodham-Smith, C., *The Reason Why* (1953) London, Constable.

Woodhouse, Annie, *Fantastic Women: Sex Gender and Transvestism* (1990) New Brunswick, Rutgers University Press.

Wright, F.L., *An Autobiography, Frank Lloyd Wright* (1937) New York, Horizon Press.

——and Twombly, Robert C., *Frank Lloyd Wright: His Life and His Architecture* (1979) New York, John Wiley & Sons.

Wyndham, H., *The Mayfair Calendar* (1925) London, Hutchinson & Co.

——*Victorian Sensations* (1933) London, Jarrold.

——*Victorian Parade* (1934) London, Frederick Muller.

——*Society Sensations* (1938) London, Robert Hale.

——*This was the News* (1948) London, Quality Press.

Wyles, L., *A Woman of Scotland Yard* (1952) London, Faber.

Wyre, R., *Women, men and RAPE* (1986) Oxford, Perry Publications.

Articles etc.

L. Alpert, 'Judicial Censorship of Obscene Literature' (1938) in 52 *Harvard Law Review*, pp. 40, 41, 43.

Herbert Asbury, 'Hatrack' in *American Mercury*, Spring 1926.

Frances Power Cobbe, 'Wife-Torture in England' in *Contemporary Review* 1878.

Susan S.M. Edwards, 'Contributory negligence in compensation claims by victims of sexual assault' in *New Law Journal*, Volume 132 (1982) 1140.

J.M. Finnis, 'The Abortion Act: What has changed?' in *Criminal Law Review*, January, 1981 p. 3.

D.F. Foxon, 'Libertine Literature in England 1660–1745' in *Book Collector* 1963.

R. Geis and others, 'Police Surgeons and rape: A questionnaire survey' in *Police Surgeon* (No. 14 Oct) 7–14.

Al-Tony Gilmore, 'Jack Johnson and White Women: The National Impact,' in *Journal of Negro History* 58 (January 1973).

Sidney A. Grant and S. E. Angoff, 'Massachusetts and Censorship' in *Boston University Law Journal*, Volume 10, 1931.

——'Recent Developments in Censorship' in *Boston University Law Journal*, Volume 10, 1931.

Richard Hauser, 'Shakespeare, Sex . . . and Dr Bowdler' in *Saturday Review*, 23 April 1955, p. 50.

Frances Kellor, 'Kellor Manuscript: Statement of the Woman's Municipal League 1909', Box 91 Lillian Wald Papers, Columbia University, New York.

C. Kenny, 'Wife Selling in England' (1929) in *Law Quarterly Review*, vol. 45 October, pp. 494–7, London.

William E. Kruck, *Looking for Dr. Condum*, Tuscaloosa, University of Alabama Press, 1982.

Dick Leitsch, 'The Hairpin Drop Heard Around the World' in *New York Mattachine Society Newsletter*, 28 June–3 July 1969.

N. Lukianowicz, 'Survey of Various Aspects of Transvestism in the light of our present knowledge' in *Journal of Nervous and Mental Disease*, January 1959.

A.N. Macksey, 'The Criminal Law and the Woman Seducer' in [1956] Crim L.R. 446.

N.M. MacLean, 'Rape and false accusations of rape' in *Police Surgeon* 15 (1979).

C.J. McAlister, 'Law and Treatment of Venereal Diseases' in *Health and Empire* 7 (1932), pp. 38–54.

Clelia Duel Mosher, 'Statistical Study of the Marriage of 47 Women in the Study of the Physiology and Hygiene of Marriage with Some Considerations of the Birth Rate' Clelia Duel Mosher Papers, Stanford University Archives.

J.S. Oldham, 'On Pleading the Belly: A History of the Jury of Matrons' in *Criminal Justice History*, Volume VI, 1985.

David Pannick, 'Homosexuals, Transsexuals and the Sex Discrimination Act' in *Public Law*, Summer 1983.

M.W. Schraenen, 'The Campaign against Medical Charlatanism – Comparison of Anti-Venereal Legislation' in *Health and Empire* 9 (1934), pp. 197–206.

Madeleine Simms, 'Abortion Law Reform; How the Controversy Changed' in *Criminal Law Review*, 1970, p. 567.

C.H. Stewart, 'A retrospective survey of alleged sexual assault cases' in *Police Surgeon*, November 1981.

Dr T.E.A. Stowell, 'Jack The Ripper – A Solution?' in *Criminologist*, November 1970.

'Symposium: the transport worker and the lorry girl' in *Health and Empire* 11 (1936).

Donn Teal, 'Stonewall Anniversary: The Riots recalled' in *Village Voice*, 12 July 1979.

E.J. Gordon Wallace, 'The Venereal Diseases Act, 1917' in *Health and Empire* 10 (1935), pp. 53–4.

A.L.S. Wood, 'Keeping the Puritans at Bay' in *American Mercury*, Autumn 1925.

Index

Other bestselling Warner titles available by mail:

☐	Bent Coppers	James Morton	£6.99
☐	A Calendar of Killing	James Morton	£7.99
☐	Gangland	James Morton	£6.99
☐	Gangland Volume II	James Morton	£6.99
☐	Gangland International	James Morton	£6.99
☐	Mad Frank	James Morton	£6.99
☐	Mad Frank and Friends	James Morton	£6.99
☐	Supergrasses and Informers	James Morton	£6.99

The prices shown above are correct at time of going to press. However, the publishers reserve the right to increase prices on covers from those previously advertised without prior notice.

WARNER BOOKS

WARNER BOOKS
Cash Sales Department, P.O. Box 11, Falmouth, Cornwall, TR10 9EN
Tel: +44 (0) 1326 569777, Fax: +44 (0) 1326 569555
Email: books@barni.avel.co.uk

POST AND PACKING:
Payments can be made as follows: cheque, postal order (payable to Warner Books)
or by credit cards. Do not send cash or currency.

All U.K. Orders   **FREE OF CHARGE**
E.E.C. & Overseas   25% of order value

Name (Block Letters) _____

Address_____

_____

Post/zip code:_____

☐ Please keep me in touch with future Warner publications

☐ I enclose my remittance £_____

☐ I wish to pay by Visa/Access/Mastercard/Eurocard

Card Expiry Date

_____